B. Fröhlich
J. Deisinger
H.-J. Bullinger (eds.)

Immersive Projection Technology and Virtual Environments 2001

Proceedings of the Eurographics Workshop
in Stuttgart, Germany,
May 16–18, 2001

Eurographics

Springer-Verlag Wien GmbH

Prof. Dr. rer. nat. Bernd Fröhlich
Lehrstuhl für Systeme der Virtuellen Realität, Fakultät Medien
Bauhaus-Universität Weimar
Weimar, Germany

DI Joachim Deisinger
Fraunhofer-Institut für Arbeitswirtschaft
und Organisation IAO
Stuttgart, Germany

Univ.-Prof. Dr. Hans-Jörg Bullinger
Fraunhofer-Institut für Arbeitswirtschaft
und Organisation IAO
Stuttgart, Germany

Typesetting: Camera-ready by authors

Graphic design: Ecke Bonk

Printed on acid-free and chlorine-free bleached paper

SPIN: 10836851

With 150 partly coloured Figures

ISSN 0946-2767

ISBN 978-3-211-83671-2 ISBN 978-3-7091-6221-7 (eBook)
DOI 10.1007/978-3-7091-6221-7

Preface

This book contains the proceedings of the joint 5th Immersive Projection Technology and 7th EUROGRAPHICS Virtual Environments Workshop. The event was held in Stuttgart from May 16 to May 18, 2001. It was organized by the Fraunhofer IAO together with EUROGRAPHICS. The workshop brought together scientists, developers, and users from all over the world to present and discuss the latest scientific advances in the field of Immersive Projection Technology and Virtual Environments.

45 papers where submitted for reviewing and 27 where selected to be presented at the workshop. Most of the top research institutions working in the area submitted papers and presented their latest results. These presentations were complemented by a key note talk from Henry Fuchs, a key researcher in the area of Virtual Environments and Augmented Reality. Panels on the impact of Virtual Environment technology in the Automotive industry and on software systems for Virtual Environments closed the workshop.

The workshop was organized in four streams: Human Computer Interaction, Software, Technology, and Applications. The largest stream, *Human Computer Interaction*, is a research area still providing major challenges for the integration of virtual environment technology into real world applications. The *Software* stream presents latest developments in system software and rendering technology for virtual environments. The *Technology* stream focuses on new devices for input and output and new hard and software technology related to projection systems. Finally, the *Application* stream presents prototype and real world Virtual Environment applications.

The editors thank everybody involved in the process of creating these proceedings. In particular we would like to mention the authors, the programme committee members, and the staff members involved in organizing the conference and creating the book. Special thanks go to Maike Maibaum and Roland Blach from Fraunhofer IAO for their valuable support during the whole preparation phase and at the workshop.

Bernd Fröhlich, Joachim Deisinger, and Hans-Jörg Bullinger

Chairs and IPC

Workshop Co-Chairs

Carolina Cruz-Neira, VRAC, Iowa State University, USA

Joachim Deisinger, Fraunhofer IAO, Germany

Bernd Fröhlich, GMD IMK, Germany

Oliver Riedel, SGI, Germany

International Program Committee

A. Bierbaum	**T. Ertl**	**S. Müller**
M. Billinghurst	**M. Gervautz**	**H. Müller**
O. Bimber	**M. Goebel**	**H Regenbrecht**
R. Blach	**M. Hirose**	**L J. Rosenblum**
D. A. Bowman	**K. Hoffmeister**	**D. Saluäär**
R. Brady	**L. Jacobson**	**D. Schmalstieg**
D. E, Breen	**H. D. Ko**	**B Sherman**
F. P. Brooks	**V. Lalioti**	**R. C. Smith**
S. Coquillart	**U. Lang**	**D. Thalmann**
B. Corrie	**J. Leigh**	**R. van Liere**
R. Darken	**R. B. Loftin**	**J. R. Wilson**
T. Disz	**M. R. Mine**	**P. Zimmermann,**
J. Duncan	**R. Moorhead**	**M. Zyda**

Table of Contents

Education and Entertainment

Software

Systems

Graphics

Technology

Devices

Immersive Projection Technology

Command & Control Cube : a Shortcut Paradigm for Virtual Environments

Jérôme Grosjean and Sabine Coquillart

INRIA
domaine de Voluceau,
78153, Le Chesnay Cedex
France
Jerome.Grosjean, Sabine.Coquillart@inria.fr

Abstract. New immersive virtual environments (VE) such as the Responsive Workbench^{TM} provide users with a very attractive way of interacting with 3D computer-generated worlds. The feeling of immersion is one of the many advantages of such configurations. Being able to interact naturally with the virtual world is a very important part of this feeling. Programs developed for the virtual environments need powerful, intuitive and rapid application control interfaces. Previous work on this topic have focused on the development of menu systems for the VEs: converted 2D menus, hand-oriented menus and 3D widgets. To our knowledge, no 3D equivalent of the quick keyboard hotkey mechanism has ever been proposed for VEs. In this paper, we propose a 3D paradigm: the Command and Control Cube (CCC or C^3), inspired by marking menus. The C^3 aims to be a rapid and intuitive mechanism for issuing a set of commands to an application.

Keywords

System control, workbench, 3D interaction, interaction styles, graphical user interfaces, user-centered design, virtual reality, virtual environment

1 Introduction

Virtual environment configurations are changing our ways of interacting with 3D objects, navigating inside 3D worlds, and controlling applications. Some of these configurations: the head-mounted display, the CAVE[5], or the Responsive Workbench[10][9] (RWB) to name but a few, have a great potential to increase the benefits of computer generated 3D worlds. Among these configurations, the *workbench* [1] is one of the most attractive for direct manipulation. The configuration provides a virtual workspace where 3D objects can be manipulated directly with the hands. Though it can be considered to be an immersive (or

[1] "workbench" is used to denote the responsive workbench as well as other similar configurations with one or two screens.

semi-immersive) configuration, users don't lose contact with their physical environment, their own body or their fellow coworkers, which is often regarded as disorienting. Many applications already running on workstations, e.g., modeler and interactive visualization of scientific data, can greatly benefit from this configuration, thanks to the head-tracked stereo display and the direct interaction with the virtual scene, for example, moving cutting planes, grabbing and manipulating objects with the hand, direct modeling, deformation of 3D objects and moving light sources.

However, porting these applications to the workbench raises two problems: interaction techniques for manipulation and system control, i.e. changing modes, variable states, issuing commands. Both have to be entirely rethought for a 3D environment. This configuration differs widely from the classic workstation. The output device of the workbench is a head-tracked stereo display allowing users to see, turn around or manipulate 3D objects due to the virtual world being superimposed onto the physical one. In contrast, for a workstation with a monitor, visualization and manipulation space are separated. The input devices are very different too. On workstations, users communicate with applications through multi-purpose interaction devices: a keyboard and a mouse. The number of available input signals is very high (102 keys on a PC keyboard). The common input devices available on workbenches are in comparison often designed for spatial manipulation only (light and wearable) and provide very few buttons, e.g. only one or two for a tracked stylus.

A now-standard application control interface has become popular and widely used for workstations: the WIMP interface (Windows, Icons, Menus and Pointing), based on the keyboard and mouse input devices. This choice of human computer-interaction is commonly accepted as the de-facto standard for these configurations. To provide lighter and faster access to the most-often used commands, shortcuts have been introduced as well. The keyboard is a good tool to issue these commands with a simple hotkey mechanism (like CTRL-S for save). Indeed the quickest way to enter a command for one's application in 2D is the hotkey mechanism associated with the keyboard.

To our knowledge no solution has ever been proposed to provide a user in 3D VE with a similar shortcut system to very rapidly issue a small set of commands to the application. In this paper we focus our work on this aspect and propose a new application control interface : the Command & Control Cube (later called in this paper: CCC or C^3). This interface has been developed for a holobench[18], a two-screen responsive workbench (see Figure 1 and Appendix). The C^3 is controlled by the user with a 6DOF tracked button. With the C^3 a user can send up to 26 different commands to the application. A two-speed mechanism similar to the marking menus[13][14][12] in 2D allows the C^3 to work in a novice mode with a graphical feedback or in an advanced mode for quicker "eyes-off" selections. In this paper we first present related work on menus and application control solutions for 3D VEs. Next, we describe the C^3 and its functions. The last section includes the conclusion and a discussion on future work.

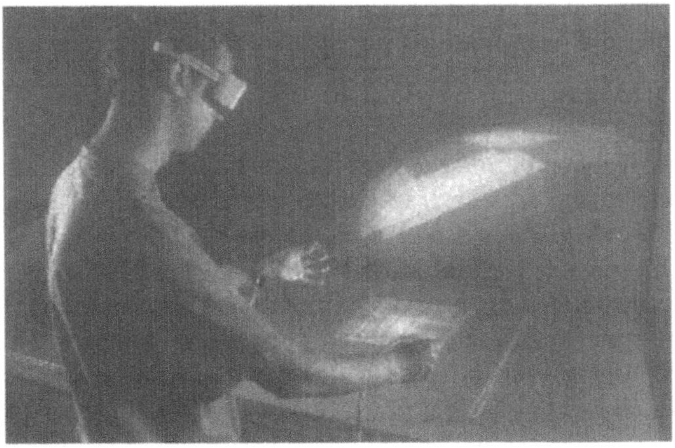

Fig. 1. The C^3 on the Responsive Workbench

2 Related work

Application control inside virtual environments is a new field of research. The first applications developed for these environments faced the immediate need to provide an interface to control functions or states of variables inside the 3D world. At the SIGGRAPH'2000 course on 3D user interface design[11], Ernst Kruijff proposed a categorisation for the current system control techniques influenced by the description of non-conventional control techniques by MacMillan et al.[19]. He divided the approaches into graphical menus, voice commands, gestural interaction and tools.

Graphical menus are the 3D equivalent of 2D menus. The following criteria should be considered when designing graphical menus: placement, selection, representation and structure.

Feiner et al.[8] is a primary source for placement issues. However Kruijff proposed a finer division of the different placement solutions. Menus can be freely placed inside the virtual world (world-referenced), connected to a virtual object (object-referenced), linked to a part of the user's body such as the head (head-referenced) or the rest of the body (body-referenced) or placed in reference to a physical object such as the borders of the workbench (device-centered).

The selection of menu items in a 3D environment is quite different from that in 2D. Selecting an item inside a set of available functions is conceptually a 1D choice system. The addition of another unnecessary dimension is in this case an added difficulty. Moving inside a plane to make a 1D choice is quite easy with a mouse despite the second dimension. It becomes more complicated when the user has in addition to control the depth of his movements. The representation of the menu (form, size, space and affordance) is another whole topic. Finally, as the number of items grows, it becomes necessary to set a mechanism to diminish the cognitive load placed on the user: hierarchical subdivision or context-sensitive menus.

In this group of graphical menus, three different categories have been distinguished by Kruijff: converted 2D-menus, hand-oriented menus and 3D widgets.

2.1 Converted 2D Menus

An intial natural approach for designers of 3D interfaces has consisted of porting 2D interfaces to the 3D world. In the 2D world (screen, keyboard and mouse) the WIMP interface is now a commonly accepted choice to control applications. Since this interface is popular and quite efficient for 2D, porting the interface has the advantage of easily providing users with a non-disturbing familiar interface. However as stated earlier, the third dimension hampers the ease of selection[1][6][20]. Using a virtual ray controlled by the hand as a pointer tool is one method to alleviate this difficulty[21]. However it is still not adapted to making quick selections (like the hotkeys of a keyboard) due to the indirect manipulation and the precision required. Another approach, based on the virtual tricorder device[23], suggests using "2D anchored menus". The 2D menu is displayed at the position of the device held in the hand. Selection inside the menu is done by pressing the mouse buttons.

2.2 Hand-oriented Menus

The two categories of hand-oriented menus are 1DOF menus, where the items are put on a circular object[15][22] and menus stored at a body-relative position, where selection of items is dependent on the hand relative position. This approach exploits proprioceptive feedback[16] [2]. A hybrid approach would materialize the plane of selection by holding a flat physical transparent palette in the non-dominant hand ([4][20]), and selecting items with the dominant one. The graphical menu is displayed directly onto the transparent physical surface (using a tracker on the palette), taking advantage of both the hand-held prop and body-centered aspects.

2.3 3D widgets

Conner et al.[3] describes widgets as the combination of geometry and behaviour. This section describes 3D widgets, including all menus whose functions can be mapped onto an object.

The C^3, in its novice working mode, is a graphical menu, hand-oriented, hand-held widget. The advanced user mode with "eyes-off" manipulation makes extensive use of proprioceptive feedback. The C^3 has been developed with the idea of exploiting the third dimension as an advantage and not a new undesirable dimension. It is based on 2D marking menus. Pie menus are in fact significantly better than linear menus when it comes to fast selection[2].

[2] Proprioception is "a person's sense of the position and orientation of his body and limbs". It provides strong advantages for direct manipulation (excellent control of one's own hand), physical mnemonics (finding body-centered objects) and gestural actions (recall of actions).

3 Description of the C^3

The C^3 proposes an equivalent of the keyboard hotkey mechanism for VE. It can also be used as a quick 3D graphical menu. Menu items are arranged into a cubic configuration, rather than the traditional 2D pull-down menus. The C^3 has roughly the appearance of a cubic volume (or *cubic structure*), divided into 3x3x3 smaller cubes (see Figure 2). Smaller cubes have the same size and are separated from each other by a fixed distance. They are associated with menu items and called "slots". A ball can be moved inside the bounding cube of the structure. The center of this ball acts as a pointer for the selection.

Fig. 2. Division of the space into 27 cubes

The C^3 is controlled by a 6DOF tracked button. The Pinch glove system developed by Fakespace[7] or the ring mouse[17] are valid devices. In essence, any device with a button attached to a tracker fits the requirements. Actually, in our experiments, we did not use a commercial system but instead built one from a simple mouse and a tracker (see Figure 3 and Appendix). The mouse buttons serve as *"pinch buttons"* placed on three fingers of the hand (although only one button was used). They can be pressed with the thumb. The tracker is attached to the user's wrist.

Whenever the user pinches, the C^3 is displayed at small horizontal distance from his hand position. It stays visible while the button is pressed and disappears when released. While the pinch button is pressed, all movements of the hand are mapped onto the ball. The ball's starting position is the center of the bounding cube, which is the center of one of the 27 slots, the middle one. By moving the hand, the user moves the ball inside the bounding cube. The ball cannot leave the cubic structure. If a user's hand movement implies that the ball should go outside the volume, then the corresponding movement of the ball is truncated so that it stops at the surface of the bounding box.

The ball can thus be moved freely inside the cubic structure and placed inside any of the 27 slots. Releasing the button when the ball lies inside a slot results

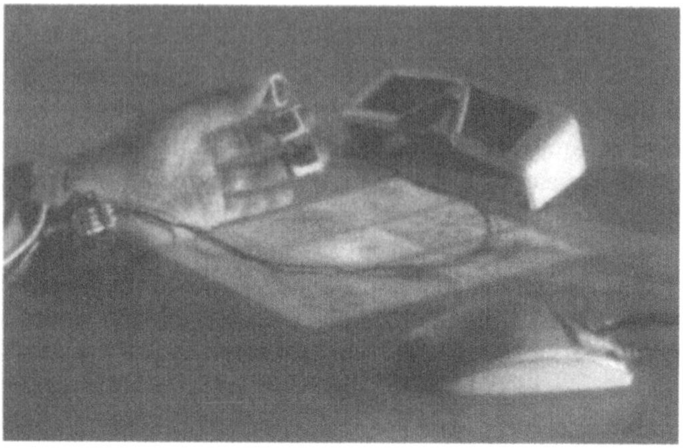

Fig. 3. The tracked buttons

in a user's selection of a menu item, the one associated with the slot. Note that the "middle slot" shouldn't have any function associated with it, to allow the user to pinch accidentally without any consequences. Furthermore, it gives the user a way to cancel the C^3 without selecting an item. There is no restriction on the user's hand movements inside the cubic volume while the pinch button is pushed down, nor is there any time limit to select an item.

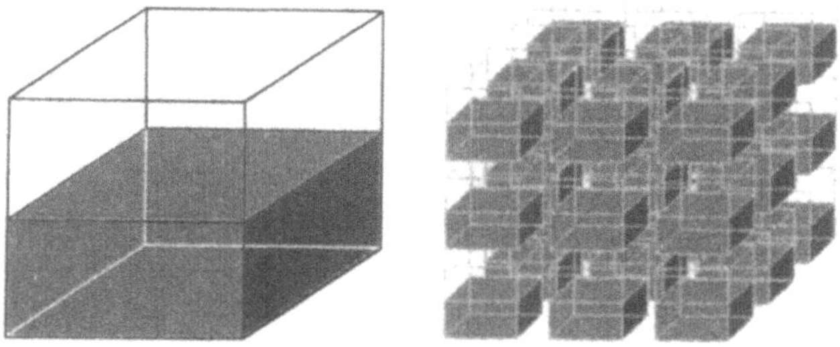

Fig. 4. Visual feedback inside a slot

Each slot is visually represented by a half cube (see Figure 4). The half cubes are transparent blue, while the ball is yellow with no transparency. Since the half cube occupies the lower part of the slot, it's possible to put a transparent texture on top of each that shows an icon, as in classic 2D menus, explaining the function of the slot. The sensitive zone for the selection is still the whole cubic volume of the slot, but the visual part of the slot lies only in the lower half. The opaque ball can be moved anywhere inside the slot to trigger the menu item and is always visible, thanks to the transparency of the slot. The center of the ball is the true pointer of the C^3. To further help the selection, the currently selected slot is highlighted.

As was previously mentioned, pinching two fingers triggers the display of the C^3. Only one horizontal plane of slots, i.e. 9 slots, are represented simultaneously. The visible plane of slots is always the one containing the pointer: the yellow ball controlled by the user's hand. Moving the hand in space moves the ball from slot to slot and triggers, if necessary, the display of another plane (see Figure 5 and Appendix). A short delay to the display of the C^3 allows "eyes-off" manipulation.

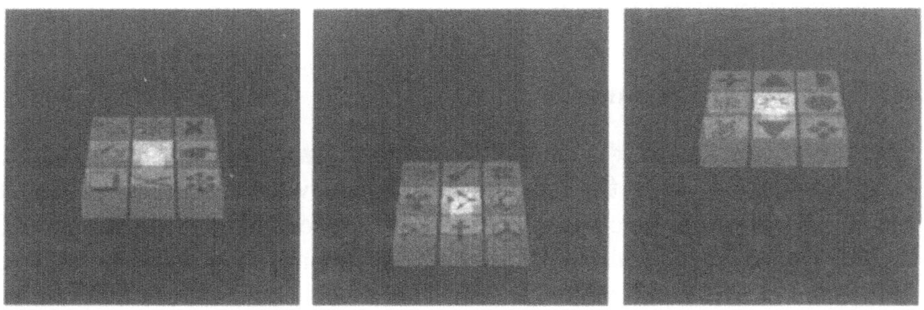

Fig. 5. The C^3 appearance when the user pinches and stands still, moves his hand down, or up.

4 Design issues

This section discusses the reasons behind the most important design choices of the C^3.

4.1 Shape

We decided to use a cubic structure to divide the space around the hand. At first the C^3 was influenced by 2D marking menus, which divided the screen around the mouse pointer into equal pie-shaped sections. We could have divided the 3D space equally around the 3D pointer (the yellow opaque ball). With a simple space decomposition into 6 parts (up, down, left, right, front, back) it would have worked well. However six is a small number of commands for a shortcut mechanism, although it could be adapted to a menu system with a hierarchical structure and was judged too limited. An equal division of the space in more than 6 directions becomes very complicated for a user to imagine. Without any mental representation of the spatial division, it's rather difficult for a user to remember and execute the correct movement with his hand for each menu item.

Thus we decided to use a simple metaphor: the cube. By dividing the space around the ball into 3x3x3 cubes we give the user an intuitive way to remember the path to each command. For example: the upper front right command, or the lower left back one. Each of the 26 available commands can be accessed by mentally figuring the cubic form of the menu and/or by thinking in terms of a combination of simple directions (up, down, left, right, front, back, middle). The task of selecting an item is facilitated by three mechanisms:

- The cubic structure (mental representation of the space)
- The proprioceptive sense (all movements start from the middle position so selecting an item equals moving the hand in one direction).
- The directions are aligned with the screen borders of the workbench (device-centered graphical menus).

4.2 Number of commands

The cube design dictates that the 27 slots are associated with the commands of an application. Since the "middle slot" is reserved for a cancel action there remain 26 options to be configured with the functions of one's application. This number is extended if all the fingers of the human hand are used to trigger different cubes (i.e. set of functions). The Pinch Glove allows 4x26 different functions to be selected. With regard to this large number, we believe the C^3 could be used as much as a shortcut mechanism than a rough 3D menu.

4.3 Visibility

Many visualization concerns have been taken into account in the design of the C^3. First, the C^3 acts as a pop-up menu, and is displayed only when a user performs a specific action: pinching two fingers. Therefore there is no obstruction of the view by 3D widgets in idle mode. The pointer is opaque and remains visible as long as the C^3 is activated. Thus all the slots are transparent and in different colors so that the ball cursor can move inside each and stay visible. The small size of the pointer allows the icon of the selected slot to be seen when the opaque ball is inside the slot (see Figure 5 and Appendix). The transparency of the C^3 does not obscure the 3D scene the user is working on. Indeed, it is still visible through the transparent slots of the C^3.

All the slots are partially "filled" in blue, although the sensitive selection zone is the whole volume. The slots are only filled in their lower half part so that icons can be placed on top of the blue transparent blocks to help the user know which command is associated to each slot. Since the user's hand, at the height the cube is displayed, is lower than the head, there is a good line of sight on the icons. The ball is also more visible with half-filled slots.

The C^3 is displayed in front of the user's hand, lower than the user's eyes. However since the multiple planes of 3x3 slots are lying one above the other, it is rather difficult to see the icons of the lower planes. To avoid this problem, only one horizontal plane (9 slots) is displayed when the C^3 is active: the plane where the ball is currently lying. Moving the ball with the hand from slot to slot triggers the display of another plane, if necessary, but there is always only one visible plane at a given time. Horizontal planes have been chosen in preference to other plane orientations, because the user's eyes are generally above the cube and because of the table-like shape of the RWB.

The size of the little cubes is roughly 10x10x10cm. Some experiments with different sizes guided this choice. The size should be adapted for each workbench with regard to the screen size and resolution.

4.4 Learning and quickness

With the help of the icons, a novice user is able to invoke the C^3 by pinching two fingers and using the cube metaphor to have quick access to 26 commands. For each command the icons provide the necessary feedback to let the user make his choice. Selecting a menu item is simple: pinching, moving the hand in one direction and releasing the pinch. As stated earlier, choosing between distinct 3D directions is easier than selecting an item inside a linear list. Movements can also be very quick and precise since they are relative to the starting position of the hand. No tracker calibration interferes in the selection process.

The C^3 approach, similar to the 2D marking menus can be improved by adding a short delay (less than a second) before displaying the menu. With this feature, the C^3 enhances the application control experience for well-trained users. Indeed, when the positions of the functions inside the cube are perfectly known it is very intuitive to blindly make a move with the hand in a specific direction to trigger the appropriate function. One advantage of this method is that the interface doesn't change between the novice level and the advanced user level. Furthermore, there is no "switch" to be activated to change from one mode to another. A novice user who begins to remember the position of his favorite functions will naturally begin to move his hand blindly. And at all times, an advanced user suddenly hesitating about the right direction to find an option would automatically trigger the display of the menu after the short delay.

In comparison to the hotkey mechanism of the keyboard, it can be argued that chain-triggering the same command with the C^3 seems slightly slower at first sight. However when the same command is not always repeated several times, results should be similar. More testing needs to be done on this issue.

4.5 Focus of attention

The non-dominant hand is used to control the shortcut system, thus leaving the dominant hand free. It is important to leave the user's dominant hand out of the shortcut process, since the main task in a VR application is usually performed by the dominant hand. We don't want to force the user to switch tools to do a simple and quick menu item selection. In addition, the *visual* attention of an advanced user is freed because he can use the C^3 blindly, thus focusing more on his main task. Actually, most of the classic menus require a user to look at a 3D widget, forcing him to break his attention.

5 Conclusion & future work

The C^3 system was initially developed with the idea of finding an equivalent solution to keyboard hotkeys for a RWB. Although in the past some solutions have been proposed to provide users with menu interfaces, to our knowledge researchers had never before focused on a shortcut approach for VE. The third dimension is used by the C^3 as an advantage to propose more menu options to the user. This addition is never an inconvenience for the user as in previous attempts to convert 2D menus into 3D menus. The C^3 has been thought of as and is indeed a real *3D* menu. Since the C^3 is controlled with the non-dominant hand, the user is not distracted from the main task, usually performed or led by the dominant one. Controlling the C^3 directly with the hand is a way to use proprioceptive feedback for a better manipulation and recall of actions. The movements of the hand can be quick and precise, because they are relative to the starting position of the hand. No tracking calibration or precision problems could interfere in the process of selection. In addition, the pop-up approach of the C^3 preserves the menu to block the view when idle.

Based on the marking menus, the C^3 provides the advantage of offering a single interface for both novice and advanced users. As the user memorizes the commands associated to each direction, he moves smoothly from the novice level where the menu is displayed, to the advanced level where he can make an "eyes-off" manipulation to select a command. Furthermore, remembering a direction is easier than remembering a position in a linear menu. An open-ended gesture is also much faster than a Fitt's law task, as in a standard linear menu. The ability to select a command blindly allows the user to rapidly control the application commands, without disturbing his attention since he doesn't have to look at an interface graphical component.

The C^3 can be extended to nx26 configurable menu items, n being the number of available buttons. This is a large number of options for a shortcut system. We found that the C^3 can then be used as a menu in itself, if the number of menu items needed by an application falls below the nx26 limit.

We are planning to add a hierarchical structure to the cube metaphor to extend the number of menu items available and to allow a better placement and recall of the application commands inside the C^3. Some discussion of the placement of the C^3 with regard to the user's hand and body and its potential visual occlusion by 3D application data is also still necessary.

The C^3 has been used in two different applications on the RWB: the visualization of a car cockpit with some basic exploration tools and a more complex visualization application for fractal models. Initial impressions of users seem positive. However we need to test the performance of the C^3 in terms of quickness of selection and accuracy for each slot, usability and to compare its efficiency on the workbench with that of the hotkeys for the keyboard. These data could help in the placement of the more frequently-accessed options inside the C^3. The C^3 has been developed on a holobench but could be extended to other VE configurations. The orientation of the cube relative to the frames of the screens should be reexamined. Some other similar considerations such as the choice of displaying horizontal planes inside the C^3 could also change, vertical planes are better for a wall display or a HMD.

References

1. J. Butterworth, A. Davidson, S. Hench, and T. M. Olano. 3dm: A three dimensional modeler using a head-mounted display. In *Proc. 1992 Symposium on Interactive 3D Graphics*, pages 135–138, 1992.
2. Jack Callahan, Don Hopkins, Mark Weiser, and Ben Shneiderman. An empirical comparison of pie vs. linear menus. In *Proceedings of ACM CHI'88 Conference on Human Factors in Computing Systems*, Menus, pages 95–100, 1988.
3. D. Conner, S. Snibbe, K. Herndon, D. Robbins, R. Zeleznik, and A. van Dam. Three-dimensional widgets. In *Computer Graphics (Proc. 1992 Symposium on Interactive 3D Graphics)*, pages 183–188, 230–231, 1992.
4. S. Coquillart and G. Wesche. The virtual palette and the virtual remote control panel: A device and an interaction paradigm for projection-based virtual environments. In *IEEE VR'99*, 1999.
5. Carolina Cruz-Neira, Daniel J. Sandin, and Thomas A. DeFanti. Surround-screen projection-based virtual reality: The design and implementation of the CAVE. In James T. Kajiya, editor, *Computer Graphics (SIGGRAPH '93 Proceedings)*, volume 27, pages 135–142, August 1993.
6. Michael F. Deering. HoloSketch: a virtual reality sketching/animation tool. *ACM Transactions on Computer-Human Interaction*, 2(3):220–238, September 1995.
7. Fakespace. http://www.fakespacelabs.com/.
8. S. Feiner, B. Macintyre, and D. Seligmann. Knowlege-based augmented reality. *Communications of the ACM*, 36(7):53–61, 1993.
9. B. Frölich, B. Kirsch, W. Krüger, and G. Wesche. Further development of responsive workbench. In M. Göbel, editor, *Virtual Environments '95*, Eurographics, pages 237–246. Springer-Verlag Wien New York, 1995.
10. Wolfgang Kruger, Christian-A. Bohn, Bernd Frohlich, Heinrich Schuth, Wolfgang Strauss, and Gerold Wesche. The responsive workbench: A virtual work environment. *Computer*, 28(7):42–48, July 1995.
11. Ernst Kruijff. 3D user interface design: Fundamental techniques, theory, and practice. SIGGRAPH 2000 Course.
12. Gorden Kurtenbach, Thomas P. Moran, and William Buxton. Contextual animation of gestural commands. In *Proceedings of Graphics Interface '94*, pages 83–90, Banff, Alberta, Canada, May 1994. Canadian Information Processing Society.
13. Gordon Kurtenbach and William Buxton. User learning and performance with marking menus. In Beth Adelson, Susan Dumais, and Judith Olson, editors, *Proceedings of the Conference on Human Factors in Computing Systems*, pages 258–264, New York, NY, USA, April 1994. ACM Press.
14. Gordon Kurtenbach, George W. Fitzmaurice, Russell N. Owen, and Thomas Baudel. The hotbox: Efficient access to a large number of menu-items. In Marian G. Williams, Mark W. Altom, Kate Ehrlich, and William Newman, editors, *Proceedings of the Conference on Human Factors in Computing Systems (CHI-99)*, pages 231–237, New York, May 15–20 1999. ACM Press.
15. Jiandong Liang and Mark Green. JDCAD: A highly interactive 3D modeling system. *Computers and Graphics*, 18(4):499–506, July–August 1994.

16. Mark R. Mine, Frederick P. Brooks, Jr., and Carlo H. Séquin. Moving objects in space: Exploiting proprioception in virtual-environment interaction. In Turner Whitted, editor, *SIGGRAPH 97 Conference Proceedings*, Annual Conference Series, pages 19–26. ACM SIGGRAPH, Addison Wesley, August 1997. ISBN 0-89791-896-7.
17. Ring Mouse. http://www.worklink.net/ringmouse.html.
18. TAN Projektionstechnologie. http://www.tan.de/.
19. McMillan G. Eggelston R. and Anderson T. Nonconventional controls. In *Handbook of human factors and ergonomics*, pages 729–771, 1997.
20. J. Sibert R. Lindeman and J. Hahn. Hand-held windows: Towards effective 2d interaction in immersive virtual environments. In *IEEE VR'99*, 1999.
21. Ron van Teylingen, William Ribarsky, and Charles van der Mast. Virtual data visualizer. *IEEE Transactions on Visualization and Computer Graphics*, 3(1):65–74, January - March 1997. ISSN 1077-2626.
22. G. Wesche and M. Droske. Conceptual free-form styling on the responsive workbench. In *VRST 2000*, 2000.
23. Matthias M. Wloka and Eliot Greenfield. The virtual tricorder: A uniform interface for virtual reality. In *Proceedings of the ACM Symposium on User Interface Software and Technology*, Virtual and Augmented Realities, pages 39–40, 1995. TechNote.

Editors' Note: see Appendix, p. 279 for colored figures of this paper

Measuring an Illusion: The Influence of System Performance on Size Perception in Virtual Environments

Jan Hofmann[1], Thomas J. Jäger[2], Thorben Deffke[2], & Heiner Bubb[3]

[1] Society and Technology Research Group,
DaimlerChrysler AG, D-10559 Berlin, Germany
jan.hofmann@daimlerchrysler.com

[2] Mercedes-Benz Passenger Car Development,
DaimlerChrysler AG, D-71059 Sindelfingen, Germany

[3] Chair of Ergonomics, Technische Universität München,
D-85147 Garching, Germany

Abstract: The effects of system performance variations on people's estimation of virtual object sizes in a multi-sided back projection virtual reality system have been explored. Seventy-seven participants adjusted the sizes of three subsequently displayed simple virtual shapes to the memorized sizes of corresponding real objects. The sizes of the virtual objects have been calibrated in real space. With low system lag (i.e., high system performance), object sizes were underestimated. With high system lag participants perceived the virtual objects significantly larger than while experiencing the high performance condition. An explanation for this effect relying on a proposed cognitive averaging process of motion-dependent size cues has been suggested. In addition, an increase in estimation variance among participants has been detected when the system lag was increased. A control experiment (real-to-real objects size comparisons) proved good applicability of the estimation method used.

Keywords: virtual environments, size perception, system performance

1 Introduction

For effective use of many existing and future applications of virtual environments (VEs), thorough knowledge about the factors influencing size and distance perception in VEs is crucial. Classic examples are applications that shall enable transfer of training and spatial knowledge from the VE to the real world (or vice versa). Others include VEs for assessing spatial properties of real world objects via analysing their virtual substitutes. The latter application is especially important in product development processes of divers industries, ranging from hand held information technology development to automobile and all the way to factory design.

1.1 Factors affecting spatial perception in VEs

Factors affecting size and distance perception in real environments have been subject to intense research for decades; see e.g. Gillam (1995) and Cutting and Vishton (1995) for reviews. Only in recent years, a number of studies has been published on factors affecting spatial perception in VEs. Various system related and cognitive factors have been analysed, including the variation of display type (e.g. Henry & Furness, 1993; Ellis & Menges, 1997; Bullinger et al., 1998; Waller, 1999), texture and stimulus size as well as navigational interface (Witmer & Kline, 1998), scene contrast (Eggleston et al., 1996), field of view (Waller, 1999; and references therein), error-corrective feedback (Waller, 1999), and distance cue type (Surdick, 1997). The majority of these studies were concerned with egocentric distance estimations, egocentric meaning that one end point of the judged distance is the observer.

1.2 Overestimation vs. underestimation

Plenty of research work has been conducted to determine the direction (overestimation or underestimation) and degree of estimation errors of distance and size judgements in real environments. Results are diverse, but as a general rule egocentric distances seem to be underestimated in many cases, whereas exocentric distances (those between objects) often tend to be overestimated (see Waller, 1999, for a concise review). This general behaviour has been observed in VEs as well. For instance, Witmer and Kline (1998) as well as Henry and Furness (1993) found strong underestimation of egocentric and mixed egocentric and exocentric distances, respectively; Waller's (1999) experiments exhibited an average overestimation in exocentric distance judgements.

1.3 Staying with us: system lag

In addition to the variation of the parameters mentioned in section 1.1, it has been suggested (Witmer & Kline, 1998) but to our knowledge not yet been shown that system performance, or system lag, has an effect on spatial perception in VEs (throughout this article, the term *system lag* is used to denote the time delay between a user motion and the corresponding adjustment of the display contents, thus including the phase lag of the tracking system, delays due to high rendering times/low frame rates, and possible other effects). Today, significant system lags are still not restricted to low-end virtual reality systems. Particularly VEs for product development and styling processes are often considered to require high degrees of pictorial realism and three-dimensional detail, thus producing a strongly perceivable system lag even using today's high end graphics engines. There is no way to rule out that the co-evolution of system power and user demands concerning handled data volumes is going to persist in the near future, underlining the importance of studying system performance-related effects.

1.4 The objective of this study

In the light of the points mentioned in sections 1.1, 1.2, and 1.3, the objective of the present paper was to investigate the effects of system lag (as induced by varied rendering frame rates) on the users' perception of exocentric distances, in this case object sizes. We did so by having participants compare the sizes of virtual objects to those of real objects seen beforehand as a mental reference. No direct perceptual frame of reference (familiar objects, grid etc.) was given in the VE.

This procedure enabled us not only to analyse effects on size estimation due to variations of system lag in the VE, but also to simultaneously compare participants' estimations to their real world size perception. The comparability to real world perception is essential for many practical applications. To ensure this comparability and to exclude a possible scaling bias caused by the tracking or projection system, we calibrated the dimensions of the virtual objects in real space.

2 Method

2.1 Participants, apparatus, and stimuli

Seventy-seven people participated in the study (9 women and 68 men). The virtual objects assessed were positioned near the middle of a cubic-shaped five-sided back projection system (2.5 m length of side). The objects were thus comfortably viewable in side-elevation while standing. The virtual environment ran on an Silicon Graphics® Onyx2™ graphics engine. The participants' head movements were tracked with a six-DOF tracker (MotionStar® by Ascension®), the left and right eye channels were separated using StereoGraphics® CrystalEyes® shutter glasses. The system lag was controlled by selectively adding a highly complex (invisible) object, slowing down the frame rate to appr. 3 frames/s (for each eye). For the high performance situation this object was removed (frame rate appr. 57 frames/s for each eye).

The three virtual objects to be assessed were a stick, a sheet, and a box (basic dimensions of (a) stick: 50 by 0.5 cm, (b) sheet: 50 by 30 by 0.5 cm, (c) box: 50 by 30 by 40 cm). No other virtual objects were displayed within the participants' field of vision in order to prevent size estimations through direct comparison. The sizes of the virtual objects could be increased or decreased by scaling factors of (n × 1.04) or (n × 0.96), respectively, along all three axes uniformly (n = 1, 2, 3...). In addition, a series of differently sized real objects of each type was provided, featuring the same scaling steps as the virtual objects.

2.2 Procedure

The participants' task was to memorize the size of a particular real object and to subsequently choose the corresponding virtual object with the size fitting their memory of the real object best. The first size displayed was slightly off the correct size. The participant had to decide whether the currently displayed object was too big, too small or correct in size compared to the real object seen just shortly beforehand. The participant gave her or his assessment aloud, and the operator immediately adjusted the size of the object by one step (of 4 % along each cartesian axis) in the indicated direction. This procedure was repeated until the participant judged the size to be correct. This size was recorded (*real-to-virtual comparison*). Having left the projection room, participants were shown a single real object again. Out of five differently sized corresponding real objects, they then chose the one that fitted the memorized size of the single object best (*real-to-real comparison*). Here, participants in both system lag groups experienced the same stimuli (control experiment).

Each participant assessed all three types of objects (stick, sheet, and box) in the two combinations real-to-virtual and real-to-real. The real-to-real comparison was included to check on the participants' performance in a corresponding task without virtual stimuli. The objects' order of presentation was randomized to prevent transfer effects. The participants were randomly assigned to the low and high system lag situations ($n_{low} = 42$, $n_{high} = 35$). Each of them experienced only one of the settings, again in order to prevent transfer effects. Prior to each experiment each participant's interocular distance was measured, enabling the software to correct for these differences by adapting the projected images.

2.3 Calibration

The aim of the calibration process was to determine the sizes of the projected virtual objects in real space. For this purpose we measured the x-, y-, and z-dimensions of the projected objects using a transparent, real ruler (n = 10 for each object and dimension, estimated reading error 0,5 cm, standard deviation 0.4-0.9 cm). For the sheet and the box, the calibration values for x- and y-directions or x-, y-, and z-directions, respectively, have been averaged as participants were able and encouraged to view the objects from different directions.

3 Results

3.1 Mean Size Estimation

The participants' size estimations were averaged separately within the twelve settings (three object types in real-to-virtual and real-to-real combinations in two system lag settings). Figures 1 (a-c) show the mean size estimation errors for each setting. The size estimation error is defined as the ratio of the size of the chosen virtual (real) object and that of the corresponding real object the size of which was to be matched. Thus, a positive estimation error indicates an *underestimation* of the size of the chosen virtual (real) object. Note that the estimation error describes uniform differences along all three Cartesian axes for all three objects. The zero lines in Figures 1 (a-c) were calibrated as described in (2.3). For each object type and within each combination, the mean values for the low and high system lag settings were subject to separate variance analyses. In the real-to-real combination, low and high system lag groups experienced the same conditions (control experiment).

Variance analysis: real-to-virtual. In the real-to-virtual combination, the variance analyses yielded significant differences between low and high system lag settings at the 0.10 level for the sheet ($F(1, 75) = 2.81$, $p = 0.098$) and the box ($F(1, 75) = 3.99$, $p = 0.050$). In both cases the participants chose bigger objects in the low system lag situation, the differences of the mean estimation errors ($error_{low} - error_{high}$) being 2.76 % (sheet) and 3.89 % (box). For the stick, the variance analysis yielded a not significant result ($F(1, 75) = 2.09$, $p = 0.153$). Though not being significant, one could argue that the tendency observed in the other two cases stays the same (bigger objects being chosen in the low system lag setting). As can be seen in Figures 1 (a-c), the mean estimation errors have relatively high positive values in the same order of magnitude for all three object types in the low system lag situation (2.91, 2.99, and

2.33 % for stick, sheet, and box, respectively). For the high system lag situation, the mean estimation errors are comparatively small (-0.37, 0.23, and -1.56 %, respectively).

Variance analysis: real-to-real. No significant differences were found across high and low system lag subject groups, as expected due to the identical conditions in this part of the experiment (stick: $F(1, 75) = 0.06$, $p = 0.807$; sheet: $F(1, 75) = 2.00$, $p = 0.161$; box: $F(1, 75) = 0.68$, $p = 0.413$).

3.2 Estimation Variance Comparison

Additionally, we compared the estimation variance within the settings across system lag situations for the real-to-virtual combination (Figure 1d). The comparison yielded significant dependencies of the estimation variance on system lag for all three object types at the 0.10 level (as well as 0.05 and 0.01 levels for box and sheet, respectively): Experimental F-values were $F_{stick} = 1.60$, $F_{sheet} = 2.55$, $F_{box} = 1.76$ (see Bortz, 1989, for F-value extraction), the corresponding theoretical F-values are $F_{90\%}(34, 41)$

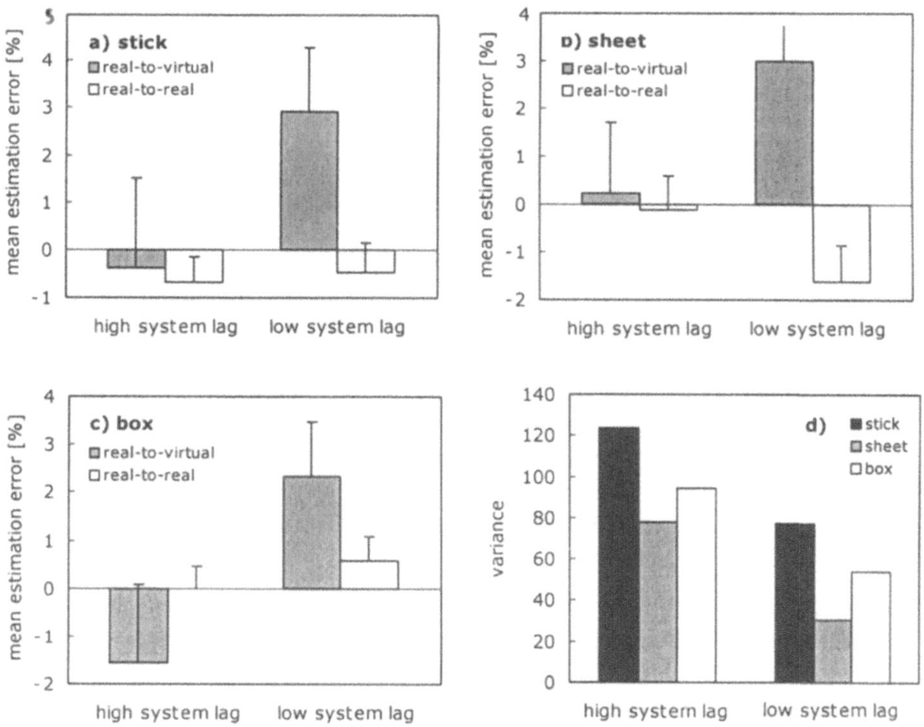

Fig. 1. (a-c) Mean size estimation errors (and standard errors of the mean) for stick, sheet, and box in real-to-virtual and real-to-real comparisons and for high and low system lags (in the real-to-real control experiment, high and low system lag groups experienced the same stimuli). Positive estimation errors denote underestimation; see the text for a definition of the size estimation error. The percentages given describe uniform scaling along all three cartesian axes. (d) Estimation variance for stick, sheet, and box in the real-to-virtual setting for high and low system lag.

= 1.54, $F_{95\%}(34, 41) = 1.74$, $F_{99\%}(34, 41) = 2.20$. In all cases the variance was smaller in the low system lag situation.

4 Discussion

Three main outcomings are to be discussed: (1) For all three geometric shapes, the high system lag situation generated a mean estimation error (as defined above) smaller in magnitude than the low system lag situation. In fact the estimation errors were well below 0.5 % for stick and sheet with high system lag. (2) Equal in direction and similar in magnitude for all three object types, a decrease of the system lag let participants perceive the virtual objects *smaller* (statistically significant for sheet and box). (3) Comparison of the estimation variance exhibited a lower variance for the low system lag (significant in all three cases).

4.1 Result one

At first glance, result (1) seems to suggest that it is the *high* system lag (which in this experiment is very high indeed) that allows *more accurate* estimations. This appears to be counterintuitive, as the high system lag situation is for sure the less 'natural' one and therefore prone to disturb normal size perception processes. The following section helps resolving this contradiction.

4.2 Result two

Why has the variation of the system lag – as described in result (2) – influenced participants' size perception? We suggest the following possible explanation.

The effect observed has to be linked directly with the participants' motion relative to the objects. If not moving, participants in the high and low system lag situations experienced exactly the same stimuli (the objects were fixed in space). The participants' motion was predominantly sideways with a slight rotation of their heads as they watched the objects from varying angles. Alternatively, they just turned their heads, looking back and forth from one side of the object to the other. To a first approximation, the turning of the head results in a movement very similar to a small sideways movement, since (1) they only slightly turned their heads to achieve this and (2) the natural axis of horizontal head rotation runs through the back of one's head. Figures 2 (d) illustrates this schematically.

Figure 2 (a) shows the geometric situation for an observer viewing a virtual object A without moving. The observer perceives it stereoscopically floating in front of her or him by looking at images B and C that are projected on screen D. Image B can only be viewed with the right eye, C only with the left. If the observer moves to the right, keeping the eyes on the same line, and only looks at the images again when the system has had enough time to adapt the display contents to the new tracker position, then the geometric situation is as shown in Figure 2 (c). Object A virtually stays in place, images A and B have been shifted (to A' and B', respectively). In an ideal system (zero lag), this adjustment is correct also *during* movements. As the objects in this experiment are very simple, our low system lag situation is close to an ideal system in this respect.

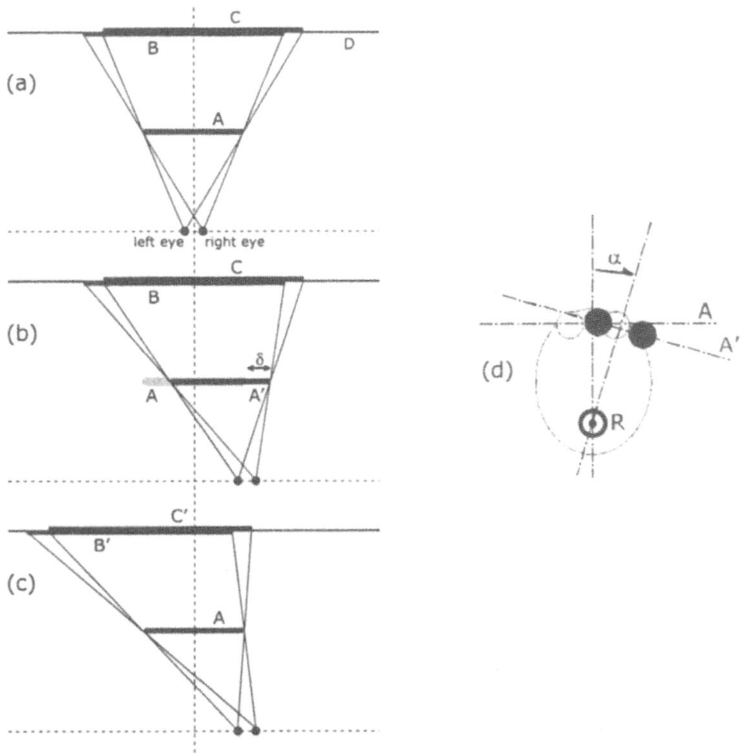

Fig. 2. (a-c) Schematic representations of a person perceiving a virtual object A by viewing a double picture B/C (B'/C') on a projection screen D. (a) Static viewing conditions; (b) intermediate viewing conditions with strong system lag, the observer has shifted to the right, but pictures B/C have not been adapted yet, resulting in a perceived shift of virtual object A by a distance δ to position A'; (c) adapted viewing conditions instantly achieved after a move to the right in an ideal system, but with a strong system lag only after a perceivable period of time. (d) Schematic overhead view of a person slightly turning her or his head. To a first approximation, a 'natural' head rotation by a small angle α (R = axis of rotation) results in a similar geometric situation as a slight shift of the head to the side.

The situation is different for a high system lag: if the observer quickly moves to the right, the system is too slow to adjust images B and C instantaneously. Figure 2 (b) shows the resulting geometric situation for the extreme case that images B and C are still in the same position as in Figure 2 (a), whereas the observer has finished her or his movement already. Thus, the observer perceives the virtual object *shifted to the right* (A'). If the observer stays in this position, the virtual objects then gradually moves back to its original position (A) as the graphics engine adjusts images B and C (resulting in B' and C'; see Figure 2 (c)). Similar effects are, of course, observed with similar movements in other directions.

This shifting of the virtual object alone does not account for the difference in size estimations as a function of system lag, as the length of A' equals that of A (intercept theorems) and their perceived distance is nearly the same (no significant change in distance cues). But taking into account that one is usually directing one's line of sight in the direction of the movement and/or rotation (looking at the right side of the virtual object while turning the head to the right), the following explanation seems plausible: With the majority of sideways movements or head rotations, the observer apparently views an object *temporarily enlarged on one side* – the side just looked at primarily (see Figure 5 for an illustration). The fact that the object is shortened by the same amount on the other side (the one not in the line of sight) seems to be neglected by the observer in comparison. Because participants were able and encouraged to view the objects from different directions, they moved a lot, thus being exposed to constantly changing size cues. The most straightforward cognitive strategy for resolving the changing size cue conflict we can think of is an averaging process. Consequently, participants might have had an overall impression of a slightly enlarged object; the degree of enlargement did then depend on their movement rate.

In the low system lag situation such an effect cannot occur. Hence, coming back to the discussion of result (1), participants' size estimations were more accurate experiencing a low system lag, as common sense had already suggested.

4.3 Result three

On the basis of the proposed explanation for result (2), a straightforward explanation for result (3) is possible as well. Given that the participants were free to choose the amount of their movement, there is good reason to believe that the amount of movement is distributed statistically across participants. If the size estimations are dependent on the overall amount of movement in the high system lag setting, the estimations should exhibit an increasing variance with increasing the system lag. This is exactly what we found in our experiments. It should be noted though that more participants were (randomly) assigned to the low system lag setting than to the high system lag situation ($n_{low} = 42$, $n_{high} = 35$), possibly enhancing the observed effect.

4.4 Why underestimation?

In the optimum estimation condition (low system lag), the sizes of the virtual objects are generally underestimated in our experiment. We currently have no explanation for this observation. A review of the literature (see section 1.2) shows divers results of similar experiments, exhibiting both overestimation and underestimation. It has to be added that the calibration process described in section 2.3 is arbitrary to some extent. A separate calibration for x, y, and z yields different zero lines in Figures 1 (a-c). Possibly, participants have given unequal weights along the different spatial axes in their estimations, either statistically varying interpersonally or even varying systematically. With the described experiment we could not account for that.

4.5 The effect of 'adding dimensions'

The F-values for the mean estimation error differences between high and low system lag settings are increasing from stick to sheet to box, reaching significance (at the 0.1 level) for sheet and box only.

The reason for this might be the following: All object types were uniformly scaled along all three axes by the same factor (n × 1.04 or n × 0.96), resulting in equal relative steps in volume for each scaling step. But since the basic stick measured only 0.5 cm in diameter and was 50 cm long, the only parameter that changed perceivably was its length. The basic sheet was only 0.5 cm thick but 50 wide and 30 cm high, resulting in a more easily recognizable change in overall size for each scaling step compared to the stick. For the box, the noticeably changing depth is added. These added cues seem to result in a lower variance of mean estimation values, finally yielding a higher F-value, as differences of the mean values between high and low system lag settings are similar across object types.

4.6 Real-to-real estimations

In the real-to-real setting, estimations have been fairly accurate with a comparatively low variance, except for the sheet estimation in the low system lag group. Additionally, no significant differences between high and low system lag groups have been detected for any of the objects. This was expected due to the identical viewing conditions. These results suggest that when comparing real objects, participants were able to relate perceived object sizes to those memorized beforehand correctly. Thus, estimation errors in our real-to-virtual experiments are due to virtual environment perception, not due to difficulties to remember and compare object sizes at all. It cannot be ruled out though that the relatively small number and narrow size range of real objects to choose from in the real-to-real task (five objects) might have diminished the variance of size estimations. In the real-to-virtual experiment, the virtual object sizes to choose from where not limited.

5 Conclusion

In the experiment described in this paper we analysed the effects of system lag variation on size perception in a high-end projection-based virtual reality system. The virtual objects were calibrated in real space. This enabled us to compare the actual projected size of the virtual objects with participants' corresponding estimates. Without the calibration, a possible scaling bias caused by the tracking or projection system could not have been excluded.

We reported three main findings:

(1) In the condition enabling the most accurate estimations (low system lag), participants systematically underestimated the sizes of the virtual objects.

(2) Increasing the system lag made participants perceive the virtual objects significantly bigger. We offered a possible explanation for this effect based on a proposed temporal cognitive averaging process of changing size cues. The changing of size cues is suggested to be a combined effect of (a) participants' motion relative to the virtual objects, (b) the system lag, and (c) participants' proposed selective attention for those parts of the virtual objects the line of sight is currently moved to.

(3) Finally we found that the variations of participants' size estimations exhibited a significantly stronger dependence on their rate of movement for high system lag

compared to the low lag condition. As movements were not restricted (which corresponds to an everyday application setting), this resulted in a higher estimation variance in the high system lag setting.

From our point of view, system performance will continue to be a topic to be concerned about even using the latest and most powerful virtual reality computing technology. Thus, we hope that our results can help designing VE applications that successfully support practical tasks. Thorough understanding of size and distance perception is essential for the effective use of many of today's and future VE applications. A lot more research work in the field of size and distance perception is though necessary. Findings so far published in the relatively small number of studies are not coherent. To get a more precise picture of the involved effects is not only interesting and important for the scientific community. It will be needed for virtual environments to gain further importance in various application fields as well.

Acknowledgments. We thank all our participants and two anonymous reviewers for their helpful comments.

References

Bortz, J. (1989). *Statistik für Sozialwissenschaftler.* Berlin: Springer.

Bullinger, H.-J., Riedel, O., & Breining, R. (1998). Perception in Different IPT-Systems. In: *Proceedings of the 2nd International Immersive Projection Technology Workshop, Iowa 1998.*

Cutting, J. E., & Vishton, P. M. (1995). Perceiving Layout and Knowing Distances: The Integration, Relative Potency, and Contextual Use of Different Information about Depth. In W. Epstein & S. Rogers (Eds.), *Perception of Space and Motion* (pp. 69-117). San Diego: Academic Press.

Eggleston, R. G., Janson, W. P., & Aldrich, K. A. (1996). Virtual reality system effects on size-distance judgement in virtual environments. In *Proceedings of the IEEE Conference – Virtual Reality Annual International Symposium (VRAIS) '96*, 139-146.

Ellis, S. R., & Menges, B. M. (1997). Judgement of the Distance to Nearby Virtual Objects: Interaction of Viewing Conditions and Accommodative Demand. *Presence: Teleoperators and Virtual Environments*, 6(4), 452-460.

Gillam, B. (1995). The perception of spatial layout from static optical information. In W. Epstein & S. Rogers (Eds.), *Perception of space and motion* (pp. 23-67). San Diego: Academic Press.

Henry, D., & Furness, T. (1993). Spatial perception in virtual environments: Evaluating an architectural application. In *Proceedings of the IEEE Conference – Virtual Reality Annual International Symposium (VRAIS) '93*, 33-40.

Surdick, R. T., Davis, E. T., King, R. A., & Hodges, L. F. (1997). The Perception of Distance in Simulated Visual Displays: A Comparison of the Effectiveness and Accuracy of Multiple Depth Cues Across Viewing Distances. *Presence: Teleoperators and Virtual Environments*, 6(5), 513-531.

Waller, D. (1999). Factors affecting the perception of interobject distances in virtual environments. *Presence: Teleoperators and Virtual Environments, 8(6)*, 657-670.

Witmer, B. G., & Kline, P. B. (1998). Judging perceived and traversed distance in virtual environments. *Presence: Teleoperators and Virtual Environments, 7(2)*, 144-167.

Presence – a global media quality metric

J. Lessiter & J. Freeman

Psychology Dept., Goldsmiths College,
University of London, SE14 6NW, UK

Abstract. In this paper 'presence' (a sense of 'being there' in a mediated environment) is proposed as a global quality metric with which to evaluate advanced multi-modal media systems. The development of a new presence self-report measure, the ITC-Sense of Presence Inventory (ITC-SOPI), is described that comprises four empirically derived scales: Sense of Physical Space, Engagement, Ecological Validity, and Negative Effects. Two applications of the ITC-SOPI are presented. Using both controlled and uncontrolled experimental designs, the sensitivity of the ITC-SOPI scales to degree of physical immersivity (e.g., large vs. small format; monoscopic vs. stereoscopic viewing condition) is demonstrated. These preliminary results suggest that the ITC-SOPI is a valid tool with which to evaluate experiential aspects of immersive technology.

1 Introduction

Evaluation is a critical ongoing process that informs the development of technology for new media systems. In terms of immersive technology evaluation, a number of issues are raised: What (construct) should be evaluated in order to optimise immersive systems? Can we identify a valid construct that is useful to developers of different types of media system? How do we measure this construct? This paper proposes one such global media quality metric and describes the development and an application demonstration of a new questionnaire to measure this construct, the ITC-Sense of Presence Inventory.

1.1 What (construct) should be evaluated in order to optimise immersive systems?

Immersive technology aims to provide mediated multi-modal stimulation, such as visual, auditory, kinaesthetic, and olfactory information. However, it is more typical for only a few of these sensory inputs, commonly visual and auditory, to be represented [1]. The ultimate goal is to render these inputs convincing and sufficiently realistic in order to replace our 'real world' sensory inputs and to fool our sensory system into 'perceiving' a mediated environment as non-mediated. This "perceptual illusion of non-mediation" has been termed 'presence' [2]. Presence has also been defined more generally as a subjective sensation of "being there" in an environment depicted by a medium [3].

1.2 Can we identify a valid construct that is useful to developers of different types of media system?

Presence is arguably a continuous, rather than a dichotomous, construct that is positively associated with physical immersion, and may therefore be evoked by a range of media to varying degrees. Indeed, Freeman and Avons [4] found that stereoscopic television viewers used terms commonly associated with virtual environment (VE) display systems, such as 'being there' [cf. 5] to describe their media experiences. For non-entertainment based immersive applications, however, task performance may be at least as important as presence in system evaluation. However, the relationship between presence and task performance is unclear.

According to Sheridan [6] three major properties of a technology (i.e., media form characteristics) can determine presence: (i) the extent of sensory information presented, (ii) the degree of control a participant has over positioning his/her sensors within the environment (e.g., a turn of the head to see or hear more of the environment); and (iii) a user's ability to modify aspects of the environment. Sheridan's theory predicts that a system which fully supports each of these criteria would elicit high presence. Other studies have empirically demonstrated that specific physical system properties can determine presence. These have included spatial audio [7]; geometric field of view [7]; stereoscopic depth cues [8, 9, 10, 11] head tracking [7]; display update rate [12]; and motion parallax [10].

In addition to media form, media content and user characteristics can also moderate the sense of presence. Media content refers to the overall theme, narrative or story depicted via a display system. Relevant content variables that have been demonstrated to enhance the sense of presence include user representations within a VE [13], life-like/natural/believable contents [14] and VE stacking (i.e., entering a VE within another VE). There is also some evidence that user characteristics such as a user's perceptual, cognitive, motor abilities and personality traits (e.g., a willingness to suspend disbelief [13]) can be important in determining presence. As presence is multiply determined, it is likely that there are trade-offs between the different determinants of presence. For instance, displays high in photorealism may compensate for an absence of control and manipulation input devices (henceforth referred to as 'interactive' displays).

1.3 How do we measure this construct?

Involvement and attention are particularly important in the measurement of presence [15, 16] as participants exposed to a media system and unfamiliar with the presence concept are likely to use these terms to describe their experience. For instance, Freeman and Avons [4] found that participants described their involvement in a 3D video presentation as 'unavoidable'.

Presence involves heightened attention towards the mediated environment ('arrival'), and conversely, decreased attention towards the unmediated environment ('departure') [17]. Thus, concentration and distraction are also key measurement variables.

The measurement of presence to date has primarily consisted of ad hoc subjective rating scales [1, 7, 13, 14] that typically relate to feeling: (a) physically located in a mediated space (b) that the mediated environment is as real as the real world and (c) that the mediated place had been 'visited'. However, these simple measures can be affected by prior experience, and are thus potentially unstable [10]. Furthermore, they offer little insight into the structure (potential multi-dimensionality) of presence that more complex questionnaires subjected to data reduction techniques afford.

There are several criteria to satisfy and issues to consider in the development of structured presence questionnaires [18], attempts at which to date [16, 17, 19], are limited. These issues and criteria include: (i) probing participants about presence-related sensations rather than presence, per se, which is an unfamiliar construct to most non-experts [4, 11]; (ii) taking care to address just one issue per question; (iii) maintaining consistency across response options to produce a user-friendly measure; (iv) tapping all characteristics that have been putatively related to presence to ensure adequate content sampling; (v) phrasing questions carefully to avoid confounds with specific physical properties and limiting generality to a range of media; (vi) ensuring broad utility by piloting the measure on participants of media systems that differ on a variety of physical parameters; and (vii) satisfying the statistical requirement of a high subject to variable ratio when using data reduction techniques such as factor analysis.

2 The ITC-Sense of Presence Inventory (ITC-SOPI)

Our research group has developed a presence questionnaire that aims to have general utility by explicitly probing the experiential qualities of a media presentation. The full development of this measure is reported elsewhere [18]. To summarise, the ITC-SOPI originally consisted of 63 items, each generated to tap one of a number of facets putatively related to presence (sense of physical space, involvement, attention, distraction, control and manipulation [i.e., autonomy], realness, naturalness, perception of time, awareness of behavioural responses, a sense of social interaction, personal relevance, arousal, and negative effects). Items are rated on a 1-5 Likert scale from 'Strongly Disagree' to 'Strongly Agree'.

2.1 Pilot sample

The 63-item measure was piloted on 604 people (51% male, mean age = 29 years; S.D. = 11.24) following their experience of one of six mediated experiences with different levels of physical immersion (IMAX 3D, IMAX 2D, conventional cinema, college film projection [GCSU], Video Short presentation on a 28'' TV, and an interactive computer games console presented on a 28'' widescreen TV housed within a controlled test platform). The content was varied to avoid confounding the results with a specific type of content. In this way, the stability of the relationships between questions, irrespective of content, could be examined. All respondents rated just one presentation.

2.2 Results

Data were entered into a principal axis factoring analysis (Varimax rotation). Four factors were extracted and labelled: Sense of Physical Space (e.g., 'I had a sense of being in the scenes displayed'; 'I felt I was visiting the places in the displayed environment'), Engagement (e.g., 'I felt involved (in the displayed environment)'; 'I felt sad that my experience was over'), Ecological Validity (e.g., 'The displayed environment seemed natural'; 'I felt that the displayed environment was part of the real world') and Negative Effects (e.g., 'I felt I had a headache'; 'I felt tired').

To refine the measure, items were dropped that (a) failed to load above 0.30 on any factor, (b) showed unstable factor loadings when separate analyses were run on a random split of the dataset and/or were deemed of low importance or relevance to their factor, or (c) elevated the internal consistency of their respective factors when deleted in the alpha check. A total of 44 items were consequently retained for the ITC-SOPI.

Preliminary validity

The first factor, Sense of Physical Space, demonstrated sensitivity to media form in an uncontrolled experimental context. Variations in factors such as naturalness of content, type of image (photorealistic vs. animated) and nature of content both within and across the conditions render comparisons for Engagement, Ecological Validity and Negative Effects, less meaningful. As indicated in Figure 1, the pattern of results correspond somewhat to the degree of physical immersivity offered by the presentation media. For instance, large field of view formats (e.g., IMAX) tended to receive higher ratings than smaller field of view formats (video shorts presented on a 28'' colour TV). The exception is the Computer Game format which is likely to have been rated more highly because it is interactive. This supports the notion that there are trade-offs between the different determinants of presence.

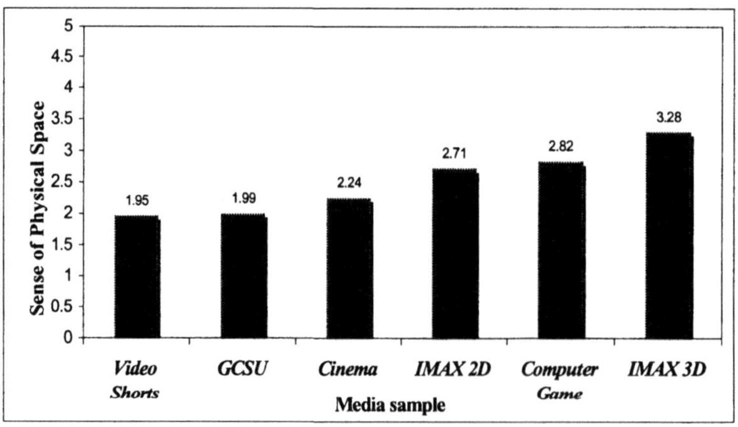

Fig. 1. Mean Sense of Physical Space scores for each of the media samples

3 Controlled experimental application of the ITC-SOPI: Stereoscopic depth cues

Our research group evaluates experiential aspects of Immersive (broadcast) TV - TV that makes the viewer feel present at a live event. By developing appropriate evaluation tools, such as the ITC-SOPI, various display configurations of the immersive system can be tested and recommendations made for its optimisation.

Stereoscopic enhancement of simple presence ratings is a robust finding [8, 9, 10, 11] that we aimed to replicate using our ITC-SOPI. We predicted that 3D presentations would receive higher ITC-SOPI ratings on Sense of Physical Space, Engagement and Ecological Validity than 2D presentations.

3.1 Method

Forty-eight students and staff or affiliates of Goldsmiths College, University of London (24 male, 24 female; aged 18-55 years, $\bar{x} = 26.6$ years, SD = 8.4) experienced one 3D and one 2D video presentation. This comprised a 120 second piece of continuous stereoscopic video footage of a rally car sequence. The sequence depicts rally car driving shot from the backseat of a car and involves fast driving along a winding dirt track with few objects in view except foliage, traffic cones and isolated buildings. The movement of the car alternates quickly between sharp bends, slow bends and occasional straight stretches of road.

Observers viewed the stimulus video on a 28" Philips 100Hz TV monitor. They viewed the display wearing Crystal-Eyes polarised spectacles. The Crystal Eyes spectacles flicker on and off (switching the visible image between left and right eye) at a rate of 100 Hz, in synchrony with the video output. When separate left and right eye video tapes were placed in the video players, the system displayed stereoscopic video to a viewer wearing the Crystal Eyes glasses. For monoscopic presentations, the left eye view was presented to both eyes. Presentation order was fully counterbalanced across the sample.

The ITC-SOPI was administered immediately following each video presentation. Four scale scores were computed by averaging the constituent items for each of the ITC-SOPI scales: Sense of Physical Space (19 items), Engagement (13 items), Ecological Validity (5 items) and Negative Effects (6 items). Each scale ranged from 1 to 5. Data were collected as part of a larger study but only the data relating to viewing condition will be reported here.

3.2 Results

Repeated measures ANOVAs were run for each of the four ITC-SOPI scales. There was a significant main effect of viewing condition for Sense of Physical Space ($F_{(1,45)} = 20.7$, $p < 0.001$), Engagement ($F_{(1,45)} = 12.2$, $p < 0.01$), and Ecological Validity ($F_{(1,45)} = 7.8$, $p < 0.01$). In each instance, 3D presentations were rated more highly than 2D presentations (see Figure 2). However there was no significant difference between the two viewing conditions for Negative Effects ($F_{(1,45)} < 1.0$, ns). Thus the prediction that 3D compared with 2D presentations would produce higher ratings for ITC-SOPI Sense of Physical Space, Engagement and Ecological Validity was supported.

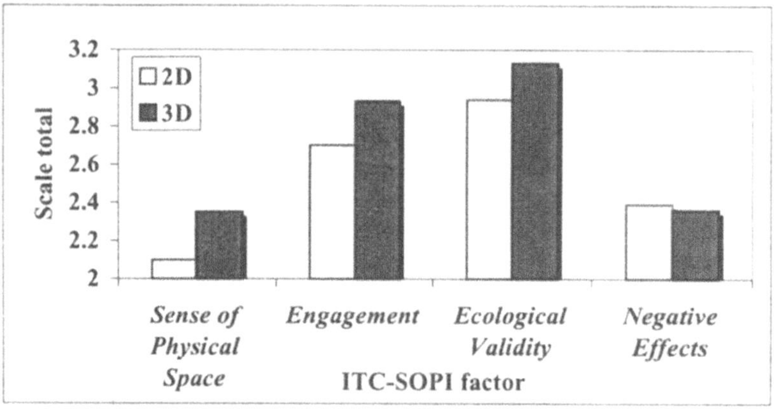

Fig. 2. The effects of viewing condition (2D/3D) on ITC-SOPI scores

4 Discussion

Immersive systems are being developed that provide viewers with an increased number of sensory inputs and enhanced fidelity within each modality. To evaluate a range of these systems a construct is required that (i) represents the goal of immersive systems and, (ii) can be measured using a reliable and valid tool which is sensitive to manipulations of system parameters.

Presence, the subjective sensation of 'being there', is proposed as a global media quality metric with which to evaluate and optimise immersive technology. The ITC-SOPI represents our research group's attempt to develop a presence questionnaire that overcomes some of the limitations faced by existing measures. A rigorous factor analysis of this carefully designed questionnaire suggested that the ITC-SOPI is composed of four scales: Sense of Physical Space, Engagement, Ecological Validity, and Negative Effects, each of which is highly cohesive. Preliminary validation of ITC-SOPI's Sense of Physical Space suggests that even in an experimentally uncontrolled context, it is sensitive to broad variations in media form. Furthermore, in an experimentally controlled context, the ITC-SOPI demonstrated sensitivity to manipulation of stereoscopic depth cues which has previously been shown to covary with simple presence rating scales. These preliminary results suggest that this measure is a promising evaluation tool.

One limitation of the ITC-SOPI is that we have not piloted this questionnaire on a broad range of what we term 'interactive' (i.e. inclusion of a control/manipulation device) displays. Nevertheless, given the high face validity of this measure, VE users should find this measure highly relevant to their experience. The revised ITC-SOPI has now been distributed to a number of VE labs across the world. Confirmatory factor analysis of this new data will enable a test of the stability of both the factor structure and its constituent items. A full exploration of the interrelationships between the factors will be undertaken.

The ITC-SOPI is currently being used in all our controlled laboratory experiments. We have planned studies to investigate, for instance, the impact of audio (number of channels, inclusion of bass, volume etc) and field of view in controlled experimental contexts. We anticipate that the results will further validate the ITC-SOPI, lending support to its use as a global media quality metric.

References

1. Slater, M. Usoh, M., & Steed, A. (1994). Depth of presence in virtual environments. Presence: Teleoperators and Virtual Environments, 3, 130-144.

2. Lombard, M. & Ditton, T. (1997). At the heart of it all: The concept of presence. Journal of Computer Mediated Communication, 3 (2), [on-line].
Available: http//www.ascusc.org/jcmc/vol3/issue2/lombard.html

3. Barfield, W., Zeltzer, D., Sheridan, T.B., & Slater, M. (1995). Presence and performance within virtual environments. In W. Barfield & Furness, T.A. (Eds). Virtual environments and advanced interface design. Oxford: Oxford University Press.

4. Freeman, J. & Avons, S.E. (2000). Focus group exploration of presence through advanced broadcast services. Proceedings of the SPIE, Human Vision and Electronic Imaging V, 3959-76.

5. Usoh, M., Arthur, K., Whitton, M., Bastos, R., Steed, A., Brooks, F., & Slater, M. (1999). The visual cliff revisited: A virtual presence study on locomotion. Presented at the Second International Workshop on Presence, University of Essex, Colchester, 6th and 7th April 1999 [http://www.cs.ucl.ac.uk/staff/m.usoh/bt.html]

6. Sheridan, T.B. (1992). Musings on telepresence and virtual presence. Presence: Teleoperators and Virtual Environments, 1, 120-125.

7. Hendrix, C. & Barfield, W. (1996b). The sense of presence within auditory virtual environments. Presence: Teleoperators and Virtual Environments, 5, 290-301.

8. IJsselsteijn, W., de Ridder, H., Hamberg, R., Bouwhuis, D., & Freeman, J. (1998). Perceived depth and the feeling of presence in 3DTV. Displays, 18, 207-214.

9. Hendrix, C. & Barfield, W. (1996a). Presence within virtual environments as a function of visual display parameters. Presence: Teleoperators and Virtual Environments, 5, 274-289.

10. Freeman, J., Avons, S.E., Pearson, D., & IJsselsteijn, W. (1999). Effects of sensory information and prior experience on direct subjective ratings of presence. Presence: Teleoperators and Virtual Environments, Vol. 8, 1-13.

11. Freeman, J., Avons, S.E., Meddis, R., Pearson, D.E., & IJsselsteijn, W. (2000). Using behavioural realism to estimate presence: A study of the utility of postural responses to motion stimuli. Presence: Teleoperators and Virtual Environments, Vol. 9 (2), 149-164.

12. Barfield, W., Baird, K.M., & Bjorneseth, O.J. (1998). Presence in virtual environments as a function of type of input device and display update rate. Displays, 19, 91-98.

13. Slater, M. & Usoh, M. (1994). Representations systems, perceptual position, and presence in immersive virtual environments. Presence: Teleoperators and Virtual Environments, 2, 221-233.

14. Welch, R.B., Blackmon, T.T., Liu, A., Mellers, B.A., & Stark, L.W. (1996). The effects of pictorial realism, delay of visual feedback, and observer interactivity on the subjective sense of presence. Presence: Teleoperators and Virtual Environments, 5, 262-273.

15. Barfield, W. & Weghorst, S. (1993). The sense of presence within virtual environments: A conceptual framework. In G. Salvendy & M. Smith (Eds.) Software and hardware interfaces. Amsterdam: Elsevier. pp. 699-704.

16 Witmer, B.G., & Singer, M.J. (1998). Measuring presence in virtual environments: A Presence Questionnaire. Presence: Teleoperators and Virtual Environments, 7, 225-240.

17. Kim, T. & Biocca, F. (1997). Telepresence via television: Two dimensions of telepresence may have different connections to memory and persuasion. Journal of Computer Mediated Communication [On-line], 3 (2).
http://www.ascusc.org/jcmc/vol3/issue2/kim.html

18. Lessiter, J., Freeman, J., Keogh, E., & Davidoff, J. (in press). A cross media presence questionnaire: The ITC-Sense of Presence Inventory. Presence: Teleoperators and Virtual Environments (Special Issue)

19. Schubert, T.W., Friedmann, F., & Regenbrecht, H.T. (1999). Decomposing the sense of presence: factor analytic insights. Presented at the Second International Workshop on Presence, University of Essex, Colchester, 6th and 7th April 1999 [http://www.uni~jena.de/~sth/vr/insights.html]

Design review and visualization steering using the INQUISITIVE interaction toolkit

L. Sastry, D. R. S. Boyd and M. D. Wilson
Information Technology Department
CLRC Rutherford Appleton Laboratory,
Chilton, Didcot, OX11 0QX. UK
{m.sastry|m.d.wilson|d.r.s.boyd}@rl.ac.uk

Abstract. This paper describes the architecture of an interaction toolkit for creating virtual environments. The toolkit contains interaction techniques, interaction objects such as menus, spanner and a runtime manager to interface to virtual reality development tools such as Maverik. The toolkit's use with a number of real-world applications in science and engineering and with different virtual reality development tools is also described. Future plans to provide an interactive interface are described.

1 Introduction

As novel technologies are absorbed into the conventional systems development methodology they usually pass through three phases: firstly, they are demonstrated in specialised stand alone systems; secondly they are demonstrated in rapid prototype environments used to elicit requirements from users unfamiliar with the potential of the technology in their domain; and thirdly, system representations and documentation for each contractually important development stage, and methods for moving between them are defined incorporating best practice. As knowledge based technologies did in the late 1980's, so Virtual Reality (VR) technologies are now moving from the second to the third of these phases, and establishing manageable system development practices that can be subject to general contractual obligations [1].

The current market for VR development tools ranges from public domain toolkits to high cost prototyping and development environments. Equally, some tools are continuing to address a generic range of VR applications, while others are becoming more focused to one application. For example, being linked as a real time interaction environment to a 3D CAD modelling tool for engineering design. In this market, VR developers have the choice of expensively maintaining the skills to support a range of tools to meet broad customer requirements, cheaply exploiting a single tool very well but thereby limiting their market, or developing their own custom toolkit layer that can be applied to a range of delivery vehicles, thereby meeting the needs of a wide customer base while also limiting the skills required by their developers to a single toolkit. The additional cost of this third option is that it usually requires development overheads calling on systems level skills that do not overlap with the VR designer's. An additional benefit of this approach in other technologies that have joined the systems development mainstream, is that such custom toolkit layers usually define API's that drive the development of market tools and form the basis of standards [2]. Rapid prototyping tools for the 2D WIMP-based (Windows, Icons, Menus and Pointer) applications aided much useful research into usability issues and eventually design guidelines. Similarly, rapid prototyping tools for the creation of interaction rich virtual environments for the experimentation of competing interaction styles or techniques are essential to the understanding of the full potential and hence the exploitation of interactions in virtual environments [3].

The aim of the Interaction Toolkit development within the INQUISITIVE project is to provide support for developing a rich set of interaction techniques for use in VR-based applications. We are approaching this from the points of view of the user's need for an appropriate, consistent and effective set of interaction techniques to carry out application-specific interaction tasks and the application developer's need to deliver this cost-effectively. The design should strive to provide easy configuration of the interaction techniques to use both existing and new input devices [4]. Interaction techniques should be flexibly adaptable by the application developer to meet the needs of a wide range of application scenarios. The toolkit should interface to existing VR run-time systems and input device drivers through defined application programming interfaces (APIs). It should support the portability of interaction techniques and input device configurations across both VR systems and hardware platforms.

The next section describes the basis from which requirements for such an interaction toolkit is derived. The architecture and components of the toolkit is described in Section 3 followed by some demonstration applications in Section 4. Future Work is briefly covered in Section 5 and Conclusion in Section 6.

2 Application and Toolkit Requirements

Our customers for VR applications are scientists and engineers [5] who have two main applications. Firstly, they wish to design and construct buildings and apparatus using 3D CAD engineering tools and undertake group design reviews using interactive real time navigation of them in VR. Secondly, they wish to visualise the data arising from scientific experiments and control that visualisation, maybe changing parameters of the visualisation process, or even steering the experiment generating the data in real time.

The users' objective is to achieve their task goals, and they are only open to using VR when it can be shown to help achieve that objective more effectively, or efficiently than alternative means. One of the advantages to the users of VR is that it allows them to do unreal things that they could not do in the real world, such as measuring between unreachable locations, or moving immovable objects. However, even in these unreal cases, the interaction in immersive or semi-immersive 3D may facilitate a speed of navigation, a precision of interaction, or a perception resulting in insight that are unattainable otherwise [6].

These users are experts in the real world domain tasks, and familiar with the real world objects and actions in their domains, but they are also highly computer literate in their own specialist tools, and accustomed to many computer domain user interface conventions. For the visualisation task, the data and its relationships have no real world representation to imitate in a virtual reality, therefore most aspects of the visualisation scene are either domain conventions or even just conventions of a previous computer representation. Consequently, the users are open to the full range of realism, and VR interaction from full presence to 2D interaction with 3D graphics.

The style of use of different user groups varies considerably; some users wish to distribute VR applications to large communities to be used around the world, so they wish to use public domain code. Others require fully certified and supported development and interaction environments that will conform to the quality control constraints on general contracts for the development of multi-million satellites systems. Therefore no single VR interaction environment will meet these requirements, so we currently use both MAVERIK [7] as a public domain tool and Parametric Technology's dvMockup VR kernels.

Local variations also exist in the requirements that cannot easily be met by both these environments requiring the development of further interaction components. For example, in one application where a public domain interaction tool is required, users wish to use an eye-level viewpoint for gross navigation around buildings and equipment, but wish to place the viewpoint at a fixed location for detailed study of experimental behaviour. Large development environments, but not the public domain interaction tools provide such facilities. A common level of implementation of these is required to meet the user requirements so as not to lock designs into the capabilities of a single development environment.

3 INQUISITIVE Interaction Toolkit

The interaction toolkit will improve support for developing user interaction within task-oriented virtual environment applications. Analysis of the interaction technique has led us to a modular design for the toolkit with defined interfaces to input devices and existing commercial and public domain VR system kernels. The interaction toolkit is being developed to provide application developers and human factors researchers with a portable toolkit of interaction techniques for navigation, selection and manipulation within virtual environments.

3.1 Toolkit Architecture

All application tasks, however complex, can be implemented in terms of a combination of tasks from the four basic classes of user interaction - navigation, selection, manipulation and data input, in virtual environments [8,9]. Each basic interaction task can be realised using a number of possible interaction techniques. For example movement can be implemented using the *magic carpet* or *point-fly* techniques. Each application will identify one or more interaction techniques appropriate for carrying out the tasks required in that application. This in turn will guide the definition of the interaction techniques needed to realise those techniques. A suitable combinations of these interaction techniques are used to achieve the application tasks. The main functional components that the toolkit must provide to cater for this are:

- a set of interaction techniques for the four classes of basic interaction tasks;
- a set of generic virtual interaction objects such as toolbox;
- a run-time interaction framework.

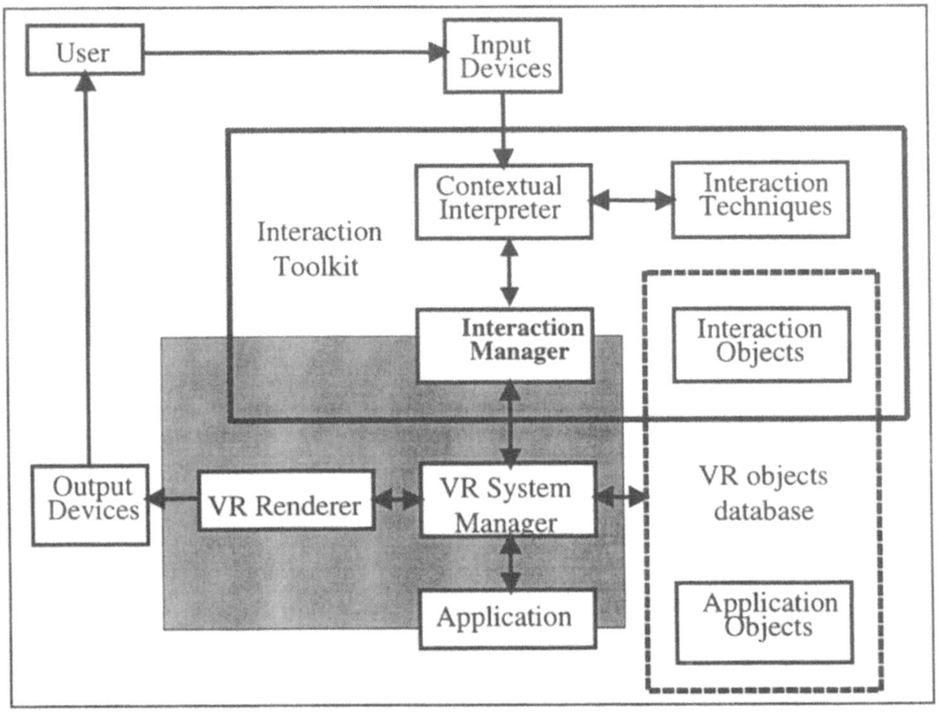

Fig.1. Relationship between interaction toolkit, input devices, VR system and application (the shaded portion represent the components of the VR kernel)

Figure 1 above depicts the detailed architecture of the interaction toolkit and how it maps on to a typical VR kernel. The toolkit provides interaction techniques for the four classes of basic interaction tasks identified above supporting a number of common interaction techniques for each. In navigation, for example, there will be interaction techniques which move the user through the VE and change his viewing direction in response to user-driven inputs from, say, a spacemouse and tracking devices attached to the user. The toolkit must also provide the capability for an application developer to implement new interaction techniques to meet specific application requirements.

Interaction objects are virtual objects with which the user is able to interact in the VE [10]. They contain methods for describing both their functional and presentational properties. The same object in different VR systems will have the same functional description because its behaviour is the same but the description of its presentational properties will be different because each VR system has its own native format for describing the perceptual aspects of virtual objects. A simple example of an interaction object is a virtual spanner, one of a number of objects which might be found in a virtual toolbox used for a maintenance training application.

The run-time interaction framework defines how the input devices and the interaction techniques are dynamically configured and how the outputs from the interaction techniques are mapped into the run-time processes provided by the VR system for implementing behaviour such as collision detection, for updating the VR object database containing the dynamic state of the VE, including the interaction objects and the virtual user, and for rendering the VE.

In its simplest definition, the interaction toolkit is a set of library routines that can be called on to implement an interaction behaviour to an object within a virtual environment. Figure 2 below shows a typical interaction technique mapped on to a specific VR kernel to elaborate how the above architecture works in practice. The example shown considers a 2D/3D mouse and virtual hand based interaction with a generic window-pane which can be used to create simple head up displays, menus, labels etc. and their characteristics and functionality on the fly as required.

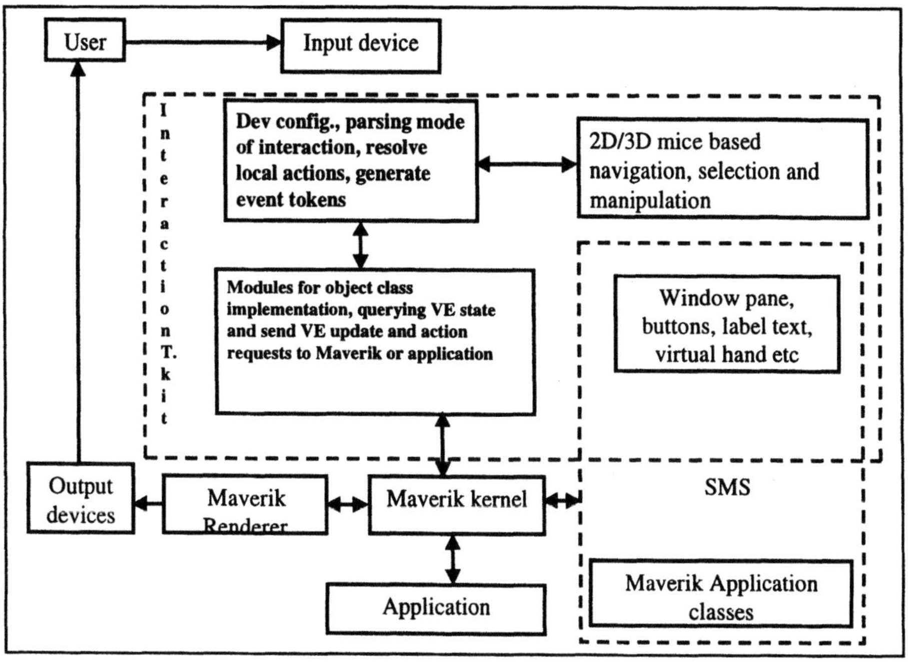

Figure 2. Relationship between window-pane/menu object class, virtual hand, the Maverik VR kernel and application.

Table 1 below shows some classes of interaction objects in the interaction toolkit. All classes of interaction object in the interaction toolkit allow VR application designers to change appearance of widgets.

When instantiated as virtual application objects the interaction objects can be: distance measuring tools, meters to read values of temperature, radiation etc.. from database underlying CAD model etc.. In the later case the display on a meter can be on a windowpane or on hand held display moving with the user depending on which interaction object is chosen. This flexibility in instantiating application objects in different ways shows the power of the interaction toolkit to both meet interaction requirements, and to allow their investigation through rapid prototyping when required.

Interaction Objects		
Window pane	Billboard – turn to user viewpoint	
	Fixed at location and presentation angle	
	Fixed to head up display location	
		Information presentation screens
		Selectable buttons – for menu of application commands, e.g. VR world creation or editing
Attachment	Red Pin calling information presentation screen on selection	
Pointer - single handed	Laser Beam to select or manipulate remote objects	
Pointer - double handed	Laser Beams to select groups of objects in 3D space	
Slider & scale	To set and show values	
Dial	To set and show values	
Constrained object	Objects with behaviour constraints (e.g. hinges).	
Constrainable Object	Objects constrained by the environment (e.g. spanner constrained to move in limited directions where the axis of movement constraint is inherited from an object it is attached to.	

Table 1: Classes on Interaction Objects in the Interaction Toolkit

4 Toolkit Demonstrations

A sample set of interaction techniques will be presented (demonstrated) which include application/user centred navigational and/or object manipulation, real-time interactive editing, querying and steering of the virtual world.

The testbed demonstrator applications include an engineering design review with an architectural walk-through and a visualisation and three-dimensional browsing of Cluster-II satellite data implemented using the interaction toolkit.

4.1 Design Review Demonstration

Engineers need to construct a new building, particle beam target, and experiments on beam lines off the target. Each component is being developed by different teams throughout Europe. The CAD models of the components have been integrated and imported into a VR environment to perform design reviews where groups of engineers jointly view the model in an auditorium with a facilitator navigating and interacting with it to identify and correct design errors.

Figure 3 shows a redlining tool for engineering design review. The red pinhead in the left-hand image is indicative of an attached annotation that can be activated as shown in the right-hand image

The group of designers undertake a variety of interactions with the model: simple navigation around the model shows design flaws (e.g. the vertical red pillar in Figure 3 that collides with the beam housing); potential design problems identified by individual designers and marked with red pinheads must be resolved by the group; distances, radiation levels, temperature levels etc. need to be measured in the overall design and checked against requirements. These interactions require the use of several of the interaction objects supported by the toolkit, and the use of the toolkit allows their development more quickly than ad hoc development has in the past. The use of the toolkit allowed the selection of interaction technique appropriate to the facilitator and group of designers at a particular meeting to investigate problems that were not specified in the initial requirements but could be responded to on the fly.

4.2 Data Visualisation Demonstration

Scientists need to study instrument calibration on a satellite, which is always a critical issue on space physics missions. To do this they wish to visualise the instrument data, navigate through it, focus in on subsets of interest, then go back to the whole set and consider it again.

Figure 4 below shows observational data from AMPTE-UKS spacecraft in NASA Common Data Format (CDF) in a hierarchy with associated metadata. The objective of the experiments is to study the distribution of chemicals in the atmosphere based on the electron density distribution in Earth's Ionosphere. The basic measurement made by the electron instrument on *AMPTE-UKS* was to count the numbers of incoming electrons simultaneously in each of eight directional sensors. The AMPTE electron measurements can be considered as a sequence of measurements of the three-dimensional velocity space distributions of the electrons - with one distribution being measured every T seconds, where T is a suitable integration time. T must be greater than or equal to the spin period of the spacecraft (approx. 5 seconds).

Interaction to select different data files, to zoom in and out of the time period being observed, and the density of the data, and to inspect the metadata – which instrument used, when by whom, which sensor, data type, references to related data etc.. so that scientists can evaluate the reliability of the data, and its relation to other data.

Figure 4: Visualisation of an electron density distribution over time (x-axis) during spacecraft flight (y & z axes) showing an event requiring detailed investigation (black rectangle).

Such discontinuous data was previously studied in 2D graphs of energy plotted against universal time where the information from the 8 different sensors are either amalgamated or presented individually. Scientists need data from all 8 sensors in single view to see how sensors are measuring data in space. Using 3D plotting in IDL gives supports inspection of data from the 8 sensors, but does not support real time navigation unless the data is so diluted as to be hard to interpret, and data context is lost from the sort buckets after focussing in. If the whole data set is inspected, then the data quantities are overwhelming.

Consequently a semi-immersive display (Crystal Eyes 3D glasses with head position sensor and SpaceMouse) driven by a VR runtime system supports the interactive real time selection and investigation of whole and part data sets. Current interaction objects for navigating through and selecting data, and requesting metadata do not meet their needs, but the INQUISITIVE interaction toolbox does, and supports tuning the interaction objects to individual user needs.

5 Evaluation and Future Work

Besides inhibiting the adoption of VR-based interaction techniques, the lack of design environments that do not constrain designs to their limited capabilities also inhibits human factors research into issues such as the utility and usability of 3D techniques for achieving user interaction goals. We will need to understand these issues in order to be able to develop design guidelines for 3D interaction comparable to those which exist for 2D desktop applications, and the INQUISITIVE Interaction Toolkit will provide a starting point in developing these.

The toolkit's functionality will be evaluated for the perceptual interfaces and interaction techniques of the testbed applications and usability guidelines developed.

This toolkit, it is hoped, together with guidelines for its use based on the demonstrations, will help user interface designers to produce more useable and productive applications thereby accelerating the exploitation of VR technology for real-world engineering product design reviews and scientific visualization applications within the Laboratory.

The toolkit is to be extended to provide a graphical user interface for low end toolkits emulating facilities provided by current high end environments for the creation from virtual worlds from within themselves.

6 Conclusion

The INQUISITIVE method and toolkit meet some of the needs of the VR developer at the stage we are in the evolution of the technology where there have been attractive demonstrations, some industrial applications, and we are moving towards the incorporation of VR technologies into conventional system development. However, both the method and the toolkit are early attempts, with the need for further refinement, and the development of design guidelines to clarify the mapping from user requirements to the design tradeoffs of VR application development.

Parts or all of the INQUISITIVE Toolkit will be made freely available to facilitate take up of the INQUISITIVE method, and promote standardisation of technology and methods in the VR field. Please contact the first author for license information.

Acknowledgements

The work reported in this paper was partly funded by the UK EPSRC through grant GR/L52406 to the INQUISITIVE (INcreasing the Quality of User Interaction for Strategic Interactive Tasks in Virtual Environments) research project.

References

1. Wilson, M.D., Duce, D.A., Simpson, D. Life cycles in Software and Knowledge Engineering: A comparative review. Knowledge Engineering Review vol.3(4) pp.189-204 (1989).

2. Duce, D., Kansy, K., Wilson, M.D. Report and Recommendations from the VRML Workshop 29/30 January 1997, Abingdon UK. ERCIM Research Report, 02/97-R049, ERCIM, France.

3. Jacob, R.J.K. A visual language for non-WIMP user interfaces, In Proc. IEEE Symposium on Visual Languages, pp.231-238 (1996). IEEE Computer Society Press.

4. Hinckley, K., Pausch, R., Goble, J.C., Kassell, N.F. A survey of design issues in spatial input. In Proc. ACM UIST'94 Symposium on User Interface Software and Technology, Marina del Rey, California, 213-222, Addison-Wesley/ACM Press.

5. Sastry, L., Boyd, D. Virtual Environments for Engineering Applications Virtual Reality vol.3 (4) pp.235-244 (1999).

6. Bowman, D., Hodges, L.F., & Bolter, J. The virtual venue: user computer interaction in information rich virtual environments. Presence,Teleoperators and Virtual Environments vol. 7(5), pp.478-493 (1998).

7. Maverik User Guide http://aig.cs.man.ac.uk/systems/Maverik

8. Hand, C. A survey of 3D interaction techniques. Computer Graphics Forum, vol. 16(5), pp.269-281 (1997).

9. Boyd, D. and Sastry, L. Development of the INQUISITIVE Interaction Toolkit - Concept and Realisation. In Workshop on User Centered Design and Implementation of Virtual Environments, (Eds.) Smith, S. and Harrison, M. pp.1-6, 30th September, 1999, University of York, York.

10. van Dam, A. Post-WIMP user interfaces, Communications of ACM, vol. 40(2), pp.63-67(1997).

On the Utility of Semantic Constraints

G. Smith and W. Stuerzlinger
Dept. of Computer Science, York University, Toronto, Canada
{ gsmith | wolfgang }@cs.yorku.ca

Abstract. Content creation for computer graphics applications is a laborious process that requires skilled personnel. One fundamental problem is that manipulation of 3D objects with 2D user interfaces is very difficult for non-experienced users. In this paper, we describe a system that uses semantic constraints to restrict object motion in a 3D scene, making interaction much simpler and more intuitive. We compare three different levels of semantic constraints in a 3D scene manipulation program with a 2D user interface. We show that the presented techniques are significantly more efficient than alternate techniques, which do not use semantics in their constraints. To our knowledge, this is the first evaluation of 3D manipulation techniques with 2D devices and constraints.

1 Introduction

Many applications are readily available in the areas of 3D modeling and scene construction, but in general, these products are difficult to use and require many hours of training. For example, products such as *Maya* (Alias|wavefront) and *3D Studio Max* (Discreet), have dozens of menus, modes and widgets for scene creation and manipulation, which can be very intimidating for an untrained user. Our efforts address these difficulties.

The task of creating a 3D scene from scratch is very complex. To simplify the problem, we choose to focus on the creation of complete 3 D scenes based on a library of existing objects. Here the challenge is to enable the user to easily add objects and to quickly position them in the environment. In general, positioning an object in a 3D scene is difficult as six independent variables must be controlled, three for positioning and three for orientation.

Our observations of humans rearranging furniture and planning environments indicate that humans do not think about scene manipulation as a problem with six degrees of freedom. The rationale is that most real objects are not placed arbitrarily in space, but are constrained by physics (e.g. gravity) and/or human conventions (ceiling lamps are almost never placed permanently onto the floor or onto chairs). This leads us to believe that an interface that exposes the full six degrees of freedom to the user makes it harder for the average person to interact with virtual environments. Many real objects have a maximum of three degrees of freedom in practice – e.g. all objects resting on a plane. In addition, many objects are often placed against walls or other objects, thus further reducing the available degrees of freedom. This implies that a two-dimensional (2D) input device such as a mouse is sufficient to manipulate objects in a virtual environment.

In our system, information about how an object interacts with the physical world assists the user in placing and manipulating objects in virtual environments. Each object in a scene is given a set of rules, called constraints, which must be followed when the object is being manipulated.

2 Previous Work

Previous work on 3D object manipulation can be classified into two categories: those that use 2D and those that use 3D input devices.

The simplest solution for a 2D input device is to decompose the manipulation task into positioning and orientation. Unfortunately, there is no intuitive mapping of these tasks with three degrees of freedom each to a mouse with three buttons.

Bier introduced 'Snap-Dragging' [1] to simplify the creation of line drawings in a 2D interactive graphics program. The mouse cursor snaps to points and curves using a gravity function. Bier subsequently applied these ideas to placing and orienting objects in a 3D environment [2]. The main features of this system are a general-purpose gravity function, 3D alignment objects, and smooth motion affine transformations of objects. Gleicher [9] built on this work and introduced a method that can deal even with non-linear constraints.

For 3D scene construction Bukowski and Sequin [7] employ a combination of pseudo-physical and goal-oriented properties called 'Object Associations' to position objects in a 3D scene with 2D devices (mouse and monitor). A two-phase approach is used. First, a relocation procedure maps the 2D mouse motion into vertical or horizontal transformations of an object's position. Then association procedures align and position the object. Although intuitive, their approach has a few drawbacks. First, associations apply only to the object currently being moved and are not maintained after the current manipulation. In addition, when an object is selected for relocation, a local search for associated objects is performed. This can result in lag between the motion of the selected object and the motion of its associated objects. Cyclical constraints are not supported.

Goesele and Stuerzlinger [8] built upon the ideas of Object Associations. Each scene object is given predefined offer and binding areas. These areas are used to define constraining surfaces between objects. For example, a lamp has a binding area at its base and a table has an offer area on its top. Consequently, a lamp can be constrained to a tabletop. To better simulate the way real world objects behave, a labeled constraint hierarchy adds semantics to the constraint process. Each constraint area is associated with a label from the hierarchy. A binding area constrains then only to offer areas whose label is equal to or is an ancestor in the constraint hierarchy. In this way, the legs of a chair can be constrained to the floor, or in front of a desk, but never to the wall. Collision detection is used to prevent objects from passing though each other.

Drawbacks of this approach include the following: Once a constraint has been satisfied, there are no means to re-constrain an object to another surface or to un-constrain it. Furthermore, the constraint satisfaction search is global, in that an object will be moved across the entire scene to satisfy a constraint, This has often-undesirable effects for the user, especially because constraints cannot be undone.

A number of authors have investigated the performance of object manipulation with 3D input devices, such as a space-ball or a six degree-of-freedom tracker. Such devices enable direct interaction with a 3D scene. In combination with devices that generate a 3D view, such systems can simulate Virtual Reality (VR).
One of the first researchers to use 3D devices to manipulate a 3D scene was Bolt in 1980 [3]. Subsequently many other researchers studied the creation and manipulation of 3D environments in VR (see e.g. [12][16]). Very few of these systems utilize constraints for object manipulation and even these support only the simplest geometric constraints (e.g. on-plane). Closest to the work discussed here is the 'SmartScene' system by Multigen [18]. This system uses tracked pinch-gloves in 3D as interaction devices.
More recently Bowman et al. [5], Mine et al. [12], and Pierce et al. [13] proposed different 3D manipulation methods that can be applied in a variety of settings. Poupyrev et al. recently also addressed the problem of 3D rotation [15]. For a more complete overview over previous work in this area, we refer the reader to [6].
While it may seem obvious that the introduction of constraints makes interaction in 3D easier, it is unclear how strong this effect is. An extensive search for literature was performed in this area, and no study that addresses was found.

2.1 Motivation

Our main motivation behind this work is that we wanted to analyze how semantic constraints affect user performance in a give task. Such constraints have been introduced to commercial products such as the Smartscene system [18], but to our knowledge, no evaluation has been performed to assess the value of these constraints. Our initial hypothesis was that semantic constraints would greatly simplify user interaction, as they make putting an object into the "right" place very simple.

3 The MIVE System

The MIVE (Multi-user Intuitive Virtual Environment) system extends the work done in [8] by improving the way existing constraints behave, and adding new useful constraints. This work concerns only the interaction of a single user; therefore we disregard the multi-user aspects of the system here.

3.1 Semantic Constraints

Every object in the MIVE system has constraints defined for it. Each constraint can be one of two types: offer or binding. Essentially, binding areas will "stick" to offer areas. Constraint relationships are stored in a directed a-cyclic graph called the scene graph. Figure 1 depicts a simple scene, and it's associated scene graph. When an object is moved in the scene, all of its descendants in the scene graph move with it.

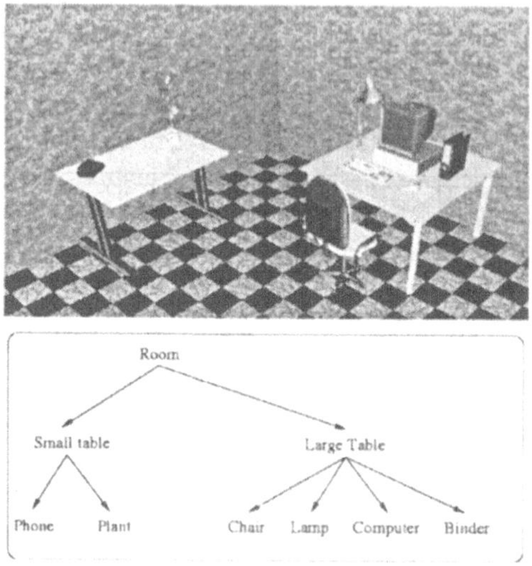

Fig. 1. A Scene and its associated Scene Graph.
Links describe constraint relations

Notice that edges in the scene graph of Figure 1 correspond directly to satisfied constraints in the scene. The user can modify the scene graph structure by interacting with objects in the scene. Constraints can be broken and re-constrained with ease by simply clicking on the desired object, and pulling away from the existing constraint to break it. This allows us to dynamically change the structure of the scene graph. Figure 2 shows the same scene as Figure 1 after the chair has been pulled away from the arge table, and dragged under the smaller table.

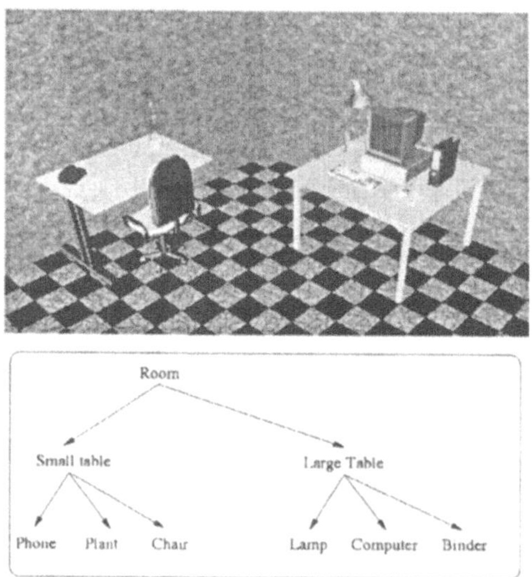

Fig. 2. Scene from Fig.1 after chair has been moved

A labeled constraint hierarchy is used to add semantics to the constraint process. The hierarchy is a tree structure, and defines the behavior of the constraint and offer areas. Each constraint area is associated with a label from the hierarchy, which defines what offer areas this constraint area is allowed to attach to. A binding area constrains only to offer areas whose label is equal to or is an ancestor in the constraint hierarchy tree.

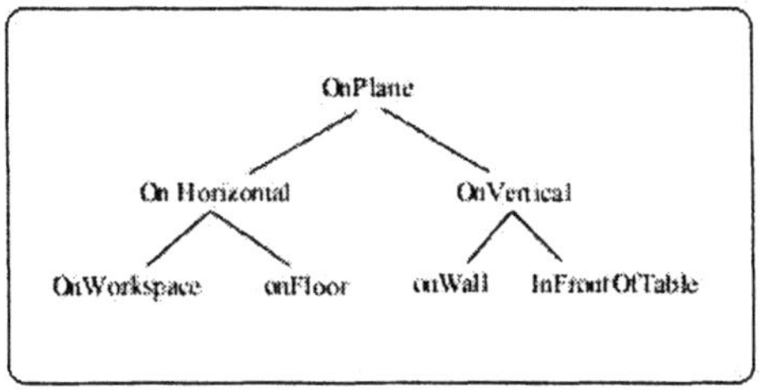

Fig. 3. Semantic Constraint tree

A simplified version of the semantic constraint tree is shown in Figure 3. This tree is used to restrict object placements and to make interactions more intuitive. For example, the phone in fig 1 has a binding area on it base, which has the OnWorkspace label associated with it, hence it can be constrained to any offer area with an OnWorkspace label, OnHorizontal label, or OnPlane label. The top of the table has an OnWorkspace label associated with its offer area, so the phone can constrain there. The phone cannot be placed on the floor, which has an OnFloor label associated with its offer area, because the label of the floor's offer area is not an ancestor of OnWorkspace in the tree. Semantics are added in a similar manner to every binding and offer area.

4 Constraint Satisfaction

For our constraint system, binding and offer areas both have a polygon and vector, which represent their effective areas and orientation. A binding area is satisfied by an offer area by aligning their orientation vectors and by translating the binding polygon so that it lies within the offer polygon (excluding the offer polygon edges). If after rotation and translation the binding polygon is not completely enclosed by the offer polygon, then the binding area is not constrained to the offer area. In addition, a binding area cannot be bound to an offer area of the same object: an object cannot be constrained to itself. In Borning's [4] terms, our system implements locally-predicate-better constraints.

To constrain an object, we attempt to satisfy all of its binding areas. For each binding area of an object, we search through the scene to find potential satisfying offer areas. Semantics restrict the offer areas that a binding area is allowed to constrain to. To prevent objects from jumping large distances to satisfy constraints, we only consider constraining an object to offer areas that are close to the object being constrained. Closeness is relative to object size, therefore we consider only objects that are within a sphere with a radius that is twice the radius of the sphere bound of the object.

Using this heuristic, constraints remain unsatisfied until an object is moved close to a valid offer area. It also ensures that objects are always locally constrained. For each binding area, if there are multiple satisfying offer areas, the closest satisfying offer

area found is chosen. The object is moved to connect the binding and offer areas. The bound object then becomes a child of the offering object in the scene graph, and the search is repeated for the next binding area.
Once an object is constrained, its motion is restricted such that the binding areas of the object always remain in contact with the associated offer areas. This essentially removes degrees of freedom from object manipulations. Constraints can be broken with ease by simply pulling an object away from its associated offer area.

5 MIVE Constraint Environments

Previous systems have used a more general constraint environment, where objects only know that they must lie on a horizontal and/or vertical surface, such as the Object Association system [7]. We hypothesize that this makes interaction less intuitive because it gives the user less control over how objects behave in the scene. For example, the chair would have a horizontal constraint on its base, and could easily be placed on a table, bed, refrigerator, or any other horizontal surface. We have implemented such a constraint system in MIVE and call it the Partially Constrained (P) mode.
Each object in the MIVE system has a set of semantic constraints associated with it. This mode uses user-defined semantics to restrict object placement to valid locations. We call this the Fully Constrained (C) mode.

6 User Testing

We designed a test where significant semantic differences between object constraints exist to see if a significant difference between the PC and FC modes would occur. Twelve pipes (3 different sizes, 4 of each size) had to be placed onto a wall. The wall had 12 different receptacles where pipes could be attached in FC mode. The test is illustrated in Figure 4.

In the task, we evaluated 3 different modes:

- Partially constrained (P) mode, where the pipes connect to all vertical surfaces (i.e. anywhere on the wall). There is no visual indication where pipes should be attached.
- Non-semantic constrained with drawn offer areas (D) mode, where a pipe can connect to anywhere on wall (as in mode P), but the correct locations are indicated visually by a small transparent green square on the wall. However, each pipe could actually be placed anywhere on the wall.
- Fully constrained (C) mode, where pipes connect only to the correct receptacle. Three different kinds of pipes existed. This is a simplified analogy to having gas, hot water and cold water pipes in a mechanical construction task, where each type of pipe is only allowed to connect to a subset of the receptacles.

Tasks were set up so that no navigation was required for any of the tests. This avoids interference with problems of participants understanding navigation in 3D.

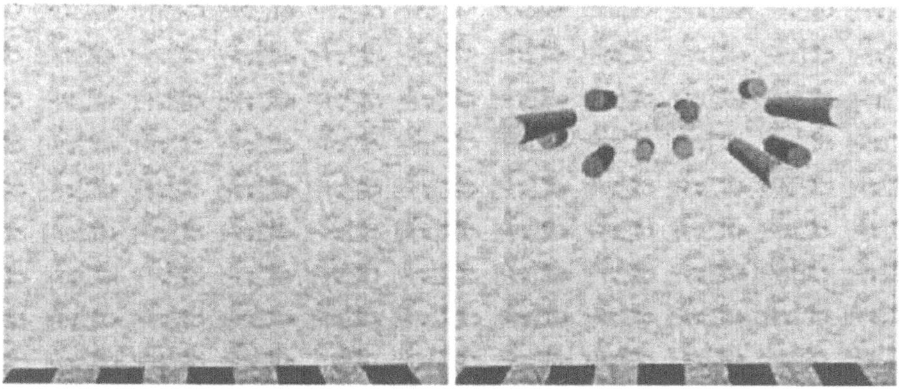

Fig. 4. The initial and target scenes for our user test

6.1 Participants

Twelve volunteers participated in this experiment. Participants were computer science students with different experience and backgrounds, different computer skills and different degrees of exposure to 3D computer graphics.

6.2 Apparatus

The MIVE interface was designed to very simple. Figure 5 shows the full user interface of the MIVE program running with its default object list.

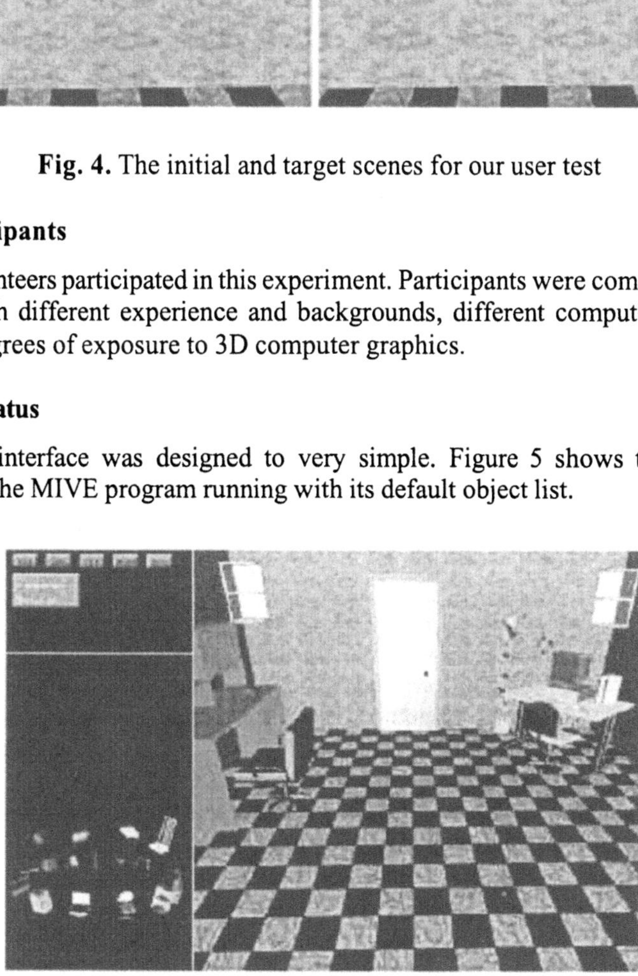

Fig. 5. The MIVE interface

The MIVE interface consists of three windows: the scene window, the object selection window, and the button window. The scene window sits on the right hand side of the screen. The participant directly interacts with objects in the scene window by clicking and dragging them.
The lower left-hand corner shows the object selection window. Objects are positioned on an invisible cylinder, which is rotated by clicking any mouse button within the

window and dragging left and right. Objects are added to the scene window by simply clicking on the desired object in the object selection window, and clicking on the desired location to add it in the scene window. Drag & Drop is supported as well. To facilitate selection of small objects all objects are scaled logarithmically.
The upper left-hand corner of the window contains buttons for performing tasks such as loading or saving the scene, deleting an object, undoing the previous operation, or quitting the program. There is also a radio button, which can be used to switch between interaction and navigation mode. This functionality was disabled for the tests in this publication.
The MIVE system is implemented in C++ and runs on an SGI Onyx2 running IRIX 6.5. It is based on the Cosmo3D [10] scene graph API.

6.3 Interaction

The interface for MIVE was designed to be as simple and uncluttered as possible. All interactions between the participant and the program are done using a 3-button mouse.
For this test, the three modes use only two of the three buttons. The left mouse button is used to move objects by clicking and dragging them to the desired new location. The middle mouse button is used to rotate the objects. The third mouse button is currently unused in these modes.

6.4 Procedure

A three-minute tutorial was given prior to the testing, at which time the experimenter gave the participant instructions on how to use the system. Each participant was then allowed to experiment less than two minutes with the system before testing started.
Each test began with the participant sitting in front of a computer monitor with a scene displayed. A target scene was displayed on an adjacent monitor, and the participant was instructed to make the scene on their screen look like that in the target scene. The experimenter supervised the participant, and when the task was deemed complete the supervisor instructed the participant to continue to the next task.
Each participant was asked to perform the task in three different modes. The order that the participant performed the modes was chosen using a Latin square method.
For each of the tests, we recorded the time taken by the participant, and the accuracy of object placement compared to the target scene. Accuracy was measured by summing the distances in centimeters between each of the object centers in the participant's final result and the target scene.

7 Analysis

At the end of each experiment task completion time and the modified scene was stored. The Euclidean distance between the participant's solution and the reference solution was computed later on.

7.1 Adjustments to Data

No adjustments were made to the collected data and no trials were excluded.

7.2 Computed Formulas

Errors are sums of Euclidean distances. We ignore rotation because no ideal measure for rotation differences exists to our knowledge. Moreover it is hard to find a meaningful combination of translation and rotation errors into one number.

7.3 Results

Figure 6 summarizes the results of the test. The thick center line of a box shows the median, the second line is the mean, the box itself indicates the 25th and 75th percentile, and the 'tails' specify the 10th and 90th percentile.
The analysis indicates a significant effect between modes C and P ($p < 0.001$). Mode P is clearly slower than mode C, by a factor of 2.5. More detailed analysis reveals that mode C is also significantly faster than mode D by a factor of 1.5. In accuracy, modes C and P do not have a significant difference, but mode C is significantly better than mode P by a factor of 8.6 ($p < 0.001$).

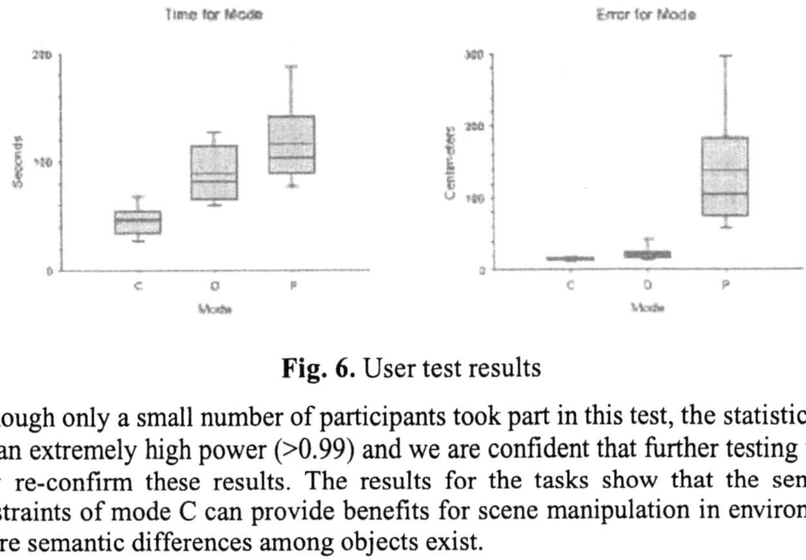

Fig. 6. User test results

Although only a small number of participants took part in this test, the statistical test has an extremely high power (>0.99) and we are confident that further testing would only re-confirm these results. The results for the tasks show that the semantic constraints of mode C can provide benefits for scene manipulation in environments where semantic differences among objects exist.

8 Conclusion

In this publication we presented a system that allows users to easily manipulate a 3D scene with traditional 2D devices. The MIVE system is based on semantic constraints, which enable an intuitive mapping from 2D interactions to 3D manipulations. The semantic constraints and manipulation techniques encapsulate the user's expectations of how objects move in an environment. Based on user tests we showed that the use of semantic constraints, as opposed to more general constraints without semantics, provide clear benefits for manipulation of 3D objects in a 2D user interface.
The benefits of our interaction techniques become very apparent when one compares the simple MIVE user interface with the complex 3D user interface in commercial packages such as AutoCAD, or Maya that are also based on 2D input devices. We can only hypothesize at the outcome of a test comparing our system with e.g. Maya, but

are confident that it is clearly easier to learn our user interface due to the reduced complexity. In fairness, we need to point out that these packages are also capable of object creation and the specification of animations, which our system does not currently address.

References

1.Bier, E.A., and Stone, M.C. Snap-dragging. *SIGGRAPH 1986 proceedings*, ACM Press, pp. 233-240.

2.Bier, E.A. Snap dragging in three dimensions, *SIGGRAPH 1990*, pp. 193-204.

3.Bolt, R., Put-that-there, *SIGGRAPH '80*, 262-270.

4.Borning, A., Freeman, B., Ultraviolet: A Constraint Satisfaction Algorithm for Interactive Graphics, *Constraints: An International Journal*, 3, 1-26, 1998.

5.Bowman, D., Hodges, L. An evaluation of techniques for grabbing and manipulating remote objects in immersive virtual environments. *Proceedings of ACM Symp. on Interactive 3D Graphics*, 1997, pp. 35-38.

6.Bowman, D., Kruijff, E., LaViola, J., Mine, M., Poupyrev, I., 3D user interface design, *ACM SIGGRAPH 2000, Course notes # 36, 2000*.

7.Bukowski, R., and Sequin, C. Object associations. ACM *Symp. Interactive 3D Graphics 1995*, 131-138.

8.Goesele, M, Stuerzlinger, W. Semantic constraints for scene manipulation. *Proc. Spring Conference in Computer Graphics* 1999, pp. 140-146.

9.Gleicher, M, A Graphics Toolkit Based on Differential Constraints. Proc. UIST 93, 109-120.

10.Eckel, G., Cosmo 3D programmers guide. Silicon Graphics Inc. 1998.

11.Mine, M., ISAAC: A Meta-CAD System for Virtual Environments. *Computer-Aided Design*, 29(8), 97.

12.Mine, M., Brooks, F., Sequin, C. Moving Objects in Space: Exploiting proprioception in virtual-environment interaction. *SIGRAPH 1997*, pp. 19-26.

13.Pierce, J., Forsberg, A., Conway, M., Hong, S., Zeleznik, R. *et al.*, Image plane interaction techniques in 3D immersive environments. *Proceedings of ACM Symp. on Interactive 3D Graphics*. 1997. pp. 39-43.

14.Poupyrev, I., Weghorst, S., Billinghurst, M., Ichikawa, T., Egocentric object manipulation in virtual environments: empirical evaluation of interaction techniques. *Computer Graphics Forum*, 17(3), 1998, 41-52.

15.Poupyrev, I., Weghorst, S., Fels, S. Non-isomorphic 3D rotational techniques. *ACM CHI'2000*, pp. 546-547.

16.Shaw, C., Green, M., THRED: A Two-Handed Design System, *Multimedia Systems Journal*,5(2),1997.

17.Shoemake, K., ARCBALL: A user interface for specifying three-dimensional orientation using a mouse, *Graphics Interface*, 1992, pp. 151-156.

18.SmartScene promotional material, Multigen (San Jose, CA), 1999.

Two-Handed *Through-the-Lens*-Techniques for Navigation in Virtual Environments

Stanislav L. Stoev[1], Dieter Schmalstieg[2], and Wolfgang Straßer[1]

[1] WSI/GRIS, University of Tübingen,
Auf der Morgenstelle 10, C9,
72076 Tuebingen, Germany
{sstoev, strasser}@gris.uni-tuebingen.de
[2] Vienna University of Technology
Favoritenstrasse 9-11
A-1040 Vienna, Austria
dieter@cg.tuwien.ac.at

Abstract. We present a tool set of techniques for navigation in virtual environments. Based on a *through-the-lens* concept, the user is enabled to simultaneously view the surrounding virtual world and an arbitrary location of the virtual world as seen through an interactively defined window. For the manipulation and the adjustment of this virtual window we propose three different strategies, loosely based on the well-known *eyeball-in-hand*, *scene-in-hand*, and *world-in-miniature* techniques. Since our technique provides a preview area with controllable size and position, the occluded part of the scene can be flexibly managed, while enabling intuitive and precise work with the proposed tools. The proposed techniques provide powerful tools that are easy to implement and can be applied in any type of virtual environments.

1 Introduction and Related Work

One of the most important features defining usability and user acceptance of a virtual environment, is the support of adequate *navigation*. Very large virtual environments make efficient navigation a key requirement. The *navigation* can be divided in three groups of techniques [12]: *Searching* is the motion to a particular location in the virtual environment. *Exploration* is defined as navigation without particular target. Finally, *maneuvering* is the high-precision adjustment of the user position in order to perform other tasks. Beside the application of these navigation techniques for performing particular tasks, each of them has a different application range. Searching and exploration techniques are utilized for overcoming large distances, while maneuvering is applied rather locally. In this work, we will present three tools each of which is suitable for accomplishing one or more of these tasks.

Various navigation techniques belonging to the above navigation types are described in the literature. Darken and Sibert [3] propose 2D maps for navigation, applying principles extracted from real world navigation aids. Stoakley et al. [10] extended this idea into the third dimension. The authors define navigation as a term covering two related tasks: movement through a virtual space and determining the orientation relative to the surrounding environment. Stoakley et al. [10] introduce in their work the *World In Miniature* (WIM)-technique for manipulating objects in the 3D space. Pausch et al. [5] extended the WIM concept to provide a navigation tool, enabling the user to directly manipulate the current viewpoint for searching and exploration tasks. However, they also reported that despite the intuitive application of the WIM, the direct viewpoint manipulation was confusing to many users. This is caused by the fact that the world surrounding the user moves simultaneously with the movement performed on the WIM. In addition, due to the applied miniaturized fixed-size copy of the virtual world, precise manipulation and navigation tasks are difficult to perform.

Another set of navigation tools is discussed by Ware and Osborne [14], who evaluate three metaphors for exploration and virtual camera control: *eyeball-in-hand*, *scene-in-hand*, and *flying-vehicle-control*. They conclude: "None of the techniques is judged the best in all situations, rather the different metaphors each have advantages and disadvantages depending on the particular task". Similarly to the WIM-technique, the main problem with the *eyeball-in-hand* and the *scene-in-hand* techniques is that the viewpoint is directly manipulated and the resulting image immediately displayed. This, however, may confuse the user or even cause loss of orientation.

The navigation tools we present in this work are inspired by the *eyeball-in-hand*, *scene-in-hand* (we call *grab-and-drag*), and WIM-techniques, but attempt to overcome their limitations. We introduced to these tools a *through-the-lens* (TTL) concept, extending their functionality and improving their usability. The idea of this concept is based on a more generalized 3D magic lens [1, 13], therefore *through-the-lens* concept. In particular, we allow the scene to be viewed from an additional (second) viewpoint, whereas the image rendered from this second viewpoint is displayed in a dedicated window. In this way, the presented navigation aids provide a set of flexible and powerful tools, covering all of the navigation categories introduced above.

The remainder of this paper is organized as follows. First, we introduce the idea of the TTL-concept, and discuss the requirements for the realization. In Section 3, we will describe in detail the three proposed tools. We will discuss their implementation, utilization, and show snapshots of the system in action. Finally, we will conclude the paper with a short comparison of the presented navigation aids.

2 Through-the-Lens Concept

The main idea of a TTL-tool is to provide an additional viewpoint and display the scene as seen from this viewpoint in a dedicated viewing window (or output window W_o) as shown in Figures 1 and 2. Thus, a preview window is provided. This window is mapped onto a pad held in the non-dominant hand of the user. For the realization of the proposed tools, we utilized the *Personal Interaction Panel* (*PIP*) concept [11, 8]. The PIP consists of a tracked palette, on which the virtual tools are displayed is such a way, that the user sees them on the pad's surface. This is accomplished either using back-projection and a transparent palette (Virtual Table, Virtual Workbench, Cave, Powerwall etc.) or front-projection (opaque and transparent head-mounted-displays). The pen is a manipulation tool for interacting with the pad. It is a physical object with a virtual counterpart used to manipulate the virtual tools on the pad.

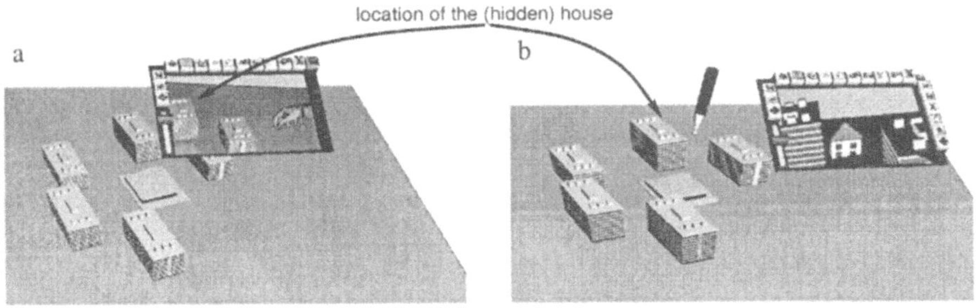

Fig. 1. The grab-and-drag tool is shown in action (Image (a)). After manipulating the additional viewpoint (shown in (b)), details invisible from the current user position become visible. The pen shows the location of the small house in the surrounding scene. Even though, the small house is in the surrounding environment, it is not visible from the current user position.

Considering the additional viewpoint and the scene seen through it (called secondary scene/world), there are two conceptually different states of the pad and the second world viewed through the window W_o on the pad: Either the secondary world is fixed in the space, or it is fixed with respect to the viewing window. In the first case, the output window W_o mapped on the pad is used to explore parts of the secondary scene (which is fixed in the space) using a magic lens (see Figure 2(c) and (d)). The window can be freely moved in the secondary world's coordinate space. In contrast, in the second scenario the window can be adjusted to show a given part of the secondary scene (location of interest), such that even if the output window W_o is moved, the virtual window W_v remains fixed in the secondary world's space (see Figure 2 (c) and (e)). Throughout this work, we will refer to these two states as "secondary scene fixed in space" and "window fixed in secondary scene". The latter scenario is only used when the TTL-WIM tool is applied, as will be shown later.

As introduced above, the proposed concept of providing an additional viewpoint for an explored scene is a more generalized 3D magic lens [1, 13] and extends the *seam* concept (spatially extended anchor mechanism) described in [9]. In contrast to the original *seam* implementation, however, in our scenario the scene viewed through the virtual window and the window itself are not fixed with respect to each other. We provide a dynamic viewpoint for exploring distant locations in the virtual world. Thus, an interactively defined *wormhole* is introduced, allowing viewing the currently explored world from an arbitrary remote location. One of the most important features of the proposed through-the-lens concept is that the surrounding virtual world remains unchanged during the two-handed manipulation of the additional viewpoint. Depending on the applied tool, the second viewpoint can be either manipulated directly (*eyeball-in-hand*) or indirectly (TTL-WIM and TTL-*grab-and-drag*), as will be discussed later.

Finally, the proposed tools are used not only to view the scene from a different point of view, but also to immerse the secondary scene through this viewpoint. Thus, a controlled "teleporting" is performed. In order to enter the secondary world as seen

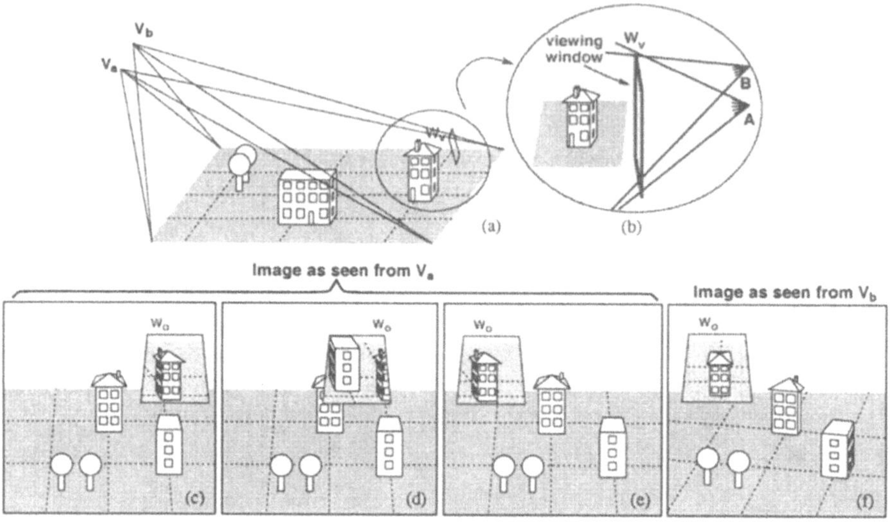

Fig. 2. The position of the virtual window (W_v) is fixed with respect to the scene seen through it, as shown in (a). V_a and V_b are two different viewing positions. (b) shows the two viewing positions A and B, derived from the current camera positions V_a and V_b. In case the virtual window W_v is fixed in the scene and the output window W_o is moved in the scene surrounding the user, the scene seen through W_o moves with the viewing window as show in (c) and (e). (d) shows the "scene fixed in space" scenario with the scene frozen as shown in (c). Moving W_o (compare (c) and (d)) allows viewing different parts of the scene. When the viewpoint changes (e.g. from V_a to V_b), the scene show in W_o can be viewed from different angles as show in (e) and (f).

from the additional viewpoint, the user has to move the pad towards the face until the image on the pad completely covers the viewing area. To facilitate the navigation, the secondary world can be immersed only if it is "fixed in the space". This is the more natural way of entering a distant world.

2.1 Realization

The hardware realization of the proposed tools requires a virtual environment setup with three tracked devices: One for the user's head position and orientation and one for each hand. This is the only information we need in order to realize the tools described in this work.

Assuming that the virtual world is organized in a scene graph-like structure, the software realization is simple as well. In order to display the virtual world as seen from an additional viewpoint V', the entire scene S, preceded by an appropriate transformation (T_a), passes the rendering pipeline once again. The projection of the output window (mapped on the pad) defines the area in which the rendering of S as seen from V' is performed. During rendering, the virtual counterpart of the physical pad is applied to fill the OpenGL's stencil buffer with an appropriate mask. Afterwards, S is rendered within the masked area as seen from V'. Further implementation details are discussed in [9].

3 TTL-Tools

As introduced above, the proposed techniques can be divided in two groups: Techniques applying direct and indirect viewpoint manipulation. In the next section, we will first describe the indirect manipulation techniques, which allow to intuitively adjust the scene seen through the second viewpoint without having to explicitly define a virtual camera position and view direction. Afterwards, we will discuss in detail the *eyeball-in-hand*-technique for direct viewpoint manipulation.

3.1 TTL Grab-and-Drag

Starting with two aligned viewpoints, this technique allows for the user to manipulate the scene seen from the additional viewpoint by grabbing and dragging the scene in the desired direction (Figure 3). This approach is similar to the scaled-world grab loco-

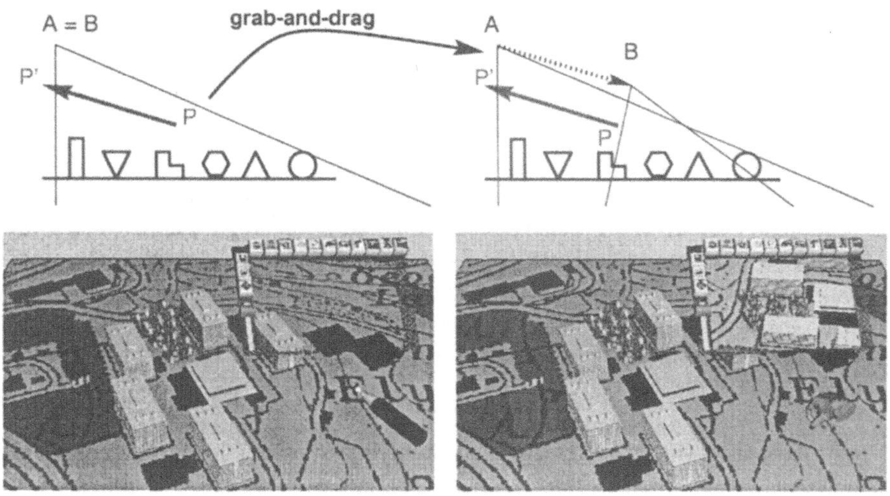

Fig. 3. Initially, both viewpoints are aligned as shown on the left. Grabbing the scene at point P and dragging to point P' corresponds to a translation (eventually combined with rotation) of viewpoint A to viewpoint B, as shown on the right.

motion metaphor described by Mine et al. [4]. Unlike the scaled-world grab where the authors apply the motion immediately, we provide a preview window. The scene seen through this window is now manipulated applying a simple grab-and-drag handle. In this way, the viewed part of the scene can be chosen very precisely, without requiring the user to physically or virtually walk/fly to the location of interest. In addition to the grab-and-drag mechanism, the user can also scale the scene if needed, hence, making this tool especially suitable for final high-precision adjustment.

Unfortunately, the application range of this technique is limited to the user's reach. When applied for viewing distant locations, the proposed technique can be circumstantial. This drawback can be overcome by combining our through-the-lens technique with other techniques for remote object grabbing (e.g. go-go technique [7], image plane techniques [6], or scaled-world grab technique [4]).

Similar to the eyeball-in-hand tool, we implemented a one-to-one mapping for the translation and the rotation originating from the grabbing tool. In this way, we can easily compute the transformation T_a. For T_a, we only need the position and orientation of the dragging handle at the beginning of the dragging motion and the current position of the handle. If another grabbing technique is applied, the transformation T_a has to be generated properly.

3.2 TTL Wim

In contrast to the original WIM tool, with the TTL-WIM we do not map the miniature copy of the virtual world *on top* of the pad. Instead, we display the latter underneath the pad's surface. Thus, the user is looking into the miniaturized virtual world through a window defined by the pad.

As introduced before, the manipulation of the additional viewpoint is indirect. The viewed part of the scene is defined by interactive dragging of a box around the target location on the pad (in the scaled down world – WIM, Figure 4). The selected part can be examined not only on the pad, but also in the virtual world surrounding the user (if visible from the current viewpoint). The size of the dragged box defines the position of the additional virtual camera, while the orientation always remains orthogonal to the virtual world (z-axis of the world) as shown in Figure 4. Thus, the virtual window is always fixed in the viewed scene.

This technique is primarily used for coarse selection of the viewed area. Once the user has adjusted the desired part of the scene to be seen through the pad, the grab-and-drag tool can be applied for precise manipulation of the additional virtual camera. In order to immerse the world seen through the output window on the pad, this world has to be "fixed in space". Since this is not the case with this tool, after selecting the location of interest, the scene has to be explicitly fixed in the space. Afterwards, the grab-and-drag tool can be used for further adjustment.

We can easily determine the scale factor and the point of interest (the middle of the dragged box), thus, the computation of T_a is simple as well. Knowing the size and location of the dragged box, the camera is positioned right over the point of interest (Figure 4).

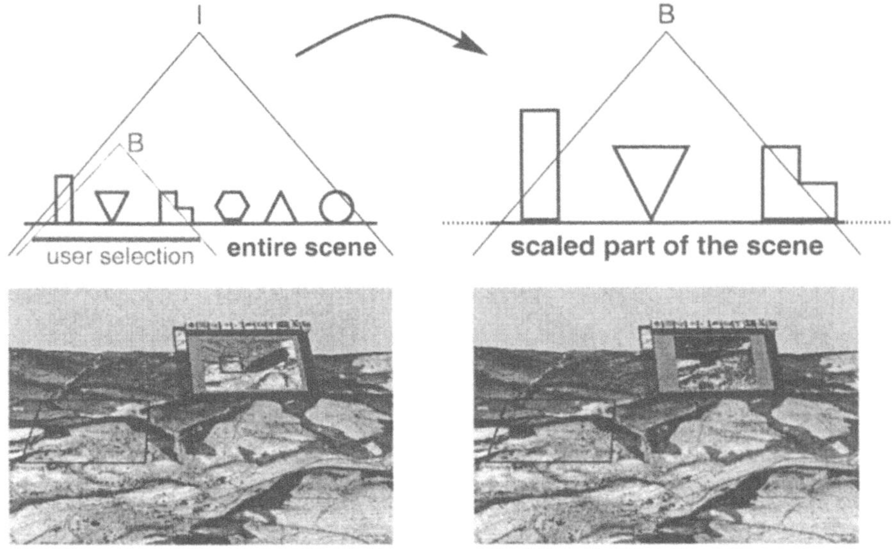

Fig. 4. Initially, a miniaturized copy of the entire scene as seen from viewpoint I is displayed on the interaction pad (do not confuse with the current viewpoint A). After interactively selecting a region of interest, the viewpoint is moved to B, such that only the selected region is visible through the pad.

3.3 TTL Eyeball-in-Hand

This technique has been introduced and explored by several researchers (e.g. [2, 14]). Despite the intuitive mental model applied with this metaphor, the main problem is the often-caused disorientation. This is due to the motion of the virtual viewpoint, which is directly applied to the current camera. Moreover, the one-to-one mapping of the hand to the virtual viewpoint makes precise adjustment of the virtual camera very hard. In addition, in order to move the camera around the scene, the user has to physically walk. Even though, the eyeball-in-hand metaphor is simple to understand and requires a simple mental model of the scene, the above limitations make it unsuitable as a sole navigation technique. In order to circumvent these limitations, while still supporting the features of this metaphor, we introduced a preview window to the eyeball-in-technique. This makes it possible to view the scene from various viewing position (in the hand's reach) without changing the current viewpoint of the user, thus, reducing confusion and disorientation.

The pen held in the dominant hand is used to define the additional viewpoint (Figure 5). It defines the position and the orientation of the new virtual camera. The scene, seen from this new viewpoint, is displayed in a window, which is mapped on the pad held in the non-dominant hand. Since the user sees the position of the virtual camera in

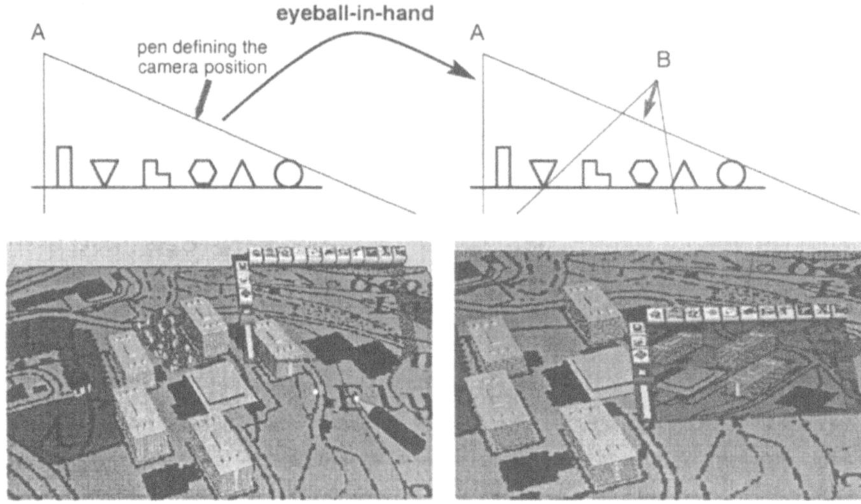

Fig. 5. Applying the eyeball-in-hand tool, the additional viewpoint can be positioned directly by defining a position and orientation of the new virtual camera B. A is the current viewpoint.

the surrounding environment and the scene as seen by the positioned camera *simultaneously*, the virtual camera can be positioned very precisely.

In order to display the appropriate part of the scene, we first compute the transformation T transforming the current position and orientation of the pen to the current camera's position and orientation. The matrix T^{-1} is now used to compute the transformation T_a.

4 Future Work and Conclusions

A topic of our future research will be the performance and evaluation of usability studies in order to make sound analysis of the proposed tools. Furthermore, we are working on an extension of the described techniques towards remote object manipulation, adjustment, and "through the wormhole" movement. Thus, we will show the versatility and flexibility of the through-the-lens display technique.

Although each of the proposed techniques has some limitations, the combination of all of them provides a powerful toolkit for exploring distant locations in a virtual world, as well as navigating in the virtual environment (see Table 1). The described through-the-lens world-in-miniature technique overcomes the main drawbacks of the original WIM-metaphor. The arbitrarily adjustable scale factor allows for the user to view large virtual worlds at a freely chosen scale. Since the miniaturized world is not displayed *on* top of the hand-held palette, the scale size is not limited to the distance between the user's head and the projection pad. The presented through-the-lens WIM is primarily used for accomplishing searching and (coarse-level) exploration tasks.

Table 1. Comparison of the proposed navigation tools.

Technique	Features	Limitations
TTL grab-and-drag	- suitable for searching tasks, and precise final adjustment tasks - intuitive viewpoint manipulation	- circumstantial for distant objects and locations
TTL WIM	- suitable for exploration and searching tasks - supports multiple scale levels	- scene cannot be entered until not "fixed in space" - improper for fine manipulations
TTL eyeball-in-hand	- requires very simple mental model - easy to use for fine precision camera adjustment	- unsuitable for exploration

In contrast, the grab-and-drag tool can be applied for all of the navigation categories introduced in Section 1. The only limitation is that it is not easily used for setting the viewpoint to very distant locations. In this case, the application of this tool has to be either preceded by the application of the through-the-lens WIM tool, or alternative techniques for remote grabbing have to be used.

The eyeball-in-hand tool is mainly used to directly define the view position and orientation in the reach of the user's hand. Hence, it falls into the category of the maneuvering-tools. This technique is very intuitive and requires a simple mental model. With the proposed preview window, this tool provides a valuable navigation aid.

In summary, we presented three tools for navigation in virtual environments based on a through-the-lens display technique. This concept allows exploring distant locations or invisible features of the virtual world without having to virtually or physically fly/walk to the remote location. It enables the viewing of locations of interest, while the world surrounding the user remains unchanged. This main contribution of the presented work will allow enhancing existing navigation aids and developing new tools exploiting the through-the-lens concept.

5 Acknowledgements

This work was partly funded by the Austrian Science Fund (FWF) under contract no. P14470-INF.

References

1. E. A. Bier, M. C. Stone, K. Pier, W. Buxton, and T. D. DeRose. Toolglass and magic lenses: The see-through interface. In *SIGGRAPH 93 Conference Proceedings*, volume 27, pages 73–80, 1993.
2. J. Brooks, F. P. Grasping reality through illusion- interactive graphics serving science. In *Proceedings of ACM CHI 88 Conference on Human Factors in Computing Systems*, pages 1–11, 1988.

3. R. P. Darken and J. L. Sibert. A toolset for navigation in virtual environments. In *Proceedings of the ACM Symposium on User Interface Software and Technology*, Virtual Reality, pages 157–165, 1993.
4. M. R. Mine, F. P. Brooks, Jr., and C. H. Séquin. Moving objects in space: Exploiting proprioception in virtual-environment interaction. In T. Whitted, editor, *SIGGRAPH 97 Conference Proceedings*, Annual Conference Series, pages 19–26. ACM SIGGRAPH, Addison Wesley, Aug. 1997. ISBN 0-89791-896-7.
5. R. Pausch, T. Burnette, D. Brockway, and M. E. Weiblen. Navigation and locomotion in virtual worlds via flight into Hand-Held miniatures. In R. Cook, editor, *SIGGRAPH 95 Conference Proceedings*, Annual Conference Series, pages 399–400. ACM SIGGRAPH, Addison Wesley, Aug. 1995.
6. J. S. Pierce, A. S. Forsberg, M. J. Conway, S. Hong, R. C. Zeleznik, and M. R. Mine. Image plane interaction techniques in 3D immersive environments. In M. Cohen and D. Zeltzer, editors, *1997 Symposium on Interactive 3D Graphics*, pages 39–44. ACM SIGGRAPH, Apr. 1997. ISBN 0-89791-884-3.
7. I. Poupyrev, M. Billinghurst, S. Weghorst, and T. Ichikawa. The go-go interaction technique: Non-linear mapping for direct manipulation in VR. In *Proceedings of the ACM Symposium on User Interface Software and Technology*, Papers: Virtual Reality (TechNote), pages 79–80, 1996.
8. D. Schmalstieg, L. M. Encarnação, and Z. Szalavári. Using transparent props for interaction with the virtual table (color plate S. 232). In S. N. Spencer, editor, *Proceedings of the Conference on the 1999 Symposium on Interactive 3D Graphics*, pages 147–154, New York, Apr. 26–28 1999. ACM Press.
9. D. Schmalstieg and G. Schaufler. Sewing worlds together with SEAMS: A mechanism to construct complex virtual environments. *Presence - Teleoperators and Virtual Environments*, 8(4):449–461, Aug. 1999.
10. R. Stoakley, M. J. Conway, and R. Pausch. Virtual reality on a WIM: Interactive worlds in miniature. In *Proceedings of ACM CHI'95 Conference on Human Factors in Computing Systems*, pages 265–272, 1995.
11. Z. Szalavári and M. Gervautz. The personal interaction panel - A two handed interface for augmented reality. *Computer Graphics Forum (Proceedings of EUROGRAPHICS'97)*, 16(3):335–346, 1997.
12. A. van Dam, A. S. Forsberg, D. H. Laidlaw, J. J. LaViola, Jr., and R. M. Simpson. Immersive VR for scientific visualization: A progress report. *IEEE Computer Graphics and Applications*, 20(6):26–52, Nov./Dec. 2000.
13. J. Viega, M. J. Conway, G. Williams, and R. Pausch. 3D magic lenses. In *Proceedings of the ACM Symposium on User Interface Software and Technology*, Papers: Information Visualization, pages 51–58, 1996.
14. C. Ware and S. Osborne. Exploration and virtual camera control in virtual three dimensional environments. In *Proceedings of the 1990 Symposium on Interactive 3D Graphics, Special Issue of Computer Graphics, Vol. 24*, pages 175–183, 1990.

Spring-Based Manipulation Tools for Virtual Environments

Michal Koutek and Frits H. Post
Delft University of Technology, Delft, The Netherlands
email: {*m.koutek, f.h.post*}*@cs.tudelft.nl*

Abstract. In this paper we present new tools for user interaction with virtual worlds, to bring more natural behavior into the manipulation of objects in virtual environments. We present some principles of physically realistic behavior of virtual objects and a set of user input techniques suitable for semi-immersive VR devices such as the Responsive Workbench. We introduce springs, spring-forks and spring-probes as new tools for assisting direct manipulation of objects in VEs. In this paper we focus on controlling rotational motions.

1 Introduction

In user interaction with virtual worlds, consistent and realistic behavior of objects is very important. We want objects to respond in a natural and predictable way to our actions. But usually VE objects are weightless and unsubstantial, and they move without friction of inertia; this leads to altogether 'unphysical' behavior and unpredictable responses, especially in semi-immersive environments such as the Responsive Workbench (RWB), where real and virtual worlds co-exist, and should follow the same natural laws.

We present a graphical force-feedback method and we provide a visual interface as an emulation of direct force input.

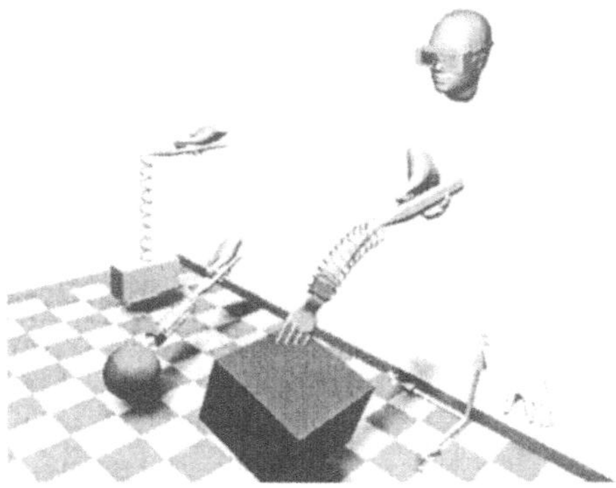

Fig. 1. Illustration of spring-based tools

We do this by the use of spring-based tools attached to objects assisting the manipulation, based on the following assumptions:

- a linear relation of force with spring compression / extension is intuitively understood and shown by the spiraling shape of a spring. Thus, even without exerting real force, a user has an intuitive notion of transforming a change of spring length to a force.

- bending and torsion of a shaft is used to show forces and torques exerted on virtual objects
- the relation between object mass and size is also intuitive, but application dependent. Specific mass of objects should be user specified. A massless world can always be created by setting all masses to zero.
- the RWB provides a natural ground plane for objects at rest.
- stability is introduced by friction and damping, reducing excessive effects of input actions on objects, and reducing undesired oscillations.
- physical contact of objects is intuitively equivalent with geometric intersection, and sound can be used to provide contact feedback.

We introduce a set of **spring-based tools** for providing the basic manipulation tasks (see Figure 1). We hypothesize that dynamics will provide intuitively consistent and predictable behavior of the objects in the virtual world, and that interactive manipulation will therefore be easier and more natural.

- **spring** is attached to the center of an object. It assists linear motions. The tool has 1 DOF (degree of freedom), the length of the spring, and controls 3 DOF (xyz) of an object.
- **spring-fork** is attached to an object and defines a contact point for transfer of forces and moments to the object. It assists translations and rotations. The tool has 3 DOF (extension, bend, torsion) and controls 6 DOF (xyz+hpr) of an object.
- **spring-probe** can be used for probing the material stiffness of an object or pushing an object. The tool has 1 DOF (length) and can control 3 DOF (xyz) or 1 DOF (pressure) of an object.

Why spring-based tools?

In VR it is just as easy to select and manipulate large and heavy objects as small ones. This may sometimes be an advantage, but it is not according to our expectations. Therefore, we will try to give the user a feeling of weight or mass of objects. We propose the use of spring-tools as a link between user's hand and a manipulated object. By this, we can obtain a natural visual feedback during manipulation.

When the user lifts a heavy object, the spring will extend proportionally to the object's weight. Also, acceleration and deceleration of the motion will affect the visible length of the spring.

The fork metaphor seems to be very intuitive. For object selection the fork has to be inserted in an object. The user can fix the position and the orientation of the fork inside the object. Then the spring part of the fork gives a visual dynamic feedback during the manipulation of the object. It is also intuitive that rotating the fork should also rotate the object. The user controls one end of the fork and the other end is influenced by the object. The fork can bend, extend (compress) or twist according to the laws of mechanics.

We will demonstrate the usage of the spring-tools with a simple object assembly task, which is easy in a real world but hard to simulate in a virtual environment; see Figure 15.

In this paper, we first review some related work and provide an overview of dynamic interaction techniques in VR. We concentrate on the use of dynamics in user interaction, especially the use of springs. New in this paper is the idea of controlling all 6 DOF of an object with a single spring-tool (the spring-fork). Crucial is control of the rotational motions. Also innovative is the spring-probe tool. With the current implementation of a micro-world we demonstrate the suggested dynamic interaction in VEs. Finally, we present areas for future work.

2 Related Work

We have studied interaction techniques used in fully immersive (CAVE, HMD) and semi-immersive virtual environments (RWB). Surveys of interaction techniques for VR systems can be found in [4, 5].

The problems of mechanics and dynamics have been studied extensively from many different points of view. It is outside the scope of this paper to review this whole field. We do not have the intention to implement a fully realistic dynamic manipulation system, but rather a limited and simplified set of basic physics to assist the manipulation of objects in VE.

In the VR literature, not much work has been published on incorporating dynamics in user interaction. Usually, haptics is used for this purpose, [3, 6]. In [1, 2], springs are introduced as a tool for direct manipulation of objects in VEs. In [1], springs are used to control the translational motions and they give a visual force feedback of applied forces. In [2], springs are also used to give a visual force feedback. They demonstrate a set of multi-spring configurations to control objects. Their force-based interaction approach allows multiple hands and users to manipulate the same object. Authors [1, 2], emphasize the problem of simulating the dynamics and collision behavior with real time frame rates.

In this paper, we will present an approach of having a set of very simple manipulation tools which reflect dynamic object behavior during the manipulation. Currently, we put our interest in single-handed manipulations.

We will extend the spring metaphor [1] to improve the user's feeling of mechanics and dynamics in virtual environments, and we will concentrate on controlling the rotation and the translation with the spring-fork tool.

3 Dynamics on the Workbench

As discussed before, we introduce the concepts of force, inertia, gravity, contact and surface friction to provide a virtual world in which objects behave more naturally. Objects behave according to physical laws and also the interaction is physics-based.

We are exploring the relevant laws of mechanics. For object collisions, there are principles of conservation of momentum and of energy, and reversible conversion between kinetic and potential energy.

3.1 Method Description

A specific mass is assigned to each object. From the volume of an object its mass is calculated. To make objects move, forces are needed. In our case, *the gravity force* and *the force exerted by the user* are acting. Counter-acting forces are *the friction force* with the surface and *the air resistance force*. For stability *a damping force* is implemented. We use a simplified implementation of the physics laws in our virtual world. We will ignore air-resistance. We will only use the static friction μ, when user drags an object across a surface. At small speeds μ is constant.

When the forces act on the object at the certain distance from the center of its mass it induces a moment and a torsion. The final rotational motion depends also on the moment of inertia of the object which corresponds to the axis of rotation. For simplicity, we will consider now that the whole mass of the object is concentrated to its center of mass and therefore the moment of inertia around axis O will be $I_O = r_O^2 m$, where r_O is the perpendicular distance of the center of mass from the axis O.

To make the simulation more realistic, it is possible to include a precise calculation of the moment of inertia for a given object and a certain axis of rotation. Here is the overview of the laws of mechanics discussed above:

Force law: $\boldsymbol{f_a} = m\boldsymbol{a} = m\frac{d\boldsymbol{v}}{dt} = m\frac{d^2\boldsymbol{x}}{dt^2}$

Gravity law: $\boldsymbol{f_g} = m\boldsymbol{g}$

Friction force: $\boldsymbol{f_r} = \mu N = \mu.m\boldsymbol{g}$

Spring force: $\boldsymbol{f_s} = -k\boldsymbol{x}$

Damping force: $\boldsymbol{f_d} = -c.\frac{d\boldsymbol{x}}{dt}$

Linear Momentum:

$$F = m\boldsymbol{a} = m\dot{\boldsymbol{v}} = \sum_{i=1}^{n} \boldsymbol{F_i}$$

Angular Momentum:

$$M = I\epsilon = I\dot{\omega} = \sum_{i=1}^{n} (\boldsymbol{r_i} \times \boldsymbol{F_i})$$

Where: m=mass, $\boldsymbol{f}$=force, $\boldsymbol{x}$=position, $\boldsymbol{v}$=velocity, $\boldsymbol{a}$=acceleration, $\boldsymbol{g}$= gravity acceleration, μ= static friction coefficient, k= spring constant and c= damping factor, ω=angular velocity, ϵ=angular acceleration, $\boldsymbol{r_i}$=force position, I=moment of inertia.

During manipulation, a spring-tool is attached to an object. Each spring-tool *(spring, spring-fork, spring-probe)* has to be calibrated with the manipulated object. That's done automatically from the weight and the dimensions of the object. The calibration procedure consists of calculating of spring and damping constants and choosing a suitable size of the spring-tool. For heavy and large objects a stronger and larger spring-tool is used, and a weaker and smaller spring-tool for light objects.

More about the basic spring-tool, the common spring, which is only used for linear motions, can be found in [1]. We will now concentrate on the spring-fork tool.

3.2 Spring-Fork

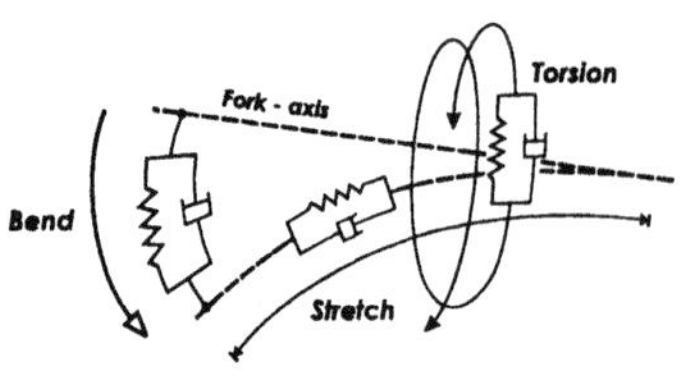

Fig. 2 Spring-damper systems for each deformation parameter of the spring-fork

We introduce here a 3 DOF spring-tool, the spring-fork. Each spring-damper in each DOF is calibrated to hold the attached object with a certain extension. In case of the spring-fork there are three spring-dampers, one for each DOF: bend, stretch, torsion.

3.3 Spring Damper

The basic component of spring-tools is the spring-damper. To reduce oscillations during manipulation, when an object is attached to a spring-tool, we have implemented a *spring mass-damper system* for each DOF.

$$m\ddot{\boldsymbol{x}}(\boldsymbol{t}) + c\dot{\boldsymbol{x}}(\boldsymbol{t}) + k\boldsymbol{x}(\boldsymbol{t}) = \boldsymbol{f}(\boldsymbol{t})$$

Here m is the mass of the object, $\boldsymbol{x}(\boldsymbol{t})$ is the extension/compression of the spring, $\boldsymbol{f}(\boldsymbol{t})$ is the force acting on the object only in $\boldsymbol{x}(\boldsymbol{t})$ direction, k is the spring constant and c is the damping factor.

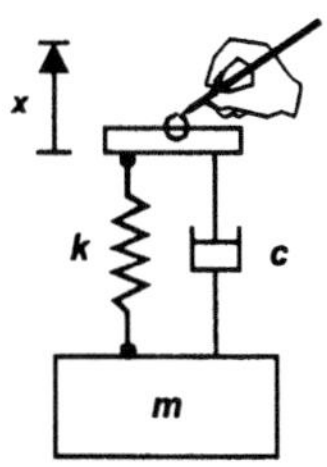

Fig. 3 Spring Damper System

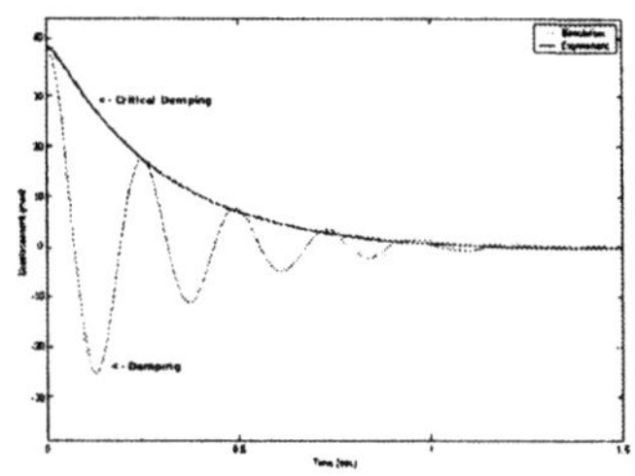

Fig. 4 Damping Comparison

If $\boldsymbol{x}_s$ is the static extension of the spring and $\boldsymbol{x}_d$ is the change of extension during the motion, we can simplify the spring-damper formula by assuming: $\boldsymbol{x} = \boldsymbol{x}_s + \boldsymbol{x}_d$ and $k\boldsymbol{x}_s = m\boldsymbol{g}$. Then we get the following differential system:

$$m\ddot{\boldsymbol{x}}_d + c\dot{\boldsymbol{x}}_d + k\boldsymbol{x}_d = 0; \qquad \boldsymbol{x}(0) = \boldsymbol{x}_0, \quad \dot{\boldsymbol{x}}(0) = \boldsymbol{v}_0$$

To avoid unwanted oscillations of the spring-damper we use a critical damping solution:

$$\boldsymbol{x}_d(t) = (A.t + B)e^{-\alpha t}; \quad with\ A = v_0 + x_0\alpha; \ B = x_0$$

$$\alpha = \frac{c}{2m}; \quad \omega_0 = \sqrt{k/m}$$

For critical damping is: $\alpha = \omega_0$ thus $c = 2\sqrt{mk}$. From Figure 4 is clear that the critical damping quickly converges to the zero but in fact it takes an "infinite" time to reach the zero. Thus when the simulation reaches a threshold, it stops. There is also another problem. Initial conditions are changing as the user moves his/her hand. Therefore, we have to re-initialize $\boldsymbol{x}_0$ and $\boldsymbol{v}_0$ each simulation time step.

4 Spring-fork Model

To implement the spring-fork manipulation, we first need to create a model of the spring-fork which would be scalable and deformable with bend, stretch and torsion deformations. The fork consists of a rigid part (the fork end) and a flexible part (the spring part), see Figure 5.

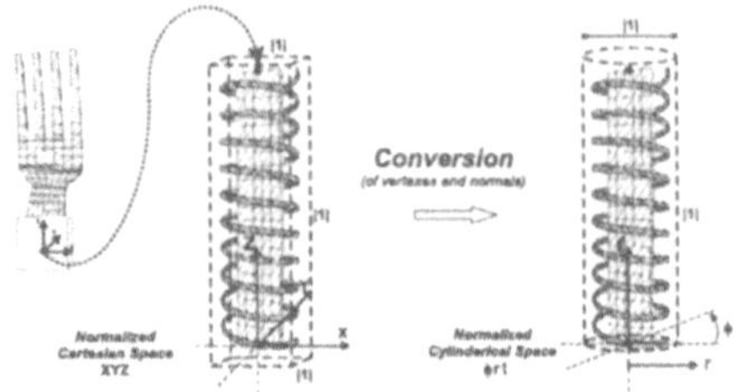

Fig. 5 Spring-fork model; Space conversions of the fork's vertexes and normals

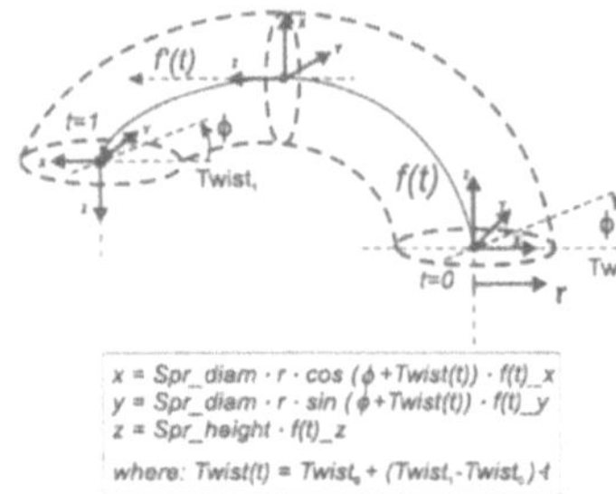

Fig. 6 Reconstruction of the XYZ coordinates of the deformed fork

The 3D model of the fork is converted to normalized cylindrical coordinate space, which is used to perform the fork deformation. All vertices and normal vectors are converted once and stored in memory as the initial and the normalized form of the fork. For a given scale of the spring-fork *(Spr_diam, Spr_height)* and a given deformation *(bend, stretch, torsion)* we have to reconstruct the final XYZ coordinates (Figure 6).

The torsion parameter of the spring-fork is the difference between $twist_0$ and $twist_1$. The bend and the stretch parameters are built in the parametric function $f(t)$. From Figure 6, it is clear how the LCS (local coordinate system) rotates along the function $f(t)$. So for each position at $f(t)$ we need to know the tangent vector, thus $f'(t)$ which corresponds to the Z-direction of the LCS. The fork-ending is attached at the end of the spring and it is aligned with the last LCS.

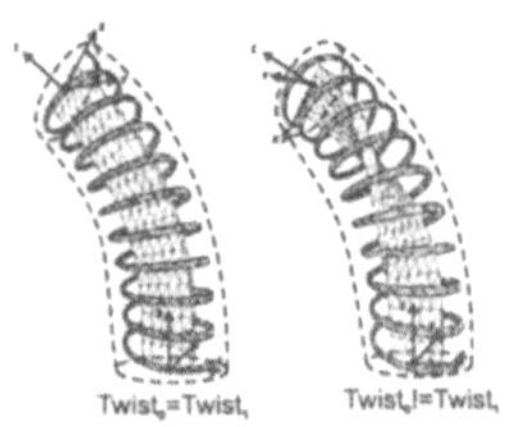

Fig. 7 Deformation of the spring-part

Fig. 8 S-shape deformation (due object collision)

Figure 7 shows deformations of the spring-part of the fork. The first example is without torsion and the second shows the both bending and torsion.

The deformation function $f(t)$ needs explanation. The problem of object or beam bending is not trivial. Bending depends on the profile along the length the object, on the material structure, on the type of load and on other parameters. In general it is a complex problem. A full general solution of the mechanical problem would be too time consuming, so we will use a simplified solution that will satisfy our needs.

We will assume that the load on the fork is concentrated. We designed an arc-length parameterized Bézier function for bending and S-shape deformation. We had to incorporate a compensation for changes in length of the arc, to keep its length constant without stretching. When the object was bent without changing length, we built the stretching ability in the deformation function. Torsion is also rather complex to perform in real time, so we also made a very significant simplification for this.

It is obvious that the deformation function needs to be calibrated to a certain range of forces, resp. to the virtual world and all the objects and their weights and forces which they could produce.

We have calibrated the spring-fork tool in our mini-world for the range of object weights *(0.0 vkg, 300.0 vkg)*, vkg = virtual kilograms. We must mention the problem of different measurement units in a virtual world and a real world where the user is standing. The real acceleration differs from the virtual acceleration, and certainly the real force applied by the user has different scaling than the virtual one of the object. The calibration procedure takes care of this problem.

Spring-fork Parameters

There are two major inputs to the spring-fork tool. Using the tracked stylus, the user controls the initial position of the tool: the fork axis and $twist_0$. The attached object applies a force and a moment to the fork-end and causes a deformation of the spring part of the tool. See Figures 9 and 10.

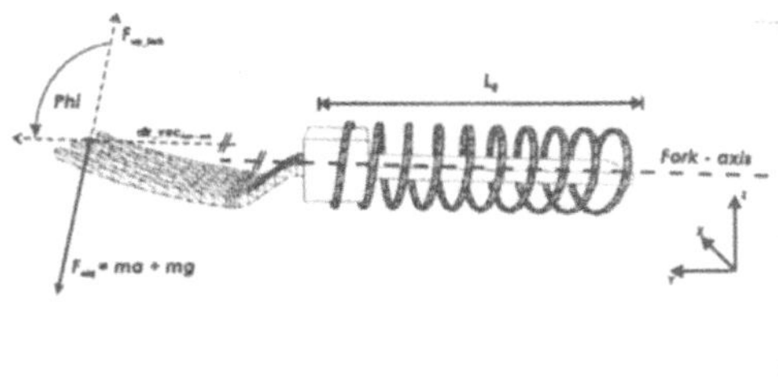

Fig. 9 Initial state of the spring-fork

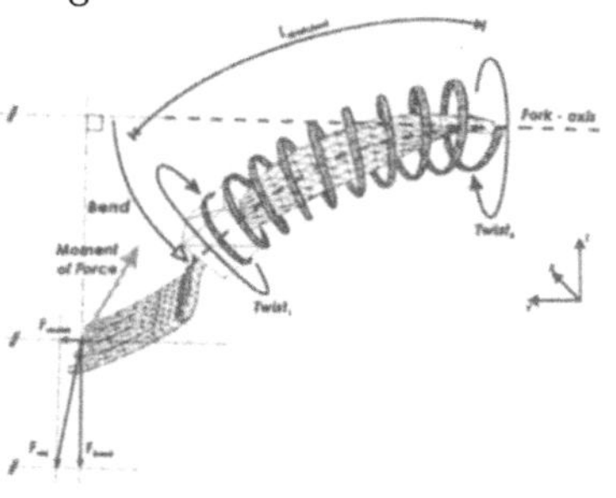

Fig. 10 Bent, stretched and twisted spring-fork

The force applied on the object F_{obj} is decomposed into the stretching force (parallel with the fork axis) and the bending force (perpendicular to the fork axis). Absolute values are calculated by using angle Phi.

We designed the spring-fork tool in such a way that it is possible to choose which of the 3 deformation DOF will be active: bending, stretching, torsion, or any combination of these. Of course, the user can change the stiffness of each DOF, for example to set up a stretch and a torsion resisting spring-fork which will easily bend only. In Figure 8, there is a torsion-free spring-fork (load: 100 vkg) showing an S-shaped bending during object collision.

5 Spring-fork Manipulation

The object selection is done by inserting the spring-fork into object. When the fork is inside the object is highlighted. The user can then still adjust the position of the fork inside the object. To begin the manipulation a button must be pressed. Manipulation stops when the button is released.

The manipulation procedure can be decomposed into several stages (Figure 12). The initial stage is the moment of selection. The position and orientation of the inserted fork will be kept for the whole manipulation. Only the spring-part of the tool will change.

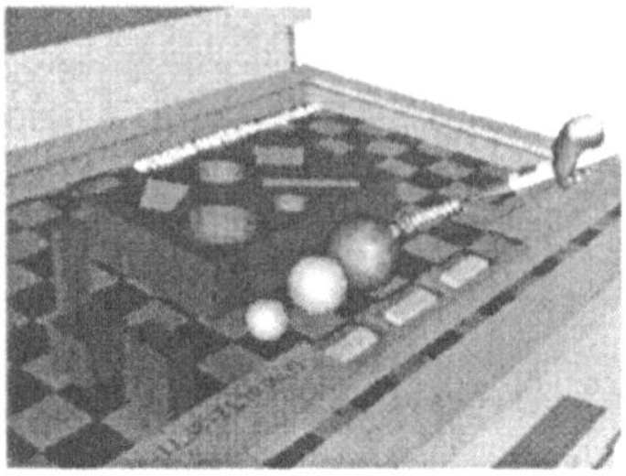

Fig. 11 Object selection

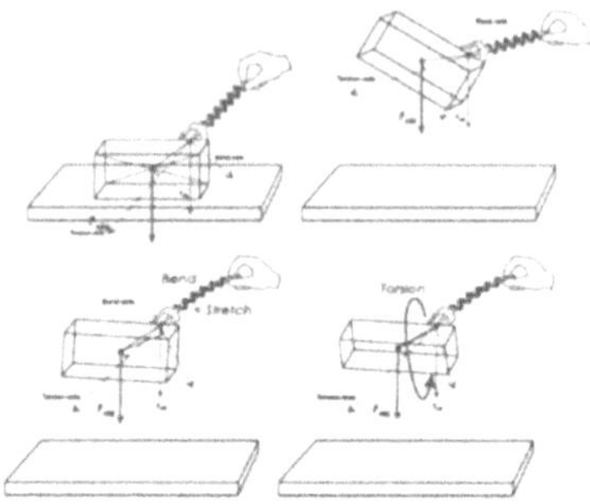

Fig. 12 Manipulation procedure

The next stage is the new position and the rotation of the user's hand and re-initialization of the spring-fork. The bend and the stretch deformations are performed first. After this torsion is calculated. This configuration (position and orientation of the object together with the deformed spring-fork) becomes a candidate for the new step, but first possible collisions with other objects have to be detected. If there is no collision, the candidate configuration will be used to re-initialize all three spring-damper systems, and they transform the current configuration to the new configuration. The spring-dampers of the spring-fork produce each new time step a new configuration of the object and the fork, but the user has meanwhile repositioned his hand. This triggers the next re-initialization of the system.

All the above steps make this simulation rather complex, especially the handling of the collisions of objects. Currently, we use a simple method for collision checking. First, we check bounding volumes collisions, then we evaluate collisions of triangles. To find the position and the orientation for the contact of two objects we use a binary subdivision collision algorithm which finds an approximate solution in 8 subdivisions.

6 Manipulation Experiments

To test the concepts of this paper, we have implemented an experimental application where the user can perform dynamic spring manipulation with virtual objects in a mini-world. The mini-world consists of several boxes and spheres which has to be assembled into the blue box (Figure 15). This task can be done either with spring-based tools or with common direct manipulation tools.

The basic concept of the RWB is that the user is standing in the real world, where the physical laws apply, and is partly immersed in the virtual mini-world which is projected on the Responsive Workbench. The user can compare the advantages of the spring-tools to the common tools (direct or ray casting manipulation). Finally, the user can also observe a visual feedback of dynamic behaviour of manipulated objects. Actual results and animations can be found at our web-site [7].

6.1 Notes on Implementation

We use the VR Responsive Workbench, based on an SGI Onyx 2, with 4x MIPS R10000, 1xIR2 graphics pipe, a stereo projection table and the Fastrak tracking system for measuring the position and the orientation of user's head and hand (stylus pointer). For implementation we have used C++ and our RWB library based on Iris Performer and OpenGL. We have implemented our scheme for collision checking, a simplified dynamic object behavior and the spring-based manipulation tools.

6.2 Spring-fork Manipulation Examples

The images in this section were created using our RWB Simulator library [7].

An object is selected by inserting the spring-fork into it (Figure 11). When the user has adjusted the fork inside the object, the manipulation can start.

As mentioned before, a user can switch the deformation DOFs of the spring-fork on and off. For example, a manipulation with a torsion-resistant spring-fork is shown in Figure 13.

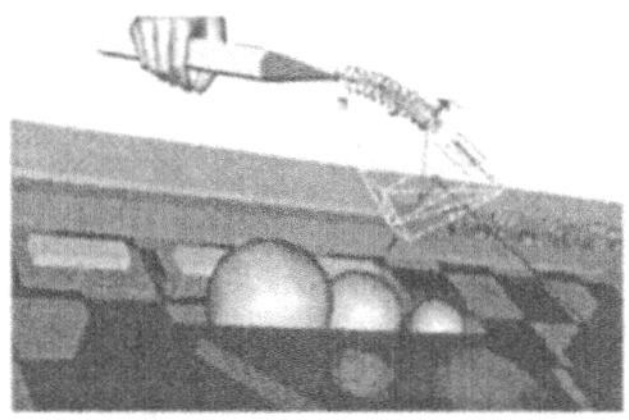

Fig. 13 Torsion resistant spring-fork **Fig. 14** Spring-fork in torsion

When the all deformation DOFs of the fork are set on the spring-fork manipulation with the box would look like in Figure 14. Torsion in the spring-fork and the rotation of the object are caused by the moment which is applied at the fork-ending. The user can compensate the rotation of the object by turning the spring-fork around its axis in the opposite direction. The spring-damper of the torsion parameter will take care of the transformation of the rotation to the attached object.

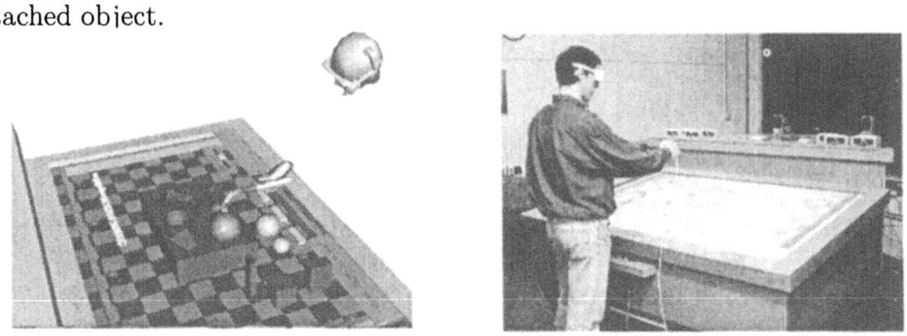

Fig. 15. RWB-overview: the spring-fork manipulation with objects in the mini-world

7 Conclusions and Future Work

We have developed a scheme of dynamic object behaviour for manipulation of objects in virtual environments. We have presented a set of spring-based manipulation tools.

We have described in detail the principles of the spring-fork, with which we can fully control both translational and rotational motions. These tools were designed to produce a realistic visual force feedback.

We did informal object manipulation tests with a group of VR experienced and un-experienced people. As expected, the spring tools were easy and intuitive to use and also the subjects performed better with the assembly task. The results show that object behaviour appears more natural and predictable than the 'unphysical' objects in most virtual environments.

However synthetic the models of the spring-tools are, they look and feel surprisingly real. The approximation of the mechanics seems to be good enough to create the illusion of mass and substance. Also the performance of the dynamic simulation keeps up with the tracker speed (50Hz). Of course, the actual performance and frame rate varies with the amount of collisions and collision behavior which seems to be the bottleneck. We are currently working on improvements and parallelization of the dynamic collision and contact behavior when an object is sliding over a surface of another object.

We can easily define a long list of extensions for future work in this area. The numerical computations for dynamic simulation can become very complex, and may put serious limits on performance. Therefore, we have greatly simplified the underlying physics. The simulation of the contact behaviour, efficient collision detection and handling, and constrained motion are areas of future work and improvement.

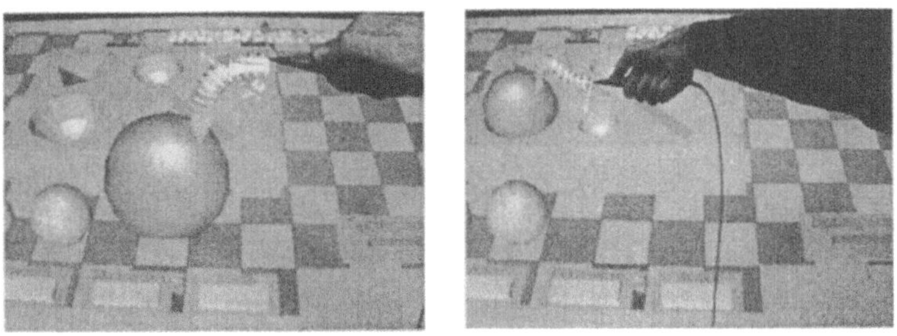

Fig. 16. RWB-detail: the spring-fork manipulation

References

1. M. Koutek, F. H. Post, *Dynamics in Interaction on the Responsive Workbench*, Proc. of Eurographics Virtual Environments, Springer, 2000, pp. 43-54
2. B. Fröhlich, H. Tramberend, M. Agrawala, D. Baraff, *Physically-Based Manipulation on the Responsive Workbench*, Proc. of IEEE VR Conference, 2000, pp. 5-12
3. B. Grant, A. Helser, R.M. Taylor II, *Adding force to a Stereoscopic Head-Tracked Projection Display*, Proc. of IEEE VRAIS,1998.
4. R. van de Pol, W. Ribarsky, L. Hodges, F. H. Post, *Interaction Techniques on the Virtual Workbench*, Proc. of Eurographics Virtual Environments '99 workshop, Springer, Vienna 1999, pp. 157-168
5. D. Bowman, D. and L. Hodges, *An evaluation of Techniques for Grabbing and Manipulation Remote Objects in Immersive Virtual Environments*, Symposium on Interactive 3D Graphics, 1997.
6. T.M. Massie, J.K. Salisbury, *The phantom haptic interface: A device for probing virtual objects*, Proc. of ASME Haptic Interfaces for Virtual Environments and Teleoprator Systems, pp. 295-301, 1994.
7. RWB Library and Simulator, Spring-tools: *http://www.cg.its.tudelft.nl/˜michal/*

Editors' Note: see Appendix, p. 280 for colored figures of this paper

Perception and Mental Rotation of 3D-Freeform Surfaces in an Immersive Projection System

Andrea Gaggioli, Ralf Breining

Competence Center Virtual Reality
Fraunhofer Institute for Industrial Engineering,
Nobelstr. 12, 70569 Stuttgart, Germany
ralf.breining@iao.fhg.de

Abstract. This paper reports on three experiments performed to examine the effects of different visualization techniques of 3D computer-generated freeform surfaces on subjects' perceptual and cognitive performance while doing CAD-related activities in an immersive VR system. Experimental perceptual and cognitive tasks included depth size estimation of a single 3D object (exp. 1), estimation of depth differences between two 3D objects (exp. 2) and mental rotation of 3D objects (exp. 3). Dependent variables were accuracy (exp. 1, 2 and 3) and response time (exp. 3). The visualization techniques we investigated were presence versus absence of binocular disparity, four different types of graphic image (wireframe, flat shading, Gouraud shading and Gouraud shading with surface normals) and two levels of shape complexity.
Results showed a positive effect of binocular disparity on perceptual performance (esp. 1), in particular when concave 3D shapes were used as stimuli (esp. 2), but a limited positive effect of stereopsis on mental rotation. Furthermore, results indicated that subjects were faster in mentally rotating 3D shapes rendered with more realistic techniques, whereas perceptual estimates were found more accurate and easier when observers were presented with less realistic rendered surfaces (exp. 1-2).

1 Introduction

A major use of 3D computer graphics is in design process, particularly for engineering and architectural systems, but almost all products are now computer designed. In the next future, CAD methods will be extensively employed in conjunction with 3D immersive displays, which may dramatically improve the possibilities of visualization and interaction offered by common 2D display CAD workstations. Thus, careful evaluation needs to be made as to how the computer-generated object is represented on 3D immersive display during the design process. It is commonly recognized that a computer-generated 3D object should be a) an accurate description of the model being designed b) presented in a realistic and integrated format, so that it can be visualized and interpreted without introducing uncertainty regarding to the represented proprieties [2]. To ensure that the displayed 3D image will satisfy these requirements, it is important focusing on which perceptual/cognitive operation is performed by the user during the design process. The main purpose of this research was to investigate the effects of stereo vision and monocular cuing techniques on subjects perceptual and cognitive abilities that are relevant in CAD-related activities, such depth estimation and mental rotation of computer-generated freeform surfaces.

Depth can be artificially simulated by presenting on a display's two-dimensional surface properties of the external world that results in the sensation of depth, called depth cues. Depth cues can be classified as monocular or binocular. Retinal disparity is an important binocular depth cue and is caused by the fact that each of our eyes sees the world from a different point of view. These two different perspectives of the same image are then combined by the brain into a single image by means of a process called *fusion*. The resultant sense of depth is called *stereopsis*. Monocular depth cues include light and shade, relative size, interposition, textural gradient, motion parallax and perspective. For some design (CAD) applications, objects are first displayed in a wireframe outline form that shows the overall shape and internal features of objects (i.e., the interior of a vehicle). Wireframe displays are useful to perform animations because the calculations for each segment of the animation can be performed more quickly when rendered surfaces of one object are not displayed. When object designs are complete, or nearly complete, realistic lightning models and surface rendering are applied to produce displays that will show the appearance of the final product [2]. Shading is used widely to depict surface structure and depends on variation of reflected light intensities according to the relationship between surface orientation and illumination direction. It relies on the ability of the human visual system to abstract shape from a physical or simulated scene illuminated from one or more light source.

Although it is known that monocular cues and steropsis can contribute individually, or in combination, to an appreciation of the object three-dimensional shape, there is little information on the relative merits of them. This is important in the case of virtual objects since incorporation of some visual cues is associated with a significant computational expense. For instance, stereoscopic vision requires two display channels to be rendered in a frame interval. Thus, an understanding of the relative benefits of these monocular and binocular coding techniques helps in judging the overall value of including a particular cue. In so doing, virtual reality application can be tuned and optimised for real time performance.

2 Experiment I: Depth Estimation of a 3D Object

The main purpose of the first experiment was to determine how stereo vision and different monocular coding techniques affect the ability to estimating depth of a 3D computer-generated object. Previous research on human distance and depth perception in 3D environments has addressed two basic questions, that is, which visual cues provide effective depth information and how does the effectiveness of given depth cues changes as a function of the viewing distance. Most studies have focused on subjects ability to estimate egocentric distance and relative distance, while there exists poor research about how depth of single objects is perceived. Real objects have depth and are located phenomenally as well as physically at different distances [3]. That is, objects have an egocentric distance (i.e., the distance of the object from an observer) and a relative distance (i.e., the distance of objects from each other). Objects also have depth in that they are perceived as three-dimensional and some parts of an object look farther away than do other parts [6]. This type of depth perception can be described as the ability of perceive variations in egocentric distance when looking at different points located on a 3D object. Stereo vision and four monocular coding techniques were investigated. Monocular coding techniques were wireframe (with hidden edges removed), flat shading, Gouraud shading [4] and Gouraud shading with surface normals.

2.1 Method

Subjects. Twenty-four subjects served as participants in the study (mean age = 29.4 years). All subjects had normal or corrected-to-normal vision and reported no experience with virtual reality, no experience with CAD software and upper-intermediate experience with computer.

Design. The experiment consisted of two types of object geometry (simple versus complex), four types of graphic images (wireframe, flat shading, Gouraud shading and Gouraud shading with surface normals) and six depth values (15, 30, 45, 60, 75, 90 cm) as completely crossed factors with stereopsis (present or absent). The serial order of depth values was determined by a Latin square arrangement and was the same for all participants. All factors were within subjects.

Apparatus and Stimuli. 3D images were created using these software 3D Studio Max, release 2.5, and displayed on the front wall of a four-walls CAVE capable of both stereoscopic and monoscopic modes. The screen is 300 cm wide and 300 cm high with a resolution of 960 x 960. Stereoscopic condition was created using CrystalEyes time multiplexed LCD shutter glasses synchronised to the display monitor. Two basic 3D free-form shapes were created (see Fig.1 and Fig.2). The simple one (a) was represented by a medusa-like object, the complex shape (b) was a terrain. Both objects were 50 cm wide. A squared base was added to the scene because during a pilot-experiment subjects reported that stimuli "floated" above the projection plane.

Fig. 1

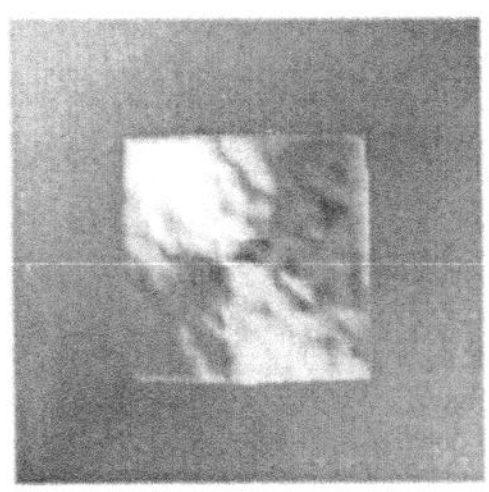

Fig. 2

Fig. 1 - 2. Stimuli used in exp. 1 (both objects are here rendered with Gouraud shading)

Procedure. Participants were told the purpose of the research and given specific instructions regarding the estimation task. In estimating depths, participants were required to report their estimates in centimetres. In order to facilitate the task, subjects were informed about their egocentric distance from the projection plane and given the edge of the square (100 cm) that represented the base of the 3D objects. Following practice, they estimated depth on each of 48 trials (6 trials for each rendering method; 24 trials for each geometry type) with stereopsis (stereo condition), took five minutes break, then estimated depth to another identical set of 48 trials without stereopsis (mono condition). From the participant's perspective, the depth value that the displayed object had on any given trial was random. In order to control the possible effect of sequence for the rendering conditions, four different sequences were arranged using a 4 x 4 latin square.

2.2 Data analysis and results

In order to analyse data, two ANOVAs were performed. The first used depth-difference estimates as the dependent measure and the second used relative errors as the dependent measure for accuracy. Relative error was calculated as follows: Relative error = (Depth estimate - True depth) / True depth.

This represents the percent error in an estimate relative to the true depth difference, with the sign indicating the direction of the error (when the sign is negative, it indicates underestimation; when the sign is positive, it indicates overestimation). Stereopsis, type of geometry, type of rendering and size of depth-difference were the independent variables in both analyses. Fig. 3 illustrates the means of the estimates in stereo and mono condition. The line with crosses represents perfect performance.

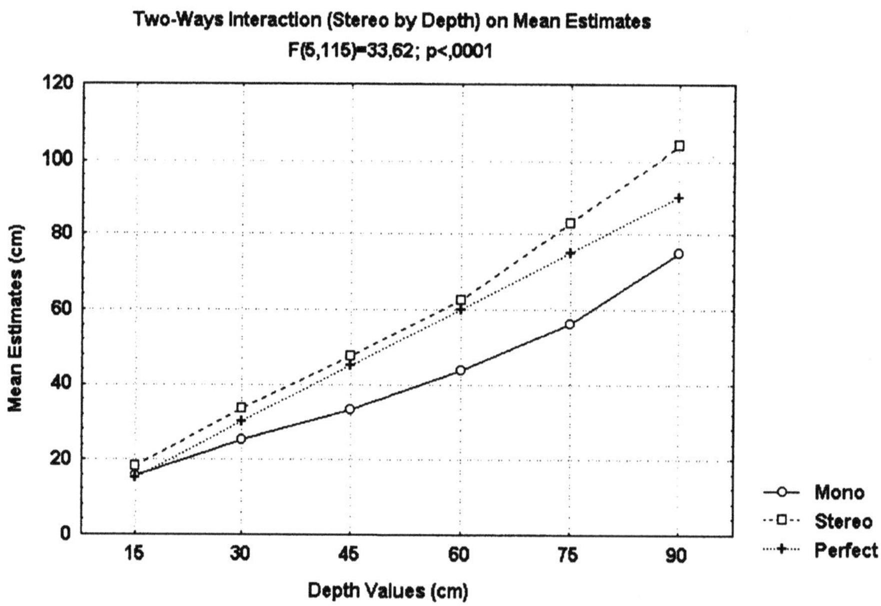

Figure 3. Effect of Stereopsis and Depth Values on estimates (exp. 1).

Fig. 3 shows that observers generally underestimated depth of 3D objects presented in mono, while performance in stereo was clearly more accurate. This is confirmed by the high significant effect of stereopsis in the ANOVA performed on relative error

(F(1,23)=69,65; p < 0,000001). The effect of object complexity on accuracy is reported in Fig. 4. This graph shows that estimates were far more accurate for the simple shape than for the complex shape.

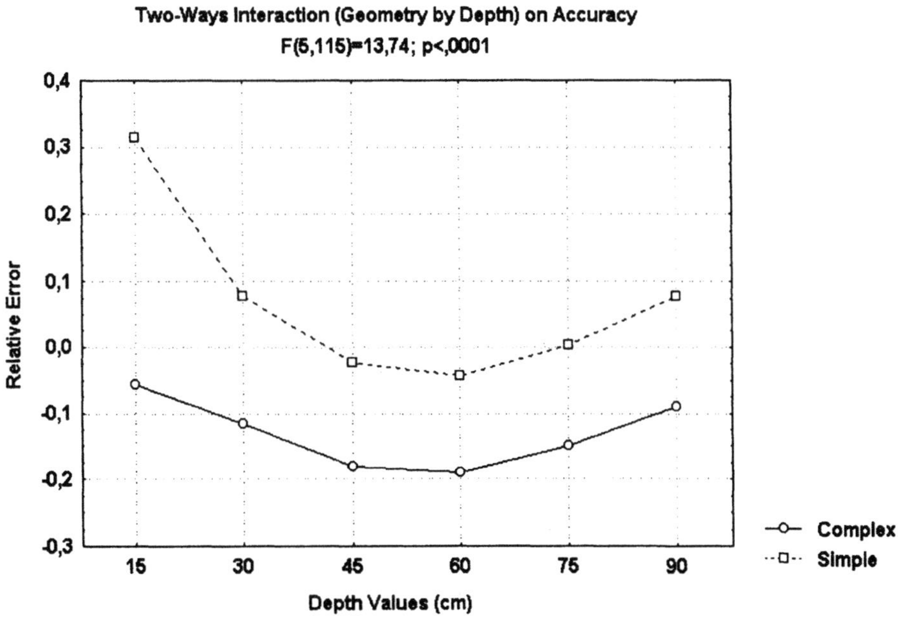

Figure 4. Effect of object complexity on relative error.

Fig.5 illustrates the effect of graphic coding techniques on accuracy. The main effect is very significant. A Tukey's HSD test was performed to assess pair wise comparisons. Results are summarized in Table 1. It was found that mean relative errors for Gouraud shading differed significantly from each other rendering method, and that there was a significant difference among Wirefame and Normals. Normals and Flat Shading determined more accurate estimates than Wireframe and Gouraud shading and the worst performance was determined by Gouraud shading.

MCT	Wireframe	Normals	Flat Shading	Gouraud Shading
Wireframe		*0,013578*	0,467195	*0,011390*
Normals	*0,013578*		0,349044	*0,000151*
Flat Shading	0,467195	0,349083		*0,000230*
Gouraud Shading	*0,011390*	*0,000151*	*0,000230*	

Note: Values indicate probability, and italic values reflect significant pair wise comparisons.

Table 1. Post hoc analysis of monocular coding techniques (dependent variable = relative error)

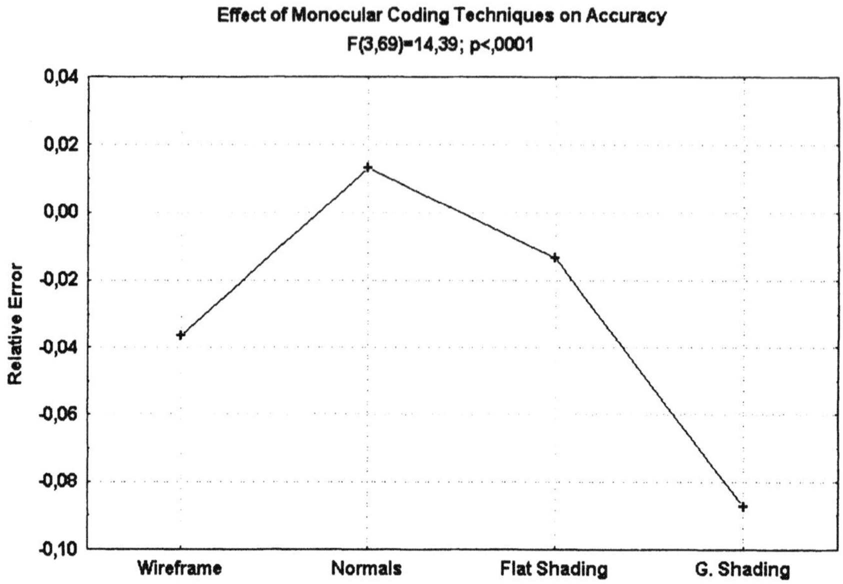

Figure 5. Effect of monocular coding techniques on relative error.

2.3 Discussion

Estimates and accuracy were significant affected by depth values, stereopsis, object complexity and rendering methods. The highest relative error was determined by the smallest depth value (15 cm). A post-hoc analysis performed on the interaction geometry type by object depth revealed that this effect was principally due to overestimation of the smallest depth value of the simple object ($p < 0,01$).

Subjects estimated depth of 3D objects more accurately when objects were displayed with binocular disparity than when only monocular cues were provided. Thus, retinal disparity confirms to be a very important depth cue, that provides effective perceptual information not only in estimating egocentric/relative distances but also in estimating distances between parts of an object that lay in different depth positions.

The effect of object complexity was highly significant. Complex objects depth was underestimated while simple objects depth - with the exception of the depth value 15 cm - was estimated more accurately. This difference could be due to the fact that irregular changes in the orientation of the surface of the complex object (a terrain-like 3D shape) did not allow subjects to detect the exact position in space of the top of the object.

Another interesting result of this study is that standard CAD monocular coding techniques affect depth estimates in different ways. Depth of wireframe objects was estimated more accurately than depth of Gouraud shaded objects but this result was inverted when normals were added to smooth shaded objects. This finding can be interpreted through results by Koenderink et al. [5] who showed that most of the relief of a shape is determined by visual contour and that shading adds very little to the "solidity" of an object if other cues are not available. Todd and Mingolla [10] performed three experiments to examine the perceptual salience of shading, texture, specular highlights and directions of light sources in providing information about the

3D structure of a cylinder. The results indicated that the shininess of the surface enhanced the perception of the curvature, but had no effect on the perceived direction of illumination, and that shading was generally less effective than the gradient produced by the texture for depicting surface in three dimensions. In our study, texture was not a surface feature but the addition of small normals across smooth-shaded surfaces appeared to be incremental to accuracy. This enhancement may depend on the fact that normals produced a gradient which served as additional depth cue. Another explanation could be that normals orientation allowed subjects to draw more detailed inferences concerning local attitude (slant and tilt) of the 3D surface. In order to disambiguate between these two explanations, however, further research is needed.

3 Experiment II: Estimation of Depth Differences Between 3D Objects

The main purpose of the second experiment was to investigate how stereo vision and different monocular coding techniques affect the ability to estimating depth differences between two 3D computer-generated forms displayed simultaneously. This task was supposed to be perceptually and cognitively more demanding than the task of Exp. 1, because subjects were to estimate depth of both objects and then to calculate their difference. Investigated factors were stereo vision, the four monocular coding techniques described in the previous experiment and type of object geometry (concave versus convex).

3.1 Method

Apparatus and Stimuli. The apparatus was the same used in experiment 1. Twelve couples of convex spheroids (Fig. 6a) and twelve couples of concave spheroids (Fig. 6b) were designed using the software 3D-Studio Max. For each objects group, the direction of depth difference was balanced: for the first six objects, the spheroid positioned on the right side of the square was greater in depth than the spheroid positioned on the left side, while for the remaining six objects the order was inverted.

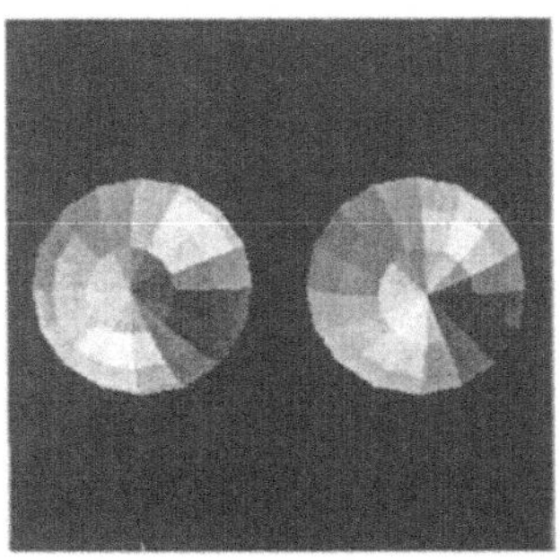
Fig. 6a

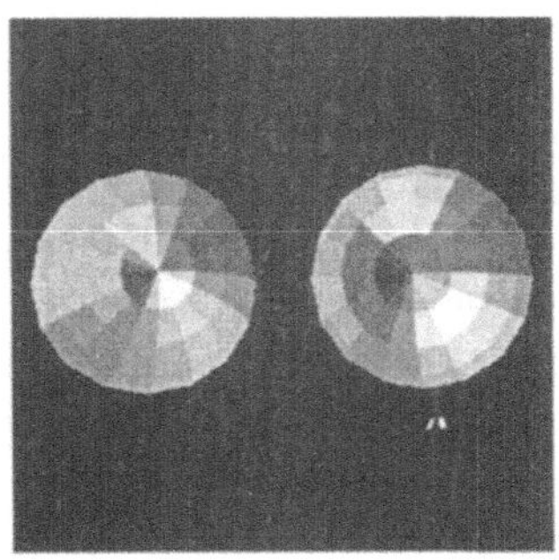
Fig. 6b

Figure 6a-b. Stimuli used in exp. 2 (both objects are here rendered with flat shading)

3.2 Data analysis and results

In order to analyse data, two ANOVA were performed. The first used depth-difference estimates as the dependent measure and the second used relative errors as the dependent measure for accuracy.

Fig. 7 illustrates the means of the estimates in Stereo and in the Mono condition. The line with crosses represents perfect performance. Fig. 7 shows that although observers generally underestimated differences in depth between the two objects, the level of underestimation was significantly reduced when binocular disparity was provided: actually, estimates in Stereo typically averaged 90% of the true depth difference, while estimates in Mono averaged 71% of the true depth difference.

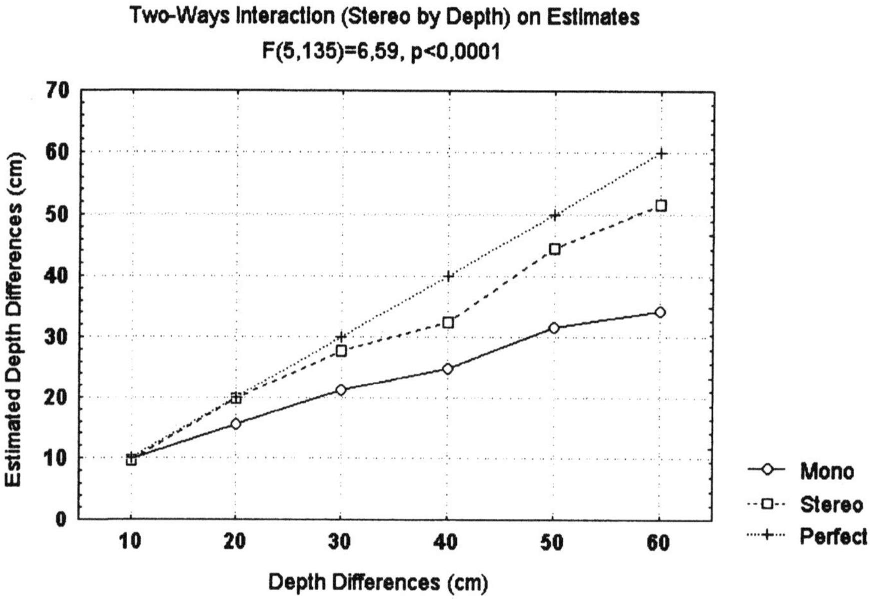

Figure 7. Effect of Stereopsis and Depth Values on estimates.

3.3 Discussion

Subjects generally underestimated differences in depth between the two three-dimensional shapes. Corroborating the results of the first experiment, the errors in depth estimation were found greater when objects were displayed without stereopsis. This confirms that stereopsis represents a powerful depth cue when the task is perceptually demanding [11]. The interaction between stereopsis and geometry type on relative error is also of particular interest. Depth differences for concave and convex objects were far underestimated in mono, and the underestimation for concave objects was found significantly greater than the underestimation for convex objects. When stereo vision was provided estimates for concave objects became as accurate as estimates for convex objects. This finding supports the assumption that the advantage of this depth cue becomes more pronounced when monocular information are ambiguous or insufficient in depicting the shape of a three-dimensional object [7].

Actually, some subjects reported difficulties in perceiving concavity without ambiguity when only monocular cues were provided, especially if concave shapes were rendered using the Gouraud shading technique. This subjective impression is corroborated by mean results for type of graphic image, that reveals a trend of underestimation of depth differences for Gouraud shaded objects, although the magnitude of the error was less significant than in Exp. 1.

4 Experiment III: Mental Rotation of 3D Objects

The previous experiments have provided evidences that participants' accuracy in estimating depth of 3D virtual objects with variable geometry is affected both by stereopsis and monocular coding techniques. In particular, it was found that the absence of binocular disparity led to an impoverished performance, whereas – more surprisingly – the use of less realistic types of graphic image (i.e. wireframe and flat shading) and the addition of surface normals improved accuracy in estimating depth. The first objective of the third experiment was to assess whether the same pattern of results could be obtained with subjects performing a more complex cognitive task, the mental rotation of three-dimensional objects. This standard cognitive task consists of presenting subjects with pairs of drawings of stationary 3D block objects and then asking participants to determine whether the presented images are different objects or different angular orientations of the same object (Shepard, 1971). In order to answer this questions, subjects mentally rotate one of the two objects into congruence with the second object for comparison. This assumption is based on the observation that the time required to make a correct judgment of "same" increase linearly with the angular difference between the objects.
The mental rotation paradigm has been applied in the computer graphics research because it represents one of the few available objective methods to assess user's cognitive performance under different visualization parameters of the computer-generated object.
The main goal of the third experiment was to further investigate the effects of stereopsis and monocular coding techniques on the cognitive manipulation of 3D structures. In particular, we were interested to assess whether the positive effect of binocular disparity observed in exp. 1-2 is strictly related to the perceptual task at hand (depth estimation), or is extended to more complicated cognitive tasks (i.e. mental rotation).

4.1 Method

Design. The experiment consisted of two levels of object geometry (simple, complex), four types of graphic images (wireframe, flat shading, Gouraud shading, Gouraud shading with surface normals) and six angles of relative rotation (0°, 36°, 72°, 108°, 144°, 180°) as completely crossed factors with stereopsis (present or absent). Each of these combinations of factors were presented to subjects in two pairs of slides. One of these pairs was a "same" pair while the other was a mirror image or "different" pair. All factors were within subjects. The 96 treatment combinations were presented to subjects in random order.

Apparatus and Stimuli. The apparatus was the same used in experiments 1-2, except that subjects were given two buttons to indicate their responses. The 3D computer generated objects (see Fig. 8) were modelled after the 3D figures portrayed in the experiment of Barfield (1988).

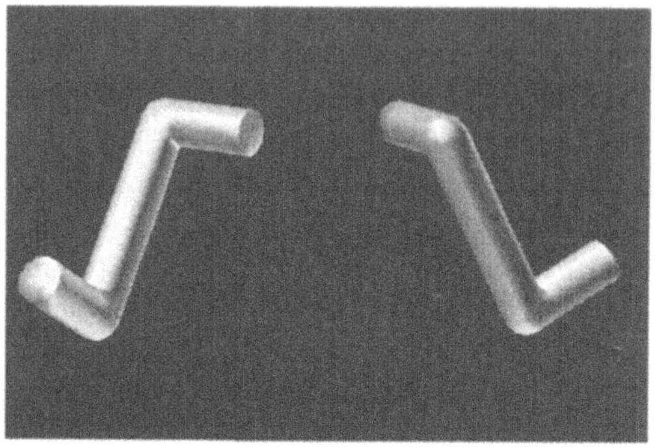

Figure 8. Stimuli used in Exp. 3

4.2 Data analysis and results

Response Time. Results of the ANOVA performed on response time data indicated a significant main effect for type of graphic image ($F(3,51) = 6{,}36$; $p<0{,}001$). A post-hoc contrast revealed that the wireframe images produced significantly slower response times than Gouraud shaded images. The ANOVA results indicated also significant main effect for angle of deviation ($F(5,85) = 13{,}85$; $p<0{,}0001$) on response time. Fig. 9 shows that response time increases almost linearly with angle of rotation, suggesting that subjects mentally rotate 3D objects. There was also a significant main effect of relative orientation, with mirror objects producing slower response time than "same" objects ($F(1,17) = 19{,}53$; $p<0{,}0005$). The effects of stereopsis and object complexity were not significant.

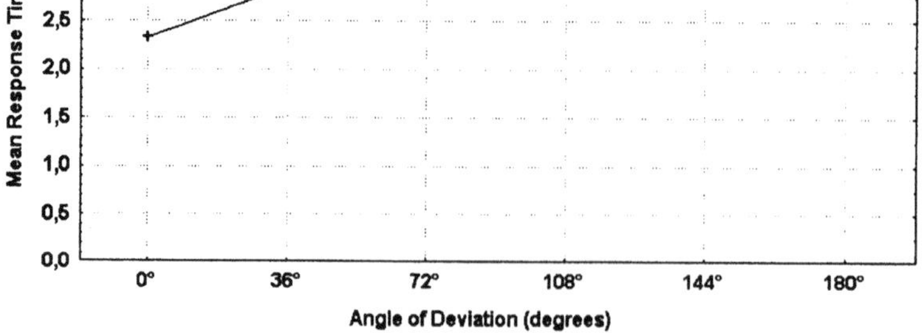

Figure 9. Mean response times across angle of deviation

Response accuracy. The overall error rate for the experiment (defined as the percentage of trials in which subjects responded incorrectly) was 7,2 %. This compares good with results from previous studies (5,9 %: Barfield [1]; 6,1%: Yuille and Steiger [12]; 3,2%: Shepard [9]). The ANOVA performed on percentage of error revealed significant main effects for stereopsis ($F(1,15) = 5{,}88$; $p<0{,}05$) with subjects more accurate in the stereoscopic condition, and for angle of deviation ($F(5,75) = 2{,}37$; $p<0{,}05$). In particular, it was found that the angle 180° was the most difficult rotation angle in the experiment, with a error rate of 10 %. The effects of the remaining factors were not significant.

4.3 Discussion

The main objectives of the third experiment were a) to assess whether providing the cue of stereopsis would help subjects to better perform a mental rotation task and b) to verify whether different monocular coding techniques of a 3D computer generated object impact performance differently. Results of this experiment indicated that the stereopsis cue helped subjects perform the mental rotation task, although this effect was limited to the accuracy with which participants discriminated 3D objects.

As concerns the effect of monocular coding techniques, results indicate that the response time was significantly slower when subjects were presented with wireframe images. This finding is in agreement with results of previous studies [1; 2] that showed that the discrimination task is better when realism cues are added to the object surface and in particular when shading procedures are used. Thus, the present study confirms that the use of advanced rendering can not only enhance the aesthetics and the form faithfulness of a computer generated object (as shown by subjective judgment studies, e.g. Sanford, 1987 [8]), but it can also improve the user's ability to visualize and mentally manipulate the structure of such object.

5. General Discussion

The most convincing conclusion suggested by the results of this research is that the stereopsis cue is useful and sometimes even necessary during CAD-related activities. As shown by experiments 1-2, subjects estimated depth of 3D objects far more accurately when objects were displayed with binocular disparity that when only monocular cues were provided.

As concerns the relative merits of monocular coding techniques, the three experiments performed produced mixed results. In particular, in exp. 1-2 it was found that the use of less realistic types of graphic image (i.e. wireframe and flat shading) and the addition of surface normals significantly improved subjects' accuracy in estimating depth; on the other hand, the third experiment indicated that the use of advanced rendering (Gouraud shading) enhanced the user's ability to visualize and mentally manipulate the structure of 3D objects. One way to account for these differences is to postulate that although both tasks imply the mental representation of the three-dimensional structure of the object, they involve different perceptual/cognitive processes. This could explain why the manipulation of specific monocular coding techniques (e.g. Gouraud shading) can determine different effects depending on which task is performed by subjects. If this assumption is correct, it would be cost-effective to give the user the possibility to customize the visualization method according to which CAD activity he/she is actually carrying out. In example, when the user is performing tasks that imply the direct estimation of the 3D object size, he could select the wireframe modus, which also has the advantage to be associated with small computational expense. Surface rendering could be applied to produce displays that assist the users in doing more cognitively demanding activities, such as rotating a figure to perform a visual interference check or to evaluate the overall aesthetic qualities of a digital mock-up.

References

1. Barfield, W., Sanford, J., Foley, J. (1988). The mental rotation and perceived realism of computer-generated three-dimensional images. *International Journal of Man-Machine Studies*, 29, p. 669-684.
2. Brown, M.E., Gallimore, J.J. (1995). Visualization of Three-Dimensional Structure During Computer-Aided Design. *International Journal of Human-Computer Interaction*, 7(1). p. 37-56.
3. Dember, W.N., Warm, J.S. (1979). *Psychology of perception* (2nd ed.). New York: Holt, Rinehart & Winston.
4. Foley, J., Van Dam, A. (1982). *Fundamentals of Interactive Computer Graphics*. Reading, MA: Addison-Wesley.
5. Koenderink, J.J., Van Doorn, A.J., Christou, C., Lappin, J.S. (1996). Shape constancy in pictorial relief. *Perception*, 25, p. 155-164.
6. Matlin, M.W., Foley, H.J. (1992). *Sensation and Perception* (3rd ed.). Boston: Allyn and Bacon.
7. Pepper, R. L., Patterson, R. (1986). Stereo TV improves operator performance under degraded visibility conditions. *Optical Engineering*, 20, p. 579-585.
8. Sanford, J., Barfield, W., Foley, J. (1987). Empirical studies of interactive computer graphics: Perceptual and cognitive issues. In *Proceedings of the Human Factors Society 31st Annual Meetting Volume I*, p. 519-523.
9. Shepard, R.N., Metzler, J. (1971). Mental rotation of three-dimensional objects. *Science*, 171, p. 701-703.
10. Todd, J.T., Mingolla, E. (1983). Perception of Surface Curvature and Direction of Illumination From Patterns of Shading. *Journal of Experimental Psychology: Human Perception and Performance*, 9 (4), p. 583-595.
11. Yeh, Y.Y., and Silverstein, L.D. (1992). Spatial judgments and stereoscopic presentation of perspective displays. *Human Factors*, 34, p. 583-600.
12. Yuille, J.C., Steiger, J.H. (1982). Nonholistic processing in mental rotation: some suggestive evidence. *Perception and Psychophysics*, 31, p. 201-209.

An Investigation into the design of an Interface for Interaction with a Virtual Environment representing a four-dimensional object

R Wellard and S.C Chapman

Physics Department, University of Warwick,
Coventry CV4 7AL
{wellard, sandrac}@astro.warwick.ac.uk

Abstract. Five methods of mapping the input from a six-degrees-of-freedom input device to the set of rotations available in four-dimensional space are evaluated with respect to how well they can be used to perform four-dimensional target aquisition tasks. Also evaluated are the user's opinions of the methods of interaction. Two of the five interaction methods perform significantly better than the rest allowing some general results to be drawn. ...

1 Introduction

4-Space is the theoretical four-dimensional vector space spanned by four orthogonal vectors. The vector space most closely associated with the universe we inhabit is three-dimensional, that is, it is spanned by three orthogonal vectors. Any position in 3-space can be described by its distance from a convenient point of origin along each of three orthogonal vectors, and illustrated in the familiar format *(x,y,z)*. For a position in 4-space to be similarly described a new variable must be introduced, the distance from the origin along the fourth orthogonal vector. The position can now be referenced as the point *(x,y,z,w)*. The properties of four-dimensional objects are very different to those of three-dimensional objects, and are well explained in works by Banchoff [3], Manning [12], and Abbott [1]. This work is only interested in controlling the extended set of rotations available in 4-space, and in particular which of the five methods of interaction presented (Section 3) form the most effective link between user and four-dimensional rotations. Although the aim of this work is to classify these methods of interaction according to how well they enable the user to control four-dimensional rotations, it is hoped that some general results for four-dimensional manipulation design can be drawn. In order to evaluate the five methods of interaction (which shall now be referred to as the five *control mappings*) an experiment was designed to test user performance under each of the control mappings, a complete description of which is provided in Section 2.

Wellard & Chapman [14] contains a brief explaination of 4-D rotations, projections through a point, and their effects on the hypercube; specifically aimed at explaining these issues in the context of this work. However, as an aid to understanding this paper, we reiterate some of the basic concepts here. Rotations in 4-Space are about a plane (in comparison with rotations in 3-space, which are about a line), and all orientations of a 4-D object can be realised by rotations about three perpendicular planes. The hypercube [2] is the four-dimensional analogy of the cube, and consists of eight cube-faces attached at their faces (cf a cube is constructed by attaching six square-faces together at their edges). With a hypercube in a certain orientation, it's 3-D projection through a point forms a cube-inside-a-cube shape ([3] p120-122).

Lessons can be learnt from work on control mappings between user and a 3-D virtual environment [13], [5], [7], and studies on input devices and their effectiveness with respect to the user [10], [11], [16]. However, the work presented here addresses an original research problem since the abstract nature of the task to be performed, and the fact that interaction is with a four-dimensional object and not with a familiar three-dimensional one, means that not all the previous results can be extended to this work.

Within this paper, Section 2 describes the experimental method; Section 3 introduces the control mappings ([14] contains a discussion of their theorized affordances and weaknesses); Section 4 presents the significant results, which are discussed in Section 5 and collated into the conclusions of Section 6.

2 Experimental Method

A within subjects 5x7 repeated measures experiment was carried out in which subjects performed seven target aquisition tasks using different control mappings. The dependent variable was *level of closeness to target achieved.* The independent variables were *control mapping*, at five levels (mappings 1 to 5), and *target orientation*, at seven levels (seven different targets presented in the same order). After completing the seven tasks using a particular mapping the subjects answered a questionnaire; resulting in a separate within subjects, repeated measures data set, where the dependent variable was *questionnaire-score*, and the independent variable was *control mapping*.

Eighteen (14M 4F) subjects were randomly selected from a set of 24 (19M 5F) physics postgraduate volunteers; as with the within subjects design, each subject completed all the tasks using every control mapping. The order in which the subjects used the control mappings was randomly[1] assigned, however the target aquisition tasks were presented in the same order for each control mapping, and for each subject. The equipment used was a FakeSpace ImmersaDesk package, which consists of a five foot by four foot stereo-projection screen, a pair of tracked CrystalEyes shutter glasses, and a tracked FakeSpace WorkWand input device with three digital buttons and a two-degrees-of-freedom analogue joystick. Together with code written specifically for this experiment; and a questionnaire

[1] a problem with the equipment meant that there was a tendency for control mappings 4 and 5 to be used after the others

constructed using the presence questionnaire developed by Witmer and Singer [15] as a guideline.

Visually the subjects were presented with the projected image of a hypercube drawn in transparent blue four feet above the ground and approximately three feet in front of them, with it's orientation in 4-space such that it's projection takes the cube-inside-a-cube form. The 'inside' cube-face of the hypercube is drawn opaque red, and it's sides labeled one to six. Also presented is the projection of an opaque green target cube that also has it's sides labeled one to six. This target cube exists in the same 4-space as the hypercube. The target aquisition task is for the subject to rotate the hypercube in 4-space so that the red cube-face of the hypercube occupies the same space (in 4-space and therefore in the 3-D projection space) as the green target cube, and the numbers on the square faces of the two cubes match up. Once this task has been completed the orientation of the hypercube is re-set, and a new target is presented.

Subjects were met individually by the experimenter and asked to read an introduction to the experiment, and then a brief set of instructions for the control mapping they were about to use. They then put on the CrystalEyes shutter glasses, were given the Workwand, and the code was started. The subjects were given two minutes to get used to the control mapping during which they were presented with a practice target so that they knew what they would have to do during the trial. After the two minutes the orientation of the hypercube was re-set and the first target was presented. Once either the subject was satisfied that the target orientation had been achieved, or they had given up, or four minutes had elapsed, the hypercube's orientation was re-set, and the next target presented. All measurements were automatically recorded by the computer. Distance from the target was calculated as the average of the linear distances, in 4-space, between each vertex of the red cube-face and the appropriate vertex of the green target cube. The minimum of this distance value during the subject's attempt to match the target was then converted into the interval scale, between 0 (distance greater than 0.24) and 8 (distance less than 0.03), *level of closeness to target.*

3 Control mappings

This section describes each of the five proposed control mappings using the following conventions and notation. The coordinate system for the three-dimensional space the user moves in consists of three perpendicular vectors, x_3, y_3 and z_3. With the user facing the ImmersaDesk, x_3 is in the direction of the user's right, y_3 increases upwards, and z_3 increases in the opposite direction to the way the user is facing. This set of axes has as its origin the centre of the Workwand; thus the Workwand itself forms a vector through the origin, and all rotations of the Workwand are about a line through the origin.

The coordinate system for the four-dimensional space, within which the four-dimensional objects are manipulated, consists of four perpendicular vectors, x_4, y_4, z_4 and w_4. The origin of this coordinate system is at the centre of the four-dimensional object. Thus all rotations of the four-dimensional object about planes through the origin do not translate the object's centre. The four-dimensional object is projected through a point on the w_4-axis onto a three-dimensional hyperplane. This projection is displayed in such a fashion that movement of a four-dimensional object in the positive x_4-direction would cause the image to move to the user's right, movement in the positive y_4-direction would cause the image to move upwards, movement in the positive z_4-direction would cause the image to move towards the user, and movement in the positive w_4-direction would cause the image to get larger. This obvious choice of projection and display-orientation, means that rotations of the four-dimensional object affecting only the x_4, y_4, and z_4 dimensional coordinates of its points will cause the projected image to rotate as a three-dimensional object (in Section 5 these rotations are referred to as *non-morphing* rotations). For example, rotating the four-dimensional object about the x_4-w_4-plane would cause the image to rotate about a line through its centre parallel to the x_3-axis.

A virtual linear slider is a one degree of freedom input device, which comprises of a handle that can be moved one-dimensionally between two end points. In the presented control mappings the position of the handle on the linear slider represents the rotation of the four-dimensional object about a particular plane. Which plane the virtual linear slider is associated to, and how it is manipulated, depends upon the control mapping.

Rotations of the Workwand are separated into two categories: rotations altering the Workwand's directional axis (a straight line through the Workwand in the direction the Workwand is pointing in), and rotations about the Workwand's directional axis. This second form of rotations shall be called twists about the Workwand's axis. For all the mappings presented, except mapping 3, twisting the Workwand will perform the expected action; that is rotating the Workwand about a certain axis has the same effect as twisting the Workwand, while that axis is the directional axis of the Workwand. With all the control mappings presented in this paper which utilise the movement of the Workwand, the trigger button will act as a ratchet button ([6], p70-71) to the movement of the four-dimensional object; hold the button down to perform a rotation, release and movement of the Workwand has no effect. This makes rotating the four-dimensional object about large angles easier, and enables the user to have the Workwand permanently in a comfortable position.

3.1 Mapping 1: Three-dimensional wand rotations with the ability to change the dimensions the rotations are mapped to

This control method maps the three-dimensional rotations of the Workwand to rotations altering three-dimensional coordinates of the four-dimensional object. For the user to be able to rotate the object fully, they are able to select which three of the four dimensions their movement affects. For example the user may rotate the Workwand in 3-space, and cause a rotation of the four-dimensional object changing only its x_4, y_4 and z_4 values; then push a button to change the dimensions their movements are mapped to, and now rotations of the wand will cause rotations of the four-dimensional object changing only its w_4, y_4 and z_4 values. Specifically, one of the four dimensions is fixed, and the other three have a one to one correspondence with the three dimensions the user is moving the Workwand in. Denoting the 4-space axes a_4, b_4, c_4, d_4; if d_4 is the fixed axis and the other three are mapped such that $x_3=a_4$, $y_3=b_4$, and $z_3=c_4$, then a rotation of the Workwand about a vector in x_3-y_3-z_3-space is mapped to a rotation of the four-dimensional object about the plane formed by the corresponding vector in a_4-b_4-c_4-space and a vector in the d_4 direction. The sub-mappings available to the user are:

(1) $x_3=x_4$ $y_3=y_4$ $z_3=z_4$ w_4 fixed
(2) $x_3=-w_4$ $y_3=y_4$ $z_3=z_4$ x_4 fixed
(3) $x_3=x_4$ $y_3=-w_4$ $z_3=z_4$ y_4 fixed
(4) $x_3=x_4$ $y_3=y_4$ $z_3=-w_4$ z_4 fixed

Mapping the 3-space axes to -w_4 is done so as to keep the other two 3-space axes mapped to their 4-space counterparts in the same direction as they are in sub-mapping 1. For example, whilst sub-mapping 1 is selected, a rotation of the Workwand about the x_3-axis corresponds to a rotation of the four-dimensional object about the x_4-w_4-plane. And whilst sub-mapping 4 is selected, a rotation of the Workwand about the y_3-axis corresponds to a rotation of the four-dimensional object about the y_4-z_4-plane. The user is able to cycle through these sub-mappings in one direction by pressing the left button on the Workwand, and cycle back through by pressing the right button. A set of axes is displayed in the lower left corner of the ImmersaDesk to indicate to the user the non-fixed dimensions, and their appropriate directions.

3.2 Mapping 2: Three-dimensional wand rotation together with change in position of wand

Under this mapping, rotation of the Workwand about a vector in x_3-y_3-z_3-space corresponds to a rotation of the four-dimensional object about the plane formed by the same vector, in x_4-y_4-z_4-space, and the w_4 vector. This is the same manipulation scheme as in sub-mapping 1 of mapping 1. But in addition to this, spatial movement of the Workwand whilst the ratchet button (trigger button) is held down also causes a rotation of the four-dimensional object thus: The change in position of the Workwand between tracker position updates forms a vector. Perpendicular to this vector is a unique plane (through the origin) in x_3-y_3-z_3-space, which corresponds to a plane in x_4-y_4-z_4-w_4-space (under the mapping $x_3=x_4$, $y_3=y_4$, $z_3=z_4$, $w_4=0$), and it is about this plane that the four-dimensional object is rotated. The length of the vector formed by the change in position of the Workwand is proportional to the angle the four-dimensional object is rotated through. For example, if the Workwand is moved along the x_3-axis (i.e. to the right), the four-dimensional object is rotated about the y_4-z_4-plane (as the y_3-z_3-plane is perpendicular to the x_3-axis).

3.3 Mapping 3: Three-dimensional rotation together with an alternative action for twisting the wand

This mapping separates the action of twisting the Workwand about its directional axis from rotating the Workwand and causing its directional axis to change. This mapping is a variation of mapping 2, described in section 3.2; instead of the change in position of the Workwand describing a vector in 3-space, the directional axis of the Workwand describes the vector. With the angle the Workwand is twisted, being equal to the angle through which the four-dimensional object is rotated, about the plane perpendicular to the described vector. All other (non-twisting) rotations of the Workwand have the same effect as those in mapping 2, and sub-mapping 1 of mapping 1.

3.4 Mapping 4: Three virtual linear sliders

As mentioned in section 1, all orientations of a four-dimensional object are achievable via rotations about three perpendicular planes. This mapping maps the position of the handles of three virtual linear sliders to the rotations of the four-dimensional object about three perpendicular planes; the z_4-w_4-plane, the x_4-w_4-plane, and the y_4-z_4-plane. The limits of the sliders represent 180° and -180° rotations of the four-dimensional object, from its original orientation, about each of the planes. For example, the virtual linear sliders are positioned horizontally, and moving the handle from its original central position, to the extreme right causes the four-dimensional object to rotate 180° in one direction about the appropriate plane. The letters "z-w", "x-w" and "y-z" are displayed above the sliders indicating which plane that slider rotates the four-dimensional object about. The user can move the handle on the selected slider by pushing the analogue joystick on the Workwand, left or right; and pressing one of the three buttons on the wand selects one of the sliders, one button per slider.

3.5 Mapping 5: Three-dimensional Workwand rotation together with one virtual linear slider

This control mapping uses the same mapping for the rotations (and twisting) of the Workwand as mapping 2, and sub-mapping 1 of mapping 1. Together with this manipulation, the user is given control over a virtual linear slider which controls the rotation of the four-dimensional object about the y_4-z_4-plane. This slider is controlled in the same way, and has the same limits, as those of mapping 4, except that it is always selected.

4 Results

Subjects *level of closeness* results were submitted to a 5 (control mappings) × 7 (target orientation) repeated measures analysis of variance. This analysis revealed highly significant effects of control mapping [$F(4,17)=15.75$, $p<0.00001$]

and target orientation [F(6,17)=33.59, p<0.00001]; with a lesser, but still highly significant control mapping × target orientation interaction [F(24,17)=5.63, p<0.0003]. Figure 1 shows the mean level of closeness together with the 95% confidence interval for each control mapping and target orientation. It is clear

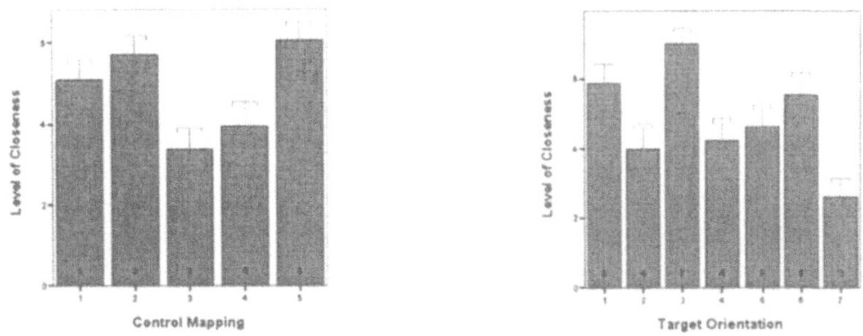

Fig. 1. Graphs showing the mean level of closeness for each (**a**) control mapping (left) and (**b**) target orientation (right). Error bars indicate 95% confidence interval

from Figure 1b that not all the targets were equally difficult to achieve. It is possible to justifiably discard one of the targets and split the remaining six into two equal sized catagories, *easy* and *difficult* targets. Targets 1, 3, 5 and 6 can be achieved by rotating the hypercube through 90° about the planes formed only by the axes, as a result the shape of the projected image of the target cube is either a cube or a truncated triangular based pyramid. Target 5 is to be discarded, as the target cube occludes the hypercube in the visual feedback, making manipulation of the hypercube unfairly difficult; the rest (targets 1, 3 and 6) form the *easy-target* catagory. Target orientations 2, 4 and 7 are more general, and the projected images of the target cubes for these orientations do not form regular 3-D shapes; these targets form the *difficult-target* catagory. Subsequently the data was collapsed across the easy and difficult target catagories and subjected to a 5 (control mapping) × 2 (target difficulty) repeated measures analysis of variance. Revealed by this analysis were strong dependencies on control mapping [F(4,17)=16.79, p<0.00001], and task difficulty [F(1,17)=146.02, p<0.00001]; together with a highly significant control mapping × task difficulty interaction [F(4,17)=18.124, p<0.00001]. Figure 2a shows the mean level of closeness together with the 95% confidence interval for each control mapping, catagorized into easy and difficult target orientations.

Questionnaire results were collated by equating an ordinal answer-score between 0 and 6 to each answer depending upon which box was ticked (0 for an answer implying that the control mapping was difficult or awkward to use). The *questionnaire-score* given by a particular subject for a particular mapping was then calculated as the mean of the individual answer-scores. Subject's questionnaire-scores were then subjected to a repeated measures analysis of variance. This analysis revealed that the questionnaire-scores were strongly dependent on the control mapping [F(4,17)=15.68, p<0.00002]. Figure 2b shows the mean questionnaire-score together with the 95% confidence interval for each control mapping.

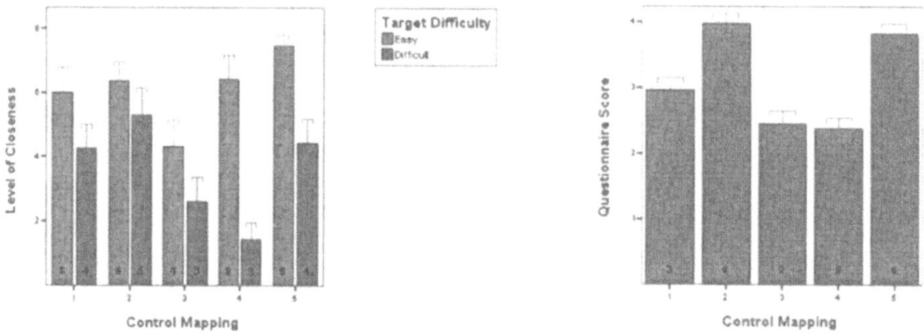

Fig. 2. **a**(left) Bars show mean level of closeness for each control mapping, catagorized into easy and difficult target orientations. **b**(right) Bars show mean questionnaire score for each control mapping. For both graphs, error bars indicate 95% confidence interval

5 Discussion

It is clear from these results that control mappings 2 and 5 form the most effective (Figure 1a), and most popular (Figure 2b), link between user and space of four-dimensional rotations; mappings 3 and 4 form the weakest and least popular link; and control mapping 1 lies somewhere in between. According to Wellard & Chapman [14] the only attributes mappings 2 and 5 have in common are that they do not treat all four-dimensional rotations equally, but rather classify them into two sets, rotations which affect the shape of the 3-D projection, *morphing* rotations, and those which do not, *non-morphing* rotations. Evident from observations whilst conducting the experiment and points of view written by the subjects on the back of the questionnaire (although no statistical evidence can be presented here), was that the subjects also performed this classification. Thus, for a control mapping to perform well it must form an effective yet separate link between manipulation of the input device and both these sets of rotations. Non-morphing rotations cause the projection to rotate as a 3-D object, therefore the most obvious way to perform these rotations is in the same way that it is done in everyday life; the rotation performed with your hand is the rotation the object undergoes. Mappings 2 and 5 have this method of controlling this set of rotations, as does mapping 1 under sub-mapping 1; but mapping 1 is weakened by the amount the user has to learn, each sub-mapping has new rules defining how movements of the workwand effect changes in the visual feedback.

Most users only learnt the effects of sub-mapping 1, and just cycled through the others until a useful effect was noticed (if one was noticed at all).

For morphing rotations the slider control was very useful, subjects had no pre-conceived ideas about the effect of moving a slider. Mappings 4 and 5 used a slider for morphing rotations; however, mapping 4 had a very cumbersome [4] method of performing non-morphing rotations. Translating the workwand under mapping 2 causes the image of the red cube-face of the hypercube to translate, from it's initial position, in the direction the workwand has been moved. This effect is reversed once the hypercube has been rotated through about 110°, but this direct link between movement of the workwand and movement of the visual feedback was very easy for the subjects to learn. Also the dimension of the space of morphing rotations available under mapping 2 (and mapping 3) is greater than that offered by any finite number of sliders. Irrespective of target orientation, the target shape of the projection can be formed by one translational movement under mapping 2, and therefore movement can always be performed towards the target. This is not the case for mappings 1, 4, and 5 where, due to the reduced set of rotations available, movement away from the target is sometimes necessary in order for the target to be achieved. Mappings 4 and 5 have the smallest set of morphing rotations available, and Figure 2a shows that these mappings have the largest difference in performance for easy and difficult target orientations, suggesting that reducing this set makes achieving difficult orientations harder.

Many subjects were not able to separate their movements of the workwand into twisting and non-twisting rotations, and therefore were not able to separate the morphing and non-morphing rotations under mapping 3. Separating these two types of 4-D rotations was easy under mappings 4 and 5, but caused a little difficulty under mapping 2, as translating the workwand often resulted in a slight rotation, and vise-versa.

The most interesting result from this experiment is the lower dependency task difficulty had on the level of closeness results for control mapping 2 (Figure 2a). For complete control over 4-D rotations, target orientation should not be a factor; if a user is performing rotation tasks in 4-space there should not be preferred orientations, as 4-space does not have preferred orientations. This low dependency on task difficulty, together with the high results for both difficulty levels, indicates that control mapping 2 forms a very strong, functional link between user and the space of 4-D rotations.

6 Conclusions

No rotary-to-rotary [10] or integrality and separability [8] [9] dependencies, as hypothesised by Wellard & Chapman [14], were found. However, some general results can be extracted from this investigation. Firstly, the projected image is three-dimensional, yet it's shape cannot be easily recognised without the ability to rotate and examine it. This, together with the separate nature of the conceptual model users form for the space of 4-D rotations, means that they must be able to separate morphing rotations from non-morphing rotations. Secondly, performing the non-morphing rotations in the manner of mappings 2 and 5 appears to be the most intuitive way. Finally, the degrees of freedom available for morphing rotations influences the ability of the user to achieve 'difficult' orientations. If the user can only perform morphing rotations about one plane (mapping 5), then they must guess the shape of the projection needed, rotate the projection to see if the shape is correct, and if it is not then repeat this procedure; ballistic movements. If they can perform morphing rotations about any plane (mapping 2), then the user can always move towards the desired shape of the projection; the shape is continuously steered towards it's target.

References

1. Abbott EA (1944) Flatland (5 ed), Basil Blackwell, Oxford
2. Strauss C and Banchoff TF (1978) The Hypercube - Projections and slicing, Currently unavailable, see http://www.math.brown.edu/ banchoff for details
3. Banchoff TF (1996) Beyond the Third Dimension, Scientific American Library, New York
4. Chen M, Mountford SJ, Sellen A (1988) A Study in Interactive 3-D Rotation Using 2-D Control Devices, Computer Graphics, 22(4), 121-129
5. England R (1995) Sensory-motor systems in virtual manipulation, in Simulated and Virtual Realities, Carr and England, ch 7, 131-117
6. Gabbard JL and Hix D (1997) A Taxonomy of Usability Characteristics in Virtual Environments, available at http://csgrad.cs.vt.edu/ jgabbard/ve/taxonomy/
7. Houde S (1992) Iterative Design of an Interface for Easy 3-D Direct Manipulation, CHI '92 Conference of Human Factors in Computing Systems, 3 - 7 May 1992, 135-142
8. Jacob RJK and Sibert LE (1992) The Perceptual Structure of Multidimensional Input Device Selection, CHI '92 Conference of Human Factors in Computing Systems, 3 - 7 May 1992, 211-218
9. Jacob et al (1994) Integrality and Separability of Input Devices, ACM Transactions on Computer-Human Interaction, 1(1), 3-26
10. MacKenzie IS (1995) Input Devices and Interaction Techniques for Advanced Computing, in Virtual Environments and Advanced Interface Design, Barfield and Furness, Oxford University Press, ch 11, 437-470
11. MacKinlay JD, Card SK, Robertson GG (1990) A semantic analysis of the design space of input devices, Human Computer Interaction, 5, 145-190
12. Manning HP (1960) The Fourth Dimension Simply Explained, Dover Publications, New York
13. Smets et al (1995) Designing in Virtual Reality: perception-action coupling and affordances, in Simulated and Virtual Realities, Carr and England, ch 9, 189-208
14. Wellard & Chapman (2000) An Investigation into Control Mappings for the Manipulation of Four-Dimensional Objects Represented within a Virtual Environment, EGUK 2000 Conference Proceedings, 4-6 April, 159-170
15. Witmer et al (1998) Measuring Presence in Virtual Environments: A Presence Questionnaire, Presence: Teleoperators and Virtual Environments, 7(3), 225-240
16. Zhai S and Milgram P (1993) Human Performance Evaluation of Manipulation Schemes in Virtual Environments, IEEE Virtual Reality Annual International Symposium Proceedings, 155-161, available at http://vered.rose.toronto.edu/people/shumin_dir/papers/VRAIS93.html

The integration of immersive Virtual Reality applications into Catia V5

D. Rantzau*, F. Maurer**, C. Mayer, R. Löffler, O. Riedel, H. Scharm, D. Banek

SGI Professional Services, Practice Immersive Solutions, Germany
[*dirkrt@sgi.com, **franzm@sgi.com]

Abstract. During the last few years a wide range of stand-alone virtual reality (VR) applications have been developed. The typical data source for most of these applications are 3D styling tools or 3D-CAD systems from which data has to be converted into a representation useful in VR software systems. The drawbacks of the stand-alone approach are well known: data conversion, loss of semantics and the problems of establishing a feedback path for updating data in the underlying CAD model from within the VR software. In this paper we will introduce our solution to this problem by proposing an integrated VR/CAD system approach based on the CATIA 3D-CAD software, more precisely the CATIA V5 application architecture [1]. We will discuss the requirements and implications from the CAD data perspective and show how the VR integration inside the CAD system can be realized. Derived from a specific end user scenario we introduce a sample application for virtual prototype reviews.

1 Introduction

Immersive Projection Technology (IPT) is getting more and more widespread in industry. Multi-wall stereo projection systems (well known as CAVE™) recently became manageable because new and powerful computer hardware technology is available and companies bringing the technology to the market are more focusing on end user solutions than simply providing raw technology.

On the software side the term Digital Mock-Up (DMU) has appeared recently, targeting at a new and innovative product development. DMU, in a broader sense, is a complete digital product description for development, design and manufacturing. One of the major data sources for DMU is 3D-CAD systems. The integration of VR technology inside existing CAD systems is desirable especially from the end user perspective: less software packages pose fewer problems with data handling and mastering different software systems. Moreover, as additional DMU functionality is becoming more and more available in standard CAD software packages, this functionality can be accessed from within the integrated "VR front-end" also.

In the following we will describe our approach taken towards the realization of an integrated VR/CAD system based CATIA V5. In the first section we begin to describe the current situation of VR software technology for engineering from the data perspective. From this we derive the requirements for an integrated system approach. We then shortly describe the component based architecture of CATIA V5. After this the integration steps of VR modules into the CATIA CAA framework is described. We then introduce a virtual prototype review application, which has been derived from a specific end user scenario.

2 State of VR Technology for CAD/DMU

Today users can choose from a lot of VR software systems exploiting different concepts such as the toolkit or framework approach found in Lightning [2], VirtualDesign2 [3], VR Juggler [4], Avango [5] or application focused systems such as EAI VisConcept [6] or Opus Realizer [7]. An interesting example of a collaborative VR system with CAD functionality based on scene graph sharing has been described by Smith et al. in [8].

However, from recent user studies [9] it is known that a number of problems still lie in the immaturity of the available software. We believe that one of the main reasons for this discovered "immaturity" lies in the stand-alone approach which is directly related to the problems of data transfer and data management. The data interfaces used today are primarily based on reading files (neutral or native formats) coming from the engineering applications, i.e. the 3D-CAD system or a styling tool.
3D-CAD systems for example generate continuous surface and volume descriptions often referred to as free form surfaces and solids. VR rendering systems deal with polygons or occasionally with voxels. The process of converting the CAD data to a polygonal representation is called tessellation. For all major CAD formats including the neutral formats IGES, VDAFS and STEP tessellators exist. Unfortunately, different problems related to this conversion process occur, which pose a burden to end users wanting to adopt VR technology in their daily productive work:

- Insufficient model quality (inconsistent normal directions, cracks by not considering topology, level of detail (LOD's) too coarse),
- unneeded model complexity (wrong SAG values, improper algorithms, tessellation of invisible details, LOD's too fine),
- poor render performance (poor culling structure, missing LOD's, unneeded model complexity),
- missing data structure (loss of logical structure, trade-off to culling structure),
- typical CAD conversion problems with neutral formats like IGES or VDAFS (least common denominator),
- poor interoperability with legacy systems, e.g. integration between VR and deployed product data management systems,
- the need for re-invention of functionality in VR software systems which is actually already available in CAD systems.

The following figure shows an abstract view of a CAD system (left) consisting of an application layer (top), and an API layer for accessing base functionality (middle) found in the graphics and kernel layers (bottom). When looking at the VR system on the right, it is interesting to note that similar layers can be discovered there. In most systems application functionality is encapsulated in one layer e.g. as modules (compiled or scriptable) which access other components through the API layer. In both cases there is a graphics component, often based on a scene graph API such as OpenGL Performer. The CAD and VR kernel are the glue between all the components. Any CAD like functionality such as measurement of distances between two points have to be re-implemented in the VR software, often with the drawback of losing a certain degree of precision due to the different data representations in each system.

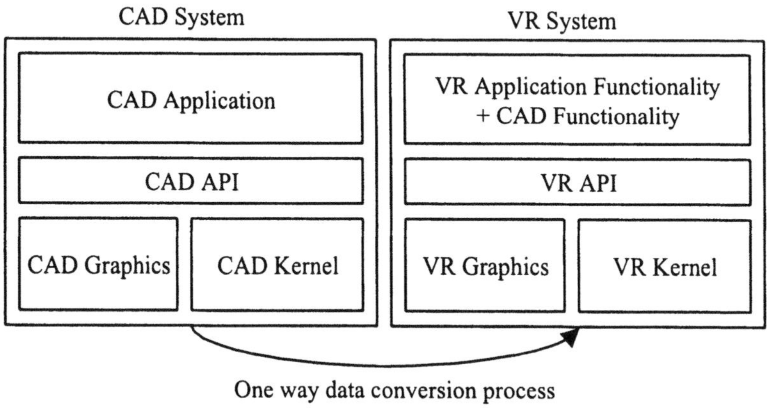

Fig. 1. Layers in CAD and VR systems

From this data perspective the idea of melting both systems into one is self evident, however several requirements have to be satisfied to provide the correct infrastructure for realizing immersive applications:

- The CAD graphics system has to be tuned for high performance rendering and should support multiple synchronized graphics pipes/channels for driving IPT systems such as CAVE's and Powerwalls.
- Support for 3D input devices needs to be added to the CAD system.
- A 3D user interface should replace or augment the traditional 2D menu driven approach when switching to the "immersive mode" using IPT.
- Effective user interaction metaphors have to be implemented to augment or extend standard CAD functionality depending on the specific end-user application needs.

While the broadly deployed CATIA CAD software in the version 4.x isn't able to meet the requirements above, the CATIA V5 software by Dassault Systèmes fulfills some of the needs already or at least provides a framework in which missing VR extensions can be implemented efficiently.

Preliminary CATIA V5 work describing the integration of a generic VR device support targeting a glove based input with BOOM based output have been proposed by Fakespace in [10] but no productive application had been realized at that time. In the following we describe our integration approach and show how this can be leveraged from applications targeting actual end user scenarios respectively specific market segments.

3 The Catia CAA architecture

Unlike traditional CAD legacy systems, which have FORTRAN based kernels reaching back 20 years ago, the CATIA V5 CAA (Component Application Architecture) has been designed using latest software design methodology. The final CAD product consists of a number of cooperating component frameworks. They can easily be extended or completely new frameworks can be added to the system. The key benefits for VR applications on top of CAA V5 are a completely object oriented C++ API and a high performance OpenGL rendering kernel.

Two kinds of CAA applications can be created: stand-alone programs which use only the CAA functionality, or CAA commands which are plugged in the runtime environment of Catia. CAA commands are encapsulated as shared objects with well known interfaces. During the program start-up phase, Catia looks in so called dictionary files for the commands that are available. This dictionary provides the link between the command and the corresponding shared object. In order to provide a technique for grouping commands of an application, Catia has the concept of Workbenches. Workbenches in the CAA context are assemblies of menu items, toolbars and commands which all belong to a certain application. After the Catia start-up the user can activate the Workbench he needs and then has access to all functions provided by the application. These concepts allow a seamless integration of immersive applications from the end user point of view.

4 Bringing VR inside the CAD system

One of the main prerequisites for integrating VR applications into a CAD software system is the capability of the rendering engine to perform interactive "realtime" visualization. One of the first steps of this work was to examine the underlying CATIA V5 system architecture in terms of event latency and renderer performance. In contrast to its predecessor CATIA V4, the renderer of the CATIA V5 CAD software is completely based on the platform independent graphics API OpenGL. Most of the graphical capabilities of V5 is located in the visualization framework which comprises the main part of the visualization model of the CATIA system architecture. Dassault Systèmes has developed a high-level graphics API, which uses a small but very efficient scene graph. Application developers can model a visualization database by composing elements such as group nodes, representation nodes (Rep), graphical primitives (GP), graphical attribute sets and so on (see also fig. 2). The scene graph can then be added to an active 3D viewer class, which is solely responsible for the actual rendering process. The viewer also manages viewpoints, lights, background colors and so forth. Furthermore the CATIA visualization provides important VR features such as:

- culling algorithms (including back face as well as occlusion)
- level-of-detail (LOD) algorithms (depth and motion)
- tessellation algorithms (the tessellation quality is adjustable by the user)

After testing the rendering capabilities of the CATIA software we came to the conclusion that V5 offers all the functionality necessary for immersive visualization. Especially the integration of the OpenGL Multipipe™ SDK [11] by SGI will enable the rendering system to generate multi-channel, multi-pipe display output. Based on these features it is possible to support every current known display configuration, including CAVE™s.

CATIA is using the Model-View-Controller (MVC) paradigm and distinguishes between the application and the visualization model. Both models are loosely coupled. The application model contains and manages all the CAD data base specific entities like the parametric information of the geometric objects or the information on how a certain part has been designed (e.g. by using sketching, filleting, chamfering or other topological operations like the subtraction of two geometries). Each visible element of the application model has its surrogate in the visualization model. Thus, based on the user settings, each visible geometry of the application model has its tessellated representation in the visualization model. The following fig. 2 sketches a rough scheme of the CATIA V5 visualization process.

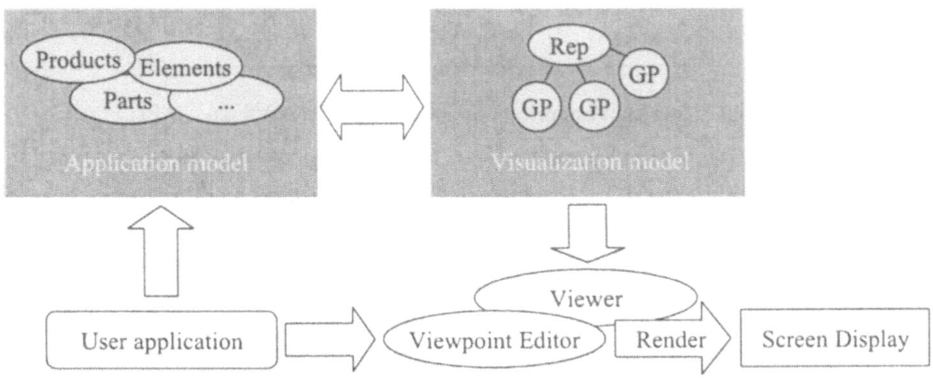

Fig. 2. The simplified visualization process in CATIA V5 using the application model and visualization model

From the VR application programmer's point of view, the separation of the application and visualization model creates the freedom to make a distinction between mechanisms that require persistent storage and operations that are only necessary during the lifetime of an "immersive session". Programmers are free to use both of the model contexts from above. In case of our first application described later, the so called "Immersive Solutions Review on CAA V5", all the user interface elements such as the 3D menu and 3D pointers are entities that reside in the visualization model only –they do not have any meaning outside the VR session. On the other hand, the annotations made during a collaborative immersive session are stored persistently in the application model and they also do have a graphical representation to indicate their position in the design model. After the immersive session has ended the user can decide whether to store the changes and additions in the same CATIA document or to use the "save as" operation of the desktop view to generate a new one.

To be able to re-use as many common VR functionality as possible, we have decided to use a layered approach in which several VR applications encapsulated as modules and sit on top of a common VR API layer. Each of these application modules is targeted towards a specific end user task or market segment like e.g. a virtual prototype review (fig. 3).

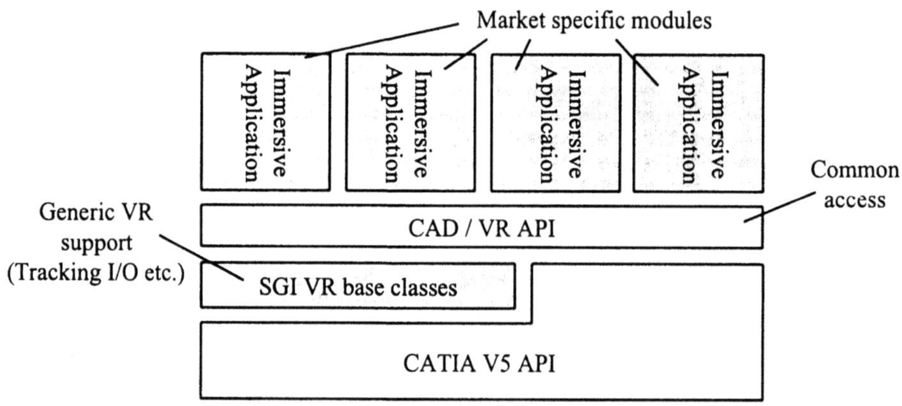

Fig. 3. Immersive applications on top of the Catia V5 CAA API

A framework with several VR base classes has been added to the system to enable easy VR application development on top of CATIA V5. These base classes offer a set of functionality that is needed in nearly every immersive application (though are not mandatory to use) such as the support for the most common 3D devices, well known 3D navigation modes like fly and examine mode as well as 3D selection. 3D selection is implemented with a newly designed 3D menu called Immunipa (fig. 4), which is very intuitively accessible and configurable from within any immersive application.

Fig. 4. Immunipa 3D menu (left), 3D selection pointer (right)

The interaction behavior inside the application is implemented as a state machine that reacts to the incoming events from the 3D-tracking or button devices. A default behavior is already realized in the base framework. This behavior can be extended or overwritten by the application.

Finally the application consists of two parts: the device daemons and the application module that is derived from the classes of the base framework. The daemons read the data of the external devices and send them as events to the VR application. An event dispatcher gets this data in the form of a small number of integer and float values and calculates the new state of interaction or triggers some action (see fig. 5). Actions can access any available function callable inside the CAD core system. This of course paves the way to implement those features that would otherwise hard or impossible to implement in a stand-alone VR system.

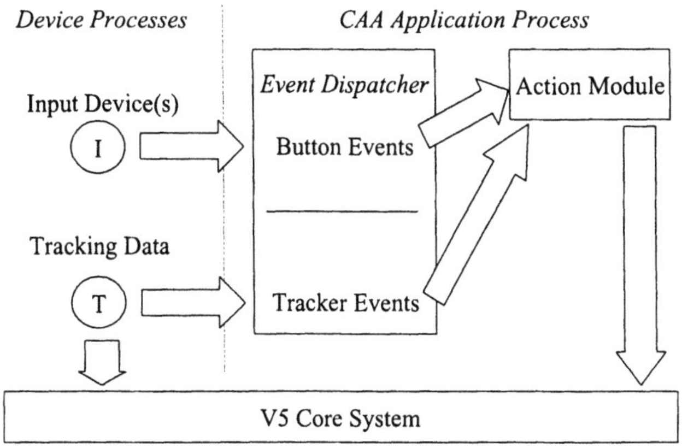

Fig. 5. Device communication between deamon and modules

From the end user perspective, the available immersive applications are accessible by the "add-in" toolbar in the DMU Navigator package. This add-in provides some commands to configure the VR session and of course one to launch the immersive mode. It is important to note that when the VR application is launched all the properties which were setup on the desktop are still valid. Vice versa, all the changes made in the VR context (like annotations) are still visible on the desktop and can also be stored as a part of the CATIA product structure for later analysis. This is what can be called the two-way communication between the DMU view of the model and the underlying CAD representation.

5 Sample application: Immersive Solutions Review on CAA V5

One of the most important lessons we have learned in the past as an immersive solutions provider is that the investment in IPT installation have the highest return-on-investment when it is possible to map existing work processes into the immersive environment as efficiently as possible. We have therefore chosen to support in the first application a widespread and proven work process in design departments, the so called DMU or virtual prototype review. The advantages of VR combined with IPT as a communication medium and tool matches perfectly with the collaborative DMU review work process.

A typically scenario involving an immersive DMU review process with the Immersive Solutions Review application could be as follows:

"A development team of different engineers is working on the design of a functional unit of a new car. Most of the team members have to interface with each other and therefore it is necessary to have regular team meetings to discuss the state of the work. Such team sessions typically include reviews based on a 3D visualization of the assembled digital mock-up consisting of the different parts provided by the team members. The team leader is therefore querying the product data management system (or the file server) and merges the latest design parts into an assembly. Since the new assembly gets to big in data size to render, he decides to reduce the tesselation quality using the CATIA product settings and to turn the material display off. One of the tasks for the session includes a comparison of two sub units, and therefore he puts one of the variants into "no show".

The meeting starts by using the immersive CAD option that is initialized by clicking on a button in the CATIA workbench which switches between the team leader's desktop console to the real-time visualization using a Powerwall in 1:1 scale mode. Soon after the group discussion begins, several design defects are encountered and improvements are discussed at the Powerwall. With the 3D-annotation tool the session moderator marks critical regions of interest with his 3D-joystick. Later on, group members will find the annotations as a part of the product structure so that they are able to work through the annotation list to improve the design for the next development cycle. An agreement within the team has been found, that the second discussed variant fits better to the functional requirements but a problem for the assembly process is discovered. The necessary space to house the units during production won't be sufficient. With the 3D-measurement tool the moderator is able to exactly ascertain the space between the critical units rapidly and it soon becomes obvious that another development team is concerned with the effects of the necessary changes. As a result of the session, team members of the other development team are informed and invited as well as member of the product management team to join the next visualization session in order to find a common decision how to circumvent the discovered problem."

Although the scenario described above is an abbreviated description of the much more complex complete DMU work process, it should become clear, how the immersive CAD application can support a simultaneous engineering approach in the car design departments. The following figures show two examples of the functionality available to the end user.

Fig. 6. Annotation feature

Fig. 6 shows the annotation feature as (numbered) markers which can be placed anywhere in the virtual model to mark the regions of interest.

Fig. 7. Distance measurement feature

In fig. 7 the straight line represents the distance between two points on the outer car body which is shown numerically above the line.
The Immersive Solutions Review application is a good example of how a simple VR interface allowing a lot of user control can expand the scope of a traditional CAD system towards a group reviewing tool. When using a 1:1 scale visualization facility

like the Powerwall, 3D navigation and annotation features can be effectively used to review the DMU models and virtual prototypes facilitating decision processes across development teams. From the functionality side we are still in an "alpha" phase where we gather valuable input from end users from the manufacturing industry to adjust the user interface to the actual work processes.

6 Conclusion

In this paper we have introduced an example of an immersive application inside a standard 3D-CAD package. Our approach of focusing on specific end user scenarios instead of developing "the" VR front-end of a CAD system reflects the results of what we have learned during the last years as an immersive solutions provider. Immersive projection technology will continue to play a significant role as the visualization technology of complex and design oriented products for the years to come. We believe that the trend towards the better integration of VR functionality into existing CAD/CAE packages is an excellent mechanism for bringing VR and IPT to a wider audience.

Acknowledgements

We'd like to thank all our partners and colleagues at Dassault Systèmes and SGI for their enthusiasm and effort bringing VR to life inside the CAD system CATIA V5, especially our friend Bob Kuehne for his valuable input.

References

1. URL: http://www.catia.com
2. Blach R., Landauer J., Simon A., Rösch A.: "A highly flexible virtual reality system", in: Future Generation Computer Systems 14 (1998), Elsevier Science, pp. 167-177
3. URL: http://www.vrcom.de
4. Just C., Bierbaum A., Baker A., Cruz-Neira C.: "VR Juggler: A Framework for Virtual Reality Development", Proc. of the IPT 98 Workshop, Ames, Iowa, 1998
5. Tramberend, H.: "Avocado: A Distributed Virtual Reality Framework", Proc. of the IEEE Virtual Reality Conference 99, Houston, Texas, March 13-17, 1999
6. URL: http://www.eai.com
7. URL: http://www.opticore.com
8. Smith, R. et al: "Collaborative Visual Eyes", Proc. of the IPT 2000 Workshop, Ames Iowa, 2000
9. Delainey, B.: "The Market for Visual Simulation/Virtual Reality Systems", CyberEdge Information Services Study, Spring 1999
10. Berta, J: "Integrating VR and CAD", IEEE Computer Graphics and Applications, Vol. 19, 1999
11. OpenGL Multipipe SDK. URL: http://www.sgi.com/software/multipipe/sdk/index.html

COVISE and the Virtual Intuitive Simulation Test bed

Andreas Wierse
VirCinity IT-Consulting GmbH

Abstract

This paper describes the developments performed in the EU-project VISiT (Virtual Intuitive Simulation Test bed). The goal of the project is the development of an intuitive simulation test bed based on Virtual Reality technology. As a new man-machine interface it will be an efficient environment for a small team of engineers and designers, that enables also the designer to evaluate and interact with the complex 3D data of simulations. The basis of the Virtual Intuitive Simulation Test bed will be COVISE, an extendable distributed software environment to integrate supercomputer based simulations, post-processing, and visualisation functionalities with co-operative working in a seamless manner. The project covers different application fields, including heating, ventilation and air-conditioning simulation in a passenger car compartment and the flow simulation in a draft tube and in an axial runner of a water turbine.

1 The Project

VISiT is an Esprit-project funded by the European Commission under the contract No. 28247. The goal of the project is the development of the interactive 3D-simulation environment VISiT by using Virtual-Reality techniques (VR) and HPCN tools developed already in other research projects. By bringing together end-users from different industries it is ensured that the VISiT environment can be effective independent from the application field.

The project-partners are BAE Systems, DaimlerChrysler, De Pretto-Escher Wyss, ICEM CFD-Engineering, University of Jyväskylä, University of Stuttgart, Valmet, VirCinity and Voith Hydro. The project started in 1998 and will continue until September 2001.

2 The Problem

The use of HPCN-technology enables industry to shorten the development time by reducing the computational time for numerical simulation considerably. The limitations for efficient use now comes from insufficient through-put by pre- and post-processing time. The time to evaluate the huge amount of 3D data produced by numerical simulation and the time to redefine or to modify boundary conditions for derived simulations are the critical bottle necks, that hinder the efficient use of simulation within the first phase of design, where fast and frequent changes or modification of the components are inherent in the process.

The whole process of the pre- and post-processing for one of the test cases is shown in figure 1. In the post-processing phase the use of Virtual Reality technology by the end user partners is already established and growing strongly. It allows the users for example to directly put particles into a velocity field similar to a wind tunnel experiment. In the VISiT project this use of VR-technology shall be extended to all simulation relevant phases in the development cycle, not only making it possible to change boundary conditions (i.e. temperature for a car climate simulation or velocity for a turbine simulation) but even some well-defined geometry changes can be performed in the Virtual Environment with a really quick update of the numerical solution.

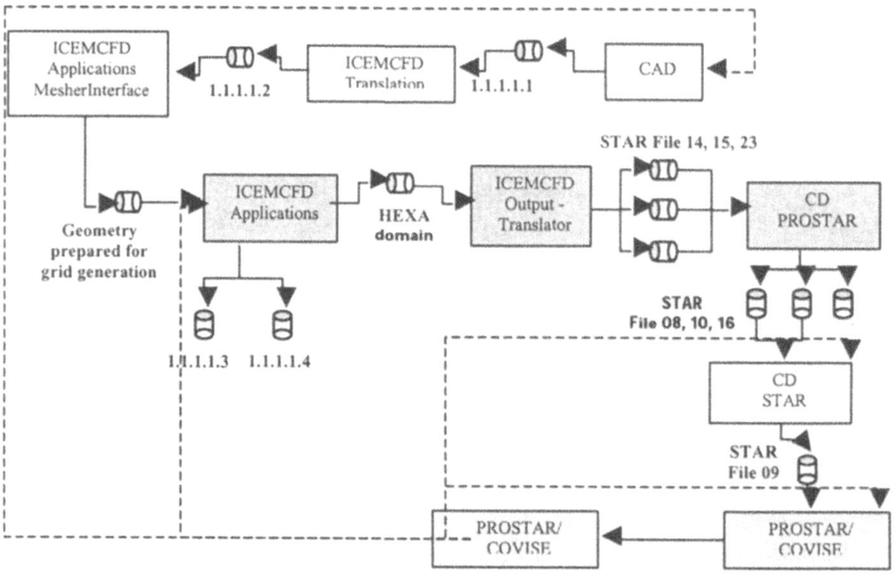

Fig. 1: The VISiT scenario

3 The Integration Platform

3.1 The COVISE Software

In the VISiT project the COVISE software has been chosen to implement the complete Virtual Environment for the analysis of numerical simulations. The COVISE approach of modular components that are based on a distributed infra structure and that are directly connected to a Virtual Reality front-end makes it very easy to integrate all the pre- and post-processing steps into a homogeneous working environment.

In figure 2 the overall architecture of the COVISE visualisation system is shown. Basically it can be structured in two parts: the basic infra structure that contains the functionality for distributed and collaborative working and the modules that are based on this infra structure and implement the actual visualisation functionality. The Virtual Reality functionality has been realised as a front-end that has been tightly integrated: an Iris-Performer based renderer can be used in addition or instead of the desktop renderer. Through a feedback loop the interaction between the user and the visualisation modules is handled.

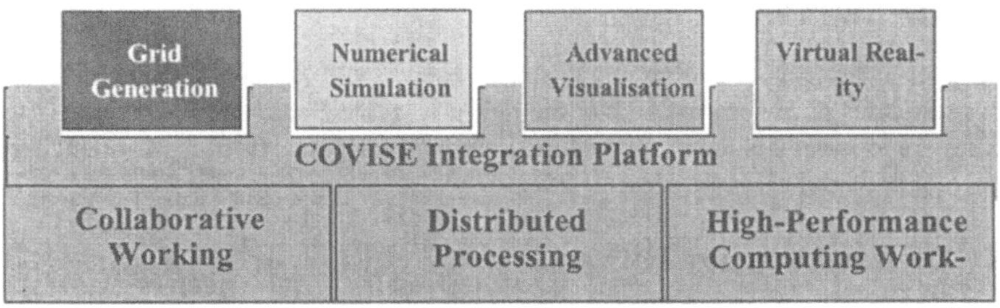

Fig. 2: COVISE System Architecture

3.2 On-Line Simulation Coupling

Since several years modules cannot only provide visualisation functionality but it is also possible to integrate numerical simulations into the platform. In 1998 a coupling to the commercial solver Star-CD has been established to directly influence the boundary conditions of a car climate simulation by changing the direction of the air vents or the air temperature.

The main difference to other projects that are working in a similar direction is, that this is no longer a proprietary coupling to a well-known simulation code whose sources are available to the project. Instead the VISiT project covers both, proprietary source code based coupling as well as the integration of commercial simulation codes into the visualisation environment. This is handled through the COVISE SimLib that has especially been designed to interface with simulation codes based on concepts like the "user subroutines" that Star-CD provides.

3.3 Integration of the Grid Generation

In the VISiT project the integration capability of COVISE is now utilized to allow the modification of the geometry to a certain extent. In a first step the geometry modification can be the movement or replacement of a sub grid that is overlaid to a basic grid. In further steps this functionality will be developed continuously to allow an ever more integrated approach to the optimisation of the product in the virtual environment.

Similar to the numerical simulation the grid generation in the VISiT project is not only based on proprietary software developments for which the source code is available, but on a commercial grid generator. The project partner ICEM-CFD has integrated its automatic grid generator Hexa as a COVISE module into the integration platform. The generic feedback loop between the Virtual Reality front end and the grid generation module allows then the intuitive control of the Hexa module.

4 The Test Cases

In order to show that this technology can be applied to many application fields, various test cases have been defined by the industrial project partners. Each partners test cases are especially chosen to reflect the important requirements of the partners. Here three of these test cases are presented:

4.1 The DaimlerChrysler Test Case

The test case provided by DaimlerChrysler is a heating, ventilation and air-conditioning (HVAC) simulation in a passenger car compartment. Normally the effectiveness of the HVAC system is evaluated with the help of measuring heating and cooling performance, of air temperatures in the cabin and by assessing personal thermal comfort votes in wind tunnel field test. To reduce the time for testing the numerical simulation is getting greater importance to investigate different cabin designs before any prototype has been build.

The VISiT result will allow the automotive engineers to simulate in an intuitive way the behaviour of the complete system under different conditions. Geometry modifications here can mean that the effect of moving the seat back or forth can be examined directly. A good climatic environment for a large person can quickly be verified for a smaller person by replacing the large body by a significantly smaller one. The location of air vents can be modified easily by simply grabbing one and moving it to the new place. Interdisciplinary teams can very quickly discuss various options from different points of view.

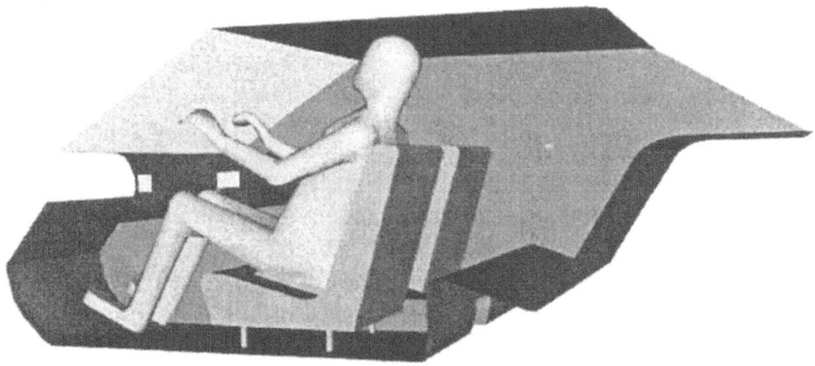

Fig. 3: DaimlerChrysler Model Car Cabin

4.2 The Voith Hydro test cases

These test cases are a draft tube and an axial runner of a water turbine. In a water turbine the runner together with the generator converts the kinetic energy of the fluid into electric energy. The main task of the draft tube is to guide the water from the runner to the tail water transferring the remaining kinetic energy of the flow into pressure. In the ideal case the only kinetic energy remaining in the flow is the one needed for the mass flow to leave the machine.

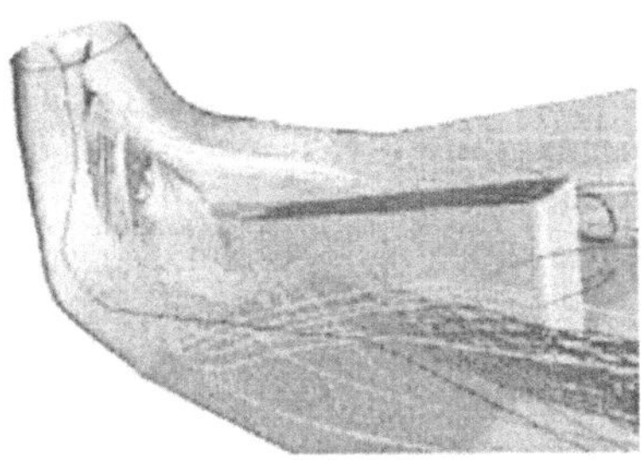

Fig. 4: Voith Hydro Draft Tube

Very important for the costs of a draft tube are the dimensions, and so one of the goals is to keep it as short as possible and to reduce the required depth to a minimum. These requirements always lead to difficult flow phenomena and the VISiT environment should enable the designer to find the optimum based on his intuition and a high quality design tool. The virtual reality environment allows the engineers to directly interact with their design while they get an immediate feedback of the effects of their changes.

4.3 The De Pretto Escher-Wyss Test Case

The test case provided by De Pretto Escher-Wyss is a Francis Turbine Runner. The design of the components of a hydraulic turbine has several goals: first the turbine efficiency and the power output have to be optimised according to the customer conditions. This has to be flexible enough to be useful for several operating points (part load, optimum, full load) and an overall weighted machine efficiency must be guaranteed. For the runner, cavitation must be prevented or at least minimized, for water resources with high particle content the effective erosion has to be minimized.

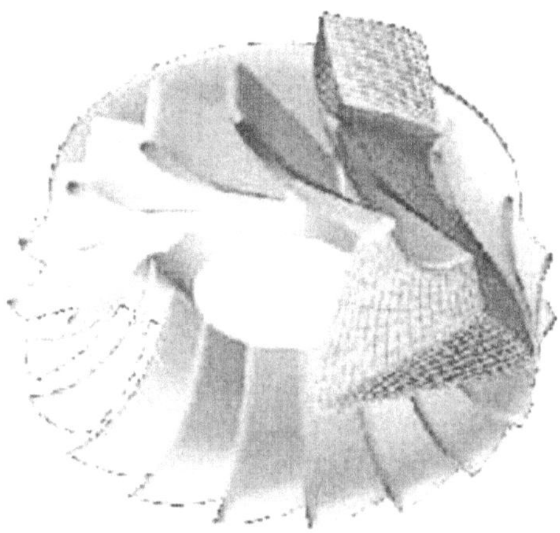

Fig. 5: De Pretto Escher-Wyss Francis Runner

The performance of a Francis runner is influenced by many parameters, e.g. the global runner dimensions, the volume flow rate, the inlet velocity profile or the meridional runner passage geometry and the blade geometry (profile, angles, etc.). All these parameters are input parameters to a special grid generator that very quickly generates a new grid for this special kind of geometries. Geometrical parameters can be changed directly at the geometry in the virtual environment, non-geometry related parameters are accessible via a 3D menu as well as through the standard window based GUI.

1. Wössner U. ; Rantzau D. ; Rainer D., „Interactive Simulation Steering in VR and Handling of Large Datasets", in: *Proceedings of the IEEE Youth Forum in Computer Science and Engineering (YUFORIC) Germany '98*, Stuttgart, 16-18th June 1998
2. Rantzau D. ; Lang U., "A Scalable Virtual Environment for Large Scale Scientific Data Analysis", in: *Future Generation Computer Systems 14 (1998)*, pp. 215-222, Elsevier Science, 1998

VIRPI: A High-Level Toolkit for Interactive Scientific Visualization in Virtual Reality

Desmond GERMANS[1], Hans J.W. SPOELDER[1], Luc RENAMBOT[1] and Henri E. BAL[1,2]

[1] Division of Physics and Astronomy
[2] Division of Mathematics and Computer Science
Faculty of Sciences, Vrije Universiteit
De Boelelaan 1081, 1081 HV Amsterdam, The Netherlands

Abstract. Research areas that require interactive visualization of simulation data tend to dismiss virtual reality due to the lack of accessible tools for application specialists. This paper presents an integral toolkit for interactive visualization in virtual reality environments. The toolkit defines a framework to build applications that allow the user to interact with arbitrary simulation software and describe virtual measurement tools for the visualized data. The approach is illustrated with a case study in medical imaging.

1 Introduction

Current trends in virtual reality show that interaction and collaboration are key research topics[14]. However, researchers working with scientific simulation and visualization seldom use these new techniques in practice[17]. This is partially due to the lack of available software.

Visualization is commonly done using a low-level graphics library and specific tailor-made libraries that supply collaborative and interactive aspects. These libraries are not suited for application experts in fields of research that are not related to virtual reality. Even though it is possible to combine existing tools and libraries to present applications in interactive scientific visualization, non-VR experts would benefit greatly from an overall high-level approach, aimed at their application domain.

This paper describes a high-level toolkit that implements interactive paradigms for visualization, analysis and measuring with virtual instruments[15]. The toolkit is aimed at non-VR experts who wish to explore simulation data using virtual reality environments, towards the idea of "Virtual Laboratories"[8]. In the rest of the paper, we will discuss related work in section 2. Section 3 describes two key issues in the acceptance of VR outside the VR community: direct interaction with a simulation program and quantifying observations in VR. With requirements from these issues, the functionality of the toolkit is described in section 4. Then, a detailed case study shows the use of the toolkit in section 5. The paper finishes with conclusions and pointers to future work in section 6. The contributions of this paper are:

- It presents a high-level interactive visualization toolkit aimed at non-VR experts.
- The toolkit integrates access to measuring paradigms and the interaction with a running simulation program.
- It demonstrates the toolkit using a real-world case study from dentistry research.

2 Related Work

tool	Scene Graph	Data Vis.	Interaction	Collab.	Multi-Platf.	VR Hardware
OpenGL	no	no	no	no	SGI+Lin.+Win.	no
Direct3D	D3DRM	no	DirectX	DirectX	Win. only	no
IRIS Performer	supported	with VTK	low-level	no	SGI+Linux	with CAVElib.
Inventor	supported	no	low-level	no	SGI+Lin.+Win.	no
VTK	no	supported	no	no	SGI+Lin.+Win.	no
CAVELibrary	no	no	low-level	low-level	SGI+Linux	supported
VR Juggler	no	no	low-level	low-level	SGI+Linux	supported
CAVERNsoft	no	no	no	supported	SGI+Lin.+Win.	with CAVElib.

Table 1. The various available libraries and their features with respect to interactive data visualization in VR.

Approaches in scientific visualization are mostly based on either application builders (like IBM's DX, or AVS[2]), application programming aids (like the Visualization Toolkit[12]) or proprietary programming. Because application builders are generally not available for immersive virtual environments, one is left with programming graphics and accessing tracking devices. A low-level starting point to address visualization issues is the widespread OpenGL graphics standard. When a scene graph (hierarchical ordering of 3D objects) is required, one can use IRIS Performer[11], a high-performance visual simulation library. IRIS Performer provides a wide variety of functionality, and is very general. However, it can only be used on IRIX machines and with limited functionality also on Linux machines. To visualize relationships and constructions, to derive data, add color, etc. the Visualization Toolkit (VTK) can be used, which runs on top of OpenGL. VTK is a complete toolkit, providing implementations of many algorithms with which the programmer can do extensive data visualization. Based on a dataflow model, where the programmer can connect objects into a data-flow graph, VTK supports data derivations, isosurface extraction, various coloring schemes, etc. However, VTK alone is not aimed at interactive and collaborative virtual reality.

Interaction in virtual environments is commonly handled through the CAVElibrary, a toolkit to access CAVE hardware (trackers and displays). An alternative to this is VR Juggler[4], an open source library that addresses similar issues. Both libraries present a small layer around the tracker hardware and ways to channel graphics on the various screens in the virtual reality setup. The user is left to program visual interaction and navigation aids for analysis and measurement.

On a higher level, Open Inventor[18] provides interactive facilities, and offers an extensive library of scene-graph related tools. Furthermore, Open Inventor is an interactive runtime system and defines the inventor file format, which is used as a basis for VRML. However, Open Inventor was not tailored for VR environments.

Collaboration is supported through numerous libraries that provide network functionality[1,3,5,7,13]. Among them, CAVERNsoft[6] presents a network infrastructure and is specialized in telepresence features, like support for several protocols, shared data management, high throughput network, avatar realization and audio/video streaming. GNU/Maverik[10] and Avocado[16] present flexible communication frameworks for larger-scale collaboration in virtual environments. Like CAVERNsoft, several issues to realize telepresence are addressed. All of these libraries approach telepresence issues at a relatively low-level. At this level, describing communication for the task is difficult for non-VR experts.

Table 1 shows features that are supported by the various libraries. Note that the table also shows a proprietary Windows-based library, Direct3D. With an increasing trend to use off-the-shelf PC clusters (for tiled displays or CAVE-like setups), the possibility to run the software in a Windows-environment becomes an issue. In Windows, most of the necessary tasks are covered by DirectX, a proprietary entertainment-related high-performance peripheral library. Direct3D is the 3D graphics part of DirectX and is to a large extent functionally comparable with OpenGL. Retained Mode Direct3D (D3DRM in the table) is a scene graph library on top of this, providing the basic needs for scene graph management. Interaction and collaboration for Windows-based machines can be handled by DirectInput and DirectPlay. Again, this only runs on Windows-based machines, and uses limited proprietary protocols and formats.

All of the above issues are described from a technical specialist's point of view. They require knowledge on the structure of computer graphics, the issues of network communication and human-computer interaction aspects. As seen from table 1, data visualization and VR hardware support can be combined with IRIS Performer. For this purpose, special versions of VTK, the CAVElibrary and VR Juggler are available. Also, IRIS Performer can cooperate with CAVERNsoft. A combination of these libraries would thus present the tools needed to write interactive visualization applications for VR environments. However, a user who is not to some extent expert in these issues will dismiss the available libraries and toolkits.

3 Motivation

Ideally, a non-VR expert would rely on the functionality of one toolkit. This toolkit provides communication, measurement paradigms and interactive VR. With very little programming effort, the programmer would create an interactive VR application that suits the needs of the apparent field of research.

To develop such a toolkit, two main steps can be identified. First, use the available toolkits to arrive at a platform-independent base level. This level should hide the platform differences between a range of different setups, and it should provide basic visualization-oriented features, like a scene graph, simple shapes, text, graph data loading, accessing trackers, etc. In our approach, we call this step *Aura*. For the second step, we need to assess and build high-level tools to provide a measuring environment on top of the base level. This takes on the shape of an interactive framework with paradigms to manipulate and measure graphical representations of data. In this paper, we describe a toolkit, *VIRPI*, that facilitates this second step.

Two aspects in the acceptance of VR outside the VR community are important:

First, *the user wishes to interact seamlessly with a remotely running simulation program.* The user wishes to rapidly understand phenomena the simulation program is mimicking. Therefore, it is highly unwanted to alter the actual source code of the simulation program by inserting probing and analyzing instructions. In some cases this is not even possible, as the source code is not available, or altering the source would introduce erroneous behavior. For VIRPI, this problem is addressed by coupling VIRPI to CAVEStudy[9]. CAVEStudy wraps an unaltered remotely running stateless simulation program, and presents a simple programming interface to the user in the VR environment. This way, the user can connect buttons and sliders in the virtual laboratory to parameters of the simulation, and read out the data from the simulation.

As a second aspect in the acceptance of VR, *the user wishes to quantify his observations.* To enable a user to do so introduces several requirements for VIRPI. Primarily, the user needs to be able to specify the type of measurement in a rapid and easy way. Also, VIRPI needs to support ways to examine the dataset visually and specify subspaces on which the measurement procedure has effect.

To summarize, the following requirements define Aura and VIRPI:

- Aura hides platform differences, provides scene graph support, simple shapes, text, graph loading and access to VR hardware.
- VIRPI communicates to remote simulation programs by incorporating CAVEStudy.
- VIRPI presents an easy interface to define interactive behavior for measurements, object examination and the selection of subspaces.

4 Functionality

Using the requirements from the previous section, we will now describe functional aspects of the toolkit. Figure 1 shows an overview of our approach. The left side shows the VR environment, and the various layers that are running there. The right side shows the simulation environment, and the connection that is made with CAVEStudy. First, we will describe the Aura and VIRPI-layers in the VR environment. Then we describe how CAVEStudy combines both environments and facilitates the communication. Finally, we show how measurement paradigms can be described in this setup.

4.1 Low-level layer: Aura

Aura is the first layer as described in the previous section. It presents a lightweight interface to underlying low-level libraries. Without noticeable decrease of efficiency, it adds features that the underlying software lacks, or it simply passes calls in a transparent way. The core of the graphical part of Aura consists, like IRIS Performer, of nodes in a scene graph. These nodes can be geometry nodes, cameras, lights, etc. Next to this, Aura defines a variety of simple shapes (cube, ball, cylinder, arrow, pyramid, etc.), can load graph data (3D model files from modelers and other polygon descriptions), fonts and textures/images (.JPG, .RGB, .PNG, etc.).

Aura can encapsulate the CAVElibrary or VR Juggler, providing a simple interface to input devices and rendering contexts. On traditional workstations, a simulator (much like the CAVElibrary simulator) fills in the missing hardware.

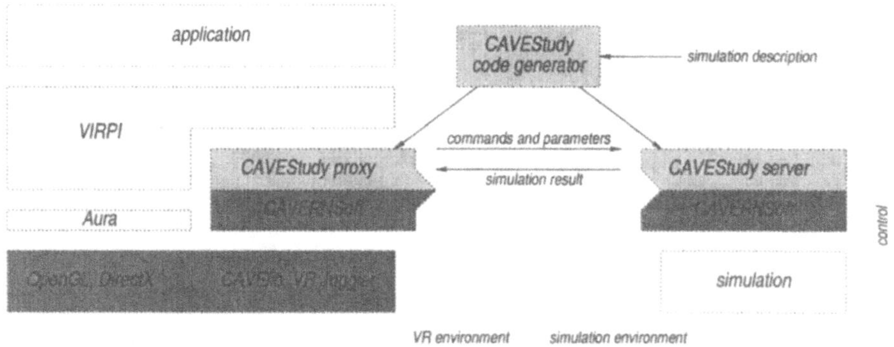

Fig. 1. The software layers for scientific visualization in VR.

In the current implementation, Aura comes as a set of libraries for various setups on different platforms. Aura is functionally the same for each setup. When the given setup is selected, simply creating the AuraVR environment object initializes the necessary hardware and tools.

To reduce complexity, Aura presents an interface where the connected hardware acts as a single environment. The interface does not present issues like multi-pipe output, multiprocessor systems and shared memory to the programmer. Instead, the Aura implementation deals with it when applicable.

4.2 High-level layer: VIRPI

Beyond the level of Aura, there are no more hardware-related issues, and platform-independence should be guaranteed. The high-level VIRPI toolkit rests on top of this level, and is identical for all platforms. VIRPI is roughly based on concepts and ideas from 2D GUIs like X or GTK. Where 2D GUIs use a hierarchical window-tree which can be used for event structuring, VIRPI uses a similar concept for hierarchical interface *views*.

A view is an atomic unit, which has a representation and can handle events. It is a tree node, so it can have a parent and one or more children. A node that contains children is called a *group*. The children of a group are called *sub-views*. Like with a scene graph, rotation, scaling and translation can be specified for each view with respect to its parent.

Like 2D GUIs, events are passed in two ways. First, events can be passed across the tree structure, originating at the root of the tree. These events are typically external events, like clicks of buttons on the pointer, movement of the pointer or other trackers, keystrokes, joystick changes, etc. Second, events can be passed directly from one view to the other, typically, to send messages between different control views.

When an event is received by a view, it is either passed down to its children, or processed. The user can overload event handlers for various types of events, adding functionality to the program. Figure 2 shows how the user can overload handling of the tracker motion event to have an object follow the user pointer (Wand, Stylus, mouse).

```
cMyApplication::OnTrackerMove(num,v,q)
{
    if(num == TN_POINTER)
        object->Translate(v);
    else
        cvApplication::OnTrackerMove(num,v,q);
}
```

Fig. 2. Code example showing how to overload a tracker move event.

The tracker motion event is defined as a tracker ID number, a vector indicating the position of the tracker and a quaternion indicating the orientation of the tracker. As soon as the tracker is moved, the `OnTrackerMove` method is invoked. When the tracker is the user pointer, the object is translated to the location of the tracker. When the tracker is something else, the inherited `OnTrackerMove` is called.

Completing the basic framework is an application base class. This is essentially a view, serving as root to the rest of the program. Writing a VIRPI program means subclassing the application class, and adding interactive features.

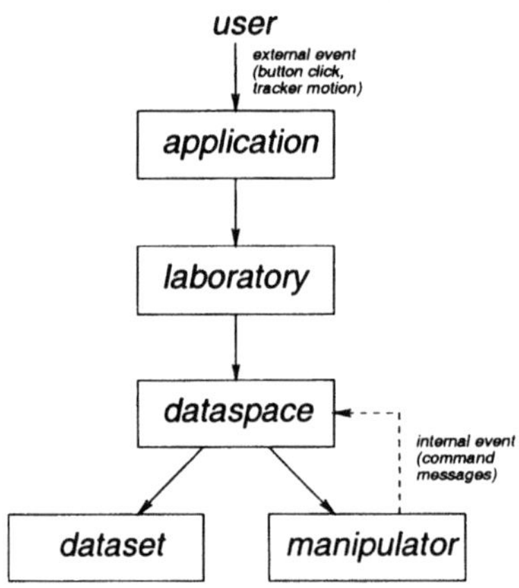

Fig. 3. An example event tree for a simple virtual experiment.

Figure 3 shows a view tree for a fictive application created with VIRPI. The application initializes a laboratory, which displays familiar laboratory surroundings and spatial references (for instance, a virtual room with a table). The laboratory creates a data space, which serves as a frame of reference in which data and measuring tools can be added. A dataset is added to the data space. Manipulating the data space will directly manipulate the dataset as well. To do this, a *manipulator* is added to the data space. The dashed line in figure 3 indicates command messages that are being sent by the manipulator to transform the data space.

Simple Controls Next to the basic structure, VIRPI provides several simple controls to interact with the user. Functional parts of 2D GUIs, like menus, sliders and (radio)buttons have a VR counterpart in VIRPI. These controls can be created, added and removed to the application at will. As the interface manifests itself in an immersive 3D environment, one can envision more new controls that are not directly related to their desktop paradigm. This, however, is beyond the scope of the paper.

```
// in the constructor:

    :
    button = new cvButton("arrow.jpg");
    AddView(button);
    :

// the message handler:
cMyApplication::OnMessage(sender,message,...)
{
    cvApplication::OnMessage(sender,message,...);
    if((message == MSG_PRESS) && (sender == button))
    {
        :
    }
}
```

Fig. 4. Code example showing how to add a button control and handle its messages.

All of these controls send events to the parent groups, indicating changes or command messages. These messages can then be processed by overloading the appropriate methods. Figure 4 shows how a button control is added to a VIRPI application. In the application's constructor, the button is created and added to the application. Furthermore, the application's message handler is overloaded. First the inherited message handler is called to process different messages, then if the message is a press-message and originates from the button, the button action is processed.

Data Manipulation An important aspect of visually examining an object is the ability to zoom in on it, move it and rotate it. These tasks are generally done with manipulators. A manipulator is a construct that interprets events from the user to make an object move, rotate or scale in an intuitive way. Internally, it is a group containing one or more handle views with which the user can interact. A handle view is a (mostly small) object, serving as interaction point for the manipulator. By dragging on a handle view, the user can scale, translate or rotate the object to which the manipulator is attached. Depending on the scheme of handle views and the functionality they provide, a manipulator can have many functions. Several standard manipulators are provided in a similar fashion as for Open Inventor.

4.3 Steering of a Simulation

As noted, one of the requirements of VIRPI is that it allows the user to interact with a running simulation. To minimize programming for the control of the simulation and the data management, the user has to describe the simulation with an XML description file. This file is processed by CAVEStudy to generate two objects, a *proxy* and a *server* (see Figure 1). The simulation is wrapped into a server object to control its execution. The server's interface provides methods to start, stop, pause and resume the simulation. The data generated by the simulation are automatically propagated to the proxy object. This object can be seen as a local copy of the remote simulation. Through the network, it reflects the input values and the commands to the server. Furthermore, it manages the incoming data from the simulation, and presents it to VIRPI.

CAVEStudy generates C++ code for the server and the proxy object, using the CAVERNsoft[5] network layer, as shown in figure 1. CAVERNsoft uses a "subscribe and publish" paradigm. A site can define keys to publish its own data, and a remote site that subscribes to these keys will automatically receive the data through call-back functions. This mechanism can be used for small data (tracker data), but also for large datasets (data-mining) using different policies.

The CAVEStudy code generator produces objects for the server and the proxy. Each of these objects contains a set of keys with their associated call-back functions to transmit input and output values. The marshaling code for all the types is generated to be able to use the system in a heterogeneous environment. A set of keys is also created for the control of the simulation (*initialize*, *start*, *stop*, *pause*, *resume*, *shutdown* methods). It is therefore possible to manipulate proxy and server entities as C++ objects, without dealing with network issues. For the server, the program is an endless loop, waiting for remote method invocations. The proxy object is embedded into VIRPI.

By using CAVERNsoft, it is possible to access one simulation with multiple VR setups. This way, a basic collaboration setup can be realized among multiple sites. Each site can, depending on their VR setup and the individual wishes of the users, display different representations of the data.

4.4 Measurement

Theoretically, measuring can be defined as a quantification of an observation in a given space. We see a virtual environment which displays the simulation results as space in which we can observe, and on which we can perform measurements. Some examples of measurements that can be done in VR are:

- In a gas simulation, dynamically count the number of atoms inside a given volume, and related to this give information about pressure and temperature.
- For a molecular dynamics simulation, measure the local electromagnetic field at a point, derived from potential data or the charge distribution from the simulation.
- From an MRI-scan of the human upper body, measure the volume and surface of a lung, or parts of a lung.

There are two key issues in making the toolkit useful for writing measurement applications as described. First, the user needs to be able to describe geometrical subsets of the data. He needs to select atoms, describe a volume, a surface, etc. Second, the user must specify the measurement itself, the calculations that need to be done on the data subset.

Basic subsets, like point sets, spherical volumes, box volumes or rectangular surfaces can be described in VIRPI by adding a selection view to the data (or rather, a data space as described in section 4.2) in an identical fashion as adding a manipulator. A combination of more subsets can be defined by means of constructive solid geometry operations.

```
cMyTool::Update(data,selection)
{
    count = 0;
    for(all atoms)
        if(selection contains(atom[i]))
            count++;
    SendMessage(display,MSG_UPDATE,count);
}
```

Fig. 5. Code example showing how to implement a measuring tool.

To describe a measurement procedure, the user can overload the `Update` method of the basic VIRPI measurement tool. This method gets called every time the dataset changes or the subset selection changes. In the `Update` method, the user has access to the elements of the dataset and the geometrical extents of the selected subset. Figure 5 shows the implementation of an example measuring tool that counts atoms in a given box volume. The `Update` method of the basic measuring tool class is overloaded, and using the selected volume, the atoms are counted. The result of this is transmitted to a display object.

5 Case Study

This section presents a case study implemented using Aura and VIRPI. The case study is representative for a range of applications in medical imaging. Furthermore, the application allows to compare results from virtual measurements with results from real-world measurements. Using this case study we describe how to setup Aura and VIRPI to examine data and quantify observations from it.

In order to clean the root canal of a patient's molar effectively, it is essential to know its exact length. Traditionally, measuring this length is done by sticking various sized files into the molar, guided by one or more X-ray photographs in different orientations. Figure 6 shows an alternative to this. By using a local CT scanning technique, the patient's molar is scanned, and a volume of 16-bit grey-scale voxels is calculated from the resulting images. An external program can produce isosurfaces for different threshold values from the volume, using VTK's Marching Cubes implementation. The isosurface is visualized by the VIRPI application, and the user measures the length of the root canal. This application was considered because it shows how the non-VR expert dental researcher is able to use VIRPI. Also, it lets the user measure on a visualized reconstruction in VR.

Figure 7 shows the setup in a VR environment for the application and the corresponding view tree. The root application group creates a data space and adds the tooth data to it. To measure the length of the inherently curved root canal, the application adds a yardstick to the data space. This yardstick is an application-specific view containing

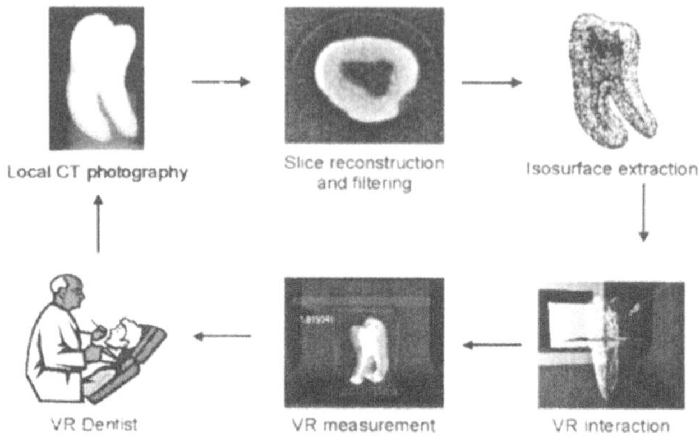

Fig. 6. The process steps from tooth to VR application.

a controlled Catmull-Rom spline representation and four interactive control points. The control points are VIRPI data subset selectors, and messages from the control points are processed by updating the spline coefficients of the yardstick.

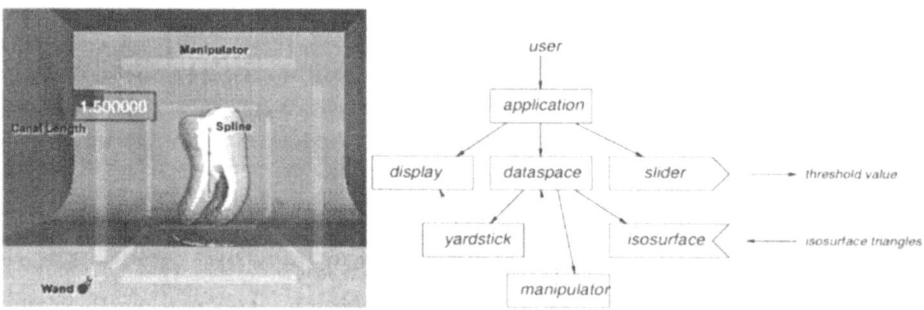

Fig. 7. Setup and corresponding view tree for the dental application.

Interaction with the simulation is implemented by adding a slider to the application. The slider's messages are passed to the CAVEStudy proxy object, which indicates changes in the threshold value to the marching cubes program.

To display the length, a display is added to the application. The display receives messages from the yardstick's `Update` method every time it changes shape (indicated by the dotted line in figure 7(b)). Finally, a manipulator is added to the data space (indicated by the cylinder cube in figure 7(a)), so the user can rotate the tooth and the yardstick, in order to view the experiment from a better angle. Dragging the edge cylinders of the cube makes the tooth rotate around the parallel axes.

6 Conclusions

The paper shows that a high-level toolkit, available on various setups, allows non-VR expert users to consider VR for their work. It also shows, by means of a case study, that it is possible to use VR as an experimentation environment where real-world measuring paradigms can be applied. Furthermore, it shows that it is feasible to implement such a toolkit for various platforms. Issues that are addressed regarding the differences in underlying operating systems and libraries present no unovercomable drawbacks. However, a lot of testing still needs to be done, as the project grows.

Towards a more complete environment which is considered useful by non-VR experts, some aspects still require attention. Currently, visualization of data in VIRPI is application-specific and limited to simple user-defined representations. An interface with data-flow visualization packages, like VTK or IBM's Data Explorer, should enable more genereral descriptions of the representations. Also, one could envision an interactive description of the representation, where the user can directly adjust the visualization data-flow to specific needs.

Next to this, although basic collaborative capabilities using CAVEStudy are mentioned, more work on this is desirable. We plan to research and implement more tight collaboration schemes in Aura/VIRPI that enable higher level telepresence aspects for measurement environments. Scientists can greatly benefit from the availability of a collaborative examining environment, in which they can discuss findings with peers around the world.

References

1. Christer Carlsson and Olof Hagsand. DIVE — A Platform for Multi-User Virtual Environments. *Computers and Graphics*, 17(6):663–669, November–December 1993.
2. I. Curington and M. Coutant. AVS: A flexible interactive distributed environment for scientific visualization applications. *Proceedings of 2nd Eurographics Workshop on Scientific Visualization*, 1991.
3. Chris Greenhalgh and Steven Benford. MASSIVE: A collaborative virtual environment for teleconferencing. *ACM Transactions on Computer-Human Interaction*, 2(3):239–261, 1995.
4. Christopher Just, Allen Bierbaum, Albert Baker, , and Carolina Cruz-Neira. VR Juggler: A Framework for Virtual Reality Development. In *2nd Immersive Projection Technology Workshop (IPT98)*, 1998.
5. J. Leigh, A.E. Johnson, T.A. DeFanti, and M. Brown. A Review of Tele-Immersive Applications in the CAVE Research Network. In *IEEE Virtual Reality'99*, pages 180–187, 1999.
6. Jason Leigh. Issues in the Design of a Flexible Distributed Architecture for Supporting Persistence and Interoperability in Collaborative Virtual Environments. In ACM, editor, *SC'97: High Performance Networking and Computing, San Jose (CA) USA.*, 1997.

7. M. R. Macedonia, M. J. Zyda, D. R. Pratt, P. T. Barham, and S. Zeswitz. NPSNET: A Network Software Architecture for Large-Scale Virtual Environment. *Presence*, 3(4):265–287, 1994.
8. B. Plale, G. Eisenhauer, K. Schwan, J. Heiner, V. Martin, and J. Vetter. From Interactive Applications to Distributed Laboratories. *IEEE Concurrency*, pages 78–90, April-June 1998.
9. Luc Renambot, Henri E. Bal, Desmond Germans, and Hans J.W. Spoelder. Cavestudy: an infrastructure for computational steering in virtual reality environments. In *Proceedings of the Ninth IEEE International Symposium on High Performance Distributed Computing*, pages 57–61, Pittsburgh, PA, August 2000. IEEE Computer Society Press.
10. R.Hubbold, J.Cook, M.Keates, S.Gibson, T.Howard, A.Murta, A.West, and S.Pettifer. GNU/MAVERIK: A micro-kernel for large-scale virtual environments. In *VRST'99, ACM Symposium on Virtual Reality Software and Technology*, 1999.
11. John Rohlf and James Helman. IRIS performer: A high performance multiprocessing toolkit for real–Time 3D graphics. In Andrew Glassner, editor, *SIGGRAPH '94*, Computer Graphics Proceedings, Annual Conference Series, pages 381–395. ACM SIGGRAPH, ACM Press, July 1994. ISBN 0-89791-667-0.
12. W. J. Schroeder, K. M. Martin, and W. E. Lorensen. The design and implementation of an object-oriented toolkit for 3D graphics and visualization. In R. Yagel and G. M. Nielson, editors, *Proceedings. Visualization '96. San Francisco, CA, USA. 27 October–1 November 1996*, pages 516–??, 93–100, 472, New York, NY 10036, USA, 1996. ACM Press.
13. G. Singh, L. Serra, W. Png, and Hern Ng. BrickNet: A Software Toolkit for Network-Based Virtual Worlds. *Presence*, 3(1):19–34, 1994.
14. Sandeep Singhal and Michael Zyda. *Networked Virtual Environments: Design and Implementation*. Addison-Wesley, 1999.
15. Hans J.W. Spoelder. Virtual Instrumentation and Virtual Environments. *IEEE Instrumentation and Measurement Magazine*, 3(3):14–19, 1998.
16. Henrik Tramberend. Avocado : A Distributed Virtual Reality Framework. In *IEEE Virtual Reality'99*, pages 14–21, 1999.
17. Andries van Dam, Andrew S. Forsberg, David H. Laidlaw, Joseph J. LaViola, Jr., and Rosemary M. Simpson. Immersive VR for scientific visualization: A progress report. *IEEE Computer Graphics and Applications*, 20(6):26–52, November/December 2000.
18. J. Wernecke and I. Mentor. *Programming Object-Oriented 3D Graphics with OpenInventor*. Addison-Wesley, 1994.

Interactive Storytelling with Virtual Identities

M. Greeff

CSIR: *i*comtek, Scientia
Pretoria 0001, South Africa
mgreef@csir.co.za

V. Lalioti

Computer Science Department, University of Pretoria
Pretoria 0001, South Africa
vlalioti@cs.up.ac.za

Abstract. Stories form an integral part of our lives. Interactive storytelling enables the participant to actively explore the story world. However, interactive storytelling has problems such as the problem of narrative flow, the character's knowledge of the world, internal consistency, time and ease of creation. We introduce the concept of using virtual identities for interactive storytelling in virtual environments and discuss how this approach solves some of the problems that are encountered with interactive storytelling. We discuss authoring tools and how we used the AVANGO framework to develop our application and the results that were achieved when the application was tested on the monitor and in Cyberstage.

1 Introduction

Since our childhood we are exposed to stories in many different forms. Legends and stories about our culture and heritage are passed on from generation to generation. The Story metaphor has been used in Multimedia and Virtual Environments to create interactive stories. Earlier systems used video, videodiscs or the television to create a non-linear story, in which the user can make a choice between different predefined paths at certain points in the story. Virtual environments are much richer both in terms of freedom of navigation and ease of interaction. In projection-based systems in particular, the user is not bound to predefined paths and can have a hands-on experience through immersion and interaction with the virtual world. However guidance is also needed in these environments in order to support the user during the exploration and facilitate the understanding of the purpose and intention of the particular virtual environment.

Interactive stories have already been used in Virtual Environments and allow the users to be actively involved in the story, since they can easily relate to it and experience joy while engaging in the interactive story world [2] [3] [12]. Although interactive storytelling gives the participant a richer experience, a number of aspects are missing from today's approaches, which relate among others to the narrative flow and internal consistency of the story. Another important issue is the ease of creation of interactive stories for virtual environments. In this paper we investigate these issues and present an approach for authoring interactive stories in virtual environments that address some of these aspects.

Our approach allows for the creation of several virtual identities through the eyes of which a user can experience the virtual world. Each identity is empowered with knowledge about itself, its perception about the virtual environment and its embodiment in the virtual world. Therefore the user can experience the same virtual world through different virtual identities being immersed each time in a different interactive story. The approach allows free navigation and interaction with respect to the particular virtual identity used. Furthermore, transitions from one virtual identity to another are possible and allow the creation of a more complex interactive story. We developed a framework and an authoring tool for defining and creating these identities, which are presented in this paper in detail. The authoring tool and the approach have been tested in a Cultural Heritage application and demonstrated in Cyberstage – GMD's surround-screen projection-based stereoscopic display system – and the results are also presented in this paper.

2 Background

The traditional methods of lectures, print, audio and video are narrative media, because they require a storyline and put the teacher in the role of the storyteller and the learner in the role of the listener. Interactive stories let the story world come alive and give the participant much more freedom. They are particularly suited for facilitated exploration and guidance in virtual environments, since they can incorporate rich interaction and free exploration, taking advantage of all the benefits and power of these environments to create a much richer experience for the user.

Although interactive storytelling gives the participant more freedom, a number of aspects relating to the character knowledge of the virtual world, narrative flow, the internal consistency of the story, the handling of time and finally the ease of creation can limit the benefits from its use in virtual environments [4] [5]. Taking a closer look at each of the aspects mentioned above reveals the following:

Character's Knowledge of the Story World

In a typical, non-interactive story, the characters understand the world and have knowledge about their world, for example a character knows the contents of the drawers and closets in her apartment and there is no need to open them to see what they contain. But in an interactive story world, the user does not have this knowledge and needs to explore the different objects as if she was a total stranger to the world. This approach can be used for the creation of interactive stories in some virtual environments, like in mysteries and heroic quests where the user will engage in new and unfamiliar worlds. However, in many applications of virtual environments it is important to provide more guidance and share some of the character's knowledge with the user. For example, in applications of virtual environments for education and cultural learning, knowledge about the story world should be incorporated in the interactive story so that the user can acquire it through this facilitated interactive experience.

Internal consistency

Any story must be coherent; that is, at any point in the story the circumstances at that specific point must be consistent with everything that happened beforehand. This does not mean that stories must be predictable, rather that they should make sense in a satisfying manner. However, the core of interactivity is freedom and therefore a conflict arises between the user's desire to do as he chooses and the story world creator's desire to impose a plot and characterisation on the user. The difficulty with using interactive storytelling in virtual environments is to ensure that a high degree of user freedom is combined with the story in a coherent way at every instance of the virtual experience.

Narrative flow

Traditionally, every story consists of an introduction, rising action, a climax, falling action and a conclusion. With non-interactive stories this can be accomplished because the author is in complete control of the story and the characters. With interactive stories the user is outside the control of the author and therefore it is very difficult to ensure that when the dramatic climax takes place in the story, the user is there and ready for it. This is known as the *Problem of Narrative Flow* [4].

Adventure games try to solve this in a number of ways:

- *Limiting the interactivity* by either cutting down the interactivity so that the user cannot stray from the plot or giving the user a lot of interactivity that is not necessarily meaningful but does not affect the plot. This solution is obviously taking away some of the power that interactive storytelling can give to the user.
- *Not taking the user's readiness for the climax into consideration* – the story world is alive and exists around the user but regardless of what he is doing. Therefore, in this solution, the user is not allowed to influence the story through any interaction.
- *Advancing the plot along with the user's advances* – the user's actions are linked to the advancement of the plot and therefore this approach absolutely guarantees that the user is ready for the climax. However, this solution is mechanistic and the story only progresses when the user performs the right actions.

Time

In traditional narrative, the story and the discourse are divided. When reading a novel, the storyline is constructed from the discourse that it is presented. Therefore, time of the narrated, time of the narration and time of the reading do not necessarily coincide.

Christian Metz, as quoted in [7], says that:
"Narrative is a ... double temporal sequence... : There is a time of the thing told and a time of the narrative (the time of the signified and the time of the signifier). This duality not only renders possible all the temporal distortions that are commonplace in narratives (three years of the hero's life summed up in two sentences of the novel or in a few shots of a "frequentative" montage in film, etc.). More basically, it invites us to consider that one of the functions of narrative is to invent one time scheme in terms of another time scheme."

It is obvious that presenting time in an interactive story becomes more complex, because of the interactive nature of the story. The representation of time and transitions in time is a particular important challenge in virtual environments were the time of the virtual experience can vary for different users or even for the same user during the repetitive use of the virtual environment.

Ease of creation

One of the main problems with using interactive storytelling in virtual environments is the difficulty in creating an interactive story. Most writers and storytellers have little or no knowledge of programming. On the other hand, the existing authoring tools for virtual environments are very specialised and require a user experienced in programming. Authoring tools are generally defined as tools for creating computer-based instruction without having to program [8]. Authoring tools for interactive storytelling should allow writers to concentrate on creating the story instead of the details of programming.

An example of an authoring tool is the *Erasmatron* [9]. It was developed to enable non-technical writers to create interactive stories without worrying about technical details, and to address the problem of exploding nodes when the *choose-your-own-adventure* approach is followed. It has editors, navigational aids and rehearsal to help the user create an interactive story world.

Authoring tools use metaphors such as paths, scenes and scripts to describe what the user experiences and what interaction is allowed with the environment. Therefore, authoring tools provide solutions to make the creation of interactive story worlds easier. They provide some internal consistency by defining what interaction is allowed in the story world, and ensure consistency using for example predefined paths. Predefined paths can also provide a solution for the *Problem of Narrative Flow*, but are still limiting the virtual experience. In addition, the problem of time and knowledge about the world remains unsolved and the user experiences the story world from only one angle, that of the specific script and path.

3 Virtual Identities Authoring Approach

In [1] we proposed the virtual identity approach to interactive storytelling. With this approach the participant experiences the interactive story through the eyes of a virtual identity. Each virtual identity is defined by the knowledge about itself, its perception about the environment and its virtual embodiment. We extended this approach by providing a framework to be used for defining the virtual identity, with the following main features:

- Characteristics that a virtual identity is born with
- Characteristics concerning the virtual identity's background
- Embodiment of the virtual identity
- Behavioural characteristics of the virtual identity

An initial approach that relates real identities to virtual identities, in terms of socio-psychological, gender and embodiment issues, presented in [1] is extended in this paper and the taxonomy (framework) will be presented in the full paper, in this section. Our authoring tool is based on this framework and it is fully described in section 4 with the authoring of an application in the Cultural Heritage area.

The Virtual Identities Authoring approach provides solutions to the problems mentioned in the introduction. We will now take a closer look at the solution for each of the problems mentioned in section 2.

Knowledge about the world

Each virtual identity is empowered with knowledge about itself, which it uses to perceive and interact with the virtual world. Therefore, although the virtual identity does not have knowledge about the story world, it does have knowledge about itself, for example its cultural background, age and gender. This partially defines its perception of the world and allows different interactions to the virtual world for each identity.

Internal consistency

Each virtual identity is allowed certain interactions with the virtual world according to its knowledge about itself. Therefore, all the user actions are coherent and go along with the story. By following this approach, internal consistency is maintained.

Problem of Narrative Flow

In our approach, the story unfolds as the user explores and interacts with the world, through the embodiment of a virtual identity. The interactive story created by this experience is not one with a specific climax and therefore the narrative flow problem is avoided.

Time

To allow change in time, we introduced transitions, both forward and backward in time. This will result either the change from one identity to another or the change of the age characteristic of the same identity. When the user interacts with an object in the virtual world that brings back memories, then a temporary change in the age characteristic of the virtual identity will result for example a flashback on its childhood, or the lowering of the height and thus the point of view of the user. In the second case, a transition from a child virtual identity to an adult identity results in a first experience through a child's eyes and then through the adult's.

4 Authoring Tool

An authoring tool enables users to create interactive stories. With our approach, the user of the authoring tool is able to create many different experiences with the use of a single model. Each virtual identity is defined by giving values to certain characteristics as described in section 3. Furthermore, certain interactions with the virtual environment are allowed in respect to these characteristics. In addition, the virtual embodiment of the identity can take many forms - i.e. video, avatar, sound, voice – which also automatically defines issues of navigation and interaction. For example, a virtual identity embodied in an avatar is not allowed to go through walls, while a voice is not allowed to grab certain objects, but can only talk about them. This approach and the inclusion of transitions in time allow a participant to have many different experiences with the same model of virtual environment (story world), and thus considerably reducing the authoring effort.

We developed the authoring tool with the AVANGO [6] framework that has been under development at GMD since 1996. AVANGO provides programmers with a scene-graph that is accessible from all the processes in the distributed application. The C++ programming language is used to define nodes or sensors (two categories of object classes). AVANGO also features a complete language binding to the interpreted language, Scheme, which is a high-level language that supports operations on structured data, e.g. strings, lists and vectors.

We tested our idea in a Cultural Heritage application. The story world is a shebeen (township tavern) in Cato Manor [10]. Cato Manor was once a vibrant Southern African community with Indian and African cultures, but in the 1950's the cumulative effects of overcrowding, deteriorating living conditions, hostility and neglect, lead to a wave of interracial violence and rebellion against the establishment. During the darkest days of apartheid it was torn down to enforce racial segregation and open up a prime piece of real estate for white occupation.

We used a 3 dimensional model of a shebeen in Cato Manor [10] developed by CSIR, under the Cultureware[1] project. The model was enhanced and imported to AVANGO, by using the hook mechanism for the objects of interest. We created three identities, namely a shebeen owner, a Zulu man and a Zulu boy. By using the same

---

[1] CSIR is The South African Council for Scientific and Industrial Research.
The Cultureware project is fully funded under DACTS (National Department for Arts, Culture, Science
and Technology of South Africa) through the Innovation Fund Programme.
http://www.cultureware.net

model (the shebeen) and allowing certain interactions in the shebeen according to the identity, the user can explore the shebeen through the eyes of each identity.

Fig. 1. The model of a shebeen (township tavern)

According to the virtual identity's age, the viewpoint of the identity as s/he explores the shebeen will be changed to provide the user with a realistic perspective of the shebeen. The Zulu boy's viewpoint is much lower than that of the Zulu man and is illustrated in figure 1.

The Zulu man is allowed to move the crates and chairs and to drink beer from the cups. The Zulu man can also click on one of the photos in the shebeen, which will then trigger a sound file to be played. The Zulu boy is allowed to also click on one of the photo's and can move the cups around, but he is not allowed to drink from the cups. Therefore, different cultural experiences can be obtained, allowing a rich cultural learning experience. We have also demonstrated this application in Cyberstage with very promising results.

(a) Zulu boy's viewpoint in the shebeen

(b) Zulu man's viewpoint in the shebeen

Fig. 2. Illustration of the difference in viewpoint of the Zulu man from the Zulu boy

5 Conclusions

In this paper we presented an approach and an authoring tool for interactive storytelling in virtual environments using the virtual identities method. In this approach, the user can have a realistic and multiple rich experiences through the eyes of the different identities. We have implemented one application in the area of cultural heritage and demonstrated it in Cyberstage – GMD's surround-screen projection-based stereoscopic display system. This approach can also be used in many application areas, such as entertainment, culture and education. We are currently improving the User Interface of the authoring tool and further extending the virtual identity approach and framework.

Acknowledgements

We would like to thank C. Jackson from CSIR for her valuable input on issues of social psychology, gender and culture and CSIR for allowing us to use the sheebeen model. Special thanks to all the members of GMD's Virtual Environments group. With their support and valuable help this work was made possible.

References

1. Jackson, C., Lalioti, V.: *Virtual Cultural Identities*, CHI-SA 2000, South African Human-Computer Interaction Conference 2000, University of Pretoria Conference Centre, Hatfield, South Africa, May 8-10, 2000.
2. Johnson, A., Moher, T., Ohlssoon, S., Gillingham, M.: *The Round Earth project – collaborative VR for conceptual learning*, IEEE Computer Graphics and Applications, Virtual Reality, Vol. 19, No. 6, Nov/Dec 1999.
3. The MIT Media Lab, *KidsRoom: Action Recognition in an Interactive Story Environment*, October 1996. http://vismod.www.media.mit.edu/vismod/demos/kidsroom/
4. Adams, E. (Gamasutra): *Three Problems for Interactive Storytellers*, December 1999. http://www.gamasutra.com/features/designers_notebook/19991299.htm
5. Juul, J.: *A Clash between Game and Narrative*, First International SKIKT Conference on Digital Arts and Culture, Bergen, Norway, November 26-28, 1998.
6. Tramberend, H.: *AVANGO: A Distributed Virtual Reality Framework*, In Proceedings of the IEEE Virtual Reality '99, JW Marriott Hotel, Houston, Texas, USA, March 13-17, 1999.
7. Genettes, G.: *Narrative Discourse*, Cornell University Press, 1980, p. 33.
8. Locatis, Ullmer, Carr, Banvard, Le, Lo, & Williamson: *Authoring system reassessed*, Educational Technology Research and Development, Vol. 40, No. 2, p. 77-82, 1992.

9. Crawford, C.: *Erasmatazz*, www.erasmatazz.com
10. Lynch, B.: *Cato Manor Development Project*, http://www.cmda.org.za
11. Hu, J.: *Spatial ability and hypermedia authoring: The attitudes of novice hypermedia developers and the characteristics of their concept maps and Authorware projects*, http://nt-hsta.hsc.wvu.edu/health/personal/AERAProposal.html
12. Bobick, A., Intille, S., Davis, J., Baird, F., Pinhanez, C., Campbell, L., Ivanov, Y., Schütte, A., Wilson, A.: *The KidsRoom: A perceptually-based interactive and immersive story environment*, PRESENCE: Teleoperators and Virtual Evironments, 8(4), August 1999, p. 367- 391.

First-Person Science Inquiry 'in the Field'

T. Moher, A. Johnson, Y. Cho, Y. Lin

Electronic Visualization Laboratory
University of Illinois at Chicago
Chicago, IL, 60607

Abstract: In this paper we describe a class of restricted simulations, virtual ambients, designed to support science inquiry learning among elementary school students. These simulations employ large multi-user VR displays to support 'first-person' collaborative exploration, data collection, and the construction of support for hypotheses in simulated environments. In order to reduce the cognitive load on learners, navigation is used instead of the traditional learning simulations' direct control of independent model variables. Users may observe phenomena in virtual environments, but cannot affect the course of the underlying simulation. We report on our early experience with second, fourth, and sixth grade students in an elementary school employing a configurable virtual ambient named 'the Field.'

1 Virtual Ambients

Elementary school science is about asking questions, collecting data that relate to those questions, and building support for answers [1, 10]. Throughout history, teachers have relied on accessible local environments to stimulate young learners' questions and to provide direct access to observable and measurable phenomena. Local environments have the advantages of convenience and salience, but they also have three important drawbacks: they may emphasize activity over learning [3], they may limit the domain of inquiry, and they may constrain teachers' ability to scaffold learning by reducing complexity.

For the past year we have been developing instructional interventions that employ 'virtual ambients' [9] as loci for children's scientific exploration. Virtual ambients are three-dimensional first person spaces within which users can navigate in space, scale, and time. Virtual ambients may include simulated scientific instrumentation, and may provide users with navigation and data collection aids. Virtual ambients may be static or dynamic, but unlike traditional simulations, virtual ambients offer users no direct control over independent variables. Nothing that the user may do within a virtual ambient can affect the course of the underlying simulation. This constraint is designed to reduce the cognitive burden of exploring complex input spaces [2, 5, 7] by limiting young learners to familiar concepts and activities: moving around, seeing things at different scales, and imagining the past and future. It does not preclude the articulation and investigation of causal hypotheses; it simply shifts the burden from artificially manipulating preconditions to finding instances of varying preconditions. This is not an uncommon model in science – astronomy has similar 'limitations.'

Fig. 1. A view of the Field from the children's perspective, showing a cluster of eight different 'plants' and one of our most recent additions – a moving turtle.

Virtual ambients are implemented on large screen VR displays to support collaborative learning experiences for small groups. Because they are deployed on scarce resources, they are carefully constructed within a pedagogical framework that combines traditional whole class and small group activities with appropriate but less frequent technology-based work [8]. In the three pilot studies described below, learners spent about 30 minutes using virtual ambients, and about three hours in whole-class and small group discussions and activities. We believe that even these simple worlds can be the source of authentic learning experiences for young learners, and are consistent with emerging frameworks for technology-supported inquiry learning [4].

We also believe that the act of collecting and transcribing data will promote conceptual understanding by making the connection between the environment being studied and the 'scientific' representations of data drawn from that environment explicit. Evidence from other domains gives credence to this theory. Holst [6] for example, found that requiring the students to do manual data entry to algebra-learning software resulted in a significantly higher level of content mastery. Such evidence highlights the need to balance between scaffolding the experience and engaging in low-level activities associated with scientific investigation.

2 The Field

In the Field, shown Figure 1, students collaboratively explore a large 'natural' terrain containing up to eight different plant types. The Field itself has limited affordances: navigation, the ability to take 'snapshots', and the ability to plant an unlimited number of biodegradable marker flags in the ground. The land mass is a square 3000 feet on a side, divided into regions in two independent ways: picket fences divide the space into a 3x3 grid, and the different patches of terrain divide the ground into regions of grass, sand, and gravel.

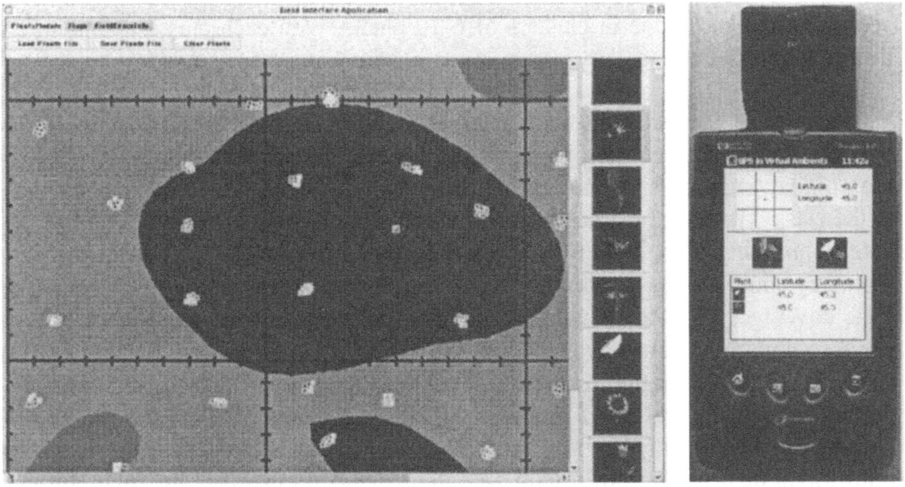

Fig. 2. The java client and the WinCE client. The java client is used to define the location of plants in the Field, as well as to monitor the users' movements and actions. The WinCE client can be carried by the children as a virtual instrument – a GPS receiver, a 'tricorder', or a note taking device, to collect data from the Field

The Field has been implemented on an ImmersaDesk® providing a wide visual field-of-view, and supporting collaborative investigations for up to four students comfortably. We are using an ImmersaDesk, driven by a 4-processor SGI deskside Onyx IR, that has been installed in the Media Center at Abraham Lincoln elementary school in Oak Park, Illinois since August 1999.

The Field has been written using YG, a scriptable language developed at EVL by Dave Pape that sits on top of SGI Performer and the CAVE library. CAVERNsoft is used for networking between multiple VR clients, and between the VR clients, the laptop-based Java client, and WinCE handheld devices. The Java client serves several purposes. Prior to the experience, it is used to set up the location of the plants in the environment. During the experience it allows us to monitor the position of the children in the space. After the experience it allows us to review their actions – the paths they took, the plants they marked, etc. This is a very useful ability, beyond what would be available in a real setting. See Figure 2.

So far 6th graders, 4th grades, and 2nd graders have had learning experiences in the Field. Jarvia Thomas' 2nd graders investigated issues of similarity and difference; Victor Baez' 4th graders learned about interpolation and extrapolation; Marilyn Rothstein's 6th graders learned to develop co-occurrence rules, and Joanna Peterson's 6th graders are currently learning to estimate population distributions.

3 Sixth Grade: Co-occurrence

Our first pilot study [9] was conducted in the spring of 1999. We configured the Field for a learning activity intended to introduce two classrooms of sixth grade students to the mathematical concept of co-occurrence. We distributed 400 plants over all nine sectors of the landscape in clusters of 6-10 plants, with each cluster containing two different types of plants.

Two groups of four students each acted as 'scouts,' making initial 20-minute forays into the Field. The scouting teams wrote general observations about the Field, and took digital 'snapshots.' The scouting team used the snapshots to make presentations to the class. Through the hour-long discussion, the class converged [11] on the task of determining the 'plant buddies' (the co-occurrence pairs). The teacher then discussed how they could ensure an accurate count within each sector; and how to ensure complete coverage. The scouts had reported that the individual sectors were too large to see across with the naked eye, and that the density of clusters was low. One girl suggested that the exploration teams could use a 'lawn mower' algorithm to ensure that the entire sector as traversed. Another girl raised the idea of using the flags to mark clusters that had already been counted. Because they suspected that the co-occurrence rules might be a function of terrain type, they decided to record, for each cluster, the two types of plants and the underlying terrain on which they were found.

The teacher organized the students into four-person teams and each team spent 30 minutes exploring their assigned sector. The students rotated through three assigned roles - navigator (made decisions on direction of travel), driver (controlled the wanda), data announcer (verbalized information about the path), and data recorder (transcribed announcer's comments and drew pictures). The use of small groups for exploration worked well; there was a great deal of interaction among team members, and their collective memories served well to recall strategies which individuals within the group had forgotten. The students said the rotation of responsibilities was 'fair' - an important consideration in an elementary school setting. See Figure 3.

Back in the classroom the individual groups aggregated their data. The final co-occurrence matrix contained only 44% of the clusters in the Field. Most of data points were lost during the exploration phase itself – partly though sloppy note-taking and partly due to their failure to follow a systematic traversal algorithm. Figure 4 shows the traversal path employed by one of the groups, which failed to explore several large regions of their assigned sector. Interestingly, when the teacher asked the students whether they believed that they had found all of the clusters in their assigned sector, all of the groups confidently reported that they had. The students were quite surprised when a checking group went back into the space and reported that a significant number of clusters had been missed. More data was lost during aggregation, principally due to a lack of common vocabulary – different groups came up with different names for the plants and it was difficult for the children to shift between these different names. All of this is not necessarily a bad thing – it was certainly a learning experience for the children to make these mistakes, and see the need for organizing this kind of survey up front. However it did seriously impact the original goal of studying correlations.

Fig. 3. A group of sixth graders exploring the Field on the ImmersaDesk

One change that we made during this first study involved head-tracking. Given that we had multiple students viewing the Field, and frequent changes of control, we decided to turn off head tracking. This allowed the students to change drivers by merely handing over the wanda rather than also needed to exchange the tracked glasses.

4 Second Grade: Similarity & Difference

The second grade students visited the field in spring 2000, focusing on similarity and difference. For this unit, only a single sector of the Field was employed, which was configured with 24 isolated plants - three each of the eight available types.

The activity began with a one-hour discussion between the teacher and the students. The teacher brought a collection of cut flowers of various types, colors, and sizes to the class. Holding up pairs of flowers, the teacher asked the children in what ways they were alike and different. The children articulated several important observations during the discussion, including the relationship between flower shapes and type, the fact that color alone might be insufficient to distinguish one type from another, and the fact that two plants of the same type might not be the same size.

The children were told about the Field, divided into eight groups of three students each, and given the task of determining how many different types of plants can be found there. They were to explore the space and come back together as a class to determine the unique plant types. Unlike the sixth grade unit, a complete survey was not expected; the children hypothesized that plants missed by one group would probably be found by another group. Because no 'scouting' activity was included, the students had no snapshots of the plants at the outset. They decided that they would need to make drawings and write brief descriptions of the plants that they found.

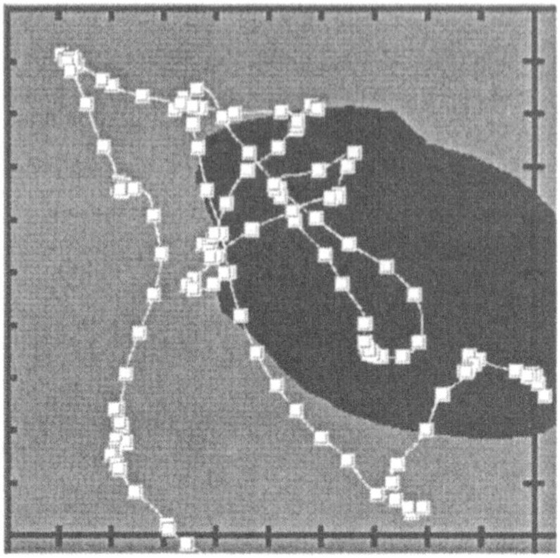

Fig. 4. Bird's eye view of the traversal pattern of one group. Instead of using a lawn-mower algorithm, the kids moved from cluster to cluster, leaving large areas of their sector unexplored.

The students were pulled out of class to participate in the exploration on the day after the discussion. Each team brought its own paper, crayons, pencils, and markers, and spent 30-45 minutes exploring. One child took the role of driver; the other two children were responsible for drawing and writing about the plants that the driver found. Again, the roles were rotated for fairness.

The next day the students sat on the floor of their classroom in their groups. Each group presented their drawing of a candidate 'new plant.' Since we knew which plants each team had found, we sequenced the groups to ensure that all the teams could introduce a new candidate. As each candidate was introduced, the class discussed whether it was really new, or simply a different picture of a plant that had already been presented. The students showed strong interest and group pride as they presented their candidate plants. In one instance, a group introduced a plant that had been previously put forward by another group. The class was evenly divided on the issue of whether the plant was new; it matched the earlier plant in colour, but differed in the number of leaves. This discrepancy led to two important discussions.

First, the teacher asked the class whether they it might be the same plant, just drawn from a different perspective. This was an interesting question as the students had paid little attention to obtaining multiple perspectives during their exploration. Typically, the students would happen upon a plant through relatively random navigation, walk up close, stop, and draw the picture. At no time did the students spontaneously articulate a strategy of walking around the plant in order to facilitate their drawing. An interesting question is whether the children would have spread out around the plant in the real world and made their drawings from several perspectives.

Second, the teacher noted that even scientists might offer different descriptions of the same phenomenon, and asked how scientists might go about resolving their differences of opinion. The class discussed - and rejected - the idea of voting to see which was correct, and articulated a strategy of sending a neutral observer back to check.

Once the class reached consensus on the set of unique plant types, each group was charged with producing an archival ('really good') drawing and description of the plant that they had introduced during the follow-up discussion. The final drawings were collected by the teacher, scanned, and combined into a montage.

The unit was well received by the children. There appeared to be little difference between the sixth and second graders with respect to use of the apparatus. The students worked well in their teams, and clearly benefited from the more detailed planning with respect to data collection tasks. They had a very clear conception of the overall process, and what was expected of them at each stage of the unit.

A major difference between the experiences of the sixth graders and second graders was the focus on tangible work products. Having the second graders to produce "archival" pictures and text greatly enriched the activity for them, and provided us with more material to characterize their learning experience.

Students were then asked to write brief answers to two questions: "What did you do?" and "What did you learn about what scientists do?" We classified each phrase in their responses to the first question into several categories based on what they referenced:

- social interaction ("Me and Jimmy went up to the media center...")
- the technology apparatus ("I put on the glasses...")
- exploration ("First we went along the fence for a while...")
- data collection ("The plant had three green petals...")

We had expected that the descriptions would emphasize the novel apparatus; we were surprised to find that it accounted for only 14% of the students' responses. Descriptions of exploration and data collection accounted for 30% of their comments, with the remaining 56% describing their interactions with their peers. To the second question, a majority of students articulated the need to "go back and look" when scientists disagree. Their responses suggest that the students truly became engaged in "doing what scientists do." For the second graders, the Field was a real place, populated by real things, where they did real work.

5 Fourth Grade: Interpolation & Extrapolation

A classroom of fourth grade students visited the Field in fall 2000, focusing on interpolation and extrapolation. Only a single sector, and only a single species of 'plant', the mushrooms, were employed. The students investigated the differential growth rates of the mushrooms based on the soil type (grass, sand, rock) and tried to predict how many mushrooms would grow by the end of the season. This was important to the students because mushrooms are the favourite cuisine of the Snookerpuss – a mysterious creature that hibernates during the summer and wakes in the fall. The students needed to find out if there would be enough mushrooms available when the Snookerpuss awoke so it wouldn't need to find other food, such as 4th graders.

The class was broken up into teams where each team visited the field in a different virtual month (June, July, etc) and counted the number of mushrooms growing on each soil type. Within two days at school, the different groups explored the same sector over eight months of growing time.

Afterwards the children collated their data and plotted the growth rates of the mushrooms on three graphs (growth in rocky soil, sandy soil, and grassy soil) as a classroom. After introducing a 'best-fit' line, they predicted of the number of mushrooms that would be available at the end of the Snookerpuss' hibernation. They confirmed their favorable prediction by sneaking into the field in October just before the hungry Snookerpuss awoke. From the graphs they also concluded that the mushrooms grew most rapidly in the grass, and recommended that next year the mushroom spores be distributed in grassy areas to maximize the yield.

In follow-up activities, the children described their surveying strategies, and developed new predictions based on hypothetical data. Although the children had not previously been introduced to linear prediction, 75% of the class was able to construct a supported prediction. The next month, when the kids were formally introduced to the concepts of linear interpolation and extrapolation, they repeatedly cited the Snookerpuss adventure.

Each child spent roughly 30 minutes using the display technology, and two hours in small group and whole-class activities. The Snookerpuss adventure accomplished two complementary learning goals. It helped the children develop their understanding of transforming between numeric and graphical representations of data, linear best-fit, interpolation, and extrapolation. In the discussion comparing the relative growth rates in different terrains, the kids even touched on issues of steepness and slope. It also helped develop skills for conducting scientific inquiry, including planning investigations, navigational strategies within a survey space, observation of phenomena and recording of data, distribution of effort within an investigational team, reporting of their results, and the aggregation of data across teams in a large-scale project.

6 Beyond the Field

The Field is the simplest kind of virtual ambient; offering a static model of an environment where users can navigate and make visual observations. We are currently enhancing the virtual ambients in several ways.

- The current field already sends data to the java application so we can track the position of the children in the space. We are also sending the data to a WinCE hand-held where we create virtual instrumentation. Adding simulated instrumentation to virtual ambients allows the study of both instantaneous and cumulative phenomena.

- It is important to extend the domain of phenomena beyond those readily accessible to learners. Fields of plants are not hard to access, the surface of Mars is.

- Nature moves and grows, and understanding dynamic phenomena is an important part of the scientific enterprise. As part of a unit on sampling and population distributions, we have created some turtles that will slowly move around the field so the children can explore differential strategies for population estimation.

Ultimately, the real question is whether science inquiry skills acquired in a virtual environment can be effectively transferred to real world situations. We will explicitly investigate this in the next school year.

We see two major barriers to sustaining the virtual ambients approach. First, the technology is far too expensive. Second, moving children to another room for the VR experience creates difficult learning and management problems for teachers, and requires the availability of additional personnel.

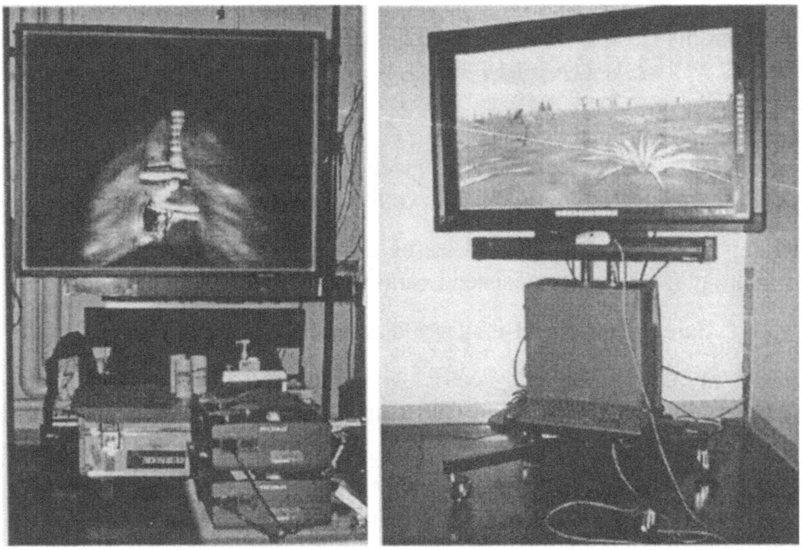

Fig. 5. Two new displays we are going to try out in the school in the next year – a passive projection screen, and a 50" plasma display, both driven by Linux PCs

We are exploring alternative delivery strategies to address these problems. YG, Performer, the CAVE Library, and CAVERNsoft work under Linux as well as IRIX, so we have ported the Field to an SGI Linux PC using a 50" diagonal plasma panel. In April 2001 we will deploy this system. We lose stereo visuals, but will maintain hand-tracking for the virtual instrumentation and the large screen allows us to continue supporting small group interaction around a shared display. A second option uses a Linux PC with a GeForce 2 MX card driving two stacked DLP projectors to project a passive stereo image. This option would use more space in a classroom, but gives us back stereo visuals. Both of these technologies represent an order-of-magnitude reduction in cost compared to our current setup, and employ consumer-driven commodity technologies with steep performance / price slopes. See Figure 5.

We envision a system that provides access to a virtual ambient for an extended period on a 'walk up and use' basis, like an ant farm, or other phenomonenaria in classrooms. As contemporary elementary school classrooms are increasingly organized around small-group activity centers, this organization allows the teacher to opportunistically provide access to the virtual ambients during regular daily activities.

Acknowledgements

We would like to thank the Lincoln schoolteachers for their partnership and friendship during this project. Thanks also to Dave Pape, and Jason Leigh for their help in implementing the Field, to Alex Hill, Janet Kim, Dave Haas, and Solomon Onomivbori for assistance during testing, and to Josh Radinsky for helpful comments and suggestions in planning the classroom discussions.

This research was made possible through major funding from the National Science Foundation, specifically EIA-9720351, DUE-9979537, and EIA-0085946. The VR research, collaborations, and outreach programs at EVL are made possible by major funding from the NSF, awards EIA-9802090, EIA-9871058, ANI-9980480, and ANI-9730202, as well as ACI-9619019.

References

1. American Association for the Advancement of Science, Benchmarks for Science Literacy: Project 2061. New York, NY: Oxford University Press, 1993.

2. de Jong, T., et al. Self-directed learning in simulation-based discovery environments. Journal of Computer Assisted Learning 14, 1998, 235-246.

3. Dewey, J. Science as subject-matter and as method. Science 31 (1910), 121-127.

4. Edelson, D., Gordin, D., and Pea, R. Addressing the Challenges of Inquiry-Based Learning through Technology and Curriculum Design. Journal of the Learning Sciences, 8, 1999, 391-450.

5. Friedler, Y., Nachmia, R., and Linn, M. Learning scientific reasoning skills in microcomputer-based laboratories. Journal of Research in Science Teaching, 27 (1990), 173-191.

6. Holst, S. Directing learner attention with manipulation style. ACM CHI 96 Doctoral Consortium, Vancouver, CA, 1996.

7. Jackson, S., et al. Making dynamic modeling accessible to pre-college science students. Interactive Learning Environments 4 (3), 1994, 233-257.

8. Loh, B., at al. The Progress Portfolio: Designing reflective tools for a classroom context, in Proceedings of CHI '98 (Los Angeles, CA), ACM Press, 627-634.

9. Moher, T., Johnson, A., Cho, Y., and Lin, Y. Observation-Based Inquiry in a Virtual Ambient Environment, in Fourth International Conference of the Learning Sciences (Ann Arbor MI, June 2000), Erlbaum, Mahwah NJ, pp. 238-245.

10. National Research Council, National science education standards. National Research Council, Washington DC, 1996.

11. Tabak, I., and Reiser, B. Activity Attributes: Steering The Course of Dialogue in Inquiry-Based Science Classrooms. Presented at AERA 1999, Montreal, Canada.

MAESTRO - a tool for interactive assembly simulation in virtual environments

Roland Steffan[1] and Torsten Kuhlen[2]

[1] Virtual Reality Center Aachen
c/o Institute of Technical Computer Science, Aachen University of Technology
[2] (corresponding author) Virtual Reality Center Aachen
c/o Computing Center, Aachen University of Technology
kuhlen@rz.rwth-aachen.de

Abstract. We introduce MAESTRO, a Virtual Reality based assembly simulation tool that comprises physically-based modeling, haptic feedback and artificial support mechanisms. The focus of this paper is on the developed support mechanisms and the evaluation of the system. The experimental results show that all three features – haptics, physics, and artificial support – considerably improve user performance and user acceptance during the completion of assembly tasks in a virtual environment.

1 Introduction

During the last years, Virtual Reality (VR) has proven its potential for the visualization and manipulation of complex data like 3-D geometries generated by means of CAD applications. An interesting and promising area of application for virtual environments is assembly simulation. Though virtual environments can already profitably be integrated into engineers' daily work, there are still a lot of disadvantages in existing VR-based assembly simulation systems, requiring trained engineers for performing interactive simulations. Especially, the lack of satisfactory feedback mechanisms in existing VR-based simulation environments complicates execution of interactive manipulations of virtual objects. In detail, suitable modeling of user-object interactions, realistic simulation of object behaviour, and intuitive presentation of information are missing. During the last 2 years, we have been developing a software called MAESTRO (**M**ultimodal Interaction Techniques for Assembly **S**imulation in Virtual Environments), where, for the first time, the following features are combined in a single, comprehensive tool:

- Realistic, physically-based behaviour of virtual objects, including automatic calculation of the objects' inherent mechanical characteristics
- Integration of force feedback into the interaction with virtual objects, operating on a unique scene graph for both, graphics and haptics
- Artificial support mechanisms like sensitive polygons, virtual magnetism, and guiding sleeves

The focus of this paper is not to describe the single algorithmic approaches of the MAESTRO features in detail, but instead to give insight into the overall MAESTRO functionality, and to demonstrate by means of a system evaluation that the combination of all features can contribute significantly to a better user performance and user acceptance during the simulation of assembly tasks in a virtual environment (VE).

The remainder of the paper will start with a short survey of existing VR-based assembly simulation tools. In section 3, our approach is compared to other simulation systems. Furthermore the physically-based modeling and the haptics component of MAESTRO are briefly described here. Section 4 illustrates the developed artificial support mechanisms, and section 5 gives an overview of the MAESTRO hardware and software. Finally, section 6 evaluates the system by means of two experiments. The paper ends some remarks about future work.

2 A Brief Survey of Assembly Simulation in VE

Basically, available systems for interactive assembly simulation in virtual environments can be subdivided into knowledge/rule-based approaches and physically-based approaches.

R. Heger [1] introduced a knowledge-based system that allows an interactive execution of manual assembly tasks in a virtual environment. The system works with the concept of reference points, i.e., single vertices within the polygon models which can be placed at connection elements (e.g., screws) or target positions. For the single reference points, assembly-specific object characteristics are stored and take care that objects are placed automatically and exactly when the user approaches such a reference point.

A similar approach was chosen by M. Grafe [2] for a virtual construction system that uses basic elements. Functional nodes can be attached to single surfaces of these elements causing, e.g., a snap-in when two corresponding nodes are approaching.

B. Jung [3] describes a knowledge-based system that allows an interactive assembly of virtual basic elements to complex modules. Here, a polygonal and a logical description are stored in two separate knowledge databases. The first one contains object characteristics which are relevant to assembly, and which are represented by so called ports. The second one serves to describe a construction goal, i.e., a kind of plan how to create modules from single objects. This knowledge allows the system to recognize assembled objects as modules and, by inference from the knowledge database, to deduce the specific use of single elements within a module.

All three knowledge-based systems are using a tracked instrumented glove and 3-D mices as interaction devices and do not provide force feedback mechanisms. In the VADE system developed by S. Jayaram [4] and an assembly system introduced by M. Buck [5], bimanual interaction is included by means of two instrumented gloves. Both systems contain a physical, constraint-based approach to achieve a realistic object behaviour. For physically-based modeling, Buck uses polygonal models of lower complexity than for visualization. When two objects intersect, the objects are simultaneously presented to the user at their physically plausible positions and, in a wireframe representation, at their intersected positions. While in the system of Buck reaction forces are visualized as vectors, the VADE system should provide a real force feedback by means of an exoskeleton glove.

R. Gupta et al. [6] introduce an assembly simulation system that provides force feedback by means of two PHANToM Haptic Devices [7]. Here, the graphical representation of the scene and the physically, constraint-based modeling are completely separated. In contrast to all other systems mentioned here, the system of Gupta is restricted to two dimensions and does not support the use of immersive displays.

3 The MAESTRO Concept

MAESTRO combines a physically-based and a knowledge-based approach in order to profit from the advantages of both strategies, i.e., realistic object behaviour on the one hand and effective manipulation of virtual objects on the other hand. The inflexibility of rule- and knowledge-based systems is avoided here, because most of the necessary knowledge is generated automatically, and because only a few assembly-relevant rules are applied. Physically-based modeling (PBM) and artificial support mechanisms, based on priori knowledge about the assembly goal, are completed by haptic feedback functionality. Our approaches for PBM and haptics are only briefly introduced in the remainder of this section, whereas the support mechanisms will be described in more detail in the next section.

Physically-Based Modeling To achieve a realistic behaviour of virtual objects by means of physically-based modeling, mass, friction coefficient, centre of gravity, and inertia tensor of the virtual objects must be known. In MAESTRO, these inherent mechanical characteristics are calculated automatically from the polygonal description of the model geometry. Since the geometries can normally be easily exported from a CAD application, MAESTRO possesses a high flexibility. In principle, the problem can be reduced to volume determination of the polygonal models. Here, we have implemented and compared different exact and approximative algorithms [8].

Starting from the mechanical object characteristics calculated in step one, we have, in contrast to other systems (see section 2), preferred an impulse-based approach to a constraint-based approach, because it allows for a consistent methodical treatment of all kinds of contact between virtual objects. Most of the algorithms we have integrated here, are well documented in the publications of B. Mirtich and D. Baraff (see, e.g., [9–11]). Whenever possible, reactions to collisions are calculated algebraically in order to fulfill the real time requirements of interactive assembly simulations. In MAESTRO, numerical integration is only applied to the simulation of sliding motions. For recumbent contact situations, a simple, rule-based approach was found.

Haptic Feedback A severe deficit of today's systems for interactive assembly simulation is the lack of multimodal, especially force feedback. The few existing systems like those of Jayaram or Gupta (see section 2) operate with a redundant haptic scene graph in order to provide stability of the haptic rendering. In contrast to these systems, our approach is based on a single scene graph for graphics as well as haptics, thus dramatically reducing modeling costs and gaining a higher system flexibility. In order to achieve stability even without a haptic description of the scene, we are operating with an interim representation of contact situations. We will decribe this approach in detail in a forthcoming paper.

4 Artificial Support Mechanisms

In order to compensate for the problems which inevitably exist in VR-based assembly operations, arising from the non-exact modeling of geometry and behaviour of virtual objects as well as from inadequacy of available interaction devices, we developed and integrated artificial support mechanisms into MAESTRO. Figure 1 illustrates how the implemented mechanisms – guiding sleeves, sensitive polygons, virtual magnetism, and snap in – are assigned to the three classical phases of an assembly process.

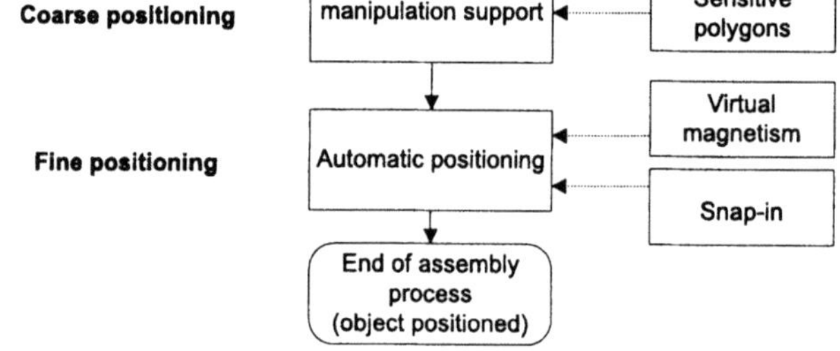

Fig. 1. Assignment of the integrated support mechanisms to the single interaction phases of an assembly process

Guiding Sleeves Guiding sleeves are a support mechanism that makes use of priori knowledge about possible target positions and orientations of objects. In the configuration phase of an assembly simulation with MAESTRO, the guiding sleeves are generated in form of a scaled copy or a scaled bounding box of the objects that are to be assembled, and then placed as invisible items at the corresponding target location. When an interactively guided object collides with an adequate guiding sleeve, the motion path necessary to complete the assembly task is animated as a wireframe representation. In addition, the target position and orientation is visualized by means of a semi-transparent copy of the manipulated object (see Fig. 2).

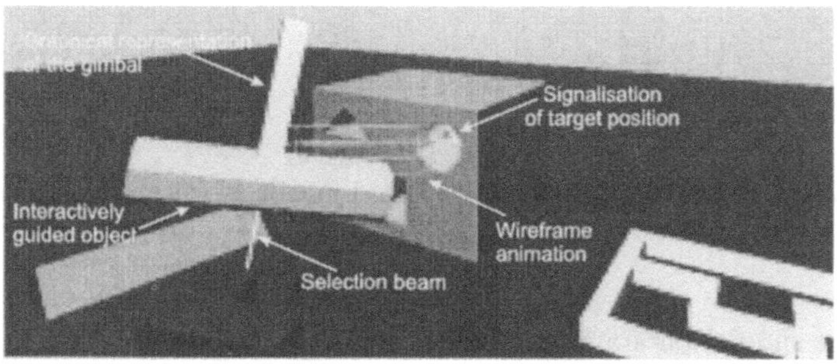

Fig. 2. Guiding sleeves support the user during the transport phase of an assembly task by means of a wireframe animation of the assembly path

Sensitive Polygons Sensitive polygons are created before simulation start and positioned at adequate positions on object surfaces. A function can be assigned to every sensitive polygon, which is automatically called when an interactively guided element collides with the sensitive polygon. We have designed sensitive polygons primarily to support the user during the coarse positioning phase of an assembly task. Among others, the polygons can be used to constraint the degrees of freedom for interactively guided objects. For instance, a sensitive polygon positioned at the port of a hole can restrict the motion of a pin to the axial direction of the hole and thus considerably facilitate the assembly task. In case of this classical peg in hole assembly task, MAESTRO creates a copy of the guided object, orientates this copy into the direction of the hole's axis, and switches the original object into a semi-transparent representation (see Fig. 3).

Virtual Magnetism In assembly procedures, it is often necessary to position objects exactly, i.e., parallel to each other at arbitrary locations, without leaving any space between them. Since in a virtual environment this task is nearly impossible to accomplish without any artificial support mechanisms, we developed the principle of virtual magnetism. The left part of Fig. 4 illustrates the effect of virtual magnetism on movable objects. As with sensitive polygons, virtual magnetism is an essential component of the the knowledge-based modeling of virtual objects' behaviour. In contrast to PBM and the other support mechanisms, a user must actively initiate it during the simulation, e.g., by a speech command.

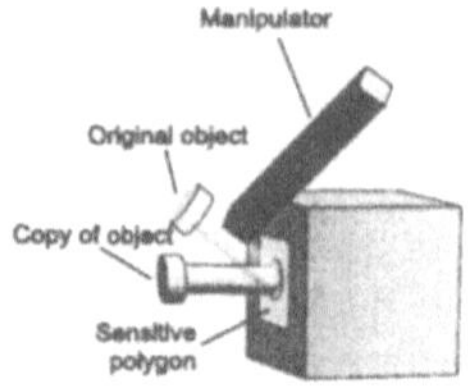

Fig. 3. Use of a sensitive polygon to facilitate the peg in hole assembly task

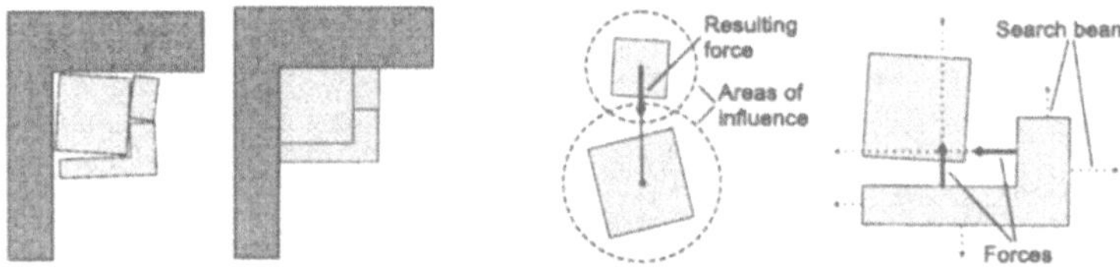

Fig. 4. Effect of virtual magnetism (left), and force components based on object distance and object surfaces

Before simulation start, an object's influence radius is calculated as a function of its volume. Whenever two of such influence areas overlap during the simulation, an attraction force is generated that consists of two components (see Fig. 4). The first component is calculated from the distance between the two objects' centers of gravity, and the second component is a function of polygon surfaces. To calculate the second component, a search beam starts from every polygon midpoint into direction of the surface normal. If such a beam intersects with a polygon of the other object, a force directed to the surface normal is created, which is proportional to the distance between the polygons. Finally, the sum of the to force components is applied to move the smaller object towards the larger one.

Snap-In As all other VR-based assembly simulation tools (see section 2), MAESTRO provides a snap-in mechanism for the final phase of an assembly process. The snap-in is activated when position and orientation difference between the guided object and the target location falls below a specific threshold.

5 The MAESTRO Prototype

Hardware Recently, we have accomplished a first prototype of MAESTRO, in which the force feedback system is a crucial component. We are using the PHANToM 1.5 from Sensable Technolgies [7], allowing a six degrees of freedom input and a simple force vector as output. Due to the rather small interaction volume of the PHANToM, we had to choose an indirect interaction paradigm, where the pencil-like manipulator ("gimbal") of the PHANToM is represented by a graphical counterpart in the VE (see Fig. 5), whose motions are adequately scaled. The PHANToM is connected to a PC that sends position and orientation data to and receives force data from the simulation computer via a 100 MHz Fast Ethernet.

In principle, MAESTRO can work together with any immersive display technology. In combination with the PHANToM, a table-like display is more suitable than a HMD or a fully immersive display like the CAVE. To accomplish the evaluation of the system (see next section), we visualized the scene on a display consisting of a horizontal and a vertical projection surface ("TAN HoloBench", see Fig. 5).

To facilitate interaction, we have furthermore integrated speech recognition that allows the user to pick up and release virtual objects, or to activate support mechanisms like snap-in or virtual magnetism, by a few simple speech commands.

So far, MAESTRO has been implemented on a Sun Microsystems E450 (2 Expert3D graphics boards) and on a SGI Onyx2 (1 Infinite Reality graphics pipe) workstation, both capable of driving a HoloBench in stereo mode.

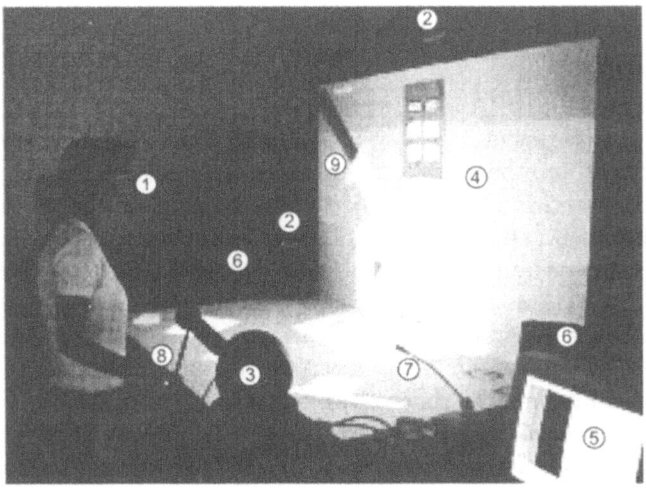

Fig. 5. Hardware setup of the MAESTRO assembly simulation system 1: Shutter glasses with receiver of electro-magnetic tracking system, 2: Infrared emitter for shutter synchronisation, 3: PHANToM Haptic Device, 4: Immersive display "HoloBench", 5: PC with haptics server and speech recognition software, 6: Stereo loudspeakers, 7: Microphone for speech recognition 8: Gimbal 9: Graphical representation of the gimbal with attached virtual object

Software MAESTRO is based on the cross platform VR software ViSTA (Virtual Reality Software University of Technology Aachen [12]) and is subdivided into three parallel processes: The graphical process is responsible for processing speech commands, applying interaction mechanisms, and rendering of the scene. It is typically running at a frequency of 30 Hz. The PBM process processes sensor values, force vectors and impulse information, recognizes collisions, and calculates physically plausible collision reactions with a sample rate of at least 250 Hz. Both processes run on different processors of the simulation computer and communicate with each other via shared memory. Finally, the haptics process runs on the PC at an update rate of 1200 Hz and communicates via UDP protocol with the simulation computer.

6 Evaluation

In order to evaluate the MAESTRO prototype, we have carried out experiments that are documented in detail in [8]. Two of these experiments shall be introduced and discussed here, with regard to effectiveness and user acceptance of the artificial support mechanisms, force feedback, and physically-based modeling. 12 right-handed subjects in the age of 24 to 31 participated at the experiments. They were asked to complete the required manipulation tasks quickly and accurately.

6.1 Experiment 1

The setup of experiment 1 is shown in Fig. 6. Two large and two small nails must be brought into the corresponding holes of a virtual block. The experiment consists of 3 phases: In phase 1, subjects had to complete the task in a "native" virtual environment, i.e., based on the 3-D visualization of the scene without any further modeling or feedback techniques. In phases 2 and 3 they were supported by guiding sleeves and sensitive polygons, respectively. Every phase was carried out twice. During the first trial, objects snapped in as far as the subject placed them into the target position below a certain tolerance. The trial ended when all objects snapped in, and the time subjects needed for completion of the task was measured. The second trial was interrupted automatically after a fixed amount of time, and the mismatches between the actual and the required object target positions were documented.

Results The results of experiment 1 show a significant time benefit with guiding sleeves in comparison to a native VE, and in turn a significant benefit when using sensitive polygons instead of guiding sleeves. In trial 2, the positions of the nails are significantly more exact for guiding sleeves than for native VEs (see Fig. 7). The subjects' judgement of task difficulty and quality of the user interface confirm the quantitative results (see Fig. 8). The snap-in mechanism has great importance with regard to the judgement of task difficulty. In case the snap-in is not available, e.g., because the target position of an object is not known, subjects judge the manipulation task as more difficult. In such cases, test persons regard the mechanisms of sensitive polygons and virtual magnetism as a useful alternative.

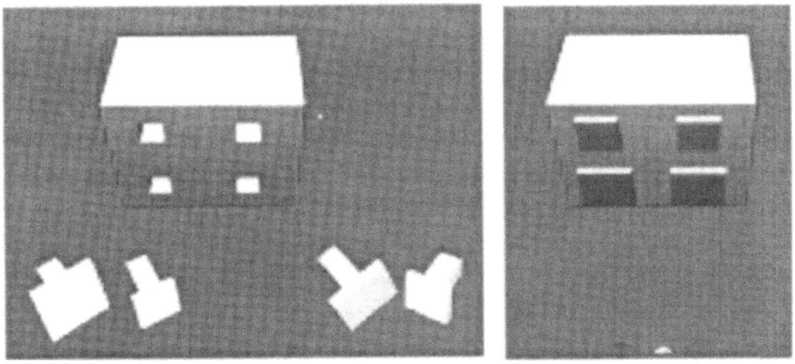

Fig. 6. Setup of experiment 1 – start (left) and target position (right) of virtual nails

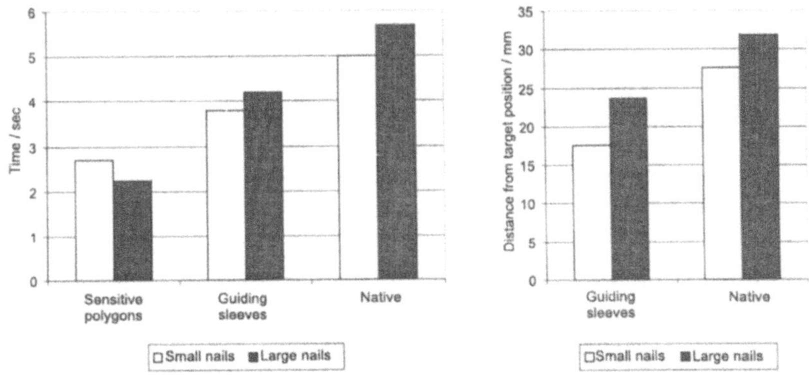

Fig. 7. Quantitative results of experiment 1 – placing virtual nails into a block. The left diagram shows the average amount of time needed until snap-in, the right diagram shows the average distance to the target position six seconds after start of the experiment.

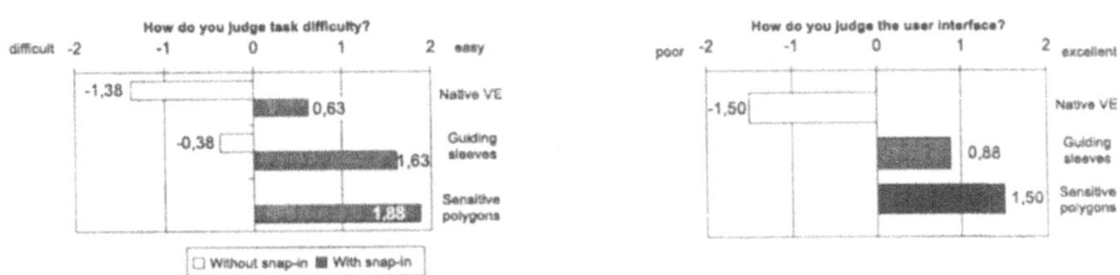

Fig. 8. Average judgement of task difficulty and user interface for experiment 1

6.2 Experiment 2

Figure 9 depicts the setup of experiment 2. Here, three virtual elements in form of the letters I, L, and T, have to be positioned into a frame. Again, the experiment consists of three phases. In the first phase, subjects had to complete the task in a native VE, where collisions between a letter and the frame are optically signaled by a wireframe presentation of the letter. During the second phase, the subjects were supported by haptic feedback. Finally, in the third phase, the subjects were asked to move the letters above their target positions and let them fall into the frame. The falling procedure, as well as the behaviour of the objects when touching the frame, have been physically modeled.

Fig. 9. Setup of experiment 2 – start situation (left) of virtual letters (I, L, T), and target position (right) in a virtual frame

Results A major result of experiment 2 is that the test persons had severe difficulties to complete the task in a native VE. They needed a dramatically larger amount of time than with support of haptics or PBM to position letter I. For letters L and T, it was even impossible to complete the task (see Fig. 10). An interview with the subjects revealed that in a native VE, they were not able to comprehend why and where exactly a collision appeared. As a consequence, they did not change their assembly strategy in a well directed manner and, instead, followed a trial and error principle, resulting in significant longer interaction times.

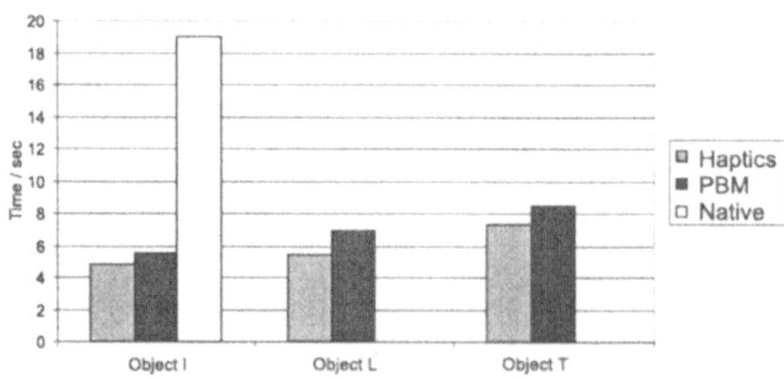

Fig. 10. Quantitative results of experiment 2 – placing virtual objects I, L, and T into a frame. The diagram shows the average amount of time needed until snap-in.

As in experiment 1, the subjects' judgements confirm the quantitative results. Both, haptic feedback as well as PBM, got a positive rating, although the test persons clearly preferred the haptic support to complete the task (see Fig. 11). Nearly all subjects praised the intuitive haptic representation of collisions. Furthermore, they pointed out that the simulated gravitational forces had a stabilizing effect onto their hand-arm-system. In a detailed judgement, haptics and PBM were nearly identically considered as important, realistic, helpful, and non-distracting (see Fig. 12).

Fig. 11. Average judgement of task difficulty and user interface for experiment 2

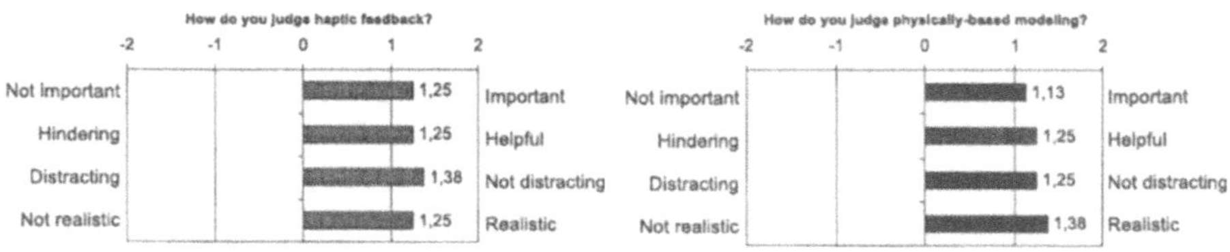

Fig. 12. Average judgement of haptic feedback and physically-based modeling (PBM)

7 Future Work

Since MAESTRO starts from the polygonal representation of a scene which can easily be exported from most CAD systems, and since most parameters needed for object behaviour, haptics, and artificial support mechanisms are calculated automatically before simulation start, MAESTRO is more flexible than most other assembly simulation systems. This benefit of a high flexibility comes along with the drawback, that MAESTRO can only handle virtual scenes of rather low complexity. The collision detection update rate is crucial to the quality of physically-based modeling and the stability of haptics. Since in MAESTRO, collision detection and all modeling are based on the polygonal object representation, the system performance is very sensitive to the number of polygons in the scene. In order to make MAESTRO applicable to assembly simulation scenarios that are relevant for industrial applications, we are working on the integration of improved collision detection algorithms and on a comprehensive parallelization of the MAESTRO software architecture.

The MAESTRO prototype makes use of a force feedback device that merely produces a force vector. However, for many manipulation tasks it is desirable to adequately present torques or even to stimulate the whole hand-arm system.

The MAESTRO algorithms are prepared for that, and in the meanwhile, haptic devices are available and should be integrated into the prototype, which produce six degrees of freedom forces.

Besides graphics and haptics, 3-D acoustics could furthermore improve the realism of an interactive assembly process and lead to a better user performance and acceptance. Therefore, we just started to work on an integration of binaural acoustics technology into MAESTRO. Here, we follow an innovative approach that is based on only two loudspeakers, producing a stable binaural sound even when the user moves in front of the HoloBench.

A considerable extension of MAESTRO's functionality is still necessary to make it attractive for real life industrial applications. Future versions of MAESTRO should allow bimanual interaction, the use of virtual tools like screwdrivers and wrenches, and provide a real-time, realistic modeling of deformable objects. Furthermore, it is highly desirable to establish a bidirectional interface between MAESTRO and product data management systems (PDMs) in order to integrate VR-based assembly simulation into the overall production process.

References

1. Heger, R.: Entwicklung eines Systems zur interaktiven Gestaltung und Auswertung von manuellen Montagetätigkeiten in der virtuellen Realität. Springer-Verlag, Berlin (1998)
2. Gausemeier, J., Grafe, M., Wortmann, R.: Interactive Planning of Manufacturing Systems with Virtual Construction Sets. 24th Annual Conference of the IEEE Industrial Electronics Society IECON '98, Aachen (1998) 2146–2151
3. Jung, B., Lenzmann, B., Wachsmuth, I.: Interaktive Montage-Simulation mit wissensbasierter Grafik. ASIM Mitteilungen **49** (1995) 20–32
4. Jayaram, S., Jayaram, U., Wang, Y., Tirumali, H., Lyons, K., Hart, P.: VADE: A Virtual Assemby Design Environment. IEEE Computer Graphics & Applications **19(6)** (1999) 44–50
5. Buck, M.: Simulation interaktiv bewegter Objekte mit Hinderniskontakten. PhD thesis, Universität des Saarlandes (1999)
6. Gupta, R., Sheridan, T., Whitney, D.: Experiments on using Multimodal Virtual Environments for Design for Assembly Analysis. Presence **6(3)** (1997) 318–338
7. Massie, T.H., Salisbury, J.: The PHANToM Haptic Interface: A Device for Probing Vitual Objects. Symposium on Haptic Interfaces for Virtual Environment and Teleoperator Systems, Chicago (1994) 295–302
8. Steffan, R.: Multimodale Interaktionstechniken für die Simulation von Montagevorgängen in virtuellen Umgebungen. PhD thesis, Aachen University of Technology (2001)
9. Baraff, D.: Dynamic Simulation of Non-Penetrating Rigid Bodies. PhD thesis, Cornell University (1992)
10. Baraff, D., Witkin, A.: Physically-Based Modeling: Principles and Practice. ACM SIGGRAPH 1997 Course Notes, Los Angeles (1997)
11. Mirtich, B.: Impulse-Based Dynamic Simulation of Rigid Body Systems. PhD thesis, University of California, Berkeley (1996)
12. van Reimersdahl, T., Kuhlen, T., Gerndt, A., Henrichs, J., Bischof, C.: ViSTA – a multimodal, platform-independant VR-toolkit based on WTK, VTK, and MPI. Fourth International Immersive Projection Technology Workshop, Ames (2000)

Spelunking: Experiences using the DIVE System on CAVE-like Platforms

Anthony Steed and Jesper Mortensen
Department of Computer Science
University College London
Gower Street, London, UK.

Emmanuel Frécon
Swedish Institute of Computer Science
Box 1263
S-164 29 Kista, Sweden.

Abstract

The Distributed Interactive Virtual Environment (DIVE) system is a mature toolkit that has been used for prototyping many collaborative virtual environment (CVE) applications [3]. Until recently, support for immersive systems has been limited to custom support for specific installations and the emphasis has been on broad support for desktop interfaces. Recently we have ported DIVE to the CAVElib™ environment† and this paper describes application programming support for immersive users and our experience in using wide-area distributed applications involving immersive projection technologies. The resulting toolkit provides a very flexible system with which to build distributed VE applications involving a variety of platforms and interfaces.

Keywords: Distributed virtual environments, virtual reality toolkits, immersive systems.

1 Introduction

One of the key requirements for the next generation of collaborative virtual environment (CVE) toolkits will be broad support of a variety of platforms from desktop through to immersive projection technologies (IPTs). Today there is a plethora of CVE toolkits boasting easy reconfiguration, broad support for devices, object-orientated programming paradigms, etc. In this paper we discuss the evolution of a mature CVE toolkit, DIVE, to support IPT displays. DIVE brings a number of useful facilities to the IPT programmer and although it does not pretend to be a replacement for low-level libraries, we suggest the framework it provides will be very useful for users wishing to prototype or explore CVE applications. In this paper we outline how DIVE has been extended to support IPTs through integration of the CAVElib™ library and we discuss some experiences of using DIVE over wide-area networks involving a variety of desktop and IPT systems.

† CAVELib is a registered trademark of the University of Illinois.

In Section 2 we give and overview of the DIVE system and in Section 3 explain how we have extended this to support IPTs. Section 4 discusses our experience in using the DIVE/CAVElib™ port in network trials and in Section 5 we discuss some distinctions between DIVE and other CVE toolkits and our plans for future work.

2 DIVE System Overview

2.1 System Services

At the conceptual and programming level, DIVE is based on a hierarchical database of objects, termed *entities*. Applications operate solely on the database abstraction and do not communicate directly with one another. This technique allows a clean separation between application and network interfaces. Thus, programming will not differ when writing single-user applications or multi-user applications running over the Internet. This model has proven to be successful; DIVE has changed its inter-process communication package three times since the first version in 1991, and existing applications did not require any redesign.

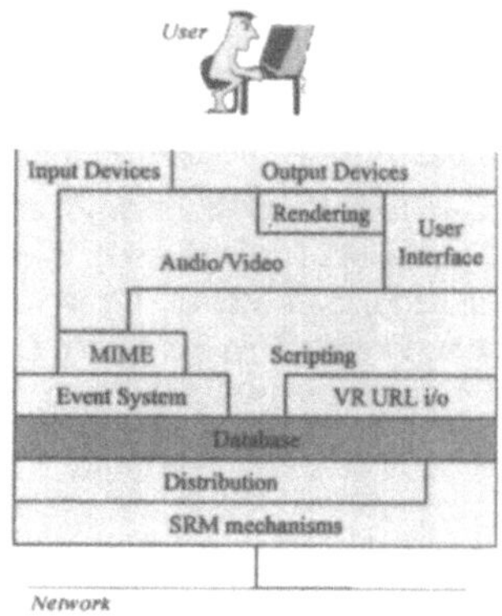

Figure 1. The different components that compose the DIVE system.

While the hierarchical model is inherited from traditional scene graphs, as used in the computer graphics community the DIVE database is semantically richer. For example, it contains structures for storing information about other users, or non-geometric data specific to a particular application. In DIVE, the database is partially replicated at all participating nodes, with a top-down approach, i.e. mechanisms are offered to control the replication of sub-branches of a given entity.

In DIVE, an event system realises the operations and modifications that occur within the database. Consequently, all operations on entities such as material modifications or transformations will generate events to which applications can react. Additionally, there are spontaneous and user-driven events such as collision between objects or user interaction with input devices. An interesting feature of the event system is its support of high-level application-specific events, enabling applications to define their content and utilisation. This enables several processes composing of the same application (or a set of applications) to exchange any kind of information using their own protocol.

A few events are local to each process, e.g. rendering events. However, most events occurring within the system will generate network updates that completely describe them. Other connected peers that hold a replica of the concerned entities will be able to apply the described modification unambiguously. Network messages are propagated using the multicast mechanisms that are built in the system. DIVE uses a variation of SRM (scalable reliable multicast [2]) to control the transmission of updates and ensure the consistency of the database at all connected peers. The SRM approach requires the transport layer to be able to ask DIVE applications to regenerate updates if necessary. Update regeneration is necessary when gaps are discovered in the sequence numbers that are associated to every entity of the database. Gaps imply that network messages must have been lost along the path from a sender to one of its receivers. A thorough description of DIVE's networking mechanisms can be found in [3]. In addition to SRM, extensions to DIVE make it possible to access any document using more common Internet network protocols such as HTTP and FTP, and to integrate these documents within the environment by recognising their media types, such as VRML.

In any application, the content of the database must be initialised. DIVE uses a module that manages several three-dimensional formats and translates them into the internal data structures that best represent their content. Usually only one peer will load, and parse, a particular file and the resulting entity hierarchy will be distributed to other connected peers through a series of (multicast) updates that describe the resulting entities. This specific mechanism differs from many other systems that rely on being able to access the description files from all connected peers.

DIVE has an embedded scripting language that provides an interface to most of the services of the platform. This language is a superset of the Tool Command Language (TCL) [9] and is called DIVE/TCL. Scripts register an interest in, and are triggered by, events that occur within the system. They will usually react by modifying the state of the shared database. Moreover, these modifications can lead to other events, which will possibly trigger additional scripts. There are numerous commands; they allow the logic of the scripts to gather information from the database, decide on the correct sequence of actions and modify the state of the database accordingly. The completeness and simplicity of the scripting interface have made it the programming interface of choice for most applications developed in DIVE.

The DIVE run-time environment consists of a set of communicating processes, running on nodes distributed within both local and wide-area networks. The processes, representing either human users or autonomous applications, have access to a number of databases, which they update concurrently. As described earlier, each database contains a number of abstract descriptions of graphical objects that, together, constitute a virtual world. A typical DIVE application will, upon connection to a virtual world, introduce a set of objects to the environment that will serve as its user-interface and start listening to events and react accordingly. One essential application of the system is the 3-D browser, called *vishnu*. *Vishnu* is the application that gives its user a presence within the environment. It introduces a new entity called an actor to the shared environment, which is the virtual representation of the real user.

2.2 User-Oriented Services

The services described previously are independent of any DIVE application. This section focuses on the different modules present within the vishnu application that render a visual and aural space and provide the users with an interface that allows them to explore and interact with this space.

The primary display module is the graphical renderer. Traditionally, the rendering module traverses the database hierarchy and draws the scene from the viewpoint of the user. This module provides for geometry and material types beyond those found in common scene description languages. Additionally, some constant frame rate techniques allows for the rendering of environments that are both large in extent and deep in details, see [7].

DIVE has integrated audio and video facilities. Audio and video streams between participants are distributed using unreliable multicast communication. Audio streams are spatialised so as to build a soundscape, where the perceived output of an audio source is a function of the distance to the source, the inter-aural distance and the direction of the source. The audio module supports mono-, stereo- or quadri-phony audio rendering through speakers or headphones connected to the workstation. Input can be taken from microphones or from audio sample files referenced by a URL. Similarly, the video module takes its input from cameras connected to the workstations or video files referenced by URLs. Video streams can either be presented to remote users in separate windows or onto textures within the rendered environment.

Users are generally also presented with a two- dimensional interface that offers access to rendering, collaboration and editing facilities. The interface itself is written using the same scripting language as offered by the world database. Consequently, CVE applications can dynamically query and modify the appearance of the 2D interface.

Finally, a MIME (Multimedia Internet Mail Extensions) module is provided to better integrate with external resources. It automatically interprets external URLs. For example, an audio stream will be forwarded onto the audio module where it will be mixed into the final soundscape.

3 Immersion Support

Previously DIVE had custom support for a small number of immersive devices to satisfy the needs of the authors. These include drivers for Ascension Flock of Birds, Polhemus IsoTrak and Fastrak and a variety of head-mounted displays. To enable support of IPTs such as CAVE™s† we have implemented a DIVE application framework that interfaces to the CAVElib™ library. The resulting application was named *spelunk*. It differs from the standard *vishnu* application in that the renderer is written in Performer rather than OpenGL and there is an extra module for interaction which we called the spelunk vehicle.

† CAVE is a trademark of the Board of Trustees of the University of Illinois.

3.1 Performer Renderer

There are implementations of the DIVE renderer for many rendering toolkits, but primary amongst these in terms of stability and functionality was the OpenGL renderer. In the COVEN project we had done extensive work on this renderer to enable scalability to very large models [7].

The choice of porting the rendering module to Performer was motivated by two major reasons. Performer is a well-designed piece of rendering software that has existed for many years. As a result, it implements a number of optimisations that DIVE will be able to benefit from, at the expense of not being able to modify and control the rendering techniques that are used. Furthermore, each Performer viewport uses a number of pre-emptive threads, as opposed to DIVE, which relies on non-preemptive threads only. Consequently, Performer makes better use of "monster" architectures by being able to place concurrent threads on several CPUs and several rendering pipelines, whenever available and applicable.

The standard OpenGL renderer was written in an immediate mode style, with each object type within the database having a different callback. The Performer renderer is written in a very different manner; it builds a Performer scene-graph when objects are created within the local database and updates them only when necessary. Fortunately the DIVE event mechanism allows us to easily obtain notification when any change affecting the appearance or form of an object occurs. We maintain the DIVE scene graph for the purposes of efficient event recreation and to support the other modules apart from rendering, such as navigation and collision detection, which require the complete geometrical description.

Some of our scalability work on the OpenGL renderer was in optimisations such as optimising triangle strips, re-ordering objects to optimise OpenGL state changes and compiling display lists. These replicate functionality built-in to Performer so we have not duplicated the effort. Functionality that is harder to replicate in Performer and is the subject of future work, are extensions to cope with massive worlds that contain many more objects than can be rendered in real-time. At the moment the Performer renderer adaptively changes the far clip distance if a frame rate target is significantly over-run by the rendering processes.

3.2 Spelunk Vehicle

A vehicle is a collection of interaction techniques and methods that respond to input events and effect locomotion, selection and manipulation within the environment. Vehicles are also commonly responsible for manipulating the pose of the avatar to reflect input. For example they may draw rays, or animate a gait pattern. Many vehicles have been implemented covering the range from keyboard and X event input through virtual widget vehicles that lie on a heads-up display, to vehicles that rely on 3D tracker information. Multiple vehicles can be activated simultaneously, though some are mutually exclusive, and not all vehicles make sense in all contexts.

For spelunk we implemented a vehicle that interfaces to the tracker input facilities of CAVElib™. The vehicle registers a callback on a local PRE_FRAME DIVE event.

The callback reads both the current tracker positions and the state of the buttons and joystick and effects interaction.

The first responsibility of the vehicle is to effect locomotion, manipulation and selection. Locomotion is a matter of changing the world co-ordinates of the avatar. Each avatar is a direct child of the root in the world's scene graph so this process is simple. We must simultaneously alter the mapping within CAVElib™ from physical co-ordinate to world modelling co-ordinates. Selection is usually effected on a button press. The default method is selection at a distance. DIVE has built-in support for ray based intersection as well as full object-object collision detection. By default, manipulation is simple attachment of the selected object to the position of the user's hand. We implement this by dynamically re-parenting the selected object under the user's hand in the scene graph.

The second responsibility of the vehicle is to animate the avatar. In DIVE avatar representation is independent of the application and users may specify a default avatar they wish to use for every session or can specify an avatar on the command line whilst starting up. It is also possible to dynamically change the avatar at run-time. It is usual for the tracker information for head and hand positions to be reflected in the position of graphical representations of the head and hands. We also provide an optional animation that can articulate the arms of tracked hands and also body to provide a more anthropomorphic-looking avatar.

The vehicle responds to several configuration variables, including default vehicle speed, mapping of wand buttons to actions, joystick dead-zone and rotation speed scaling. Configuration variables can be changed from module and plugin C/C++ code, and TCL code associated with the interface or objects in the current world.

Internally the spelunk vehicle relies on its own callback registration mechanism. The vehicle was designed this way to allow easy extension of the spelunk vehicle to support other interaction techniques. Thus plugins can register and over-ride callbacks on different CAVElib™ events. We have used this for example to build a plugin that over-rides the default spelunk selection metaphor of "selection at distance" to the "go-go" interaction technique [5]. Note that because plugin can register TCL functions, and since the spelunk menu system is built in TCL/TK we were able to dynamically change the spelunk menus to add options to change the behaviour of the go-go technique at run time. We used this mechanism to have the plugin optionally provide menus to configure the threshold and scaling factors associated with the go-go technique.

3.3 Desktop & Immersive Menu Interfaces

A DIVE application may or may not create a user interface when it starts up. Most DIVE applications are linked with TCL/TK so as to provide scripting of objects within worlds and thus it is natural to use TCL/TK to build a user interface. TCL/TK desktop DIVE applications such as *vishnu* will build a TCL/TK window structure and then delegate rendering of particular windows to the renderer by passing it a window context. An example of the *allinone* application's interface is shown in Figure 2 (*allinone* is a variant of the *vishnu* application). The *allinone* interface allows access to a very wide range of functionality: world and object loading, scene graph editing, avatar loading, system configuration (including audio, video, network behaviour), object editing, text and audio chat groups, subjective views and world, bookmark and viewpoint menus and participant activity summary. The main *allinone* window contains a menu and location bar at the top, rendering window below that, and viewpoint, participant and text-chat panes surrounding the rendering window.

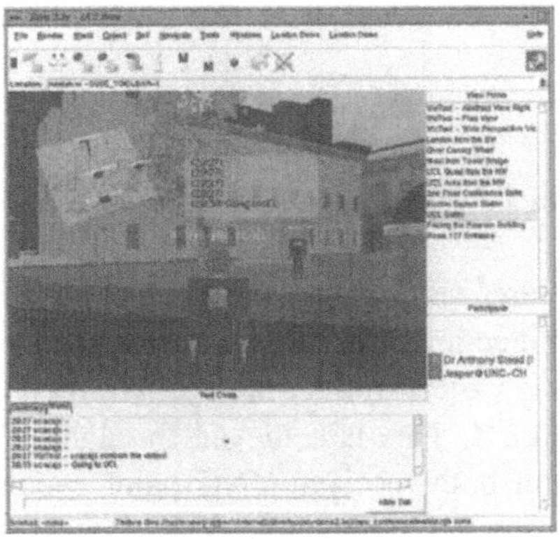

Figure 2. *allinone* desktop interface to the *vishnu* application

With the spelunk application we build a user interface on start-up and display it to a user-specified display. The spelunk interface consists simply of the menu and location bars from *allinone*, though the viewpoint, participant and text chat windows as still available. Keyboard input in still active so a person sat at the console can drive the user around independently of the joystick controls. Note also there are also other 2D widget based vehicles that can be used, the viewport menu allows the console user to teleport the immersed user about and the participant window allows teleportation to other users. This functionality is very useful when demonstrating immersive systems in network situations.

Of particular interest within the spelunk menus is the *Navigate* menu that allows access to control features of various vehicles. This allows us to enable and disable vehicles at run-time and control parameters of the vehicle by through the DIVE/TCL APIs or by setting configuration parameters. For example for the CAVElib™ vehicle the spelunk menu allows the console user to change the velocity, planar constraints, button control mapping, direction of motion and collision detection response.

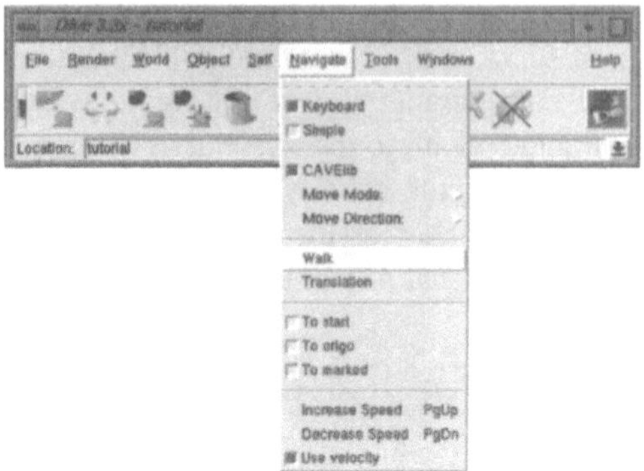

Figure 3. Spelunk menu system displayed to a desktop

These console menus therefore give the console user significant power to modify the world and the user's interaction with the world at run-time. To enable world editing work within IPT systems we can reflect the spelunk menus onto surfaces within the world as shown in Figure 4. This is achieved through a DIVE plugin that acts as a VNC† client. The plugin both receives VNC paint events and maps selection and manipulation events on the 3D surface into VNC input requests. To enable this, the spelunk menus are displayed to a VNC server rather than an X display, though it is possible to access the menus simultaneously from desktop and IPT by using a standard X or Windows VNC client as well as the DIVE plugin VNC client.

Figure 4. Using spelunk menus within the UCL ReaCTor

4 Distribution Support and Network Trials

We have used the desktop and custom immersive versions of DIVE for several years on collaborative projects. With the new CAVElib™ port we have been able to very rapidly bring our new IPT systems into these collaborative trials and perform trials

† Virtual Networking Computing, AT&T Laboratories Cambridge, available from http://www.uk.research.att.com/vnc/

and experiments using a variety of platforms. DIVE is a very useful platform for prototyping CVE applications since it takes a world-centric program approach, with individual worlds being constructed from a collection of standard sources such as VRML97 files, with behaviour being scripted in TCL/TK. The actual client applications change very little, and then usually only through initialisation time configuration through plugins. Note object behaviour scripts can check for the existence of a plugin and can alter their behaviour accordingly or warning the user that certain functionality will be disabled.

Given the interpreted nature of world programming, it is very simple for us to interactively edit a world in a distributed manner. A common editing practice is to load a world on both the IPT system and a desktop machine. The immersed user can enter the world, whilst the desktop user interactively edits the world with immediate effect on the immersed user's experience. Furthermore through DIVE/TCL programmers can remotely access interface and plugin functionality on other clients and can use this to reconfigure clients as necessary. Example uses of this is to dynamically add or delete items from the heads-up display of other users (e.g. the miniature map in Figure 2), or force them to re-align to world coordinates if they get lost.

4.1 DIVEBONE

Distribution in DIVE is based around multicast communications. For networks where multicast is not available, DIVE supports an application level bridge called the DIVEBONE [4]. A process called *proxyserver* can listen on multicast groups and transmit packets in a unicast manner. DIVE processes (including other proxyservers) can then connect directly to the unicast port on the proxyserver. Typically this might be used to connect together multicast "islands". We use this mechanism extensively in the trials described in the following two sections.

4.2 Internet2

As part of the Collaboration in Tele-Immersive Environments project funded by UKERNA we have been testing DIVE over transatlantic experimental academic networks. Our interest in these tests has been to investigate requirements for effective communication in virtual worlds. In these trials we are collaborating with laboratories at MIT (Massachussetts Institute of Technology) and UNC-CH (University of North Carolina Chapel Hill). Figure 5 illustrates the network setup in these trials.

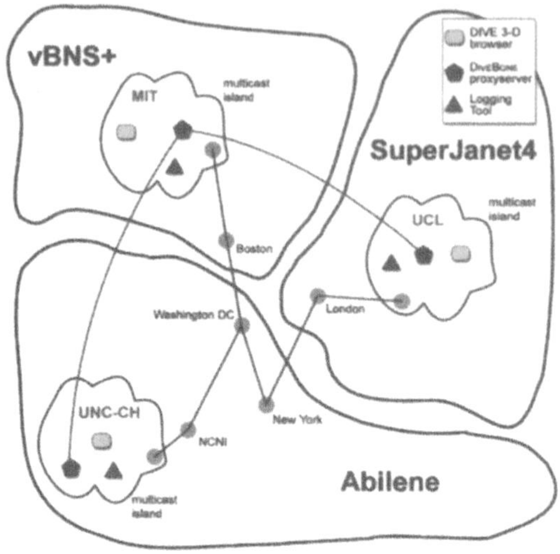

Figure 5. Network topology

Approximately eight afternoon trials have been held so far using a variety of models with aural communication. We use the DIVEBONE to connect together three multicast pools, one at each site. We have used a variety of machines, including Windows NT3.5 & 2000 and SGI O2 in desktop mode, SGI Onyx2 at UCL driving the ReaCTor and SGI Onyx2 at UNC-CH driving HMD's. Over this test-bed we get very stable round-trip times of ~130ms on average and ~90ms at best from UCL to UNC-CH (and similar RTT's to MIT). In our situation the gross bandwidth is not an issue except at model load time. Network performance analyses on the 14 hop path between UCL and UNC-CH (using pchar†) have shown that the bottleneck in this setup is the 10Mbps LAN link between the Onyx2 driving the ReaCTor at UCL and the external Cisco router at UCL and the sustained bandwidth achieved in tests is ~7.4Mbps between these two sites (similar performance between UCL and MIT). We have experimented using the London Traveller application [7] between these sites without any difficulty (see Figure 2). This model is ~107MB and is loaded across the transatlantic link in ~2 mins.

The low latency and absence of significant jitter means that collaboration between the sites is very natural. We plan to continue these trials looking at requirements for latency and jitter for visual, audio and haptic interaction.

4.3 ReaCTor to VR-CUBE

As part of a collaboration between UCL and Chalmers Technical University, Gothenburg, Sweden, we have been running a series of trials between two IPT systems. The IPT system at Chalmers is a TAN VR-CUBE consisting of four walls and a floor driven from a 14 processor Onyx with 3 InfiniteReality2 pipes. Tracking is

---

† pchar is written by Bruce A. Mah of Cisco Systems, it is based on the algorithms of the pathchar utility written by Van Jacobson, formerly of Lawrence Berkeley Laboratories.

done with Polhemus Fastrak and there is a tracked Wanda controller.

We installed spelunk on the Chalmers VR-CUBE in early October 2000. The only configuration required beyond normal DIVE installation was an adjustment of the dead-zone for the joystick. We tested several simple applications between the two sites and between mid-October and early-December we ran 7 afternoons of experiments using spelunk.

The network situation between UCL and Chalmers was very different to the Internet2 trials. Again the DIVEBONE was used to connect the sites together. This time UCL ran a proxyserver and Chalmers connected directly to this over a unicast connection. This allowed UCL to monitor activity by adding a desktop user as a 3rd client. The desktop user had an invisible avatar so the participants were not aware of their presence. Network latency varied between ping times of 160 and 380ms. Users did not notice any lag in the animation of the avatars, though when jitter was high occasional drop outs in audio occurred.

The experimental situation was similar to that reported in [8] with two users collaborating in the solution of a cube assembly puzzle. Our initial results indicate that collaboration between users of IPT systems is much more fluid and natural than either collaboration between IPT system and desktop or between two desktop users. Setting up and controlling the experiment was much more simple than our experience with running distributed experiments with other CVE toolkits [6]. The experimental scenario was ported from a different CVE toolkit in two ½ day sessions, one of which was a collaborative review to investigate different lighting effects and avatar representations.

5 Discussion

5.1 Comparison to Other Toolkits

DIVE provides two principle levels at which to program: custom C/C++ applications using the DIVE core libraries and C/C++ plugin based extension of one of the standard processes in combination with world files and interpreted DIVE/TCL scripts.

Most CVE toolkits that support IPT displays such as VRJuggler [1] support the former paradigm. Thus a CVE is set up between custom applications, and the CVE toolkit provides a framework for building such applications. Although DIVE does support many of the same library facilities as recent toolkits, it was not primarily designed to be used this way. However the plugin interface goes a long way to providing the types of initialisation-time extension that is required by most programmers, and the scripting interface encourages programmers to think about writing plugins that provide services that can be exposed through the DIVE/TCL scripting interface rather than build monolithic applications.

DIVE's origins were in workstation based 3D applications for distribution over wide area networks. Thus two areas are well developed: desktop interfaces and multicast networking. As has been discussed in previous section support for desktop interfaces is very wide, with run-time reconfiguration of interfaces being exploited in many applications. The multicast support is also mature, with support for real-time audio and video transmission as well sharing of the world-database.

5.2 Future Work

The current version of DIVE including CAVElib™ support will be available shortly from http://www.sics.se/dive/ as version 3.4x of DIVE. This release will be a maintenance release. A new branch of work, that will probably lead to version 4.0, has now started at SICS. This will focus on general improvements to the internals of DIVE such as an entire rewrite of the database and event system and moving many of the current modules in to plugins that will be dynamically loaded as required at run-time.

DIVE's focus on multicast networking does mean that currently it is not well suited to large-volume data visualisation problems. Currently the database is geometry centric, with bulk transfer of data taking place over ftp or http. This is being addressed in a number of manners. First the internal database and renderer are being re-engineered for more generic object type support. Second we are investigating model transfer protocols that take into account pre-computed visibility within the models. We will also revisit the issue of scalability support in scenes where there are many more objects in the scene than can be rendered at a reasonable frame-rate at any level of detail.

References

1. Bierbaum, A., "VR Juggler: A Virtual Platform for Virtual Reality Application Development". MS Thesis, Iowa State University, 2000.
2. Floyd, S., Jacobson, V., Liu, C., McCanne, S. & Zhang, L. (1997). "A Reliable Multicast Framework for Light-weight Sessions and Application Level Framing", *IEEE/ACM Transactions on Networking*, 5(6), 784-803.
3. Frécon E., Stenius M., "DIVE: A Scaleable network architecture for distributed virtual environments", Distributed Systems Engineering Journal (special issue on Distributed Virtual Environments), Vol. 5, No. 3, Sept. 1998, pp. 91-100. See also *http://www.sics.se/dive*
4. Frécon, E., Greenhalgh, C. & Stenius, M. (1999), "The DIVEBONE - An Application-Level Network Architecture for Internet-Based CVEs", *Proceedings of the ACM Symposium on Virtual Reality Software and Technology'99* (pp. 58-65), London, UK: ACM Press.
5. Poupyrev, I., Billinghurst, M., Weghorst, S. and Ichikawa, T. (1996). "The Go-Go Interaction Technique: Non-Linear Mapping for Direct Manipulation in VR". In Proceedings of ACM Symposium on User Interface Software and Technology (UIST '96), pp. 79-80.
6. Slater, M., Sadagic, A., Usoh, M. and Schroeder, R. "Small Group Behaviour in a Virtual and Real Environment: A Comparative Study". Presence: Teleoperators and Virtual Environments. 9(1), 37-51, 2000
7. Steed, A., Frécon, E., Avatare-Nöu, A., Pemberton, D. & Smith G. (1999). "The London Travel Demonstrator", *Proceedings of the ACM Symposium on Virtual Reality Software and Technology'99* (pp. 58-65), London, UK: ACM Press.
8. Wideström, J. Abelin, Å. Axelsson, A-S, Nilsson, A., Schroeder, R., "The Collaborative Cube Puzzle: A Comparison of Virtual and Real Environments". CVE 2000, the Third International Conference on Collaborative Virtual Environments. 2000.
9. Ousterhout J. (1994), "TCL and the TK toolkit", Addison-Wesley, ISBN 0-201-63337-X.

Towards a Scalable High Performance Application Platform for Immersive Virtual Environments

Matthias Bues, Roland Blach, Simon Stegmaier, Ulrich Häfner, Hilko Hoffmann, Frank Haselberger

Competence Center Virtual Environments
Fraunhofer Institute for Industrial Engineering (IAO)
Nobelstr. 12, D-70569 Stuttgart, Germany
phone: +49-711-970-2232, fax: +49-711-970-2213
Matthias.Bues@iao.fhg.de
http://vr.iao.fhg.de

Abstract. Software for the development and generation of virtual environments used to run on specialized and expensive hardware. This situation has dramatically changed in the last two years. This paper describes a scalable high performance application platform for immersive environments using commodity hardware. Scalability will be obtained with a coarse cluster of specialized nodes, with emphasis on distributed real-time rendering. As data synchronization method a distributed shared memory approach is used. Dedicated to this hardware setup, a modular component oriented design is presented.

1 Introduction

Virtual Reality (VR), in our understanding, is an interface technology which allows direct multimodal interaction with dynamic and responsive computer generated or so-called virtual environments. Immersive virtual environments (VE's) should operate in real-time and consider the spatial superposition of user and data-environment, that is, the response time and update rate of the system is high enough that it generates an experience of continuity and a perceptible 3D-environment. This requires not only 3D-based real-time computing and render systems but also real-time spatial registration of the user and his behavior.

We see the main purpose of VR-technology in the enhancement of human computer interaction. Especially in problem domains of high complexity the use of immersive virtual environments enables more direct perception and manipulation. Obvious application domains are complex evaluation or planning tasks like architecture or design, medical training, fluid dynamics in engineering, assembly planning, etc..

One of the major obstacles for broader research and development was definitely the usage of specialized and expensive hardware which does not scale adequately. Also network bandwidth restricted the distribution of real-time systems.

Nevertheless there have been various approaches to distributed virtual environments. Common usage were multi-user environments like the DIS/HLA [Kuhl99] based military simulations which focus on large scale multi-user applications. Similar systems are described in [Singhal99] which gives a good overview of the state of the art. Another important domain was the coupling of super-computer-based simulations with immersive visualization systems. But it was not very common to use these distributed systems for single user purposes as an substitute for expensive high end graphic real-time systems.

This has changed dramatically in the last two years. The availability of an open source operating system on commodity hardware platforms with sufficient graphic power has started a serious approach to commodity hardware based VE research and development. On the one hand it promises more fine grained and cost effective scalability as with specialized workstations. On the other hand new bandwidth problems induced by the multi-purpose design of the hardware architecture require new creative solutions for real-time systems. This suggests a design of virtual environment system software closer dedicated to a commodity hardware based computer cluster.

Our target application domain is a single/few user system in a local distributed environment for the sake of pure performance scalability. We do not intend to create large scale networked virtual environments.

2 Conceptual Overview

The choice of the granularity of system components seems to be a crucial factor for the usability on the application development level, as we have experienced with the Lightning VR System [Blach98].

Our approach tries to bundle functionalities to coherent units of hard- and software. These units gain a certain autonomy and independency which makes the whole system more robust and manageable. To spend a complete hardware system for even simple but computationally intense tasks seems to be affordable because of the comparative cheapness of commodity hardware. To achieve this level of independence of the system components an asynchronous approach to communication is necessary.

For many applications, the most important scalability aspect is the scalability of graphics output, ranging from variable channel count of the display environment to scalability of overall graphics throughput, and parallelization of special rendering tasks. A distributed approach combining multiple graphics subsystems on multiple hosts is pursued to overcome the limitations of the PC architecture.

Other important abilities are rapid configuration, run-time access and prototyping of applications where the introduction of an interpreted scripting language has proven useful. Therefore two levels of the application developer interface should be considered:

- A C++ native object extension, to extend the system with a kind of plug-in structure. As long as the shared memory based data pool can be accessed other languages are also conceivable.
- A scripting layer for easy configuration and runtime access.

We will experiment further with a multi-language support. In real world applications obviously only one language will be reasonable. The language of choice must be able to build and maintain larger applications. Our experience with Tcl [Ousterhout93] has shown that it is a very convenient choice for small and medium size applications but seems not to be able to help structuring large scale applications.

3 An Early Prototype: Personal Immersion (Lightning 1.7 distributed)

Commodity hardware like the PC architecture implies some limitations in comparison to classic graphics workstations, namely concerning bus bandwidth, memory bandwidth, and multiprocessor capabilities. A PC-based scalable graphics architecture therefore requires a distributed approach.

A first prototype of a scalable distributed VE System is the Personal Immersion System. Based on the Linux port of Lightning 1.7, it is capable of driving single- or multi-wall immersive projection environments. It is based on a distributed scene graph/application approach. As a result, the network bandwidth needed for synchronization is kept at a minimum, independent of the amount of actual per-frame scene graph updates. Standard 100MBit Ethernet components are used for cluster interconnection. To keep the synchronization of the buffer swaps of each graphics channel as tight as possible, an additional light-weight synchronization using the handshake lines of a serial port is established. One node in the cluster acts as a master; it acquires tracking and input device data and propagates these data to the other hosts in the cluster. Usually, the master node also runs a full application/rendering task. If the data acquisition overhead is considerable, e.g. from computationally intensive calibration tasks, the master can also be fully dedicated to data acquisition and preprocessing.

In current configurations, passive stereo projection is used; a typical single-wall configuration runs on two nodes, each generating one eye view. Each node is equipped with one graphics card, allowing to exploit the immediate-mode throughput of modern PC graphics accelerators to the maximum extent possible. Fig. 1 shows a block diagram of this configuration.

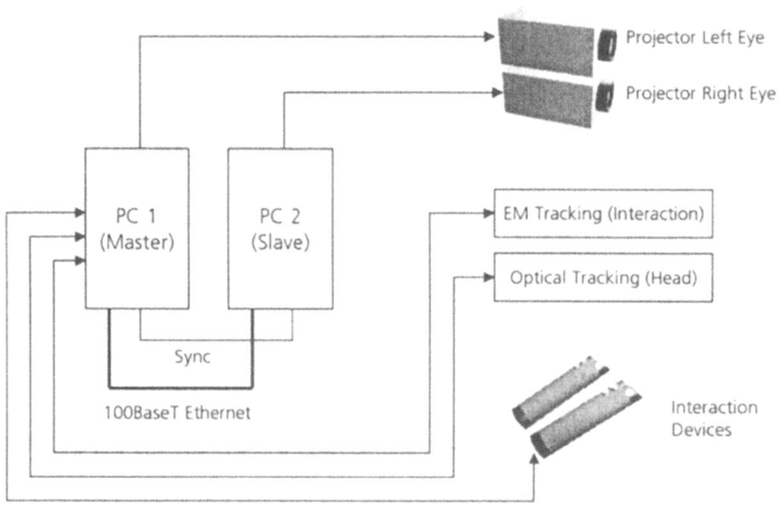

Fig. 1 Personal Immersion configuration

The Personal Immersion System was evaluated in various application environments [IPTW2000], proving its usability being comparable to traditional high-end configurations. Advantage of the approach pursued with Personal Immersion is its compatibility with existing Lightning Applications on high-end platforms. Since the full set of the underlying scene graph API can be used, even applications performing much run-time modification to the scene graph can be ported to the Personal Immersion platform with minimum effort. An application example are immersive surface or volume modeling systems.

Drawbacks are the replication of the computational tasks of the application on each image generator node, which is unnecessary in most cases, and the limited granularity in distribution of image generation and application-side computational tasks.

4 A Scalable Personal Immersion System

4.1 Interactive Core System

The interactive core system is able to model and therefore abstracts all components and the communication behavior of immersive interactive applications in virtual environments. It is in itself a complete system for the definition and description of the interactive behavior of such environments. The specific device or render modules should be as loosely coupled as possible.

The main goal is to achieve a real-time behavior of the application control module with a timing being independent of I/O specific limitations, namely graphics throughput.

Consider the situation that an independent device process is used and that this process is fast enough to register all input events sent by any device subsystem, e.g. a spatial tracking device. A commonly used scene graph API, OpenGL|Performer™, uses a pipelined multiprocessing model consisting of the stages application, cull and draw, each running in a separate process in the full multiprocessing configuration [Rohlf94]. However, theses processes are synchronized at frame boundaries, resulting in the frame rate of the entire system being limited by the process with the longest frame time. Preprocessing of interaction data and application control is performed in the application stage. In practice, this means that in case of heavy graphics load, a double click event can easily be lost. There are two main directions to tackle this problem. A history buffer for input streams can be introduced, from which all events accumulated during the last frame are processed in the current frame. Major drawbacks of this solution are the immanent overflow problem, and the application process frame time still limiting system frame rate. The second way, which is our approach, is to run the application control loop asynchronously from the renderer main loop. [Grimsdale 91] describes a similar method. The application control loop processes the inputs and control related functions in real-time and possible render modules/devices sample the specific system state at a certain time and processes it as fast as possible. This can probably be applied to other function modules, e.g. collision detection or physical simulation.

Although custom solutions for most load balancing problems as described above can be found, these solutions do not apply for the general case.

Concerning control and data flow, we extend the data flow model of the VR system Lightning [Blach98]. So-called Application-Objects hold the main functionality. The state of the system is completely contained in so-called fields which are actually attributes of the Application-Objects. These fields can be linked to other fields or procedurally set from elsewhere. The structure of the linked objects and their behavior describe the application. Every object has a central update function which reads incoming data, processes it and updates the object state. This is similar to other data flow oriented systems as e.g. [VRML97]. We introduced container objects which control other objects and have the possibility to run their own autonomous simulation loop via threading. One key container object type has the role of the update manager of objects it owns. There is no central hidden update manager as in the VR system Lightning because we found that in most applications, the sequence of the data propagation is not only manageable by the application developer but wanted. Another important container object type is the renderer which abstracts the various hardware and library specific renderer.

The Object Database Pool resides completely in shared memory. Unrelated processes can easily access this database. This offers the opportunity to modularize the application components on binary level which makes them easier to develop, control and maintain. The communication protocol is string based and timestamps are used for synchronization. Reference counting is the only security mechanism which allows to control the usage of the database objects. The synchronization of object state across host boundaries relies on mirroring the shared data pool via a distributed shared memory approach which can use various networking technologies for transportation, as described in section 4.3.

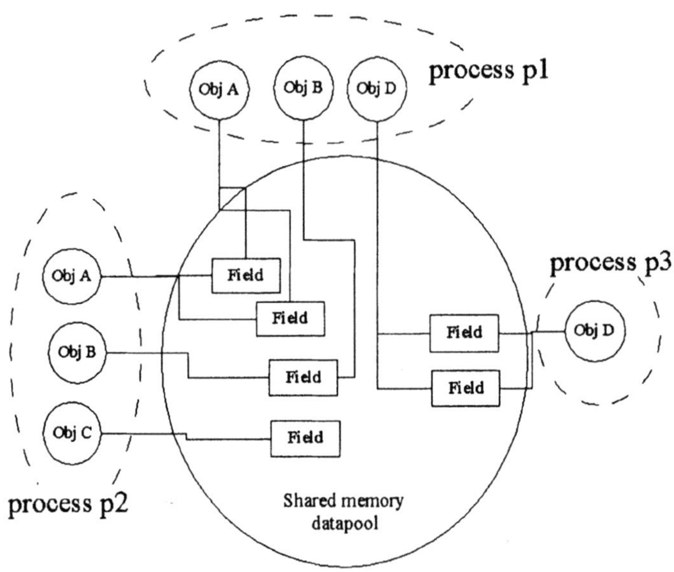

Fig. 2 Shared memory data pool as central repository of system state

The scripting and configuration system consists up to now of four different language bindings Tcl/iTcl, Java, Javascript and Python. Which one will be the language of choice for productive application development has to be proven in the near future. The interpreter is also an object which runs in its own thread where commands can easily be sent from external processes. The usage of various interpreters in the same application is conceivable but does not seem reasonable to us.

4.2 Graphics/IG System

On the graphics/image generation side, a coarse-grained scaling approach similar to the granularity of Personal Immersion is pursued in a first approach. This means one single node and graphics pipe per output channel; of course, multiple channels per node are also possible if the respective node provides appropriate hardware resources. The scene graph is completely replicated on all nodes; scene graph updates are propagated on a per-frame basis. This approach can easily be implemented using the distributed object database pool as described above, running multiple visual renderers on the various nodes, each registering interest in the visual objects in the shared data pool. The multiple visual renderers can be synchronized at frame boundaries to drive stereoscopic and multi-channel displays.

To overcome the limitations of this distribution approach, a more fine-grained distribution of image generation tasks is pursued in parallel, based on tiling a single output channel and recombining the final image. An network protocol independent of a particular Scene Graph API is designed to distribute scene graph updates across the visualization cluster. This allows the rendering hosts to run on various operating system platforms. For combining the final output image, commodity graphics hardware allows two approaches of accessing frame buffer data. First one is reading back the framebuffer through the host interface of the graphics card and conveying it via a high speed network to the host being in charge of output image reassembly. Samanta et al. [Samanta00] have shown the feasibility of such an approach. The second way is to use the video or DVI output of the graphics card, using custom hardware to reassemble the final image. An example of this is described by Humphreys et al. [Humphreys2001]. Such solutions have the huge advantage of yielding the entire system bus and networking bandwidth for other tasks; however, the need for custom hardware contradicts to the commodity hardware paradigm of our approach. This is the main reason for us to prefer the a system bus/networking based architecture.

4.3 Distributed shared memory

A flexible and high-performing distribution and shared memory model is a key building block of our system.

Interprocess-communication is simple and fast as long as the communicating processes have access to the same physical memory. Distributed shared memory

(DSM) implementations aim at providing the same simplicity when communicating between processes on different nodes with no shared physical memory.

Page-based DSM implementations extend the capabilities of the well known shared memory mechanisms available in most of today's operating systems to inter-node communication. That means a DSM segment is as usually first created with an API call. Every statement of the programming language can then be used to manipulate the segment's data. The modifications made by a process become visible to other processes, which may - in contrast to ordinary shared memory - even reside on a different node.

Most page-based DSM implementations use a pull scheme: A process works on the local data as long as possible, requesting data from remote nodes only when needed. Major drawback of this technique is that if multiple processes are interested in the newly created data of another process, the data has to be transferred repeatedly to all these nodes; no multicasting takes place. This algorithm provides the same strict consistency as ordinary shared memory. But this strict consistency isn't needed. The so-called "release consistency" is sufficient and allows multicasting. Release consistency has already been implemented in the shared variable DSM-system *Munin* [Bennet90].

Communication using shared memory requires synchronization. This means that prior to any modification on a shared data object, a lock is set on this object. This lock is released after modification. Propagation of the modifications is postponed until the release operation is completed. This allows to accumulate the modifications made between a pair of synchronization operations and multicast them together in one large chunk via multicasting to all nodes sharing the respective object.

This approach may perform a little bit worse compared to common implementations of DSM that delay the transmission until the data is really needed when communication only takes place between two nodes but should perform much better when applied to an environment like ours, where interest of multiple nodes to a particular data object is a common case.

By combining usual UNIX shared memory and the techniques described it is possible to achieve latencies nearly as low as and throughput nearly as high as those using the UNIX shared memory API system calls. The implementation therefore may well eliminate the need for using this API as an application programmer. This is – indeed - the very goal of our efforts.

For inter-node communication, both latency and throughput will suffer considerably when using off-the-shelf networking hardware. Nevertheless we intend to support Ethernet networks to provide a low-cost communication layer for applications with modest requirements. For applications with high bandwidth and tight synchronization requirements, we need something "with a little more kick". We have chosen SCI, the

Scalable Coherent Interface, for this purpose. SCI not only provides extremely low latencies of a few microseconds and a throughput of more than 100 MBytes/,) but also has the advantage of implementing DSM directly in hardware. Using SCI, the main task in implementing the DSM is therefore reduced to the design of an abstraction layer and the implementation of a DSM mechanism for low-cost networking hardware.

4.4 Implementation details

The current core system prototype runs on x86-based Linux Systems. For special purposes (e.g. image generation or audio) the usage of other hardware-software combinations are likely. The basic node configuration is

- AMD Athlon at 1 GHz
- VIA KT133 chipset.
- NVidia GeForce2 or Quadro gfx card
- Dolphin DC330 SCI card, Dolphin Interconnect

The current implementation of the visual renderer uses OpenGL|Performer™ from SGI.

5 Conclusion and future work

Our approach has lead to a scalable, simple and lightweight system for interactive applications in immersive virtual environments. The core system is small and has the freedom for maximal extensibility. Nearly all components can easily be exchanged because of the quasi-autonomous approach of the communication.

First prototypes are already implemented and the further modularization has proven already very helpful for the development process, especially control user interfaces, which are not part of the immersive simulation loop.

The next steps are the evaluation of the adequate scripting language and extensive testing and performance evaluation, especially in real world application contexts. Here we hope to gain insight how to distribute and modularize application components on the cluster. Do we need specialized nodes and which are these? How complex can such systems and applications grow to stay manageable?

All these topics will be questions for the next stage of the virtual environment research - the personal immersion stage

6 References

[Bennet90] Bennet, J.K, Carter, J.B., and Zwaenepoel, W., Munin: Distributed Shared Memory Based on Type-Specific Memory Coherence. In: Proc. Second ACM Symp. on Principles and Practice of Parallel Programming, ACM 1990, pp. 168-176

[Blach98] Blach, R.; Landauer J., M.; Simon, A.; Rösch, A.: A Flexible prototyping Tool for 3D Real-Time User-Interaction. In: Virtual Environments 98, Proceedings of the Eurographics Workshop, 1998 pp. 195-203

[Grimsdale 91] Grimsdale, C. (1991). dVS-Distributed Virtual Environment System. In Proceedings of Computer Graphics, Computer Animation, Virtual Reality, Visualisation, (pp. 163-170): Blenheim Online.

[Humphreys01] Humphreys, G., et al.: WireGL – a Scalable Graphics System for Clusters. Submitted to SIGGRAPH '01.

[Kuhl99] Frederick Kuhl, Richard Weatherly, and Judith Dahmann, Creating Computer Simulation Systems - An Introduction to the High Level Architecture, Prentice Hall, Upper Saddle River, NJ. 1999.

[Ousterhout93] Ousterhout, J., Tcl and the Tk Toolkit, Addison-Wesley, Reading, Massachusetts, 1993

[Rohlf94] Rohlf, J., Helman, J.: IRIS Performer: A High Performance Multiprocessing Toolkit for Real-Time 3D Graphics, Proceedings of ACM SIGGRAPH '94, Orlando, FL, pp. 381-394.

[Samanta00] Samanta, R., et al.: Hybrid Sort-First and Sort-Last Parallel Rendering with a Cluster of PC's. SIGGRAPH/Eurographics Workshop on Graphics Hardware, Interlaken, Switzerland - August, 2000

[Singhal99] Singhal, S.; Zyda M.: Networked Virtual Environment – Design and Implementation, Addison Wesley acm Press, 1999

[VRML97] The Virtual Reality Modelling Language (VRML) Specification 2.0 ISO/IEC CD 14772, 1997

Remote View-Dependent Rendering

Jihad El-Sana

Department of Computer Science, Ben-Gurion University, Beer-Sheva 84105, Israel
el-sana@cs.bgu.ac.il

Abstract. In this paper we are presenting a novel approach that enables rendering large-shared datasets at interactive rates on a remote inexpensive workstations. Our algorithm is based on view-dependent rendering and client-server technologies. In our approach, *servers* host large datasets and manage the selection of the various levels of detail, while *clients* receive blocks of update operations which are used to generate the appropriate level of detail in an incremental fashion. We assume that servers are capable machines in term of storage capacity and computational power while clients are inexpensive workstation that have limited 3D rendering capabilities. To avoid network latency we have introduced two powerful mechanisms that cache the adapt operation blocks on the clients' side and predict the future view-parameters of clients based on their recent behavior history. Our approach dramatically reduces the amount of memory needed by each client and the entire computing system since the dataset is stored only once in the local memory of the server. In addition, it decreases the load on the network as a result of the incremental update contributed by view-dependent rendering.

1 Introduction

Recent advances in computer and communication technologies have dramatically increased the number of computers connected to the Internet, thus extending usage of the Internet as a media to exchange and share knowledge. The increased need for more information and the limited bandwidth of the shared network has been calling for smart application and algorithms to bridge the increasing gap between hardware capabilities and the large amount of data that resides in various servers all over the world. In addition, advances in three-dimensional shape acquisition, simulation, and design technologies have led to a generation of large polygonal models and virtual environments that are beyond the local storage of the Internet clients and cannot be downloaded in a reasonable amount of time.

The structure of the Internet as an enormous number of computers connect via global network has led to development of various distributed application. These applications include multimedia, three-dimensional graphics, and virtual environments that require a transmission of large data over short periods of time. Distributed three-dimensional games, virtual museum, and virtual walk-through are good examples of such applications. These distributed applications usually manage very large datasets that clients can not download either because they are too large to fit into their local machines' memory or because these datasets are shared by other clients. On one hand, most of these applications are required to run at interactive or semi-interactive rates. On the other hand, the time it takes one machine to send a request to another machine and receive an answer may be too long for interactivity or even unpredicted. In the network community they refer to this time interval as *network latency*. Level-of-detail rendering could be used to reduce the size of the shipped three-dimensional datasets. El-Sana [5] has shown that view-dependent rendering dramatically reduces the traffic load over a local network by using a client-server technology. View-dependent rendering has been introduced to enable seamless and adaptive level-of-detail representations on real-time for polygonal datasets. The level-of-detail selection is based on view parameters such as view location and illumination. However, view-dependent rendering may not be enough to overcome the latency problem, which is the major obstacle in extending view-dependent rendering to work over the Internet. In addition, traditional view-dependent rendering schemes usually increase the size of the dataset, require the existence of the entire dataset in main memory, and do not enable different users to share the dataset currently in memory. To overcome the memory size drawback El-Sana and Chiang [2] have developed an external memory view-dependent rendering. However, their approach provides only a single-user solution and requires an additional level of preprocessing.

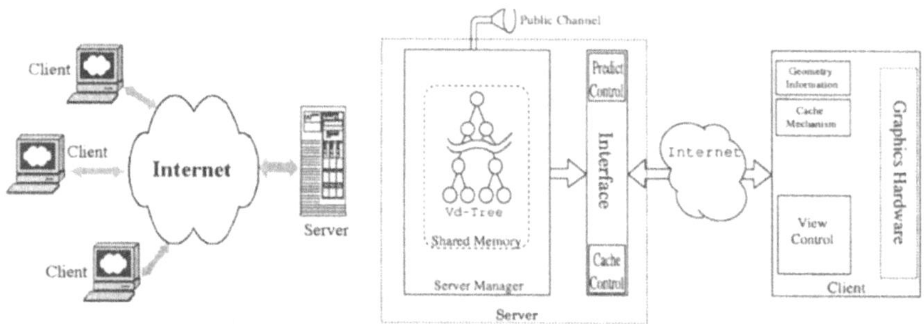

(a) Client-Server network (b) Client-Server View-dependent rendering

Fig. 1. Systems Configuration

In this paper we have developed a remote view-dependent rendering for large datasets over a wide area network. Our approach is based on the view-dependence tree data-structure [7] and a client-server technology. The view-dependence trees are stored in a remote and capable machine in terms of memory size and computation power. We shall refer to this machine as *server* which are accessed by different remote inexpensive machines that we will refer to as *clients*. To overcome the latency problem in wide area networks we have introduced two powerful mechanisms that provide caching of adapt operations and prediction of future view-parameters of the associated client. Our architecture enables inexpensive workstations to take advantage of view-dependent rendering to visualize large remote 3D datasets. In addition, it reduces the memory needed by each client machine, improves the rendering frame rates, and dramatically reduces the communication load.

2 Previous Work

Our system is based on two main ideas: view-dependent rendering and a set of users who share the visualized dataset. Next, we will briefly discuss some of the previous work in these two fields.

2.1 View-Dependent Rendering

Recent advances in level-of-detail rendering have taken advantage of temporal coherence to adaptively refine or simplify the polygonal environment from one frame to the next in a view-dependent manner. In particular, adaptive levels of detail have been used in terrains by Gross *et al* [8] and Lindstrom *et al* [14]. Hoppe has developed the concept of progressive meshes [10] which are based upon two fundamental operators – edge collapse and its dual, the vertex split.

Merge trees have been introduced by Xia *et al* [22] as a data-structure built upon progressive meshes to enable real-time view-dependent rendering of an object. Hoppe [11] has developed a view-dependent simplification algorithm that works with progressive meshes. This algorithm proceeds to construct a vertex hierarchy over a progressive mesh in a top-down fashion by minimizing an energy function. Luebke and Erikson [15] define a *tight octree* over the vertices of the given model to generate hierarchical view-dependent simplifications. De Floriani *et al.* [4] have introduced multi-triangulation(MT). Decimation and refinement in MT are achieved through a set of local operators that affect fragments of the mesh. Klein *et al* [13] have developed an illumination-dependent refinement algorithm for multiresolution meshes. El-Sana *et al* [6] have developed Skip Strip: a data-structure that efficiently maintains triangle strips during view-dependent rendering.

View-dependence tree [7] is a compact multiresolution hierarchical data-structure that supports view-dependent rendering. In fact, for a given input dataset the view-dependence tree construction often leads to a forest (set of trees) since not all the nodes can be merged together to form one tree. View-dependence trees are constructed bottom-up by recursively applying the vertex-pair collapse operation (see figure 2). The order of the collapses is determined by a predefined simplification metric.

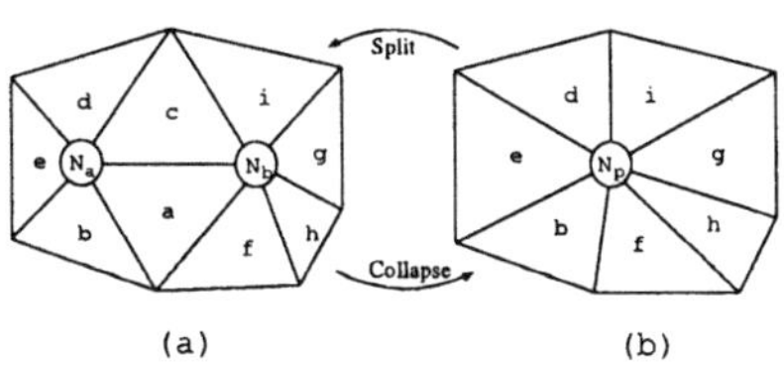

Fig. 2. Vertex-pair collapse and vertex split operations.

View-dependence trees are able to adapt to various levels of detail. Coarse details are associated with nodes that are close to the top of the tree (roots) and high details are associated with nodes that are close to the bottom of the tree (leaves). To be able to handle non-manifold cases, a more general scheme is used so that when a vertex split occurs more than two new adjacent triangles can be added. The reconstruction of a real-time adaptive mesh requires the determination of the list of vertices of this adaptive mesh and the list of triangles that connect these vertices. Following [7], we refer to these lists as the list of *active nodes* and the list of *active triangles*. At each frame the *active nodes* list is traversed to adapt to the appropriate level-of-detail representation of the given scene.

2.2 Distributed Interactive Systems

Experimental distributed systems have also been developed for real-time iteration in shared virtual environments such as Maverik [12], WAVE system[19], Shastra[1], NPSNET[16], and Cspary[18], and RING system[21]. Man and Cohen-Or [17] have developed a selective pixel transmission for navigating in remote virtual environments [17]. Hesina and Schmalstieg [9] have suggested a network architecture for remote rendering. Chim *et al* [3] have suggested algorithms on caching and prefetching of virtual objects in distributed virtual environments. Schmalstieg and Gervautz [20] have developed a demand-driven geometry transmission for distributed virtual environments.

Recently, El-Sana [5] has introduced a multi-user view-dependent rendering approach that allows multiple clients to visualize in a view-dependent manner large datasets that resides in a local server. Even though this approach shows a good improvement over external memory view-dependent rendering however, it has failed to handle the wide area network since it lack any prediction or caching mechanism.

3 Our Approach

Our approach provides a novel solution that enables Internet users to take advantage of view-dependent rendering. The technique of view-dependent rendering provides a mechanism to accelerate the rendering process as well as the transmission process.

On one hand the Internet becomes "the place" of shared-large media including large 3D models. On the other hand, Internet users' machines usually lack the memory size and the rendering capability to interact with large dataset by themselves. In fact the vast majority of the Internet clients use low-end PC machines.

Our algorithm is based on a *view-dependent server* and a set of *view-dependent clients*. In our current implementation, we assume that the large dataset resides in a *view-dependent server* which has enough memory and computation power to store and handle the entire multiresolution representation. The *view-dependent clients* visualize in a view-dependent fashion the dataset that currently resides in the server through the Internet using inexpensive machines. Each client receives only the level of detail required to visualize a dataset with respect to its current view-parameters and its machine computation capability. It is important to note that clients interact with the large dataset without downloading the entire dataset into their local machines' memory because of memory size, consistency, or security issues. In addition, our approach aims to reduce the load on the wide area network and avoid undesirable slowdown.

4 Adopting View-Dependence Trees

View-dependence tree [7] is a compact multiresolution hierarchical data-structure that supports view-dependent rendering. To use view-dependence trees in remote shared multi-users environments we have added new functionality and performed several changes.

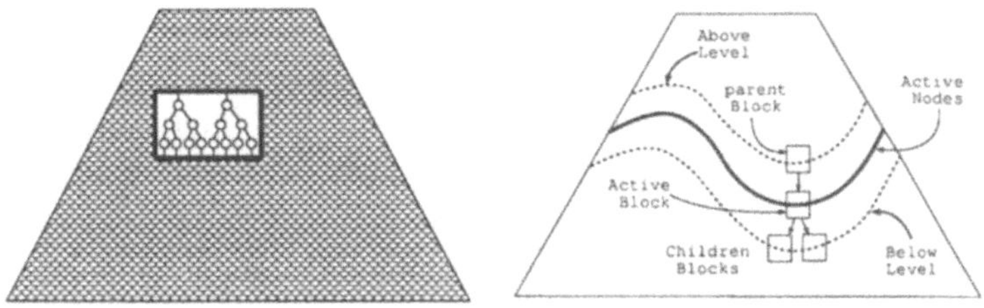

(a) A View-dependence block (b) Above and below cache levels.

Fig. 3. View-Dependence Tree

We have divided the view-dependence trees into blocks based on parenthood and sibling relation in the view-dependence trees, as depicted in Figure 3(a). This blocking scheme is similar to the one developed by El-Sana and Change [2] to support external memory view-dependent rendering. Our blocking scheme improves the transmission time, make it possible to take advantage of compression, and paves the way for a successful caching scheme. We shall refer to each block as *view-dependence block* and to blocks that contains at least one active node as *active blocks*. Instead of using active-nodes list as in traditional view-dependence tree we use active-blocks as a list of pointer to the active blocks in the blocked-view-dependence trees.

To allow multiple users to access the same view-dependence trees concurrently we have separated the active-blocks list from the view-dependence trees. Recall that implicit dependencies [7] have been developed to prevent foldover at runtime by carefully assigning *id*-es to the nodes of the view-dependence tree. In addition, we have found that the implicit dependencies enable the separation of the active-nodes from the view-dependence tree. This separation enables multiple interfaces to have different active-blocks while sharing the same view-dependence tree.

The size of the transmitted data determines partially the transmission time, therefore we compacted the view-dependence tree by making the geometry of a parent node identical to one of its children's geometry. Such a scheme of the view-dependence trees stores geometry information such as vertex position, normal, and color on the leaves of the tree. Each Internal node only keeps a pointer to the appropriate address where its geometry information is stored. These changes reduce the overhead of storing a view-dependence tree to only 2/3 times more than the 3D representation of the original mesh.

5 Our System Configuration

In this section we shall review the configuration of our system which is based on a view-dependent server and clients that access this server via the Internet. Next we shall overview our view-dependent server and client architecture.

5.1 View-Dependent Server

The view-dependent server is responsible for delivering three-dimensional objects in view-dependent fashion over the Internet. Since servers on the Internet should provide services for multiple clients, the view-dependent server should also send different appropriate level-of-detail to the seeking-service clients.

The server loads a view-dependence trees [7], then based on the view-parameters of each client, it delivers an appropriate level of detail for the loaded dataset. We shall refer to the main process that sets the public communication channel, initializes the shared memory arena, and loads the view-dependence tree into memory as the *server manager*. The *server manager* also listens, on a public channel, for requests for connection by new clients. For each calling client, the server creates a new thread, which is responsible for the interaction with the calling client. We will refer to this thread as an *interface*.

Each interface stores the characteristic parameters, maintains the active-blocks list, and handles the view-parameters changes of its associate client. On each change of the client's view-parameters its interface updates the active-blocks list to adapt to a better representation of the viewed scene. The interface is also responsible for packing and sending the view-dependence blocks with the proper additional data to its associate client.

The active-blocks list should match the active-nodes list that depends on the view parameters such as camera position, view direction, and illumination. Instead of watching for changes on the view parameters the interface receives only a *switch-up* and *switch-down* operations which reflect the changes on the view-parameters. On receiving the switch operations, the server updates its active-blocks list and transmits the added blocks to its associate client.

5.2 View-Dependents Clients

Clients should receive and maintain the minimum amount of information needed to maximize the visualize appearance of the inspected 3D dataset. In our implementation, clients maintain a small fraction of the view-dependence trees in a form of blocks; an active-nodes list as a list of pointers into nodes in the active nodes list; and active-triangles list which is sent to the graphics hardware at each frame. Practically, the active-nodes and triangles lists represent the appropriate level of detail of the visualized dataset with respect to current view parameters of the client.

Periodically, the client scans its active-nodes list and tries to converge to the best visual appearance of the currently visualized dataset by increasing or decreasing the resolution in various regions. For split operations that produce nodes that are in the lower quarter of the active-block, the client sends a *switch-down* message to its interface. And for merge operations that activate nodes in the top quarter of the active block the client sends *switch-down* message to its interface.

5.3 Messages and Session Phases

Our current implementation relies on the data-network layer hence, we assume that the connection is sequential and reliable. Nevertheless, our system maintains a timeout on the data channel to check for critical simple-detected errors such as communication breakdown.

Clients take advantage of the memory and computation power of the server to acquire the ability to visualize large datasets over the Internet. Because our system is distributed over a wide area network, it involves several different phases of interaction. In the setup phase the server loads the view-dependence trees and sets the public communication channel at which it listens for clients' requests for connection. On receiving a *request-for-connection* message the server creates an interface to handle the connection with the calling client. The interface, which has access permission to the shared memory, then establishes a private data channel shared with the calling client.

As soon as the client and the interface have established a connection the interface initializes its active-blocks, active-nodes, and active-triangles lists using the root-nodes list of the view-dependence trees. Then it sends the created lists to its associate client. On receiving the data, the client initializes its data-structures and buffers and both the client and its interface enter the *adapt dialog* phase. The client-server dialog allows the client to converge to the best possible visual appearance of the inspected scene with respect to its computation power, local memory, and rendering capabilities. During this phase the client updates its active nodes-list and sends switch messages based on its view parameters. Based on the received switch messages the interface sends blocks of view-dependence nodes.

To terminate the connection session the client sends to the server a *disconnect* message. On receiving this message, the associate interface releases its allocated resources, returns an acknowledge message, and terminate the session.

6 Overcoming Network Latency

Distributed applications over the Internet take advantage of sharing computation power and storage space, but they suffer from the disadvantage of the Internet latency. Latency of a network link is the time delay between a transmitted packet and its associated acknowledge. The disadvantage of latency becomes very severe for interactive applications.

We have chosen to tackle the problem of latency by caching some information on the client side and predicting the future view-parameters. We have also developed a new adapt-operation form that is used for performing a split and its dual merge without sending additional data. Caching adapt operation on the client's local storage not only reduces the amount of transmitted data but it can also avoid transmission of a complete group of adapt operations. The prediction of future view-parameters allows the server to send more data to the client without waiting for its reply.

6.1 Caching the Adapt Operations

By using view-dependent rendering we manage to reduce the transmitted data by orders of magnitude, but to avoid the latency problem we should try to avoid transmitting data when possible. We have achieved that by caching previously sent blocks and reuse them instead of re-transmitting.

Our cache algorithm is based on the blocking scheme of the view-dependence tree we have introduced in section 4. The client caches every block it receives from the server as long as it has enough memory space (note that a cache could also be on an external media). We assume that clients keep at least the active-blocks list in its local memory. In order to be able to converge to the appropriate visual appearance of the visualized scene we cache one level of view-dependence blocks above the current active-blocks list and one level of view-dependence blocks below the active-blocks level as shown in Figure 3(b). We maintain these addition levels in a lazy manner by taking advantage of the cached blocks and by transmitting blocks that have a better chance to be used in the near future. In such a scheme the same block could be transmitted multiple times from a server to the client during one session. We could often avoid such cases by caching every block transmitted either in local memory or on an external media as long as we do not reach the cache buffers' limit.

We manage the cache by maintaining two level buffers: local and external memory. In addition, we maintain the booking of the received blocks in a hash table based on the unique *id* of each view-dependence block. Before asking for any block, the client checks its local-memory and external-memory buffers respectively to verify that the needed view-dependent block does not exist.

Since we have used limit cache buffers we had to come up with a scheme that manage removing items form the cache buffers and switch blocks between the local and external memory. With each block we store its level on the view-dependence trees, then we give priority to blocks according to the distance between their level and the current active level. We keep blocks with higher priority on the local memory and the ones with lower priority on the external memory.

6.2 Prediction Mechanism

Sine the user is the human factor in the real-time interaction, idle time is almost inevitable. In these intervals the client and server often do not exchange any data over the communication channel. We utilize these intervals by performing operations that reduce the need for data transmission in the future. We shall refer to the performed operations as *prediction*. The server's interface utilizes its idle time by predicting the future view-parameters and sends view-dependence blocks needed for the predicted view-parameters. For better prediction, the server's interface tracks the speed, velocity, and tangent of the client's motion. Then a client chooses whether to cache the predicted adapt-operation and notify the server or discard them.

6.3 Client Server Synchronization

Assume that a server has an idle time and it sends future predictions to a client. Concurrently, the client's camera moves and sends switch messages to the server. Both the client and the server cannot determine which action took place first and each one thinks its action happened first. Choosing the incorrect order for the two events order may cause the to consider the arriving prediction for its new view-parameters. To avoid such a problem we synchronize the server and client to ensure the consistency of the view-parameters they both consider.

Clients consider predications that are either accurate or lead to transmission of uncached blocks. In our scheme, it is not easy for clients or servers to measure the "goodness" of prediction because the server is not aware of the exact view-parameters and both – client and server – do not keep a history of the switch messages. Practically, we do not need to determine the relation between the sent switch messages and the received view-dependence blocks. It is sufficient to determine where in the partial view-dependence tree in the client side the received block will fit. We use the unique *id* of each block to determine its position on the partially cached view-dependence trees. In such a scheme, a server may send blocks that is already cached in the client side. In such case, the client discards these blocks as soon as they arrive.

7 Implementation and Results

Similar to [5] the server allocates shared memory buffers to store the view-dependence tree. The server interfaces have a read-only access to the shared memory to maintain their active-blocks list. Active-blocks list keeps a record for each active block that includes a pointer to the actual node of the view-dependence tree. View-dependent rendering algorithms usually store in the local memory the multiresolution hierarchy on the rendering machine. Instead, our approach keeps a set of active blocks that include the selected level of detail in the rendering machine (the client machine). Such a technique usually provides more memory space which enables the selection of more detailed representation for large datasets. In addition, the display process and the adaptation process run completely in parallel since they live in two different machines.

We have also tested the performance of our unoptimized implementation on different hardware using various datasets and have received encouraging results. Next we are reporting some of the acquired results. For security reasons we were not able to conduct test outside the state of Israel, therefore all the reported results were carried out in two geographically distributed regions within the same country. In such a wide area network we can at the maximum, get either 2Megabit/second or 10 Megabit/second (depends on the client position) but in our experiments we have never exceeded 1 Megabit/second. For each experiment session, we periodically check the latency of the network.

One of the major advantages of view-dependent rendering is the ability to takes advantage of coherence between consecutive frames. Therefore, we have

Dataset	Original		Average/frame			
	Vertices	Triangles	Triangles (K)	Split/Merge (K)	Blocks Sent(KB)	Time(ms)
Dragon	151 K	300 K	72	1.6	0.5	240
Terrain	262 K	522 K	80	1.8	0.6	230
Palace	280 K	760 K	83	2.3	0.64	243
VR-City	612 K	1,250 K	91	2.6	0.68	260

Table 1. Run time over a sequence of frames for various datasets.

chosen to compare its performance over sequences of frames and not over one isolated frame. Hence, the reported results were obtained using sequences of frames.

In table 1 we report the average number of split/merge operations, data sent over the data channel, number of triangles at each frame, and the average time for a frame. These results were obtained using the configuration: the server runs on an SGI ORIGIN 200 and the client runs on an Pentium III machine with 128 MB. As can be seen from Table 1 we have achieved acceptable frame rate even for large datasets. In the same time the average amount of data transmitted at each frame is quite small.

Figures 4 and 5 show images generated by our system. Figure 4(a) show the original dragon model. Figure 4(b) shows in small window on the top-right corner the image seen by a user and the other window is the global view of the dataset. In Figure 5(a) we see the full resolution of a Terrain dataset and in Figure 5(b) we show a low resolution view of the same Terrain dataset.

8 Conclusion and Future Work

We have presented a novel approach for view-dependent rendering of large datasets on an inexpensive workstation. Our idea is based on a client-server architecture over a wide area network. We have adapted a compact-multiresolution-hierarchy data structure that supports view-dependent rendering that is known as *view-dependence trees*. The view-dependence trees reside in a remote Internet server that runs the view-dependent server. A client that may run on an inexpensive machine establishes a connection with a server and sends its view-parameters to the server which provides the client with the appropriate level-of-detail representation of the scene with respect to the sent view parameters.

We see the scope for future work in designing virtual environment application that allows typical Internet clients to enjoy navigating through very large datasets at reasonable interactive rates. In addition, our approach could be used to promote remote touring, virtual museums, and remote shopping malls.

9 Acknowledgements

We would like to acknowledge the Weiler Family Fund, which helped in purchasing some of the equipment used in this project. We would like to thank the reviewers for their insightful comments. We also would like to thank 3DCafe and the Stanford Computer Graphics Laboratory for providing datasets.

References

1. V. Anupam and C. Bajaj. Shastra: An architecture for development of collaborative applications. *Intern. Jour. of Intell. and Cooper. Info. Sys.*, 3(2):155–172, 1994.
2. J. El-Sana Y. Chiang. External memory view-dependent simplification. In *Computer Graphics Forum*, volume 19, 2000.
3. J. Chim, M. Green, R Lau, H. Leong, A. Si, and A. Si. On caching and prefetching of virtual objects in distributed virtual environments. In *ACM Multimedia*, pages 88–91, 1998.
4. L. De Floriani, P. Magillo, and E. Puppo. Efficient implementation of multi-triangulation. In *Proceedings Visualization '98*, pages 43–50, October 1998.
5. J. El-Sana. Multi-user view-dependent rendering. In *IEEE Visualization '2000 Proceedings*, pages 335–342, 2000.
6. J. El-Sana, E. Azanli, and A. Varshney. Skip strips: Maintaining triangle strips for view-dependent rendering. In *IEEE Visualization '99*, October 1999.
7. J. El-Sana and A. Varshney. Generalized view-dependent simplification. In *Computer Graphics Forum*, volume 18, pages C83–C94, 1999.
8. M. Gross, R. Gatti, and O. Staadt. Fast multiresolution surface meshing. In G. M. Nielson and D. Silver, editors, *IEEE Visualization '95*, pages 135–142, 1995.
9. G. Hesina and D. Schmalstieg. A network architecture for remote rendering. In *Inter. Workshop on Dist. Inter. Sim. and Real Time App.*, pages 88–91, 1998.
10. H. Hoppe. Progressive meshes. In *Proceedings of SIGGRAPH '96*, pages 99 - 108. ACM SIGGRAPH, August 1996.
11. H. Hoppe. View-dependent refinement of progressive meshes. In *Proceedings of SIGGRAPH '97 (Los Angeles, CA)*, pages 189 - 197. ACM Press, August 1997.
12. R. Hubbold, D. Xiao, and S. Gibson. Maverik – the manchester virtual environment interface kernel, 1996.
13. R. Klein, A. Schilling, and W. Straßer. Illumination dependent refinement of multiresolution meshes. In *Computer Graphics Intl*, pages 680–687, June 1998.
14. P. Lindstrom, D. Koller, W. Ribarsky, L. Hughes, N. Faust, and G. Turner. Real-Time, continuous level of detail rendering of height fields. In *SIGGRAPH 96 Proceedings*, pages 109–118. ACM SIGGRAPH, 1996.
15. D. Luebke and C. Erikson. View-dependent simplification of arbitrary polygonal environments. In *SIGGRAPH '97*, pages 198 - 208, 1997.
16. M. Macedonia, D. Brutzmann, M. Zyda, D. Pratt, P. Barham, J. Falby, and J. Locke. Npsnet: A multi-player 3d virtual environment over the internet. In *Symposium on Interactive 3D Graphics*, pages 93–94, 1995.
17. Y. Mann and D. Cohen-Or. Selective pixel transmission for navigating in remote virtual environments. *EUROGRAPHICS 97*, 16(3):201–206, 1997.
18. A. Pang, C. Wittenbrink, and T. Goodman. Cspray: A collaborative scientific visualization application. In *Multimedia Computing and Networking*, 1995.
19. K. Rick. Making waves: On the design of architectures for low-end distributed virtual environments. In *IEEE Virtual Reality Intern. Symp.*, pages 443–449, 1993.
20. D. Schmalstieg and M. Gervautz. Demand-driven geometry transmission for distributed virtual environments. *EUROGRAPHICS 96*, 15(3):421–433, 1996.
21. F. Thomas. Ring: A clientserver system for multi-user virtual environments. In *Symposium on Interactive 3D Graphics*, pages 85–92. ACM Press, 1995.
22. J. Xia, J. El-Sana, and A. Varshney. Adaptive real-time level-of-detail-based rendering for polygonal models. *IEEE Transactions on Visualization and Computer Graphics*, pages 171 - 183, 1997.

Editors' Note: see Appendix, p. 281 for colored figures of this paper

Volume Rendering in a Virtual Environment

Jürgen Schulze-Döbold, Uwe Wössner, Steffen P. Walz, Ulrich Lang

High Performance Computing Center (RUS/HLRS), University of Stuttgart, Germany
{schulze,woessner,walz,lang}@hlrs.de

Abstract. This paper describes a flexible rendering system for scalar volume data which has been integrated into the visualization system COVISE. It allows direct volume rendering based on texture mapping hardware on both the desktop and in projection based virtual environments. Special care has been taken for the design and usability of the virtual reality user interface and for interactive frame rates. It features a new slider-less interaction window for the manipulation of the transfer function and methods for direct interaction with the volume data, such as a sub-volume probing mode. The interface has been evaluated in collaboration with a group of potential end users.

1 Introduction

Volume rendering has become an important visualization method, predominantly in the fields of scientific and medical visualization. Due to the usually large amount of data it is difficult to analyze it in a suitable way. Our approach is to display the volume graphics in a virtual environment, and to provide the user with suitable interaction techniques. The color and opacity transfer functions can be edited interactively from within the virtual world by a 3D user interface. It is designed for CAVE-like environments such as the CUBE at HLRS, but it could also be used with other VR systems after slight modifications.

The volume data is displayed using graphics hardware accelerated texture mapping, which allows the concurrent display of volume and surface graphics in a straightforward way. The most challenging issue was to provide the user with both an intuitive and easy to use interface for the manipulation of the transfer functions, and additional methods to display only those sections of the data which are of interest to the user.

2 Previous Work

Several developments were required to create our volume rendering system in a virtual environment. The underlying visualization framework COVISE is described in [Ran95], details about the integrated VR renderer COVER can be found in [Ran98].

The volume rendering capabilities were added by developing a volume rendering library, which uses 3D texturing hardware for direct volume rendering, as described in [Cul93]. This development was necessary because none of the publicly available volume rendering packages met our requirements, which are multipipe support and availability of an API. For VolPack, 3DDataMaster, Amira, TeleInVivo, VoxelView and VTK this was investigated in [Woh00], SGI's OpenGL Volumizer could not be used because it lacks multipipe support when used with Performer.

The most interesting developments of user interfaces for volume rendering include the Crumbs tool [Bra95] and the StudyDesk interface [Woh00]. None of them allow modification and display of both the color and the opacity transfer function in one window, and they are not designed to be used in conjunction with a traditional visualization system.

3 COVISE

COVISE is a modular visualization system, designed to support collaborative visualization of data in virtual environments as well as on the desktop. The architecture of COVISE allows developers to extend the existing functionality by integrating new code as modules. In a visual application builder, these modules are connected to form a dataflow network (see Fig. 1).

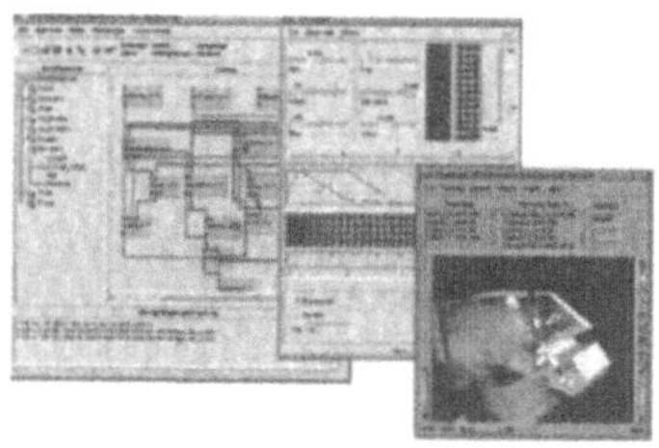

Fig. 1. COVISE desktop user interface and OpenInventor renderer

At the end of the pipeline there is a render module, which can either be a desktop renderer, based on Open Inventor, or the VR oriented render module COVER, which is Performer based, see section 5. Existing modules can be used to visualize geometry, cutting surfaces, iso surfaces, streamlines, etc. New modules have been introduced to sample data from unstructured or non-uniform structured grids to uniform grids. Unlike in the medical field, in technical environments simulation domains are usually modeled using unstructured grids. Existing modules have been extended to support value blanking, which is useful for representing regions containing no data in uniform grids. Finally, both render modules have been extended to support direct volume rendering of uniform scalar fields by integrating VIRVO.

4 Volume Renderer

The volume rendering library VIRVO (Virtual Reality Volume Rendering) provides an API for texture-based volume rendering. The API manages the volume data, provides file I/O and conversion routines, and renders the volumes using OpenGL routines. The renderer supports texturing using 2D or 3D textures. For interactive frame rates the volume data sets have to fit into texture memory entirely, bricking is not supported. The volume data is displayed by drawing equidistant planar texture slices.

4.1 Slice Orientation

The VIRVO system only allows for arbitrary texture slice orientation when the hardware supports 3D texturing. Then the following strategy for the slice orientation is used: Without head tracking, the texture slices are drawn parallel to the screen. For volume rendering in virtual environments, VIRVO uses two different methods to find the texture slice normals. Whenever the center of the user's eyes is outside the volume boundaries, the normals are set parallel to the line from the volume center to the center of the eyes. If the user's eyes are inside the volume, the normals are set parallel to the current viewing direction, which yields the least amount of artifacts.

The reason for using two different methods is that although the least amount of artifacts occurs in the latter case, the constantly changing slice orientation while looking around the scene turned out to be irritating.

4.2 Interactive Classification

For an interactive classification, the mapping from scalar values to RGBA (red, green, blue, alpha) values has to be done using look-up tables, because otherwise the volume data would have to be reloaded into texture memory for every change. Depending on the volume size, this would take up to a few seconds, due to the limited throughput rate from main memory to texture memory (see measurements in [Vol00]).

Our SGI Onyx2 system provides the texture color table extension, which allows interactive changes of the look-up table. This gives instant feedback to the user on transfer function modifications.

4.3 Slice Distance and Opacity Correction

Current graphics hardware is limited in the pixel fill rate. Thus the number of texture slices used to draw the volume is the critical factor for maintaining a certain frame rate, which in turn defines the slice distance. Since we need to achieve interactive frame rates to sustain the effect of immersion, linking the slice distance to the frame rate is a fast method to keep the rendering time low.

In order to retain the correct overall volume opacity when changing the number of slices, VIRVO adapts the opacity values in all slices accordingly by using look-up tables for the opacity values (see section 4.2) and by re-computing the tables whenever the number of slices changes. The required opacity correction formula is derived in [Wei00].

5 COVER

The virtual environment renderer COVER was originally developed as a VR renderer for COVISE, but it can also be used as a standalone VR renderer with full VRML97 capabilities. It supports all major tracking devices and arbitrary projection-screen configurations. Additionally, it is extensible through a flexible plugin system. It is based on the multiprocessing graphics API OpenGL Performer, which introduces several difficulties when trying to include custom rendering code. The plugin interface provides access to all three Performer processes (Application, Cull and Draw) as well as to the COVISE module interface. A plugin was developed which uses VIRVO to render volume data and which provides the 3D user interface described in section 6.

The actual rendering of the volume has to be done in the Draw process, but the user interaction and the interface to the COVISE pipeline is done in the Application process, thus various information has to be passed between these processes. This is done through a shared data structure which includes queues and shared states for the data objects, the user's position and orientation, the probe position, etc.

The plugin uses a custom Performer node to represent the volume objects in the Performer scenegraph. Thus the view frustum culling features of Performer can be exploited, and draw buckets can be used to ensure the correct order of rendering as for a combination of volume and polygonal objects the correct drawing order has to be maintained.

The volume plugin is based on OpenGL routines instead of Performer commands in order to be system independent and to take advantage of the latest OpenGL extensions. Thus, special care had to be taken to ensure that the Performer state is not changed after the execution of OpenGL commands.

6 Transfer Function Editor

The transfer function editor was designed specifically for use in immersive virtual environments such as the CAVE, see [Cru93]. Currently a three button input device is required, we are using a three button 3D mouse. Starting at the mouse position, a "laser" beam of infinite length is cast into the pointed direction. The current interaction element is determined by its intersection with this beam.

The editor and all input elements are placed on a floating menu, see Fig. 2. In the entire editor, we explicitly do not use any sliders to modify scalar values. Instead, we created rotary knobs, which are manipulated by clicking on them and then twisting the hand, similar to real knobs. There are three advantages to this technique. First, the human hand can accommodate twists much more precisely than translations. Secondly, rotary knobs do not have a limited value range, they can be rotated multiple times for manipulation of unconstrained values. Thirdly, the accuracy of the adjustment is independent of the user's distance from the knob.

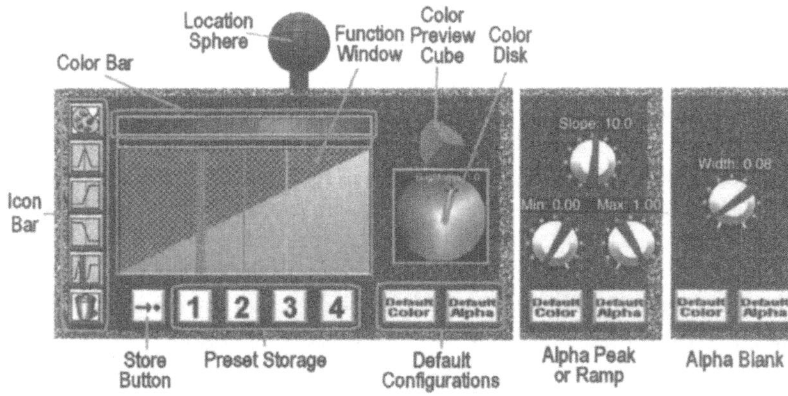

Fig. 2. Transfer function editor

6.1 Editor Position

A sphere on top of the floating menu can be used to set the location of the editor within the virtual world. Dragging it with the left mouse button down, the menu always points to the user; using the right button additionally modifies the orientation. The middle button is used to resize the menu.

6.2 Transfer Functions

The color and opacity transfer functions are modified in a two-dimensional window. The scalar values are assumed to be located horizontally with the smallest value on the left. The transfer functions assign both a color and an opacity to each scalar value. The resulting RGBA values, as applied to the volume data, are displayed in the color bar above the function window. Opacity, which equals the alpha value, is perceived by a varying visibility of the window background texture.

Color Selection. Changing the color value (R, G, and B components) requires setting a control point (pin) in the function window, which is done by clicking on the color palette icon and then clicking on the desired scalar value position in the function graph. The colored disk, which appears to the right of the function window, is designed according to the HSV color model. The hue and saturation components are selected by clicking the left button on the desired location in the colored disk, the brightness is modified by pressing the middle button in the colored disk and twisting the input device.

Both color and alpha pins can be selected by clicking next to them with the left mouse button, they are shifted by dragging with the right mouse button. If more than one pin is located closely together or on top of each other, repeated left mouse button clicks cycle through them. Removing a pin is done by first selecting it and then clicking the trash can icon.

Alpha Selection. Alpha pins, which describe the opacity function, can be set independently of color pins. Setting an alpha pin requires selecting a pin of the desired type in the icon bar and dragging it to a scalar position in the function window. There are three basic types of alpha pins: peaks, ramps, and blanks. Peaks and ramps have a slope, a minimum, and a maximum value. They are used to gradually fade in or out scalar ranges. If peaks or ramps overlap, the maximum value determines the resulting alpha value. Alpha blanks only have a width, they force a scalar range to be transparent. Blanks dominate peaks and ramps.

The properties of alpha pins can either be adjusted by the rotary knobs to the right of the function window (see Fig. 2, middle panel for peaks or ramps, right panel for blanks), or they can be adjusted by twisting the mouse while pressing the middle mouse button with the pointer in one of the three sensitive areas around the pin position. The extent of these areas is displayed in a horizontal bar, located between the function window and the color bar.

Preset Functions. Up to four pairs of transfer functions can be stored for later use. This can be done by first clicking the store icon and then clicking the desired storage number icon. Stored functions can be retrieved by clicking the respective storage number icon directly.

Some commonly used default color and default alpha pin configurations can be applied by clicking the Default Color and Default Alpha buttons. Multiple clicks on these buttons cycle through a number of default configurations.

7 Other Features

The transfer function editor only allows editing the transfer function related parameters. More features can be addressed by the Volume Menu, which is a conventional COVER style menu, and which does not provide rotary knobs instead of sliders. This menu is needed to select the probe mode, the clipping plane, and the frame rate, and it provides an interface to set the animation parameters for time-dependent data sets. The following sub-sections describe these features more detailed.

7.1 Animation

Time dependent data sets can either be displayed in single frame mode or as an animation with adjustable speed. The volume data for the time steps are entirely loaded into texture memory whenever they are to be displayed. If the texture memory is insufficient to accommodate all time steps, OpenGL automatically caches the data in main memory, thus slowing down animation speed considerably. Fig. 3 shows seven time steps of a statistical FE simulation.

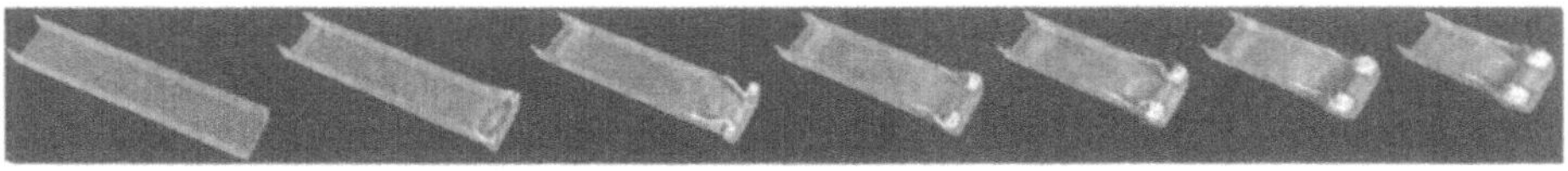

Fig. 3. Time steps of FE statistics simulation

7.2 Image Quality

The default image quality mode is the adaptive mode (see section 4.3) in which the number of volume slices is automatically adjusted, so that the user selected frame rate is maintained. Whenever the user wants to see the image in a better quality, he can click a mouse button while holding the mouse above his eye level to trigger the High Quality Mode (see Fig. 4). In this mode no downsampling is performed on the volume data. Since in High Quality Mode usually no interactive frame rate can be achieved, the user must press a mouse button again to return to the adaptive mode.

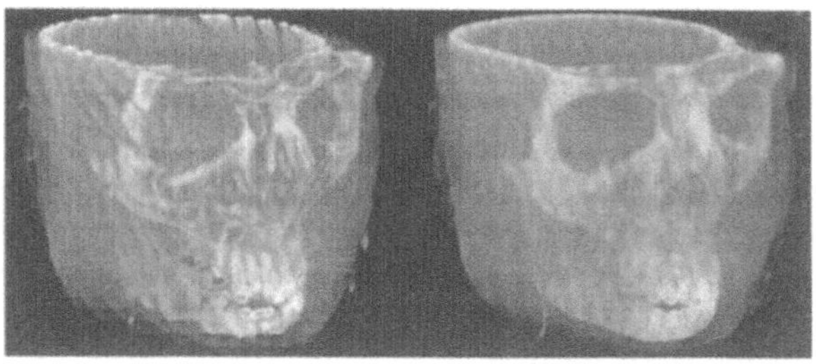

Fig. 4. Adaptive Mode (left) compared to High Quality Mode (right)

7.3 Clipping Planes

OpenGL clipping planes cut off all geometry on one side of the plane. Thus when applied on volume data displayed with the slicing technique, artifacts occur at the clipping plane, whenever the plane is not parallel to the slices. Therefore our clipping approach does not use an OpenGL clipping plane. Instead, in clipping plane mode, we match the volume slice orientation with the clipping plane orientation, and we clip the volume by not drawing the slices on one side of the plane. Furthermore, the volume slices are shifted so that there is always a slice drawn at the clipping plane location. Multiple OpenGL clipping planes can be used additionally.

7.4 Probe Mode

Motivated by the clear boxes in [Bra95], we developed the probe mode (see Fig. 5). When it is selected, the volume data boundaries are displayed and only a cubic subset of the volume is rendered. The user can drag-and-drop the cube with the left mouse button, its size is changed by twisting the mouse while pressing the middle button. Interactive speed is obtained because the volume data in texture memory is not changed but only the texture coordinates are set according to the current position.

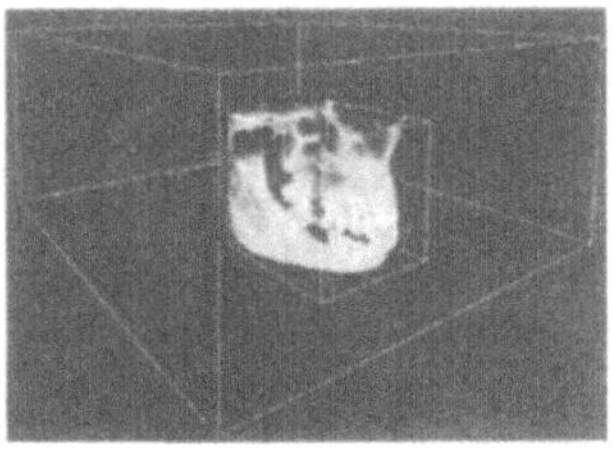

Fig. 5. Probe Mode

8 Evaluation

Derived from [Swa99], our evaluation process consisted of two main phases: a usability inspection and a scenario-based evaluation. Both phases were slightly modified in order to better suit our needs.

8.1 Phase 1: Usability Inspection

In the usability inspection, a specialist from HLRS, who was not involved in the system's development process, reported obvious flaws in the design of the user interface and made redesign suggestions to the developers, who decided on their implementation. The above described volume rendering system already includes these changes.

8.2 Phase 2: Scenario-Based Evaluation

Before the external users were invited, a pilot study of the system was performed by an in-house expert. We detected several problems with e.g. the chronology of the evaluation procedure, the number of tasks, and the understanding of the questionnaire. Then we optimized these factors.

Chonology. The evaluation was put into the following order:

1. *Self-Rating Questionnaire.* In a conference room, the users filled out a questionnaire asking them to self-rate personal skills and knowledge, based on a Likert scale with a value range from 1 to 5, see [Lin99]. We also asked users about their gender, age, and physical constraints such as glasses.
2. *Introductory Presentation (Briefing).* On several slides we gave a brief introduction to volume rendering and the CUBE. We explained the functionality of the transfer function editor in detail and finally presented two application scenarios.
3. *Passive Introduction.* The users were brought to the CUBE, where three evaluators were present: M, V, and P. V and P sat outside the VE. Evaluator M explained the functionalities of both the CUBE and the volume rendering system. The passive introduction averaged around 5 minutes. Evaluator V videotaped Steps 3 to 5, P conducted Participant Observation during the same time.
4. *Active Introduction.* The users were handed the 3D mouse and started exploring scenario #1 with M still explaining. This step seamlessly faded into Step 5, it averaged to 5 minutes.
5. *Exploring the Scenarios.* M left the CUBE and served as an expert mediator, but only helped users when asked to. About 10 minutes before the end, it was switched to scenario #2. This step was aborted when the total elapsed time of steps 3 to 5 reached 30 minutes.
6. *Follow-up Questionnaire.* Back in the conference room, users filled out a questionnaire. Ten questions asked for the overall usability of the user interface, 24 dealt with single components of the volume rendering system. These questions were based on Likert scales. Five additional questions were posed as multiple-choice questions.
7. *Focused Expert Interview (Debriefing).* Finally, a focused expert interview was conducted by P. It mainly addressed the system's functionalities and direct interaction. This interview took between 20 minutes and 1.5 hours. The users' comments were hand-noted.

Scenarios. We chose the following two scenarios in which the users could explore the volume rendering system:

- Scenario #1 was the skull of the male Visible Human CT Data Set [Spi96] (see Appendix, Plate A). It was proposed to emboss the ivories, the auditory canal, or the spine.
- Scenario #2 was a volume data set representing the temperature distribution in the interior of a passenger car (see Appendix, Plate B). The car body, the seats, and the driver were rendered with polygons. It was proposed to visualize the air conditioning output or particularly hot areas.

8.3 Evaluation Results

In this section we present the outcome of the evaluation analysis.

Self-Rating. The evaluation proved that there was the expected range of users' skills (see Table 1). Twelve volunteer users participated in the evaluation. They stemmed from either related departments at the University of Stuttgart, or they worked with visualization software professionally.

Table 1. Self-Rated experience on a Likert-Scale from 1 (low) to 5 (high)

Type of Experience	Average Score
CAVE or CUBE	2.83
Volume Rendering	1.90
Scenarios	1.13
Scientific Visualization	2.33

Follow-Up Questionnaire. We found the following significant answers from the questionnaire:

- For 2 users the image quality was not detailed enough, 7 users did not mind the poor image quality with large volumes.
- 11 users found the High Quality mode useful, 1 found it awkward to use.
- 11 users thought the automatic alignment of the editor menu was useful.
- 10 users liked the layout of the user interface components.
- 1 user had trouble interacting with the rotary knobs.
- For 9 users, defining the alpha function with pins made sense.
- All users found the probe mode to be helpful, 10 users thought it was easy to use.
- 9 users found the clipping plane beneficial, 8 users thought it was easy to use.

Overall usability satisfaction with the system scored from 55 % to 90 %. The numbers are based on a composite measure derived from a System Usability Scale [Bev91].

Table 2. Overall Usability Issues

Issue: RS:	Alpha and color pins are hard to differentiate when both are gray. Use striped alpha pins.
Issue: RS:	Mouse button assignment is confusing when working with pins. Assign selection and dragging to the same button, with an additional undo-function.
Issue: RS:	Imprecise pin positioning in the transfer function field. Introduce a magnification mode and a numeric display of scalar values.
Issue: RS:	When entering the probe mode, users were unaware of the active clipping plane mode. Give feedback on clipping plane position.
Issue: RS:	Users wished for a rectangular or trapezoidal alpha pin. Introduce an additional alpha pin type.
Issue: RS:	Invisible colors in color bar resulting from transparent regions in the alpha function made it difficult to set the color of color pins. Separate the color bar into two regions with and without alpha representation.
Issue: RS:	After deletion of all color pins the volume turns black and thus becomes invisible on a black background, even with opaque regions in the alpha function. Use white as the default color instead of black.

Overall Usability Issues. After having consulted both quantitative and qualitative data, we filtered the most important key findings occurring across all investigative methods. Issues are separated into a short description and a redesign strategy (RS), see Table 2.

9 Performance Numbers

Table 3 shows the slice numbers which are achieved on our SGI Onyx2 system with two Infinite Reality2 pipes. Full size means the object fills one wall entirely, half size means that the object fills only a quarter of a wall. The test object is the 256x256x120 voxels skull, which was also used in the evaluation's scenario #1.

Table 3. Rendering Performance

Frame Rate [fps]	#Slices, Full Size	#Slices, Half Size
1	381	381
2	172	381
5	65	255
10	32	93
15	16	53
20	9	19

10 Conclusion and Future Work

We have presented a volume rendering system for virtual environments which includes interaction elements for adjusting the transfer function, a probe mode, and a clipping plane. The evaluation of the system shows its general usability, but it points out a number of issues to be solved in future versions. We were surprised at how little the users were disturbed by the relatively poor image quality of large volumes, but this may in part be due to the existence of the high quality mode.

Beyond solving the usability issues, future work on the system should concentrate on two fields:

First of all the rendering quality must be improved. This can either be accomplished by using faster texturing hardware, so that more texture slices can be drawn for each frame. Or the rendering algorithm can be improved, for example by applying level-of-detail strategies.

Secondly, a more diverse set of direct interaction techniques with the volume data and more functionality for the transfer function editor needs to be developed. The evaluation showed that different kinds of user groups have entirely different requirements, resulting from their profession, which cannot be solved with one single implementation.

11 Acknowledgements

This research is supported by the Deutsche Forschungsgemeinschaft within the SFBs 382 and 374. The car cabin data set is courtesy of the DaimlerChrysler AG. The Visible Human Data Set is courtesy of the National Library of Medicine and the Visible Human Project. The statistical FE simulation data was used with the kind permission of J. Marczyk, EASi, and SGI. The COVISE visualization system is a common development of the HLRS Visualization Department and its spin-off company Vircinity, which offers COVISE commercially.

12 References

[Bev91] N. Bevan, J. Kirakowski, J. Maissel, "What is usability?", in H.-J. Bullinger (ed.), Human Aspects in Computing: Design and use of interactive systems and work with terminals, Amsterdam, 1991

[Bra95] R. Brady, J. Pixton, G. Baxter, P. Moran, C.S. Potter, B. Carragher, A. Belmont, "Crumbs: A Virtual Environment Tracking Tool for Biological Imaging", IEEE Symposium on Frontiers in Biomedical Visualization Proceedings, 1995

[Cru93] C. Cruz-Neira, D.J. Sandin, T.A. DeFanti, "Surround-Screen Projection-Based Virtual Reality: The Design and Implementation of the CAVE", SIGGRAPH 1993 Proceedings

[Cul93] T.J. Cullip, U. Neumann, "Accelerating Volume Reconstruction With 3D Texture Hardware", Technical Report TR93-027, University of North Carolina, Chapel Hill, 1993

[Lin99] R.W. Lindeman, J.L. Sibert, J.K. Hahn, "Towards Usable VR: An Empirical Study of User Interfaces for Immersive Virtual Environments", CHI 99 Proceedings, pp. 64-71

[Ran95] D. Rantzau, et.al., "Collaborative and Interactive Visualization in a Distributed High Performance Software Environment", Proceedings of the International Workshop on High Performance Computing for Graphics and Visualization, Swansea, Wales, 1995

[Ran98] D. Rantzau, K. Frank, U. Lang, D. Rainer, U. Woessner, "COVISE in the CUBE: An Environment for Analyzing Large and Complex Simulation Data", Proceedings of the IPTW 1998

[Spi96] S. Spitzer, M.J. Ackerman, A.L. Scherzinger, D. Whitlock, "The Visible Human Male: A Technical Report", Journal of the American Medical Informatics Association, 1996

[Swa99] K. Swartz, U. Thakkar, D. Hix, R. Brady, "Evaluating the Usability of Crumbs: A Case Study of VE Usability Engineering", Proceedings of the IPTW 1999

[Vol00] W.R. Volz, "Gigabyte Volume Viewing Using Split Software/Hardware Interpolation", IEEE VolViz 2000 Proceedings

[Wei00] M. Weiler, R. Westermann, C. Hansen, K. Zimmermann, T. Ertl, "Level-Of-Detail Volume Rendering via 3D Textures", IEEE VolViz 2000 Proceedings

[Woh00] W. Wohlfahrter, L.M. Encarnacao, D. Schmalstieg, "Interactive Volume Exploration on the StudyDesk", Proceedings of the IPTW 2000

Editors' Note: see Appendix, p. 282 for colored figures of this paper

Adaptive Networking for Tele-Immersion

Jason Leigh+, Oliver Yu, Dan Schonfeld, Rashid Ansari,
Eric He, Atul Nayak, Jinghua Ge, Naveen Krishnaprasad,
Kyoung Park, Yong-joo Cho, Liujia Hu, Ray Fang,
Alan Verlo, Linda Winkler, Thomas A. DeFanti

+spiff@evl.uic.edu

Electronic Visualization Laboratory **(EVL)**
Dept EECS, MC 154, 1120 SEO, 851 S. Morgan St.

University of Illinois at Chicago
Chicago, IL 60607, USA

Abstract. Tele-Immersive applications possess an unusually broad range of networking requirements. As high-speed and Quality of Service-enabled networks emerge, it will becoming more difficult for developers of Tele-Immersion applications, and networked applications in general, to take advantage of these enhanced services. This paper proposes an adaptive networking framework to ultimately allow applications to optimize their network utilization in pace with advances in networking services. In working toward this goal, this paper will present a number of networking techniques for improving performance in tele-immersive applications and examines whether the Differentiated Services mechanism for network Quality of Service is suitable for Tele-Immersion.

1 Introduction

Tele-Immersion is the integration of collaborative virtual reality (VR) with audio and video conferencing in the context of data-mining and significant computation. The ultimate goal of Tele-Immersion is not only to reproduce a real face-to-face meeting in every detail, but to provide the "next generation" interface for collaborators, world-wide, to work together in a virtual environment that is seamlessly enhanced by computation and large databases. When participants are Tele-Immersed, they are able to see and interact with each other in a shared virtual environment. They are able to query and visualize data stores and steer complex scientific and engineering simulations[1].

One of the challenges of Tele-Immersion is that it poses diverse requirements of the underlying networks. For example, to convey audio and gestures of virtual participants (avatars,) low network latency is required; to distribute state updates, low latency but reliable data transmission is preferred; and to distribute data sets high-speed bulk data transfer is needed. In this paper, we will present our most recent work in exploiting advanced networking techniques to optimize data distribution in Tele-Immersion. We will describe our experiences in using Quality-of-Service-enabled high-speed networks for supporting Tele-Immersion. We will structure this work by proposing an adaptive networking framework to allow application developers to map their data distribution requirements to suitable networking services. We believe that as networking technology becomes more complex, application developers will have to rely increasingly on intelligent adaptive systems to make decisions on how to optimally distribute their data over them. The work discussed in this paper serves as a starting point toward that ultimate goal.

2 Adaptive Networking for Tele-Immersion

We propose an intelligent adaptive networking system (Fig. 1) consisting of a Strategy Selector, Adaptive Controller and three supporting services: a Resource Monitor, a Quality of Service (QoS) Provisioner and a collection of network transport mechanisms. The Strategy Selector's role is to take application-specified data delivery requirements (e.g. bandwidth, latency, jitter, reliability, etc) and translate them into networking and computational resource allocations needed to meet the applications' demands. The Strategy Selector must monitor the current state of the network, select an optimal transmission protocol, and make QoS requests (if available.) Some protocols such as Forward Error Corrected UDP or Parallel TCP (described later) may pose additional computational overhead, which the Strategy Selector must take into account. If QoS is available, the Strategy Selector must contact the Admission Control system to determine if the available bandwidth is available, and then make a reservation using the Reservation Controller. Once a strategy has been activated, the Adaptive Controller must monitor the progress of the data transmission and adjust networking and computational parameters to sustain the desired performance. To accommodate multiple simultaneous and heterogeneous network flows, the Adaptive Controller may alter some of the low-level transport protocol parameters (such as buffer or window size,) or may adjust QoS reservations dynamically.

It is clear that the realization of such a system is an ambitious endeavor. In this paper, we will present several steps we have taken towards understanding the issues and creating the necessary building blocks towards such a system. These include:

- a study of the behavior of the Differentiated Services QoS with respect to the requirements of real-time tele-immersive applications;
- the development of a collection of advanced data delivery mechanisms as part of our CAVERNsoft Tele-Immersion toolkit[2, 3]. These include Reliable Blast UDP for bulk data transfer, and Forward Error Corrected UDP for semi-reliable, low-latency state transfer.

3 Quality of Service for Real-time Collaborative Applications

Network Quality of Service (QoS) refers to the ability of an application to request a guaranteed level of networking service in the form of bandwidth, latency or jitter. There are two well-known types of QoS: Integrated Services (IntServ) and Differentiated Services (DiffServ). IntServ achieves QoS by having intervening routers maintain the state of a particular network link between two end points[4]. While this method can provide a hard guarantee on QoS, it is ultimately not scalable to the larger Internet. DiffServ, on the other hand, takes the approach of marking network traffic with a priority level that can be interpreted by the router to effect special treatment of the data packet[5]. In particular, the marked packets are promoted to a higher priority queue in the router and, as a result, spend less time in the router. Packets that are not marked are attached to a lower priority queue, and in some cases may be dropped when congestion arises. A more detailed description of DiffServ may be found in the paper by Foster et al [6].

The common misconception in the field of collaborative virtual reality (CVR) is that QoS, once it is available, will solve all of CVR's networking problems. At the same time networking experts believe that bandwidth provisioning is the only form of QoS needed by applications. The experiments described below were performed as a joint project between collaborative virtual reality and networking experts in order to shed some light on these common misconceptions.

A series of experiments were performed over a wide area DiffServ testbed as part of the EMERGE project. EMERGE [7] is a Department of Energy funded project for designing, deploying and testing Differentiated Services on an IP/ATM Regional GigaPoP Network interoperating with ESnet for applications in Combustion, Climate and High-Energy Physics. The main participants of the experiments were EVL and Argonne National Laboratory (ANL)- approximately 30 minutes away by car.

Cisco 7507 DiffServ routers at ANL were connected to DiffServ routers at EVL as shown in **Fig. 2**. The router at EVL had Weighted Fair Queueing enabled; and the routers at ANL had Priority Queueing enabled to produce DiffServ's Expedited Forwarding behavior. Several experiments were performed over this testbed, but in the interest of brevity, we will report on the results of only one experiment. The reader is encouraged to peruse the detailed technical report at [8]. The goal of the experiment was to observe whether DiffServ is able to maintain bandwidth allocations while keeping latency low, especially during periods of high network congestion. The experiment began with the transmission of a steady foreground stream of UDP data at the networks saturation point (25Mbps) from ANL (Tundra) to EVL (Laurel). After some time, 25Mbps of competitive networking traffic was transmitted from Fjuk to Laurel to increase congestion over the inter-domain link between EVL and ANL. Then DiffServ was enabled on the foreground stream to determine if bandwidth and latency recovery would occur. GARA (the General-purpose Architecture for Reservation and Allocation,) developed by ANL was used to make the DiffServ reservation[9].

In Fig. 3 the dip in the top graph shows that when competitive traffic is injected the throughput of the foreground stream suffers. However, when DiffServ is enabled the throughput is brought back to near its original levels. This shows that DiffServ is effective in providing bandwidth guarantees. However, the second graph shows that latency was only partially restored. Note also that the restored (*one-way*) latency is at approximately 150ms, which has been shown in the past, to be intolerably high for real-time tightly coupled interactions in Tele-Immersion. Park et al [10] have found that the *roundtrip* latency threshold where human performance begins to noticeably degrade is approximately 200ms. The results suggest that while DiffServ is suitable for making bandwidth guarantees it is unable to reliably make latency guarantees *under heavy network congestion.* We have performed the same experiment over uncongested links (from EVL to ANL over an 80Mbps private virtual circuit) and have not observed the same performance degradation[8].

We believe the increased latency under heavy congestion maybe due to queueing that is occurring at the interior router (Aruba.) Priority queueing would ensure that the DiffServ marked packets would receive priority transmission, however since priority queueing is not pre-emptive on Cisco's 7507 router it must wait for all the packets in the non-priority queue to be forwarded before it can concentrate on priority traffic.

Finally to confirm our results in the context of a real tele-immersive application, we repeated the experiment using the Tele-Immersive Data Explorer (a collaborative VR application for querying data mining servers)[11]. In this experiment, low-bandwidth avatar data represented the foreground traffic. Again over a congested network, we observed the same increase in latency, as in our previous experiments [8].

4 Advanced Data Transport Techniques for Tele-Immersion

CAVERNsoft is an open source, cross-platform, C++ toolkit for building tele-immersive applications[2, 3]. Although its initial intended audience was developers of VR applications, CAVERNsoft's decoupled networking tools has made it useful in building networked applications in general. CAVERNsoft supports a broad collection of low-level to high-level data distribution tools. Low-level tools include classes for basic UDP, TCP and multicasting. Mid-level tools consist of classes for remote procedure calls, key/value database, parallel sockets, UDP and TCP reflectors, and remote file transfer. High-level tools include C++ classes for rendering articulated avatars, audio conferencing, and shared scene graphs. As one of the intended audiences for these tools are computational scientists, a 64-bit version was implemented- for example the 64-bit remote file transfer API allows the transfer of files greater than 2 Gigabytes in size. Finally, since optimal network utilization requires careful monitoring of network performance, every CAVERNsoft network class has been instrumented to measure bandwidth, latency, jitter and burstiness.

In our continuing efforts to expand CAVERNsoft's networking services, we present below, schemes for reliable low-latency state transmission, and high throughput bulk data transfer.

4.1 Reliable Low-Latency Data Transfer for Tele-Immersion

For long distance networks such as international networks, latencies are high (on the order of hundreds of milliseconds). In Tele-Immersion we would ideally like state updates in the shared environment to occur with a minimum amount of latency and with a high degree of reliability. A scheme is therefore needed to transmit data reliably over long distances without requiring the acknowledgement typically used in protocols such as TCP. Forward Error Correction (FEC) provides a promising solution to this problem. FEC works by collecting between 1 and N (typically 2 or 3) data packets and performing a bit-wise operation on the packets (such as XOR) to generate a "redundant" packet. This packet is delivered along with the regular UDP traffic as a separate UDP stream. If any data packets are lost, FEC packets can be used to reconstruct the missing packet. A detailed description of the encoding algorithm can be found in [12].

To evaluate our FEC implementation we performed a series of experiments between EVL and SARA (SARA- Stichting Academisch Rekencentrum Amsterdam) over STAR TAP (the Science and Technology Advanced Research Transit Access Point- a National Science Foundation funded project to interconnect international high speed networks.)[13]. The experiment involved comparing the latency, jitter and packet loss of basic UDP, TCP and UDP augmented with FEC. Details on the experimental setup can be found in [12].

Fig. 4 shows the results of the experiment using an FEC scheme that generated 1 redundant packet for every 3 consecutive UDP packets. Notice that FEC does appear to incur lower latency than TCP but slightly higher latency than UDP. Also, note that the benefits of FEC are greatest at small packet sizes since it takes less time to accumulate and encode 3 small packets. The goal in future work would be to bring FEC performance closer to UDP performance while maintaining maximal reliability. Fig. **4** also shows the variation of latency (jitter) between TCP, UDP and FEC. Notice that FEC produces lower levels of jitter than TCP but higher levels than standard UDP.

Finally, to observe packet loss of UDP versus FEC, packets were sent at a rate of 50Mbps over a 100Mbps link between EVL and SARA. Then an additional 50Mbps of congestion traffic was injected. The results in **Fig. 5** shows that FEC was quite effective at recovering lost packets. However, note that while our FEC scheme is good at recovering intermittent lost packets it cannot recover from the loss of large consecutive blocks of packets. To recover from this the selection of encoding packets must be more widely distributed across the data stream. This unfortunately has the effect of increasing latency. Another drawback of FEC is that the FEC packets themselves can become a source of congestion. Hence, careful selections of FEC parameters need to be made to ensure optimal performance. For the purposes of transmitting real-time state information in tele-immersive applications, the recommendation is to encode few (like 3) and small (like 1Kbyte) consecutive packets over networks that have the capacity to sustain the additional bandwidth needed by FEC.

4.2 High Throughput Techniques for Tele-Immersion

Quality of Service is designed to guarantee a level of service (mainly bandwidth) for the networked application. It does not however guarantee that the networked application will be able to take full advantage of the bandwidth, even when it is made available. Since tele-Immersive applications are so highly interactive, the expectation is for the retrieval of distantly located data sets, such as 3D models, to be equally expedient. This can only be achieved by being able to maximally use the available bandwidth to deliver the data.

To support high-bandwidth bulk data transfer we have developed two techniques- Parallel TCP Socket Striping and Reliable Blast UDP. These two schemes allow applications to overcome what is classically known as the Long Fat Network (LFN)

problem[14]. The LFN problem occurs over long, high-bandwidth networks, such as those between the United States and Europe or Asia. The high round-trip latencies in these networks (at best 120ms) will result in gross bandwidth *under*-utilization when default TCP is used for data delivery. This is because TCP's windowing mechanism imposes a limit on the amount of data it will send before it must wait for an acknowledgement. The long delays that occur over international networks means that TCP will spend an inordinate amount of time waiting for acknowledges, which in turn means that the client's data transmission will never reach the peak available transmission rate of the network. Traditionally this is "remedied" by modifying TCP's window and buffer sizes to match the bandwidth * delay product (capacity) of the network. For example, for a 45Mbps link between Chicago and Amsterdam, with an average round trip time of 150ms, the capacity is 45*0.15/8 = 0.84Mbytes.
Unfortunately adjusting TCP window size is problematic for two reasons: firstly, on some operating systems (such as IRIX for the SGI,) the window size can only be modified by building a new version of the kernel- hence this is not an operation a user-level application can invoke. Secondly, one needs to know the current capacity of the network in order to set the window size correctly. The current capacity varies with the amount of background traffic already on the network.

Parallel TCP Socket striping overcomes the LFN problem by partitioning a payload and delivering it over multiple TCP connections. Reliable Blast UDP overcomes the LFN problem by literally "blasting" UDP packets over the networks and then transmitting an acknowledgement only after the full payload has been transmitted. Our experiments between Chicago and Amsterdam (at SARA) will illustrate how each of these schemes can significantly improve throughput over LFNs. In the interest of brevity we refer the reader to Park et al [3] for information on our Parallel TCP socket striping scheme and performance results.

Reliable Blast UDP (RUDP)

When operating over QoS-enabled networks the probability of packet loss is low. To take advantage of this we have implemented an alternative reliable data transmission scheme using UDP augmented with acknowledgements. The scheme works by "blasting" the contents of a data file at just below the available bandwidth without asking the remote site to acknowledge any of the packets. Hence, all the bandwidth is used for pure data transmission. At the remote site, a tally is kept for all the packets that have arrived and, after some timeout period, a list of missing packets is sent back to the sending client. The sender reacts by resending all the missing packets and again waiting for another negative acknowledgement.

Fig. 6 shows the results of using RUDP to deliver a 50M file over a 100Mbps link between EVL and SARA. Since QoS is currently not available between the two sites, we chose to send data at rates well below the maximum available bandwidth of the network link- in essence emulating a smaller reserved QoS link. The table shows the bandwidth at which RUDP data was transmitted and the effective throughput of the total file transfer. Notice that on an over-provisioned network, effective throughput is almost as high as the sending bandwidth. This is in contrast to TCP, which typically incurs a 20% bandwidth loss by requiring frequent acknowledgements. Note also that as we approach the bandwidth limit of the link, performance begins to decrease-however performance is no poorer than what is expected of optimally tuned TCP. Remember that these experiments were conducted without the benefit of QoS. Hence, interference from competing traffic streams was possible and likely. We predict that our results would yield even better performance with QoS.

5 Conclusion

The work presented in this paper serves as a beginning for our research in adaptive networking. While our interest has been driven mainly by our need to provide better networking services for Tele-Immersion, the results we have presented are generalizable to other networked applications.

Future research on our adaptive networking framework will consist of the following goals:

1. To define QoS from the point of view of application developers. For example QoS may mean: "reliable low-latency transmission," "faster download," "faster realtime response," "guaranteed delivery by a deadline."
2. To characterize transmission protocols, QoS mechanisms and computational resources as a set of parameters or functions.
3. To find suitable mappings that will translate application-level descriptions of QoS to characterizations of required network services. Ie. To map from item 1. to 2. to guarantee optimal application and network performance. Heuristics may be used initially. For example:
    - If data requires low latency but can tolerate much loss use UDP
    - If data requires low latency and can tolerate low loss use Forward Error Corrected UDP
    - Else use TCP
    - If data set is large and requires reliable delivery:
        - Use TCP and adjust window size and buffer size to match network capacity if possible;
        - Else use parallel TCP socket striping;
        - If QoS is available- use Reliable Blast UDP
4. To find prediction models that can be used to predict the consequences of making mapping decisions during dynamic network situations.
5. To test our predictions on real applications and on real networking testbeds.

Our QoS experiments have shown that Differentiated Services is able to provide bandwidth and latency guarantees when the network is not over-subscribed. However, if the network *is* over-subscribed then only bandwidth guarantees are possible. We believe that Integrated Services QoS should be able to overcome the limitations of DiffServ. However the main drawback of IntServ is that it is not scalable to the larger Internet. We, as well as other researchers have proposed that a scalable solution might require the use of IntServ at the edge routers (where the clients connect,) and the use of DiffServ in the core routers (where the excess bandwidth resides.)[15] We are in the process of constructing a network testbed to firstly, examine IntServ, and then a combination of IntServ and DiffServ.

Finally, we are in the continual process of translating our research results into useable tools for the computational science community. CAVERNsoft [2, 3], our open source toolkit for building networked applications, already has built-in performance monitoring, and parallel socket striping capabilities. Modules for Forward Error Correction and Reliable Blast UDP will be incorporated in the near future.

6 Acknowledgements

We would like to graciously thank our collaborators at SARA, CERN and Argonne National Laboratory without whom these experiments would not have been possible. We would also like to thank our collaborators at the National Center for Data Mining for sharing their parallel socket algorithm.

The virtual reality research, collaborations, and outreach programs at the Electronic Visualization Laboratory (EVL) at the University of Illinois at Chicago are made possible by major funding from the National Science Foundation (NSF), awards EIA-9802090, EIA-9871058, ANI-9980480, ANI-9730202, and ACI-9418068, as well as NSF Partnerships for Advanced Computational Infrastructure (PACI) cooperative agreement ACI-9619019 to the National Computational Science Alliance. EVL also receives major funding from the US Department of Energy (DOE), awards 99ER25388 and 99ER25405, as well as support from the DOE's Accelerated Strategic Computing Initiative (ASCI) Data and Visualization Corridor program. In addition, EVL receives funding from Pacific Interface on behalf of NTT Optical Network Systems Laboratory in Japan and Microsoft Corporation.

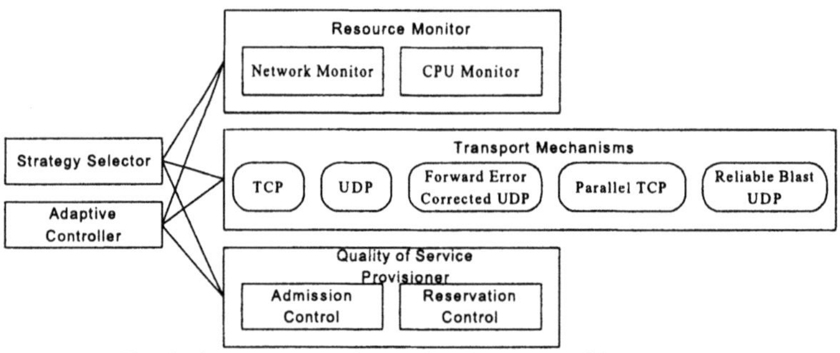

Fig. 1. Components of an Adaptive Networking System

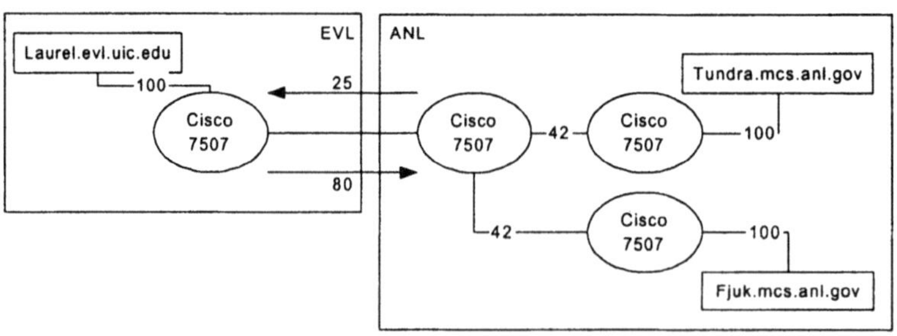

Fig. 2. Simplified diagram of EMERGE DiffServ Testbed. Numbers on the links represent bandwidth levels.

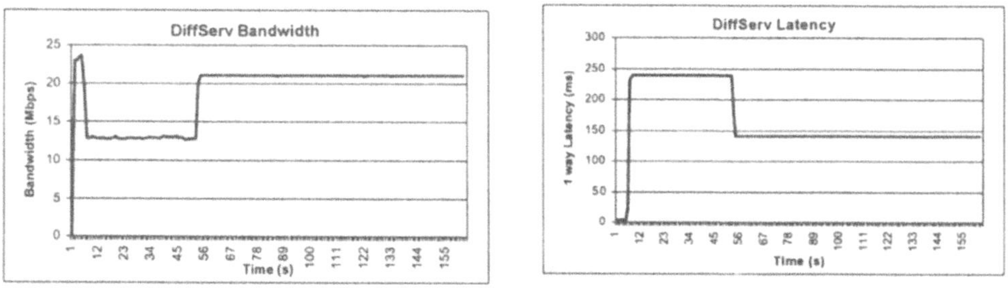

Fig. 3. Results showing that DiffServ, while being able to make bandwidth guarantees, may not always provide latency guarantees.

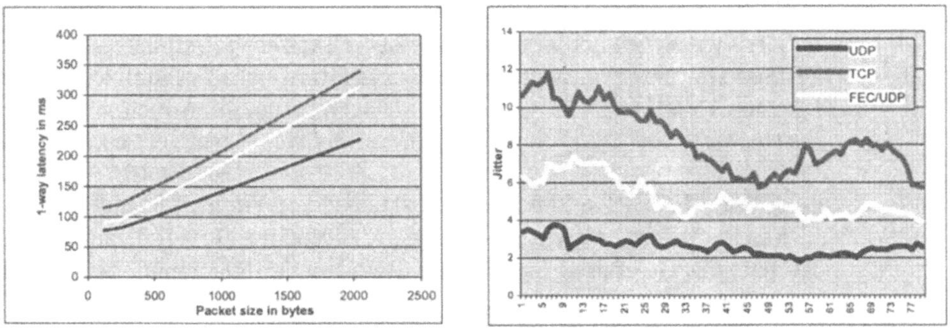

Fig. 4. The graph on the left shows the transmission of 100 packets under TCP, UDP, FEC/UDP. The FEC scheme derives its greatest benefit when packet sizes are small as larger packet sizes incur additional buffer processing time. The graph on the right shows that FEC also introduces jitter in the data stream. Jitter is computed by first calculating the short-term latency over every 20 data points and then computing the average deviation of the instantaneous latency as compared to the short-term latency.

	Packet Loss
UDP	1.90%
FEC	0.05%
UDP with congestion	17.40%
FEC with congestion	4.15%

Fig. 5. Comparison of Packet Loss in UDP vs. FEC over an uncongested and congested network.

Sending Bandwidth (Mbps)	**Effective Bandwidth**	**Number of NAKs**
20	19.7	0
40	38.5	0
60	54-57	1
80	56-70	2
90	61-77	3

Fig. 6. Comparison of transmission bandwidth vs. effective throughput using Reliable Blast UDP over a 100Mbps non-QoS provisioned link between Chicago and Amsterdam. When the

network is over provisioned performance is good. We anticipate the best results of RUDP to occur in conjunction with the use of a QoS scheme such as DiffServ or IntServ.

7 References

[1] J. Leigh, Johnson, A., DeFanti, T., et al., "A Review of Tele-Immersive Applications in the CAVE Research Network," presented at IEEE VR99, Houston, Texas, 1999.

[2] J. Leigh, Cho, Y. J., Krishnaprasad, N., Nayak, A., Fang, R., "the CAVERNsoft Tele-Immersion Toolkit : http://www.evl.uic.edu/cavern/cavernG2."

[3] K. Park, Cho, Y., Krishnaprasad, N., Scharver, C., Lewis, M., Leigh, J., "CAVERNsoft G2: A Toolkit for High Performance Tele-Immersive Collaboration," presented at ACM Symposium on Virtual Reality Software and Technology, Seoul, Korea, 2000.

[4] IntServ, http://www.ietf.org/html.charters/intserv-charter.html.

[5] DiffServ, http://www.ietf.org/html.charters/diffserv-charter.html.

[6] I. Foster, Kesselman, C., "Globus. A Metacomputing Infrastructure Toolkit," *International Journal of Supercomputing Application*, vol. 11, pp. 115-128, 1997.

[7] EMERGE, "EMERGE : http://www.evl.uic.edu/cavern/EMERGE."

[8] J. Leigh, Yu, O., Verlo, A., Roy, A., Winkler, L., DeFanti, T. A., "Differentiated Services Experiments Between the Electronic Visualization Laboratory and Argonne National Laboratory : http://www.evl.uic.edu/cavern/papers/DiffServ12_12_2K.pdf," 2000.

[9] I. Foster, Sander, V., Roy, A., "A Quality of Service Architecture that Combines Resource Reservation and Application Adaptation," presented at 8th International Workshop on Quality of Service (IWQOS, 2000.

[10] K. Park, Kenyon, R, "Effects of Network Characteristics on Human Performance in a Collaborative Virtual Environment," presented at IEEE VR, Houston, Texas, 1999.

[11] N. Sawant, Scharver, C., Leigh, J., Johnson, A., Reinhart, G., Creel, E., Batchu, S., Bailey, S., Grossman, R, "The Tele-Immersive Data Explorer: A Distributed Architecture for Collaborative Interactive Visualization of Large Data-sets," presented at 4th International Immersive Projection Technology Workshop, Ames, Iowa, 2000.

[12] R. Fang, Schonfeld, D., Ansari, R., Leigh, J., "Forward Error Correction for Multimedia and Tele - immersion Streams : http://www.startap.net/images /PDF/RayFangFEC1999.pdf," 2000.

[13] T. A. DeFanti, Goldstein, S., "STAR TAP, http://www.startap.net."

[14] W. R. Stevens, "TCP/IP Illustrated," vol. 1: Addison Wesley, 1994, pp. 344-350.

[15] O. Yu, "Dynamic QoS and Routing Support for Real-time Multimedia Applications over Next Generation Internet," presented at Proceedings of IEEE International Conference on Multimedia and Expo 2000, 2000.

COMPUTER GRAPHICS OPTIQUE
Optical Superposition of Projected Computer Graphics

Aditi Majumder and Greg Welch

Department of Computer Science,
University of North Carolina at Chapel Hill, NC, USA
{majumder,welch}@cs.unc.edu

Abstract. We present some ideas and demonstrations for a hybrid projector-based rendering and display technique we call *Computer Graphics Optique*. Instead of partially overlapping projected images to achieve a wide-area display, we completely overlap projected images on top of each other to achieve the addition of light and color in an "optical composition buffer." The idea is to use the optical composition to replace some analytical computation, to increase rendering speed, gain flexibility, intensity range, and intensity resolution. Where projector-based displays are appropriate, potential uses include the optical realization of certain effects normally requiring a digital accumulation buffer, the optical composition of heterogeneous lighting techniques, and the ability to use heterogeneous graphics engines, in parallel. In addition one can make use of the optical projector control of focus augmented with the optical superposition to achieve effects that are otherwise computationally expensive. We believe that this technique offers the possibility of a new paradigm for combined rendering and projector-based display.

1 Introduction

Light projectors have been used in computer graphics for almost as long as graphics has been around. During all of this time they have been used almost exclusively to construct wide-area and high-resolution tiled displays [17, 7, 10, 15, 13]. A typical design goal for such systems is to maximize the usable display area, and so overlap between projectors is minimized. Recently however we wondered what might be gained by *maximizing* the overlap between multiple projectors—that is, by "stacking" or *superimposing* the projector images on top of each other to achieve addition of light and color *optically*.

For example, this optical superposition certainly yields brighter displays. Taking advantage of this property, many popular projector vendors like Sony, Panasonic, Epson and others are now providing features to 'stack' 2-3 projectors to achieve two or three times brighter images. They are also providing lens shift controls to facilitate the alignment of imagery from multiple projectors right on top of each other.

It appears that optical superposition of imagery was being done in a limited fashion even a century ago. In 1888 Emile Reynaud created a machine called *Theatre Optique* (Figure 1), a revised version of his earlier invention, the *praxinoscope*. In Theatre Optique a subsidiary light called "magic lantern," was used to project a stationary background on the same screen where the action film was projected. In more recent times,

Fig. 1. Theatre Optique

the flight simulator community used a similar method called *calligraphic lights* to superimpose high intensity and brighter runway lights on a projected scene.

Beyond increased brightness, we believe optical superposition augmented by some optical effects like blurring (available in most projectors), can be used in modern computer graphics to replace expensive *computation*, to increase rendering *speed*, to achieve *flexibility*, and to increase intensity *range* as well as *resolution*. We like to call such a hybrid projector based rendering and display technique *Computer Graphics Optique* (CGO) in deference to Reynaud's Theater Optique.

At this point, one might reasonably wonder about achieving similar effects with specialized graphics hardware, for example by compositing results from multiple rendering boards like the PixelFlow machine [16], using interconnected parallel graphics cards like Quantum3D [1], or composition/interconnect systems such as the Lightning-2 system at Stanford University [5]. What we hope to convey is at the very least an interesting *alternative* to specialized or monolithic graphics engines when projector-based displays are appropriate, an alternative that leverages the effective "bandwidth" into the "optical buffer," i.e. the projector screen or display surface.

In this paper we present a number of ideas for the uses of optical superposition in projector-based interactive computer graphics. While we have experimented with all of the ideas, some are more well developed than others. For these we have done some preliminary analysis of their usefulness, and we have developed some relatively simple methods for implementing them. The practical utility of some of the less-developed ideas are yet to be proven, however we also present those ideas with the hope of sharing them with the graphics community to obtain feedback that will help us to better assess their utility and target our efforts.

2 Interactive Depth of Field via Optical Blurring

We believe there is a significant advantage to using the optical controls on a pair of projectors to achieve computationally-intensive realistic effects like blurring at *inter-*

active rates, which is not currently possible even using specialized graphics hardware. Using the projector optics one can achieve *depth of field* (DOF) effects at interactive rates, something that would add valuable realism to projector-based environments for flight simulation and training, scientific visualization, immersive virtual environments, architectural walkthroughs, and entertainment. Beyond a lack of realism, the absence of DOF effects leads to eye strain as *fusion stimuli* are generated for objects outside the limited depth of focus of the eye. DOF effects are also sometimes used as depth cues. For example for night-vision training of helicopter pilots, pilots rely on DOF cues near the ground to compensate for the narrow fields of view of night vision goggles. By some simple experiments, we demonstrate how optical blurring and superposition can be used to achieve a DOF effect in real-time.

2.1 Algorithm

We use two projectors whose images overlap completely. We designate one projector as the *focused* projector and the other as the *defocused* projector. We then adjust the optical focus of the latter to correspond to the maximum circle of confusion for the application. At run-time we use a two pass rendering approach. After the image is rendered by the traditional graphics pipeline in the first pass, each pixel is divided into two complementary components based on its distance from the focal plane in the second pass. Thus we get two images: one to be sent to the focused projector, and the other to the defocused projector. When projected, the two overlapping images combine via optical superposition, resulting in a single image with depth-dependent blur (Color Plate).

In effect we use the projector optics to perform two samples of the image convolution, and then we use optical superposition to blend a weighted combination of the results. We can vary the depth of the focal plane in real time. One could do so based on a user's head position for example, or ideally (if available) eye tracking could be employed [18] to adjust the focal plane.

We can use a similar technique to achieve a focused inset region in a blurred 2D image (or visa versa). We use a focused projector to render the inset region, and a defocused projector to render the rest. We can move the focused inset around in the image interactively by moving a pattern in the alpha buffers (Color Plate).

2.2 Analysis

In this section, we analyze what we are actually getting using this method and how similar it is to the ideal depth of field effect.

Depth of Field Effect : Based on a *thin lens model* for the human eye, Figure 2 helps explain the blurring of the retinal image of points beyond the limited DOF. We let r be the distance between the lens and the retina, e be the aperture of the eye lens, and b be the focal or fixation depth. An object point at depth b will form a focused spot (circle of radius 0) on the retina, while an object point P at some other depth z, will form a (blur) circle of radius c on the retina. In general the *thin lens equation* relates focal length, the distance to the object point, and the distance to the focused image as

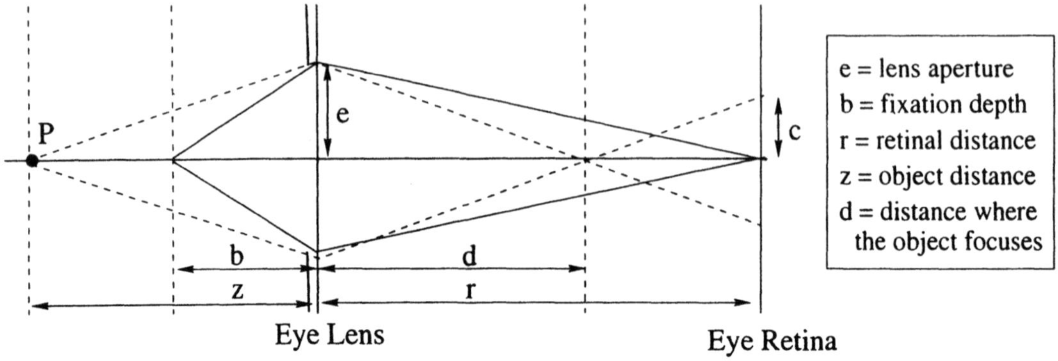

Fig. 2. The Depth of Field Effect in Human Eye

$$\frac{1}{object\_dist} + \frac{1}{image\_dist} = \frac{1}{focal\_length} \quad (1)$$

Using this expression, the principle of *similar triangles*, and the fact that an object at depth z focuses at a distance d from the lens, we can obtain the following expression for the radius c of the corresponding circle of confusion in Figure 2:

$$c_z = |er(\frac{1}{b} - \frac{1}{z})|. \quad (2)$$

Relative Radius of Confusion : Let us assume we are rendering a scene with near and far plane at depth n and f respectively. We can say that the *maximum* radius of a circle of confusion, c_m, will occur for an object point on the far plane when the focal plane is coincident with the near plane, or vice-versa. Hence, from Equation 2

$$c_m = \left| er\left(\frac{1}{n} - \frac{1}{f}\right)\right| \quad (3)$$

We define the *relative radius of confusion*, c_r, for a point at depth z as the ratio of c_z and c_m as follows.

$$c_r = \frac{c_z}{c_m} = \left|\frac{\frac{1}{b} - \frac{1}{z}}{\frac{1}{n} - \frac{1}{f}}\right| \quad (4)$$

Notice that c_r is zero for an object point at b and increases as the distance of the object from the fixation depth increases.

Second Rendering Pass : In the traditional graphics pipeline, the perspective transform z' of depth values z for a 3D scene with a near and far plane at $z = n$ and $z = f$ respectively, is given by

$$z' = \frac{f(z - n)}{z(f - n)} \quad (5)$$

Let us assume that we are rendering a scene when the focal depth is $z = b$. It turns out that relative radius of confusion c_r for any z can be obtained by simply subtracting b', the perspective transform of b, from z' obtained from the z-buffer.

$$|z' - b'| = |\frac{f(z-n)}{z(f-n)} - \frac{f(b-n)}{b(f-n)}| = \frac{|\frac{1}{b} - \frac{1}{z}|}{|\frac{1}{n} - \frac{1}{f}|} = c_r \tag{6}$$

During the first pass at runtime we copy the *desired image* (just rendered) in texture memory. In the second pass, we read the z-buffer values and then generate an *alpha mask* for the defocused projector by calculating the c_r at every pixel by subtracting b' from the values read from the z-buffer. We simultaneously generate a complementary alpha mask for the focused projector. Finally we use *alpha blending* and texture map the desired image on the projector's image plane using the respective alpha masks.

Summary : Thus, an ideal DOF effect is generated in a graphics systems by blurring each pixel by their relative radius of confusion. However, our method achieves this effect by the constant radius of confusion produced by the defocused projector while limiting the amount of light from the defocused projector to be proportional to the relative radius of confusion. We project the rest of the light from the focused projector with the hope that this will perceptually create a circle of confusion equivalent to the ideal one.

3 Parallelism and Flexibility in Rendering

Wile conventional graphics hardware has achieved significant performance in the years, it has done so while effectively restricting interactive computer graphics to specialized APIs and rendering paradigms. It is currently difficult, if not impossible, to match and mix between different rendering styles while rendering the same scene. We believe that optical superposition has the potential to liberate us from this rigidity and give us a new flexibility to simultaneously combine rendering methods for the same imagery. Even for one or more similar rendering methods the technique could potentially be used to exploit parallelism, improving rendering speed by sharing tasks between independent "optical pipelines."

Separating Lighting Components : One universal aspect of computer graphics where superposition inherently plays a fundamental role is virtual scene illumination. Such illumination is typically modeled as a sum of independent terms that are added together. Separating these components offers the flexibility of using different lighting effects in parallel for the same scene. For example, we can optically combine diffuse lighting from a global illumination algorithm with specular lighting from a simple Phong model. As a proof of concept, we compute the diffuse and specular lighting using two different graphics pipeline, and project the images asynchronously on top of each other from two different projectors. One might extend this to separate lighting into different spatial regions and resolutions also. For example, lower resolution computation and projectors for ambient or diffuse lighting, and higher resolution for specular effects or hard shadows.

Stages in Graphics Pipeline : There is often no reason for texture mapping to be coupled to lighting, which normally depends only on the surface normal and material properties. In some cases each could be computed with a different platform or pipeline, and projected asynchronously.

Multi-Pass Rendering : Many algorithms have multiple rendering passes which are independent of each other, and the *accumulation buffer* [9] is used to add colors. All such algorithms can have their different rendering passes implemented in multiple graphics pipeline in parallel, each being output to a projector, and the results can be combined in an *optical accumulation buffer*. For example, Diefenbach achieves effects like shadows, reflections and refractions in [4] using an accumulation buffer and a multi-pass rendering method. Or, for example, sometimes software and computational resources place practical limits on the number of lights that can be used in a scene (OpenGL is limited to eight lights). Thus an interactive ray-traced scene with 50 lights would probably take multiple rendering passes. Here also, we can render subsets of lights in parallel on separate graphics pipelines, and then optically combine the (projected) results (Color Plate) to achieve highly specular and photorealistic scenes without compromising on the interactive rates.

Synchronization Issues : In Bastos's *superposition rendering* [2], where all lighting computation is sequential and synchronized, Bastos notes that the computation of the glossy reflections is the primary rendering bottleneck. While we believe we can help by decoupling tasks, rendering them in parallel, and re-combining them optically, we need to develop an understanding of the perceptual effect of such asynchronous rendering. We are unable to find directly relevant user studies in the literature, and therefore intend to undertake this investigation.

4 Higher-Fidelity Imagery

The color range in conventional graphics ranges only from $0 - 255$. Here we show that a display made up of superimposed images from multiple projectors is not only brighter but has a higher intensity resolution which can be used to render outdoor/natural scenes more realistically.

A display d capable of producing a lowest intensity $I(0) = L$ (the black level) and highest intensity $I(n-1) = H$ (the white level), is characterized by the following.

- *Range:* The difference between the highest and the lowest intensity levels, $H - L$.
- *Dynamic Range:* The ratio of the highest and lowest intensities, $\frac{H}{L}$.
- The *number of levels*, n, between the highest and lowest intensities, which is typically 256. This is the number of unique discrete colors that can be produced.
- *Intensity Resolution:* Levels per unit intensity, $\frac{n}{H-L}$. This is true only for devices with a linear response. Thus, we assume that all our projectors have been corrected for different kind of non-linearities [10].

With the use of multiple overlapping projectors, the *range* is the sum of the individual projector ranges. The *dynamic range* is approximately the same as that of the individual projectors. It can be shown that a CGO display made up of m projectors each having n discrete intensity levels can have a minimum of $O(mn)$ and a maximum of $O(n^m)$ discrete intensity levels. As a result, we get a higher *intensity resolution* from a CGO display.

The number of levels (n) that is sufficient for a *monochrome* display is given by $1.01 = (H/L)^{1/n}$ [8]. Based on the response curves of multiple projectors [11] we find that $n = 500$ would be sufficient for a monochrome projector. Further, [3] says that humans are $3 - 4$ times more sensitive to luminance differences in the presence of color. Thus, the problems arising from the low value of n offered by current projectors can be addressed to some extent by CGO. Further, the larger range will result in higher quality images. We demonstrate this by using three overlapped projectors to render a high dynamic range scene (Color Plate).

5 Limitations

The CGO idea is not without limitations. The most significant limitation is that it is only useful when a projector-based display is appropriate. Further, since today's projectors do not produce zero intensity for a corresponding zero input, optical superposition increases perceived "black level." However, it is reasonable to expect this to improve with new technology [6]. A potential limitation when using CGO with parallel optical pipelines is that one might need to explicitly manage certain occlusions, instead of relying on the hardware to resolve them. Finally, while there may be concerns about luminance/color uniformity and geometric blending issues, we have used the methods of [11] to achieve results that are comparable to a single-projector setup.

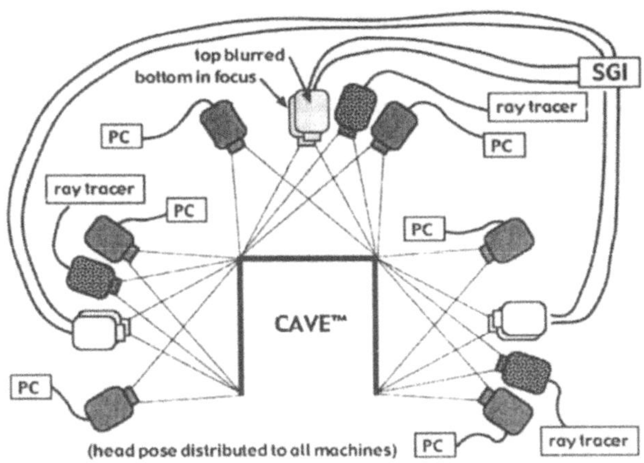

Fig. 3. A hypothetical CGO CAVE setup.

6 Conclusion

To summarize, we believe that optical superposition (CGO) offers a new hybrid rendering and display paradigm for immersive virtual environments (Figure 2), one that replaces some computation, offers greater rendering flexibility, and facilitates rendering parallelism. In support of this belief we have conducted some simple demonstrations of a few CGO applications. It appears at the least that the most valuable use is the generation of DOF effects at interactive rates for projector based systems. However we do also believe that the remaining CGO applications we have identified (and others we have not) can be used to achieve higher-fidelity projector-based imagery. We anticipate finding and/or developing a mathematical framework appropriate for the additive superposition of light, so that we can more rigorously find and characterize the uses and usefulness of CGO.

References

1. "Mercury: Realtime anti-aliasing 3d graphics sub-system," Technical Report, http://www.quantum3D.com/products%20pages/mercury.html, [cited Jan 2000].
2. Rui Bastos. *Superposition Rendering : Increased Realism for Interactive Walkthroughs*. PhD thesis, University of North Carolina at Chapel Hill, Department of Computer Science, 1999.
3. R.A. Chorley and J. Laylock, "Human factor consideration for the interface between electro-optical display and the human visual system," In *Displays*, volume 4, 1981.
4. Carolina Cruz-Neira, Daniel J. Sandin, and Thomas A.Defanti, "Surround-screen projection-based virtual reality : The design and implementation of the cave," In *Proceedings of ACM Siggraph*, 1993.
5. "Flash : Graphics System and Architecture,"Department of Computer Science, Stanford University, [cited on Jan 2001] Available from http://graphics.stanford.edu/projects/flashg/,
6. White Pages of ColorVision, http://www.colorvision-lasers.com/, [cited Jan 2001].
7. P. Diefenbach and N. Badler, "Pipeline rendering : Interactive refractions, reflections and shadows," In *Displays(Special Issue on Interactive Computer Graphics)*, 1994.
8. J.D. Foley, A. Van Dam, S.K. Feiner, and J.F.Hughes, *Computer Graphics Principles and Practice*. Addison Wesley, 1990.
9. Paul E. Haeberli and Kurt Akeley, "The accumulation buffer: Hardware support for high-quality rendering," *Computer Graphics (Proceedings of SIGGRAPH 90)*, 24(4):309–318, August 1990.
10. G. Humphreys and P. Hanrahan, "A distributed graphics system for large tiled displays," In *Proceedings of IEEE Visualization*, 1999.
11. Aditi Majumder, Zue He, Herman Towles, and Greg Welch. "Achieving Color Uniformity Across Multi-Projector Displays," In *Proceedings of Visualization*, 2000.
12. Thomas L. Martzall, "Simultaneous raster and calligraphic crt projection system for flight simulation," In *SPIE Proceedings,Electroluminescent Materials, Devices, and Large-Screen Displays*, volume 1910, 01/31/1993 - 02/05/1993.
13. R. Raskar, G. Welch, M. Cutts, A. Lake, L. Stesin, and H. Fuchs, "The office of the future: A unified approach to image based modeling and spatially immersive display," In *Proceedings of ACM Siggraph*, pages 168–176, 1998.
14. Ramesh Raskar, "Immersive planar displays using roughly aligned projectors." In *Proceedings of IEEE Virtual Reality 2000*, 1999.
15. Samanta Rudro, Jiannan Zheng, Thomas Funkhouse, Kai Li, and Jaswinder Pal Singh, "Load balancing for multi-projector rendering systems," In *SIGGRAPH/Eurographics Workshop on Graphics Hardware*, August 1999.

16. S.Molnar, J. Eyles, and J. Poulton, "Pixelflow : High-speed rendering using image composition," In *Proceedings of SIGGPARH*, pages 231–240, 1992.
17. M. Lacroix, "A HDTV Projector for Wide Field of View Flight Simulators," Presented at *IMAGE VI Conference, Scottsdale, AZ*, July 14–17, 1992.
18. K. Talmi, J. Liu, "Eye and Gaze Tracking for Visually Controlled Interactive Stereoscopic Displays," Proceedings of *Image Communication*, 1998.

Editors' Note: see Appendix, p. 283f. for colored figures of this paper

Comprehensive Calibration and Registration Procedures for Augmented Reality

A.L. Fuhrmann, R. Splechtna and J. Přikryl

VRVis Competence Center for Virtual Reality and Visualization,
Lothringerstraße 16/4, A-1030 Vienna, Austria
e-mail: [fuhrmann|splechtna|prikryl]@vrvis.at

Abstract: Augmented Reality - best described as adding computer-generated virtual content to the real environment – needs more adjustments to work properly than immersive virtual environments. To be perceived as an augmentation of reality, the virtual environment has to be properly aligned to the real world. This *registration* process has to be done at least once for every hardware set-up, but may have to be repeated in part or completely for each user, prop or device to be included both in the real and the virtual world. In this paper, we propose a comprehensive process for registration and calibration tasks necessary to implement correct augmentation. This includes procedures for calibrating projective and head-mounted displays, tracking systems, tracked input devices and props. Our method unifies the necessary tasks of world-to-augmentation alignment, display calibration and registration of tracked and static props in one, interactive set-up process, which can easily be conducted by the untrained user.

1 Motivation

The *Studierstube* augmented reality system [1] uses different techniques to overlay computer graphics onto a user's view of the real world. Primarily we have been using see-through head-mounted displays to accommodate individual viewpoints for a multi-user scenario, but *Studierstube* also supports projection display devices such as the Virtual Table or a stereo projection wall. Our concept includes at least two tracked interaction devices per user: a pen and pad combination called the *Personal Interaction Panel* (PIP) and supports tracking technologies ranging from magnetical to optical and inertial methods.

Since each hardware set-up can consist of almost any combination of the display and tracking technologies mentioned above, most of the parameters of display and tracking system will depend on the set-up. Altering the hardware or setting an environment up in a new location will require a complete registration process.

Studierstube is already in use as development environment in different research institutes in Europe and the United States, but not two of them are employing exactly the same display/tracker/input device combination. In most cases the calibration and registration process proved to be the biggest obstacle when setting up a new site. Even when using the same hardware in a different location – e.g. as demonstration at a scientific conference or a trade show – altered position of tracker origin and projector lead to unnecessary delays in the set-up.

The aim of the described method is to provide a fast, comprehensive calibration and registration procedure. The method should present itself to the user as an interactive sequence of simple, independent tasks, which can easily be performed even without knowledge of the actual parameters they modify. Setting up an augmented reality installation becomes therefore a reliable and reproducible routine.

Fig. 1 illustrates the complexity of this task. While by itself each of the shown transformations is easily grasped, their concatenation leads to non-intuitive results. The determination of all these transformations by hand, even when excluding projective distortion of the display is an error-prone and cumbersome task. Discrepancies between the movement of the stylus and its virtual counterpart for example can be caused by the world-to-tracker transformation (wt), the world-to-screen transformation (ws), or the tracker-to-eye transformation (te). Finding out which part of the registration is to blame can be difficult, especially when the misregistration results in a completely blank screen.

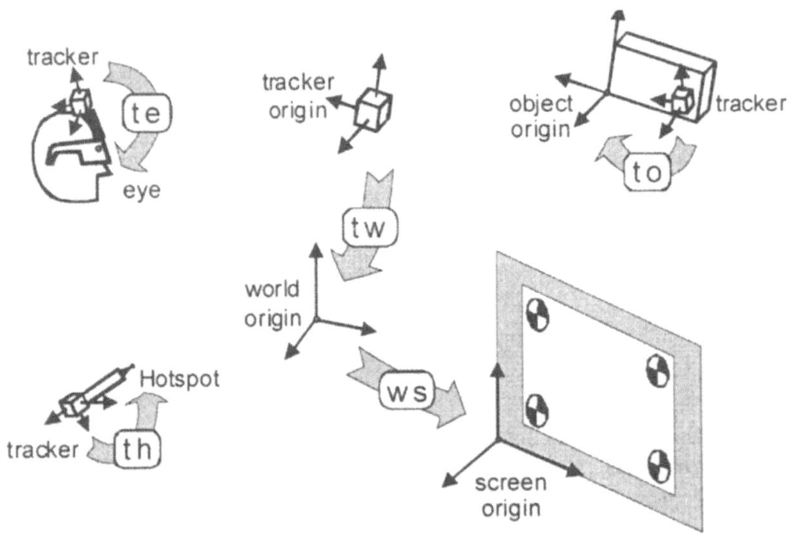

Fig. 1: registration parameters

2 Related Work

Some of the here-discussed problems have already been addressed separately:

Holloway [2] analyzed different aspects of registration error and Hoff and Vincent [3] presented analysis of head pose accuracy for AR applications.

Bajura [4] proposed calibration for video see-through systems based on tracking known features in the working environment. Interactive calibration methods for see-through HMDs have been described by McGarrity and Tuceryan [5], Fuhrmann et al. [6], and Tuceryan and Navab [7]. Czernuszenko et al. [8] describe a tracker and camera calibration approach for back-projection systems. Summers et al. [9] address registration and calibration of an experimental see-through projection-based system that employs shutter glasses.

Whitaker et al. [10] describe a pointer calibration method together with two different object calibration methods for augmented reality. Automatic, image-based object identification and registration methods have been proposed by Billinghurst [11] and Rekimoto [12]. Image-based methods have the potential to work completely without user intervention, but imply a video-based AR set-up, which until now has not been integrated in Studierstube.

The innovative aspect of our method lies in its unification of separate but connected problems: calibrating the HMD or shutter glasses (te) or projection screen for example, works only when the stylus' hotspot has been registered (th), but is independent of the world-to-tracker transformation (wt). The sequential execution of the different steps of our method takes these interdependencies into account.

A further advantage of our method lies in its simplicity as perceived by the user: every sub-task consists of an easily performed gesture, or the touching of a displayed marker. Additionally all of the used algorithms have fail-safe mechanisms: if the user wrongly positions his head during display calibration, it is detected via the head-tracker and the step is repeated; if the fitting algorithm when registering a prop or the stylus shows discrepancies, a notification message is displayed.

3 Method Description

Our method implies two prerequisites:

First, a tracking system capable of delivering accurate results over the working volume. In the case of a magnetical tracking system, for example, one has to assure linear behavior by appropriate methods like Kindratenkos [13] or Livingston et.al. [14].

Second, a tracked pointing device with one button and precisely defined hotspot (i.e. a point that defines where an action is executed when pressing the button).

We divide the registration process into four distinct tasks:

- Calibration of the registration stylus' hotspot (th)
- Registration of tracker coordinates to the world coordinate system resulting in transformation (wt)
- Calibration of display, providing us with the proper orientation of the screen coordinate system (ws), linear image distortions (e.g. caused by off-center projection), correct eye distance for stereo, and — in case of a head tracked system — the tracker-to-eye sensor offset (te).
- Registration of the tracked interaction devices relative to their tracking sensors (to) and position of the static props – e.g. desks, walls – in world coordinates

4 Stylus calibration

Stylus calibration determines the offset of the tracker sensor as measured to its tip or hotspot (th). This has to be done at the start of the whole process if thc tracking system does not provide an implicitly calibrated stylus, e.g. a digitizing wand.

We can accomplish this quite easily by fixing the stylus' tip in a small pit drilled into a table (Fig. 2), and moving the tracker sensor on a hemisphere measuring its position. Having fitted a sphere to the measured sensor positions, the center of the sphere gives us the position of the hotspot with respect to the sensor.

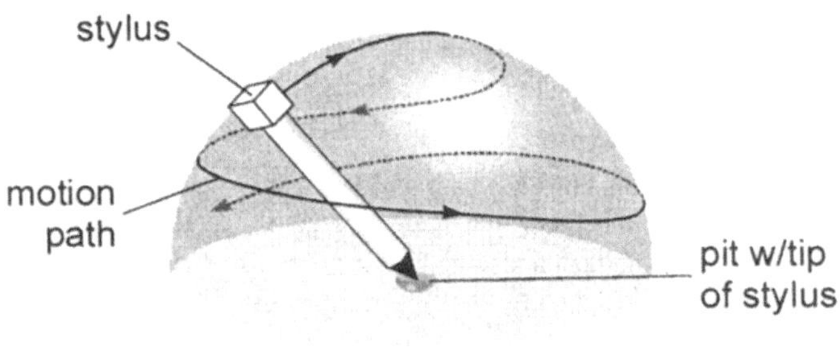

Fig. 2: calibrating the stylus

For fitting an optimal sphere to the measured data points, we optimize the offset vector from tracker sensor to the stylus' hotspot (th, see Fig. 1) using the variance V of the hotspot positions for the measured data points as a metric:

$$V = \sum_{n} (th_n - th_{mean})^2$$

This gives us a least-squares fit solution for the hotspot offset th. To enforce stability of the solution, the user has to cover a large part of the hemisphere, ideally by sweeping the sensor along two orthogonal great-arcs.

5 Registration of World to Virtual Coordinate System

The first step in the proposed calibration method is registration of the tracker system so that it corresponds to the selected world coordinate system, i.e. the transformation tw.

The registration process consists of three steps (Fig. 3):

First, the world coordinate system origin is determined by placing the stylus' hotspot to the desired location of the origin and pressing the stylus' button. Knowing the origin of the coordinate system, the up-vector can be defined by lifting the pen with pressed button along a vertical axis.

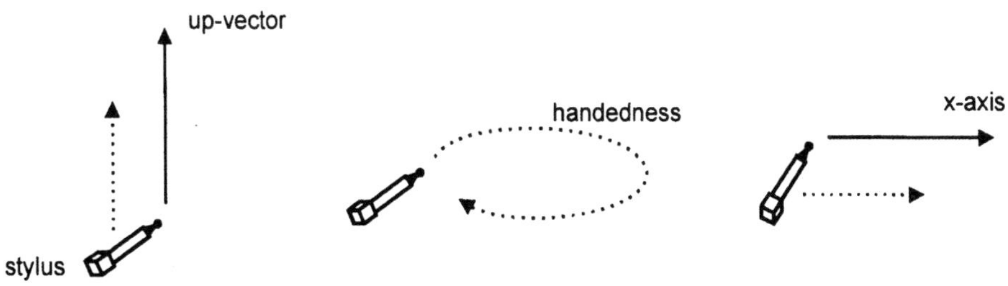

Fig. 3: registering world-to-tracker coordinate transformation

If an axis of the tracking coordinate system lies reasonably near this direction, the user will be asked if the up-vector should be changed to this axis on the assumption that the tracking system has been intentionally aligned. If this is not the case, the manually specified direction is used.

In order to determine whether the coordinate system is left- or right-handed we ask the user to circumscribe a clockwise-oriented circle in a horizontal plane of the world coordinate system.

Then the user is asked to move the pen horizontally to the right to determine the last remaining degree of freedom, the rotation around the up-vector. This step can be skipped for projection-based displays, where an alignment to the projection screen is mostly preferred.

6 Display device calibration

As already mentioned, the *Studierstube* system permits the use of see-through head-mounted displays (HMDs) or different kinds of front or back projection displays. Although both setups are to some extent similar, we shall address the calibration processes for projection and HMD setup separately.

6.1 Calibrating projection systems

Here we use a variation of the calibration method we applied to HMDs in [6], which differs from Czernuszenkos [8] method in the use of the stylus instead of a transparent reference grid, which would have to be built for each site.

First the position and orientation of the display screen has to be determined (transformation ts, Fig. 1). This is done by projecting reference markers near the corners of the screen and measuring their position with the tracked stylus. This gives us the absolute position and orientation of the projection plane in tracker coordinates (Fig. 1, right).

To determine interpupillary distance and eye to tracker offset we project two or more markers — of which we now know the absolute location in tracker coordinates — on the screen. The user now brings the tip of the stylus in alignment with each marker (Figure 4) and presses the button time accordingly. This is repeated for each eye and gives us their absolute positions in tracker coordinates.

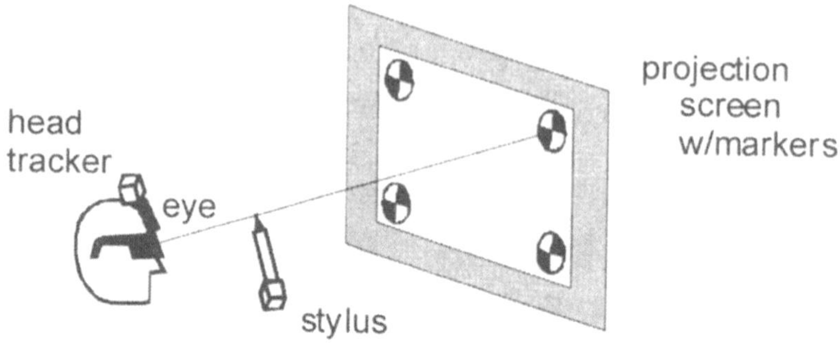

Figure 4: calibrating a projection set-up

For each measurement we now have:

- head position
- stylus' hotspot position
- marker position

Hotspot and marker define a line in space, which we transform into head-relative coordinates relative to the actual head position at sample time. By this we remove the influence of the users head position. The gathered lines can now be used to determine the users eyes' position relative to the head-tracker (te in Fig. 1).

Since in most cases the lines will not precisely intersect, we use an optimization procedure as we used in [6], resulting in an eye position with minimal distance to all measured lines.

Two criteria for positioning the stylus during data acquisition have to be observed by the user:

- the stylus should be much nearer to the users eye than to the marker on the screen
- the users head should always point in the general direction of the screen center (not in the direction of the active marker)

These rules guarantee a valid sample of measurements. We are going to implement some warning messages to notify the user of discrepancies.

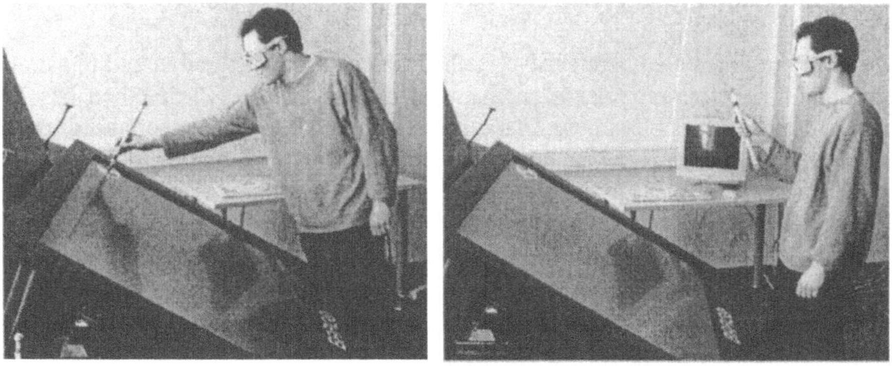

Fig. 5: Calibrating the Virtual Table: projection plan calibration (left), eye position calibration (right). For illustration purposes, the displayed marker has been enhanced.

Figure 5 depicts the two typical user gestures during calibration: touching the marker on the screen during projection plane calibration and sighting along the stylus' tip during eye position calibration.

6.2 Calibrating head-mounted displays

For the calibration of the head-mounted display we use the method developed by Fuhrmann et al. [6]. This method is guides the user through a sequence of tasks the same way that the whole registration procedure does.

Generally, this HMD calibration consists of displaying points in corners of each HMD display and aligning these points with the hotspot of the stylus. The measured data gives us all the necessary calibration information - eye position, view-plane distance, and aspect ratio. Redundancy in the measurements allows us to detect user errors and repeat steps accordingly.

7 Calibration of Props

Stationary props — e.g. desks, walls — have to be included in the registration process by specifying features on the objects, which can be used as calibration points. These features can be corners or attached markers, which can easily and unambiguously be touched with the stylus. The positions of these features have to be described in the virtual representation of the prop, allowing for inferring the position of the prop in the real world by an appropriate fitting algorithm.

The registration of tracked props — e.g. a pad, or a mock-up of an object to be augmented — is performed accordingly; only the measurements are taken in the objects tracker coordinate system instead of the absolute world coordinate system.

8 Conclusions and Future Work

We have presented a comprehensive method for the usual calibration and registration procedures necessary for using an augmented environment. The method has been implemented as an applet in our *Studierstube* system, allowing inexperienced users to properly set up their working environment. The only information that has to be specified when starting the calibration applet is the setup type (HMD or projection). The applet then guides the user through the calibration and registration process and produces all necessary XML files for our unified tracker interface, *OpenTracker* [15]).

As test setup we used our virtual table (BARCO BARON, Fig. 5), a back-projection desk specifically designed for VR applications.

The precision of our method depends heavily on the input data:

We tested it – as worst-case scenario - with an uncompensated magnetical tracker, which delivers extremely bad precision near our projection setup. The resulting errors amounted up to a few centimeters, essentially making the results unusable. By using our optical tracking equipment [16], which delivers results with about 3mm precision, eye positions were calculated within the same precision range (2-6mm).

A further contributing factor is of course the precision of the users input samples. We are at the moment evaluating different marker combinations and filtering techniques to minimize this error component.

Java3D [17], a high level API for writing three-dimensional graphics applications and 3D applets in Java, supports user interaction with the virtual world for different types of application setups through its unified view model. Since this API supports standard computer displays, (multiple-) projection display rooms, and head-mounted displays, as well as interaction using 6DOF trackers and joysticks, it can be applied for augmented reality applications needing registration. We plan to adapt the output of our applet to generate the files defining the Java3D view branch, which declares display method and tracking of camera and interaction devices.

Acknowledgments
Special thanks to Dieter Schmalstieg for his constructive criticism and help.

References

[1] Dieter Schmalstieg, Anton Fuhrmann, Gerd Hesina, Zsolt Szalavári, L. M. Encarnaçao, Michael Gervautz, Werner Purgathofer: The Studierstube Augmented Reality Project. Technical report TR-186-2-00-22, Institute of Computer Graphics and Algorithms, Vienna University of Technology, Austria, December 2000..

[2] Richard L. Holloway: Registration Error Analysis for Augmented Reality. Presence, vol. 6, no. 4, August 1997, pp. 413–432.

[3] William A. Hoff, Tyrone Vincent: Analysis of Head Pose Accuracy in

Augmented Reality. To appear in IEEE Transactions on Computer Graphics and Visualization, vol. 6, no. 4, 2000.
[4] Michael A. Bajura: Merging Real and Virtual Environments with Video See-Through Head-Mounted Displays. Dissertation, UNC, 1997.
[5] Erin McGarrity, Mihran Tuceryan: A Method for Calibrating See-through Head-mounted Displays for AR. Proceedings of the 2nd IEEE International Workshop on Augmented Reality (IWAR 99), San Francisco, CA, October 1999.
[6] Anton Fuhrmann, Dieter Schmalstieg, Werner Purgathofer: Practical Calibration Procedures for Augmented Reality. Proceedings of the 6th Eurographics Workshop on Virtual Environments, Amsterdam, Netherlands, June 2000.
[7] Mihran Tuceryan, Nassir Navab: Single point active alignment method (SPAAM) for optical see-through HMD calibration for AR. Proceedings of the IEEE and ACM International Symposium on Augmented Reality, Munich, Germany, October, 2000, pp. 149–158.
[8] Marek Czernuszenko, Daniel Sandin, Thomas DeFanti: Line of Sight Method for Tracker Calibration in Projection-Based VR. Proceedings of the 2nd International Immersive Projection Technology Workshop, Iowa State University, May, 1998.
[9] Valerie A. Summers, Kellogg S. Booth, Tom Calvert, Evan Graham, Christine L. MacKenzie: Calibration For Augmented Reality Experimental Testbeds. Proceedings of the 1999 symposium on Interactive 3D graphics, Atlanta, GA, April 1999, pp. 155–162.
[10] Ross T. Whitaker, Chris Crampton, David E. Breen, Mihran Tuceryan, Eric Rose: Object Calibration for Augmented Reality. Proceedings of Eurographics'95, Maastricht, Netherlands, 1995, pp. 15–28.
[11] Mark Billinghurst, Hirokazu Kato: Collaborative Mixed Reality. Proceedings of the First International Symposium on Mixed Reality, Yokohama, Japan, March 1999, pp. 261–284.
[12] Jun Rekimoto: Matrix: A Realtime Object Identification and Registration Method for Augmented Reality. Proceedings of Asia Pacific Computer Human Interaction 1998, Japan, 1998.
[13] Volodymyr Kindratenko: Calibration of electromagnetic tracking devices. Virtual Reality: Research, Development, and Applications (The VRS Journal), vol. 4, 1999, pp. 139–150.
[14] Mark Livingston, Andrei State: Magnetic Tracker Calibration for Improved Augmented Reality Registration. Presence, vol. 6, 1997, pp. 532–546.
[15] Gerhard Reitmayr, Dieter Schmalstieg: OpenTracker — An Open Software Architecture for Reconfigurable Tracking based on XML. Poster, IEEE Virtual Reality 2001, Yokohama, Japan, March 2001. Extended version available as technical report TR-186-2-00-18, Institute of Computer Graphics and Algorithms, Vienna University of Technology, Austria, June 2000.
[16] M. Ribo, A. Pinz, A.L. Fuhrmann: A New Optical Tracking System for Virtual and Augmented Reality. To appear in proceedings IEEE IMTC®/2001 (May 21-23, 2001, Hungary)
[17] Michael F. Deering, Henry A. Sowizral: Java3D Specification, Version 1.0. Technical Report, Sun Microsystems, August 1997.

Using Exercise Cycle as a Haptic Input Device in a Virtual Environment

Pasi Välkkynen, Juhani Heinilä, Sari Lainio, Sami Lakaniemi, and Antti Väätänen

VTT Information Technology
Sinitaival 6
P.O. Box 1206
FIN-33101 Tampere
Finland
Pasi.Valkkynen@vtt.fi,
WWW home page: http://www.vtt.fi/tte

Abstract. Virku (Virtual Fitness Centre) is a study, in which an exercise cycle is used for navigating in a virtual environment. The cycle acts as a haptic bodily user interface between the user and the simulation. The simulation takes the terrain of the virtual environment into account in order to provide better feedback of the environment for the user. We have found out in usability tests that this kind of interface enhances the user's feeling of immersion in the virtual environment.

1 Introduction

Virku (Virtual Fitness Centre, see Figure 1) is a research and development program in which a prototype of a fitness game played with an exercise cycle in a virtual environment has been produced[10]. Virku includes also a Fitness Monitoring Program for testing the user's fitness level and for supporting long term fitness monitoring and training.

The purpose of our research is to study bodily user interfaces and the use of a computer game to enhance motivation to keep fit. In this paper, we will concentrate on the bodily user interface and especially on how to use an exercise cycle as a haptic input device in a virtual environment.

2 Background

2.1 Bodily user interface

With the bodily user interface we mean an interface, which allows the user to interact with the interface using other methods than the traditional input devices, such as a mouse or a keyboard. The user can also react with other senses along with his visual or aural perception.

Bodily user interface is not a very defined term and there are sometimes difficulties in determining, whether an interface is a bodily user interface. A

Fig. 1. Virtual Fitness Centre

fitness computer game is a good example for illustrating these difficulties. We do not usually consider a bicycle racing simulation played with mouse to be using a bodily user interface. We could, however, replace the mouse with a handle-bar. Does this make the interface a bodily one? What if we make the user sit on a bicycle seat and give him pedals for controlling the speed of the cycle in the game?

In our research, we have used (somewhat vaguely) the term bodily user interface for an interface in which the user uses his whole body for controlling the system. In Virku, the user moves the pedals with his leg muscles and steers the bicycle with his hands. Whole body weight can be used for example for riding uphill in order to gain more power for the pedaling.

Bodily user interfaces are clearly useful for fitness purposes since they force the user to move, instead of only sitting in front of the computer. We also show in this paper that a haptic bodily user interface helps the user feel more immersed in a virtual environment.

2.2 Haptic user interface

We usually get information from the computer systems by seeing and hearing, and input information by manipulating a mouse and/or keyboard with our hands. These modes of communication neglect our other senses, touch, taste and smell. Of these three, smell and taste are more difficult to include in human-computer interaction, but this does not necessarily have to apply to touch.

According to Tan [8], the term "haptics" refers to sensing and manipulating through the sense of touch. He divides haptic sensations into two categories: sense of touch and sense of posture, both of which are important in a bodily user interface. The sense of posture can be especially effective in a fitness application, like Virku, in which whole body is used for controlling the interface.

In a virtual environment, haptics are an important part of the immersion, the feeling of "being there". In our terms, haptics are a part of the bodily user interface. Its purpose is to enhance the virtual environment's resemblance to natural environment and thus make the whole experience more vivid, enjoyable and captivating.

2.3 Other bicycle simulators

Using a bicycle as an input device has been studied, for example, with the Peloton simulator[1], which was developed as a virtual environment for athletic training and competition. There are also virtual reality systems, which use a bicycle as their input device, such as Jeffrey Shaw's Legible City [7] and the Diamond Park [11]. Legible City can be considered as an art installation and Diamond Park as a study of social virtual reality.

Other bicycle interfaces with simulators are commercially available and their purpose is usually to improve the users' fitness. These include RealBitz.com, WebRacing and CompuTrainer. RealBitz [6] uses a movement sensor, which is attached to the user to sense the speed of his movements. WebRacing [12] supports the use of VR helmet and it has a multiplayer game, which can be played via the Internet. CompuTrainer [2] adds the possibility to design one's own training courses.

Virku differs from these systems by taking the terrain of the virtual environment into account in its haptic response and by allowing the user to navigate anywhere in its virtual world. In the user's point of view, the purpose of Virku is to help him improve his fitness [5].

In Virku, it is possible, but not required, for the users, to compete with each other or against a clock. Instead, they can also enjoy the game just by cycling around the generated landscape and enjoying the nature and the views. This is an important difference between the commercial, more competition-oriented games played with exercise equipment, and Virku.

3 Virtual Fitness Centre and Research Objects

In Virku, the bodily user interface is an essential part of the interaction between the user and the exercise cycle. In our research we used a Tunturi T6 cycle [9], which can be used both as an input and an output device. The T6 cycle uses an asynchronous RS interface to move data in and out of the cycle. It is capable of increasing its resistance according to commands sent from a computer via the serial line, and it can tell the computer its resistance, torque and the heart rate of the user. We can use this information for modifying the training session so that the training will be optimal. The user navigates in the virtual world entirely with the exercise cycle. The cycle has two buttons for steering, and the torque of the pedals affects the movement speed.

The visual part of the virtual environment is presented on a computer monitor or it can be projected with a data projector onto a large screen. We use SimCore[3], a commercial 3D engine, to render the scenery. The scenery depicts a rural environment from the northern Finland generated from digital map information. Virku uses a multichannel sound system, which creates an illusion of threedimensional sound. The user gets feedback from the game also in the form of resistance. The resistance is increased when the user rides his bicycle uphill and decreased when riding downhill.

Virku is designed to be usable in a fitness centre or a gym. Typically, these are environments in which head-mounted displays can not be comfortably used, because of sweat, humidity and heat. With the traditional fitness devices, VR equipment is not needed, so the users would also have to put them on or remove them every time they wanted to use some other training device in the gym. This is why we did not want to use intrusive equipment. Therefore, we could not use, for example, stereo images of the landscape. So, the bodily user interface has to enhance the immersion in order to compensate for the possible loss of visual realism.

The Virtual Fitness Centre also includes a fitness monitoring program to assist the user in long term exercising. It gathers information from the exercise sessions and uses it to give training recommendations for the user. The purpose of the fitness monitoring program is to support the overall concept of enhancing the users' motivation for adhering to a certain training programme, whereas the purpose of the game is to help the users with short term motivation.

4 Evaluation and results

We applied the Human-Centred Design (HCD) approach in the development of our system. The Human-Centred Design is an iterative approach to design where an active involvement of the users and a clear understanding of the user and the task requirements are emphasised [4].

We tested the fitness game with nine people, seven women and two men. They were especially familiar with computer games or virtual environments. All of them trained at least somewhat actively (minimum once a week). The tests were conducted in the Usability Laboratory of VTT Information Technology. We arranged an environment, which consisted of the exercise cycle, a computer and a large screen onto which the scenery was projected with a data projector. The users were asked to ride through a predetermined course in the virtual environment after which they were allowed to explore it themselves. The test data was gathered by observing the users and interviewing them.

The users felt that they were exercising rather than playing a computer game. They liked the game and felt thet it was more entertaining than using an exercise cycle without a game. The interface was natural and intuitive to use; the users knew immediately how to navigate in the virtual environment with the exercise cycle. They also told that they had a feeling of immersion. At times, some users' behaviour suggested that there was a feeling of riding a bicycle in a natural environment. Some users, for example, were afraid to ride down a ridge (see Figure 2), or they stood up on the exercise cycle to see better over obstacles in the terrain. In the interviews, they told that the immersion was due to the combination of a large, impressive and realistic visual system and the bodily user interface. The experience of the bodily interface was achieved by both the haptic response and using the whole body to control the navigation.

Fig. 2. A view down a ridge

One problem with the haptic interface is that the resistance does not adjust according to other terrain features than the slope. Useful bases for adjusting the resistance would be at least surface and vegetation. This is an important feature to improve in a cross-country bicycle simulation, and it will be dealt with in the next version of the game.

We must keep in mind that following a fitness program is a long task. Therefore, we can not expect to gain long term results until we have conducted a prolonged field test study. The first impressions of the users, however, suggest, that this kind of system motivates them in adhering to a training program. The reason is that a fitness computer game adds entertainment value and naturality to the exercise session compared to traditional exercise cycling.

5 Conclusions

In conclusion, we found out that the bodily user interface was a tremendous addition to the virtual environment and the game. Users can feel immersed in the environment without any intrusive VR equipment and stereo imagery. It seems to us, that in this kind of application, a haptic bodily interface is at least as effective as the traditional approach with the head-mounted displays.

6 Future work

We will continue to develop the interface and the game during this year and the next; at the time of this writing we are about halfway through our research and have another fifteen months ahead. The improvements will include at least developing a multiplayer game in a local area network, in which many users can train together in a common session. The haptic response will be improved by taking into account other terrain features such as the surface and vegetation. We will also consider other extensions to the bodily user interface and implement them if they seem appropriate. The Human-Centred Design approach will be used in this work; design solutions will be tested with the users.

References

1. Carraro, G. U., Cortes, M., Edmark, J. T., Ensor, J. R.: The Peloton Bicycling Simulator. Bell Laboratories (1998)
2. CompuTrainer. `http://www.computrainer.com`. CompuTrainer.com (2001)
3. Instrumentointi Oy, IVS - Insta Visual Solutions. `http://www.instrumentointi.fi/ivs/english_about_ivs.htm`. Instrumentointi (2001).
4. Kaasinen, E., Kantola, K. and Olphert, W.: Human-Centred Design Process. In Concejero, P. et al. Usability in the Information Society - How to design user-friendly products and services. USINACTS project. European Commission. (CD-ROM) (March 2000)
5. Lainio, S., Väätänen, A., Välkkynen, P., Heinilä, J., Lakaniemi S., Mänttäri, A., Mäenpää, S.: Virku - Virtual Fitness Centre. In Abstract Book of International Congress on Bridging Sport, Exercise and Lifestyle Activity for Health. The Finnish Society for Research in Sport and Physical Education (2001).
6. RealBitz.com. `http://www.eloton.com` and `http://www.realbitz.com/fitness.htm`. RealBitz.com (2001)

7. Shaw, J.: Legible City. Interactive installation (1988)
8. Tan, H. Z.: Haptic Interfaces. Communications of ACM, March 2000, Volume 43, Number 3, pp. 40-41. ACM Press (2000)
9. Tunturi Oy Ltd. http://www.tunturi.com. Tunturi (2001).
10. Virku WWW pages. http://www.vtt.fi/tte/tutkimus/tte5/tte51/virkuwww_eng.htm VTT Information Technology (2001)
11. Waters, R., Anderson, D., Barrus, J., Brogan, D., Casey, M., McKeown, S., Nitta, T., Sterns, I. & Yerazunis, W.: Diamond Park and Spline: A Social Virtual Reality System with 3D Animation, Spoken Interaction, and Runtime Modifiability. Mitsubishi Electric Information Center America (1996)
12. WebAthlon. http://www.fitcentric.com. FitCentric (2001).

Invisible Interface for the Immersive Virtual World

Tetsuro Ogi[1,2,3], Toshio Yamada[1], Koji Yamamoto[3], Michitaka Hirose[2]

[1] Gifu MVL Research Center, TAO
Iutelligent Modeling Laboratory, The University of Tokyo
2-11-16, Yayoi, Bunkyo-ku, Tokyo 113-8656, Japan
{tetsu, yamada}@iml.u-tokyo.ac.jp
[2] Research Center for Advanced Science and Technology
The University of Tokyo
4-6-1, Komaba, Meguro-ku, Tokyo 153-8904, Japan
hirose@cyber.rcast.u-tokyo.ac.jp
[3] Mitsubishi Research Institute
2-3-6, Otemachi, Chiyoda-ku, Tokyo 100-8141, Japan
koji@mri.co.jp

Abstract. Immersive projection technologies such as CAVE can generate a high presence virtual world. However, it is difficult for the user to experience the immersive virtual world in the real workplace, such as the design room or the conference room, because this type of display system requires a large space in order to install the screen. In this study, an invisible interface was developed for the immersive virtual world by integrating a transparent immersive projection display and cellular phone interface technologies. By using this system, the user in the real world can experience the high presence virtual world in an immersive environment. This system was applied to several fields of application, such as augmented reality and telecommunications.

1 Introduction

Virtual reality technology is advancing from the conception stage to practical use in various fields of application. For example, the three-dimensional design model of a new product is often visualized in the virtual environment, or remote researchers are able to communicate with a high quality of presence in the shared virtual world [1][2]. In these practical applications, it is desirable for the user to be able to experience the virtual environment in the real workplace [3].

On the other hand, immersive projection technologies such as CAVE and CABIN have become very popular as virtual reality display systems [4][5]. These display systems project high-resolution stereo images onto large screens, and generate more highly immersive virtual worlds than those experienced with the ordinary head mounted displays. However, this kind of display system needs a large space in which to set up the equipment, because it consists of large display screens. Thus, when the user wants to use an immersive projection display, he must go to the particular room in which CAVE or CABIN is installed. Therefore, it is difficult for the user to experience the immersive virtual world using CAVE or CABIN in the real workplace, such as the design room or the conference room.

In this study, an invisible interface that allows the user to experience the immersive virtual world was developed by integrating the transparent immersive projection display and cellular phone interface device technologies. In this system, the user in the real workplace can experience the virtual world in the immersive environment. This paper describes the concept of the invisible immersive interface, system configuration of the prototype system and some applications using this technology.

2 Invisible Immersive Interface

The invisible immersive interface is a concept of a computer-augmented environment in which the user can experience a high presence virtual world in the real workplace, such as the design room or the conference room. For example, it means that the designer can visualize the three-dimensional model of a new product in his design room or that remote researchers can communicate with a high presence in the conference room. Figure 1 illustrates the concept of the invisible interface for the immersive virtual world.

In order to realize this concept, the components of the virtual reality system, such as the display and the interface device, should be hidden in the real workplace without disturbing the user's view. Namely, it should be constructed as an invisible interface so that the user in the real world can experience the immersive virtual world.

Although an augmented reality system, such as the see-through head mounted display, is often used to experience the virtual world in free space, this method cannot generate such a high presence sensation as that generated by an immersive projection display [6]. In addition, special interface devices, such as the wand or the data glove are used in ordinary virtual reality and augmented reality systems. However, from the standpoint of the invisible interface, it is desirable for the user to experience the virtual world by only using a device that might be carried in their daily life.

In this study, a prototype of an invisible immersive interface was constructed that enables a user in the real workplace to experience the high presence virtual world by applying the immersive projection technology. In particular, the transparent projection display and cellular phone interface technologies were developed to realize this concept.

Fig. 1. Concept of Invisible Interface for Immersive Virtual World

Fig. 2. Appearance of HoloPro Screen

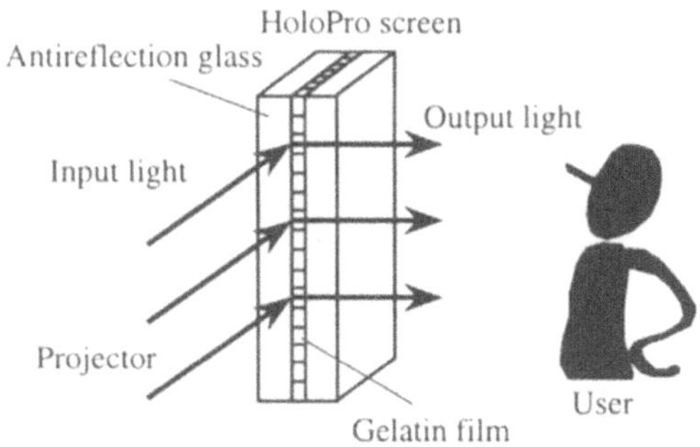

Fig. 3. Structure of HoloPro Screen

3 Transparent Immersive Projection Display

In order to generate a projection based immersive virtual world in the real workplace, a large screen display is necessary that does not obstruct the user's view. In this study, a transparent rear-projection screen known as HoloPro is used, which is made by G+B Pronova GmbH [7]. Figure 2 shows the appearance of the HoloPro screen, and Figure 3 shows the structure. Since this screen is constructed by laminating a gelatin light-directing film inside anti-reflective multi-layer glass, the screen itself is nearly invisible. Therefore, the image projected onto the transparent HoloPro screen appears as if it is floating in the air.

In this system, when the image is projected onto the screen from a specific angle between 35 degrees and 40 degrees, the incoming light is redirected in the direction of the viewer. Therefore, the projector can be placed on the floor or on the ceiling, hidden from the user's view. Moreover, since the polarization of the light is preserved when it goes through the screen, a polarizing filter method using high brightness projectors can be used to generate three-dimensional stereo images. This screen can also be used outdoors in daylight, because the projected image is hardly affected by the ambient light. By

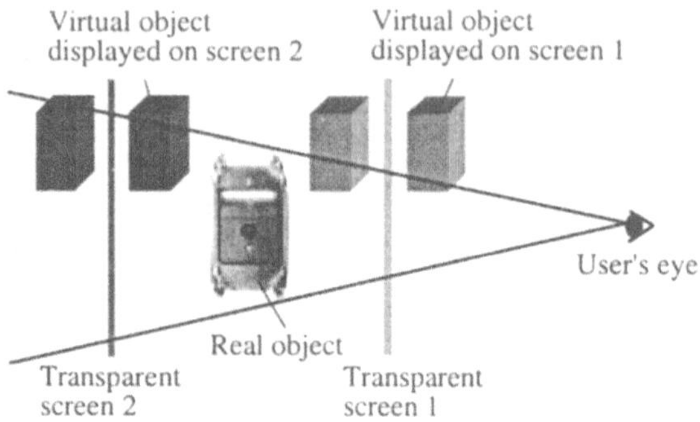

Fig. 4. Transparent Screen and Occlusion

using this transparent screen, a user in the workplace can experience an immersive virtual world that appears to be part of the real world as the need arises.

In addition, since the HoloPro screen itself is transparent, the black part of the displayed image would be see-through, and the user can therefore view both the projected image and the background of the real world simultaneously. Therefore, this screen can be used as an augmented reality system utilizing the optical see-through function.

This kind of transparent immersive projection display has some additional features compared with other augmented reality systems. For example, in the case of an optical see-through head mounted display, the real object cannot occlude the virtual object, because the screen plane is located in front of the user's eye. On the other hand, when a projection-based augmented reality system is used, the virtual object cannot occlude the real object because the screen is placed behind the object. In a transparent immersive projection display, a real object placed in front of the screen plane can occlude the virtual object, and the virtual object can occlude a real object placed behind the screen plane, as shown in Figure 4. Therefore, the real object and the virtual object can be located in various positional configurations by considering the position of the screen in the real world.

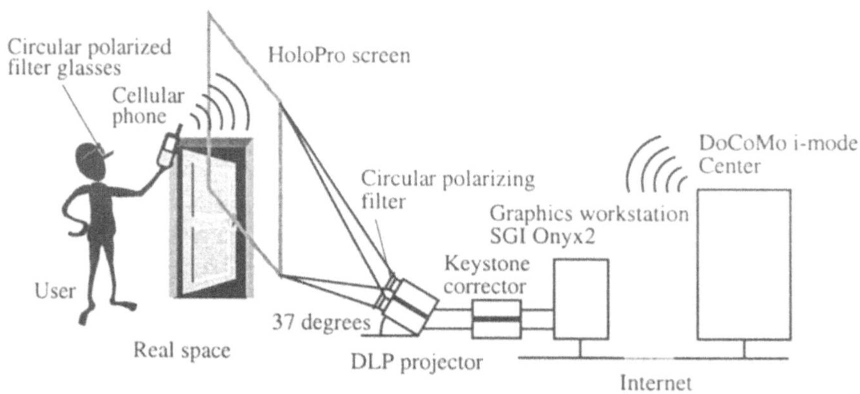

Fig. 5. System Configuration of Invisible Interface for Immersive Virtual World

Thus, by using the HoloPro screen, the user can experience the three-dimensional immersive virtual world and the augmented reality world in the real workplace. Figure 5 shows the system configuration of the transparent immersive projection display system constructed in this study. The diagonal size of the HoloPro screen is 50 inches (1000mm x 750mm), and an SGI Onyx2 graphics workstation is used to generate parallax images for the left and right eyes respectively. These two images are transmitted to the NEC LT140J DLP(Digital Light Processing) projectors through the Analog Way Keystonix KC-100 keystone correctors, and are projected onto the screen from floor level at the angle of 37 degrees. Circular polarizing filters are attached to the lenses of the projectors, and the user can then see the stereo images by using circular polarized filter glasses.

4 Cellular Phone Interface

Along with the transparent screen, the development of interaction technology with the virtual world displayed on it has been necessary. In general, in the CAVE-like immersive projection display, a special interface device called the wand is used [8]. In the real workplace however, it is desirable to employ an everyday device that is used in daily life for interactions with the virtual world. Therefore, in this study, we developed an interface technology using the i-mode function of the cellular phone.

The i-mode is an Internet access service for the cellular phone provided by NTT DoCoMo Inc., and which is currently used by about twenty million people in Japan [9]. For example, the user can access the Internet web pages by inputting the URL characters or selecting a bookmark using the dial buttons, and the information on the web page is displayed on the LCD of the cellular phone. Since this LCD window can also be used to display the menu or to confirm the characters that have been entered, the user can input a command using local feedback from the LCD without displaying the three dimensional input window in the virtual world.

In this study, this Internet communication function of the cellular phone was applied to running the virtual reality application and communicating with the virtual world. Figure 6 shows the software construction of the i-mode interface with the virtual world. In this system, in order to experience the virtual world, the user accesses the web server

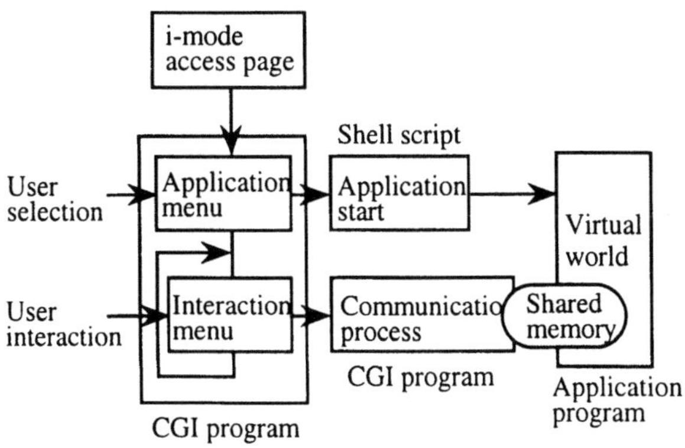

Fig. 6. Software Structure of i-mode Interface

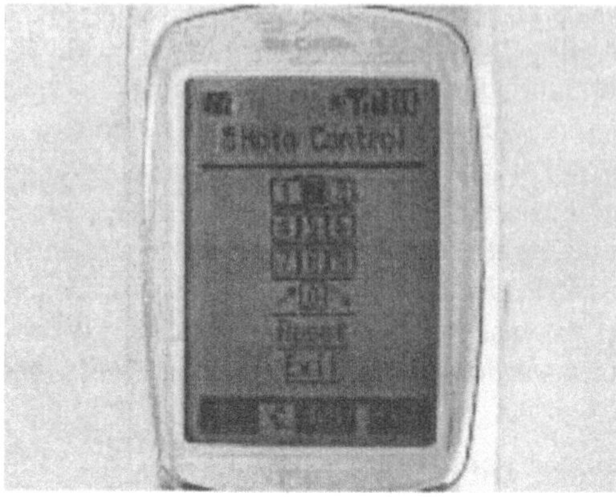

Fig. 7. i-mode Menu for Walk-through Control

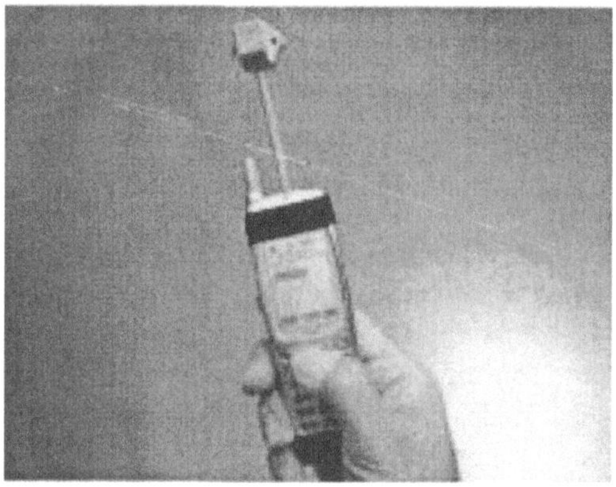

Fig. 8. Cellular Phone Interface with Pointing Function

of the SGI Onyx2 graphics workstation from the cellular phone through the DoCoMo i-mode Center. Selecting a menu item in the i-mode page starts the virtual reality application program. This i-mode page is written in CGI (Common Gateway Interface) script, and when the user selects the menu item, the shell script runs that starts the virtual reality application. By using this i-mode function, the virtual world suddenly appears by only operating the cellular phone without a computer terminal.

In the virtual reality application program, the user can also interact with the virtual world by using the cellular phone interface. After starting the application program, the CGI program displays the interaction i-mode page in the LCD on the cellular phone. When the user inputs characters or selects commands on the interaction page using the dial buttons, the communication process is generated and it transmits the interaction command to the application program through the shared memory. By using this method, the user can interact with the virtual world using the i-mode function.

For example, Figure 7 shows the interaction i-mode page for walk-through control in the virtual world. Although the i-mode web site is basically written using subsets of HTML, it also supports some individual functions corresponding to the cellular phone device. In this example, each key of the dial button is assigned to several movement functions, such as "go ahead", "turn right", "turn left", "go up" and "go down". Therefore, the user can walk through the virtual world freely by operating these keys.

In addition, the cellular phone can also be used as a pointing device as well as a key-input device by attaching a position tracker to it. In this system, a Polhemus electromagnetic sensor is used to track the position of the cellular phone. However, when the cellular phone communicates with the Internet to send the interaction command, it generates an electromagnetic wave that causes a tracking error. Therefore, the position tracker was attached about 8 cm away from the body of the cellular phone in order to reduce the influence of the electromagnetic wave as shown in Figure 8.

Thus, the type of cellular phone that is carried around in daily life can be used as an interface device that can provide both keyboard and wand functions. In this system, since the user can use his or her own cellular phone as the interface device, it can easily be manipulated to interact with the virtual world.

5 Application of the Invisible Interface

5.1 Experience of the Immersive Virtual World

In this study, by integrating a transparent immersive projection display with cellular phone interface technologies, an invisible interface was constructed with the immersive virtual world, and it was applied to several fields of application. Figure 9 shows an example of how the experience of the immersive virtual world can be displayed in the real world. In this example, a three-dimensional virtual town appeared before the user's eyes in the real world when he accessed the application program using the i-mode control, and he could walk-through the virtual town by operating the cellular phone in the immersive environment.

Fig. 9. Experience of Immersive Virtual World

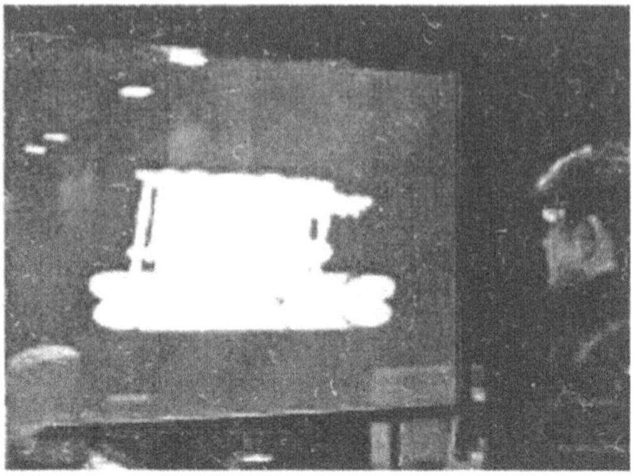

Fig. 10. Visualization in Augmented Reality World

Fig. 11. High Presence Communication Using Video Avatar

5.2 Experience of the Augmented Reality World

Figure 10 shows another example of the application being used to the experience the augmented reality world. In this example, since the background image of the three-dimensional model that is being displayed is black, the real object behind the screen can be seen through the transparent screen. In this case, the user can view the three-dimensional computer graphics model as if it was floating in the real world. By applying this method, the designer would be able to visualize a three-dimensional design model in the real workplace of his design room to inspect and discuss it.

5.3 High Presence Communication

The authors have been studying a high presence communication method using the video avatar in the shared virtual world generated in the immersive projection displays at CABIN and COSMOS [10]. In this technique, the user's image is captured by a stereo video camera, and then the user's figure is segmented from the background as a three-dimensional live video image. This video image is transmitted to the other site via the broadband network, and is superimposed on the shared virtual world. By using this method, remote users can communicate with each other with a high quality of presence. In this study, the video avatar technology was applied to communications in the networked real world. Figure 11 shows an example of video avatar communication in the real workplace. In this example, remote users could communicate with each other in the real world by projecting a transmitted video avatar image onto the transparent screen without superimposing on the virtual world.

In these examples, an invisible immersive interface was used effectively to experience the virtual world or augmented reality world in the real workplace.

6 Conclusions

In this study, an invisible immersive interface was constructed as a framework in which the user could experience the immersive virtual world in the real workplace by integrating transparent immersive projection display and cellular phone interface technologies. Since the three-dimensional virtual world can apparently be displayed in the air by using the transparent wide screen, the user in this system can experience an immersive virtual environment in the real world. In addition, since the type of cellular phone that is regularly carried in daily life is used as the interface device, the user can interact with the virtual world using an implement that he or she is accustomed to using. This system was applied to several fields of application, such as accessing the immersive virtual world, experiencing the world of augmented reality and for high presence communications. Future work will include the application of this technology to practical applications to evaluate the effectiveness of this method.

References

1. Scharm, H., Breining, R.: How Automoive Industry Uses Immersive Projection Technology, 3rd International Immersive Projection Technology Workshop (1999) 133-144
2. Leigh, J., DeFanti, T.A., Johnson, A.E., Brown, M.D., Sandin, D.J.: Global Tele-Immersion: Better Than Being There, ICAT'97 (1997) 10-17
3. Encarnacao, L.M., Barton III, R.J., Bimber, O., Schmalstieg, D.: Walk-up VR: Virtual Reality beyond Projection Screens, IEEE Computer Graphics and Applications, Nov./Dec. (2000) 19-23
4. Cruz-Neira, C., Sandin, D.J., DeFanti, T.A.: Surround-Screen Projection-Based Virtual Reality: The Design and Implementation of the CAVE, Proceedings of SIGGRAPH'93 (1993) 135-142
5. Michitaka Hirose, Tetsuro Ogi, Toshio Yamada: Integrating Live Video for Immersive Environments, IEEE Multimedia, Vol.6, No.3, July-September (1999) 14-22
6. Fuchs, H., Ackerman, J., Displays for Augmented Reality: Historical Remarks and Future Prospects, Mixed Reality, Ohmsha (1999) 1-40
7. http://www.holopro.com/
8. Browning, D.R., Cruz-Neira, C., Sandin, D.J., DeFanti, T.A., Edel, J.G.: Input Interfacing to the CAVE by Persons with Disabilities, Virtual Reality and People with Disabilities (1994)

9. http://www.needocomo.com/i/index.html
10. Tetsuro Ogi, Toshio Yamada, Ken Tamagawa, Michitaka Hirose: Video Avatar Communication in Networked Virtual Environment, INET 2000 The Internet Global Summit Proceedings (2000)

Control Software for the productive Use of distributed IPT Installations

H. Scharm*, F. Maurer**, D. Neuber, R. Löffler, D. Rantzau, D. Banek

SGI Professional Services, Practice Immersive Solutions, Germany
[*holgers@sgi.com, **fmaurer@sgi.com]

Abstract. Over the last few years the number of industrial immersive projection technology (IPT) installations has grown rapidly. Most of these systems are powered by one or more SGI Onyx graphics computers with several independent graphics pipes and quite a few CPUs. Since these machines represents a big investment, many installations are designed to make use of the Onyx graphics power at different presentation areas and meeting rooms. In this paper we will introduce a new client/server approach for controlling such distributed IPT installations where multiple presentations and work sessions run simultaneously and where different users access the resources of the facility in parallel. We first discuss the necessity of multiple configurations of the IPT hardware for different kinds of presentations and applications. After this, we explain the special requirements for the control of distributed multi-user Reality Center™s ("Reality Center" is a trademark of SGI). We then present the client/server architecture of our new Reality Center management software (RCMS). Finally, we will give an outlook for possible future extensions of the software to meet individual requirements.

1 Introduction

Over the past few years the automotive industry as well as the oil and gas industry have adopted immersive projection technology (IPT) in productive scenarios. Virtual Reality (VR) installations are used as a communication tool and work place for inter-disciplinary engineering groups working on different tasks. The benefits of VR technology combined with IPT are beginning to be visible throughout the engineering process. Multi-channel projection systems known as Powerwalls and CAVE™s are setting the new standard for collaborative, interdisciplinary visualization in virtual product development processes. It is interesting to note that especially in productive industry sites, the number of the IPT systems implemented is growing. Today it is common, that several autonomous IPT installations are placed in one VR service center as a sharable resource for the whole site and sometimes also the companies suppliers. A good example for this trend is the VR Center of the DaimlerChrysler AG, MTC in Stuttgart, Germany [1]. It features five independent IPT systems driven by a single large SGI Onyx 2 image generator (currently 14 pipes, 60 CPUs) and quite a number of media devices. The usage of such centers is typically not only limited to VR related work, it is merely used as an universal media center, where slide presentations, video or DVD playback, video conferencing and different – not only VR - software applications co-exist at the same time. Engineers use these facilities on a daily basis in parallel, while utilizing the available media resources in an intensive manner.

The problem that arises with the growing size of centers is the necessity to control the complex set of interconnected devices and media systems. Especially in a service oriented work model it is an absolute requirement that even users without detailed knowledge of the system are able to switch the installation to the operation modes they need, without depending on trained VR center staff. By providing a flexible control software as a part of the SGI Professional Services in Reality Center [2] projects, we believe that we can strongly contribute to the acceptance of immersive projection technology in places with high productivity needs.

2 State of the Art: Media Control Applications

Media center control is not a new kind of application. Today, there are quite a number of commercial and research solutions available, although they do have selective objectives. One of the more popular commercial solutions is to use dedicated control hardware and touch panels to operate media centers ([3] as a representative for this kind). One disadvantage of this technology is the need for extra, proprietary hardware, and therefore additional expenses. Additionally, these solutions generally offer no management of concurrent user access and no control support for more sophisticated hardware, like an SGI Onyx2 or Onyx3000.

The majority of installed center control solutions is based on client/server web technology, where a web server acts as the central control instance. On the client side any web browser can be used to access the system. The actual device driver controls are encapsulated in CGI web server scripts and the center logic is mapped on HTML (see figure 1).

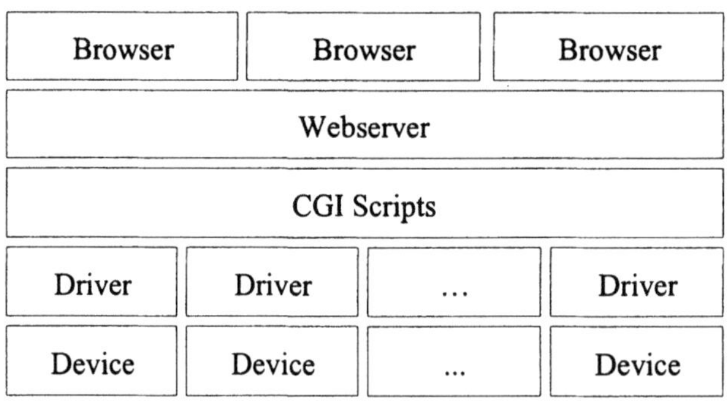

Fig. 1. Typical HTML/CGI control software architecture

Normally it is also possible to create macros (for example with a scripting language like PERL) to setup the hardware configuration for a particular application. These modes can be invoked smartly by a single button click in a web browser. Some of the web pages also use Cookies and/or Javascript code.

In the past, SGI Professional Services has delivered this kind of software based on HTML, CGI and PERL scripts along with most of the Reality Center projects. Figure 2 illustrates the web interface of the center control for an installation in the automotive area. On the left side a navigation bar, with a list of control possibilities can be seen. The entry point for the user is a center control web page (as currently visible) for the most common tasks, additional pages are available for device control and individual tasks. Users can choose the operation mode they need and with some optional parameters, they can switch to the new mode just by one single button click.

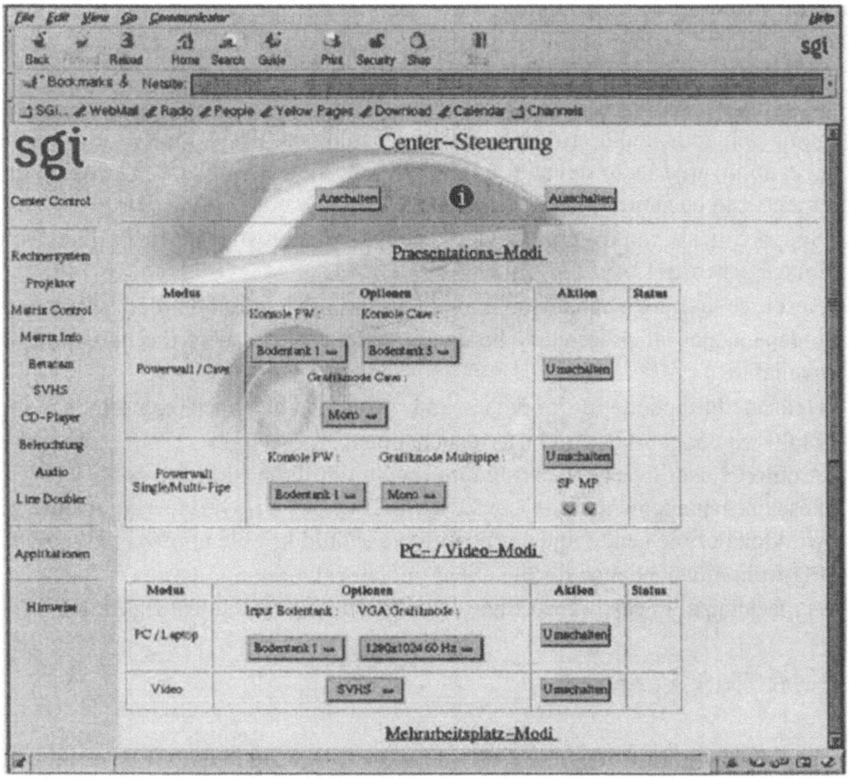

Fig. 2. Example of a web based center control software

Nevertheless, the software as presented before was not able to grow in the same way as the center installation. Due to technical limitations, the HTML based approach is not able to fulfill the new requirements and demands. One major disadvantage is the lacking support for proper status updates to indicate system changes inside the web page (as push technology is required therefore). Another drawback is the enormous maintenance effort necessary, if the underlying HTML/PERL code base has to be expanded and adapted to the growing center environment needs.

3 Requirements for distributed IPT Installations

The main challenge with controlling a distributed IPT installation is that different users will try to make use of the same hardware resources at the same time. Some of the available resources are actually sharable such as a video switching matrix with multiple input sources and output streams, others are atomic per se such as a simple video recorder device. Accessing resources without a dedicated resource locking mechanism causes frustration since work sessions and presentations could be interrupted unintentionally. Another problem is the protection of confidential data. This critical content could be disclosed by broadcasting the video signals of a presentation to another projection system. Last but not least a differentiated access to IPT resources can hardly be implemented using a HTML client.

Changing demands, requirements and the technological limitation of the available approaches motivated us to develop a new kind of control software. The functional requirements can be summarized as follows:

- Support of all controllable devices, including sophisticated ones, like the Onyx image generators.
- Resource locking mechanism to avoid a sharing violation on media resources.
- Independence of proprietary hardware. 'Make best use of the hardware already available'.
- Dedicated functionality for device and system maintenance operations.
- Multi-user capabilities and user management.
- A tailored user interface, taking into account different skill levels.
- Session management. Users must be able to get an overview about the current workload of the center and administrators should be able to manage the sessions.
- Platform independence for the client implementation.
- A mechanism to easily reconfigure and extend the system configuration.

4 The RCMS Approach

As a consequence from above, we introduce the following client/server architecture as a new kind of control software for IPT installations (see figure 3). The implementation based on this architecture uses the internal working title 'Reality Center Management System' (RCMS).

The RCMS server consists of the modules:

- User management (authorization handling),
- Resource management (resource locking and releasing),
- Device management (device control plug-ins) and
- System configuration (device and mode description in XML)

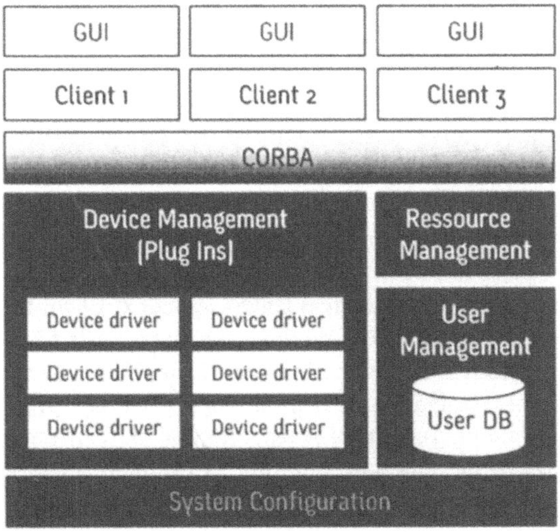

Fig. 3. The RCMS architecture

Both client and server are implemented with JAVA2 technology [4]. For the communication between client and server a CORBA layer is used. This has led to the following features:

- Clients can run on different platforms (Windows, Linux, IRIX and others).
- The server can run on different hardware platforms.
- No additional proprietary hardware is needed (provided that all controllable devices have a serial connection to the server platform or to a standard terminal server).
- Users cannot disrupt other sessions since all used resources are locked.
- A login procedure for all users secures the access to the system.
- The client GUI behavior can be customized using XML.
- National languages are fully supported (standard properties).
- A hardware upgrade does not result in programming effort. The reconfiguration can be done using XML.

To reflect the diversity of IPT installations, a plug-in concept is used for the user interface as well as for the interface to the hardware, which has to be controlled. This approach offers a maximum in flexibility and extensibility, while leaving the core system untouched if the software is adapted to new installations. The setup of the software is done via XML files. These files store the following information:

- The configuration of every single device (Fig. 4)
- The configuration of the client user interface
- The different application modes of the installation (Fig. 5)
- A hierarchical set of resources

The hierarchical structure of resources is used to be able to lock single devices like a projector as well as whole parts of an IPT installation like a Powerwall.

The configuration of the devices is described using an XML scheme. An example of a single device configuration is illustrated in figure 4. By using the reflection API of the Java programming language, it is possible to extend the system setup with new or modified device drivers without affecting the application core system. Therefore it is necessary to incorporate the Java device driver class as an attribute of the XML device element. The devices used in center installations are completely different, starting from simple ones up to very sophisticated 'devices' like an Onyx. Therefore it is not possible to define a generic XML device scheme, that fits for all devices. For that reason the parsing of the XML device file is performed by a generic parser. Each time a new device element is parsed, a corresponding device XML parser class is loaded at runtime and the concrete parsing task is passed to it. The attribute "stub" of the device element is a feature to test the configuration of the devices without having physical devices attached to the system. This is a very useful feature to test the complete system configuration before deploying it at a customer's site. The "config" element contains some attributes and physical settings of the device, like the number of input and output ports of the video media switch. The "in" and "out" elements that follow, establish the mapping between the physical cabling of the media matrix and the input and output ports of the matrix switch.

```
<device id="videomatrix" class="com.sgi.ccvis.server.devices.AutopatchYDM" stub="true">
  <config port="/dev/ttyd14" chassis="1" inputs="16" outputs="16" timeout="100"/>
  <in nr="1" resource="onyx3000.pipe0.channel0"/>
  <in nr="2" resource="onyx3000.pipe0.channel0"/>
  <in nr="4" resource="onyx3000.pipe1.channel1"/>
  <in nr="5" resource="onyx3000.pipe1.channel1"/>
  <in nr="14" resource="media.linedoubler"/>
  <in nr="15" resource="patchpanel1.vga_in"/>
  <in nr="16" resource="patchpanel2.vga_in"/>
  <out nr="1" resource="data_proj"/>
  <out nr="4" resource="pwall.upper_center_proj"/>
  <out nr="5" resource="pwall.lower_center_proj"/>
  <out nr="10" resource="pwall.right_proj"/>
  <out nr="11" resource="design.plasma"/>
  <out nr="12" resource="craftmansship.plasma"/>
  <out nr="14" resource="patchpanel1.plasma"/>
  <out nr="15" resource="patchpanel1.monitor"/>
  <out nr="16" resource="patchpanel2.monitor"/>
</device>
```

Fig. 4. Example device (video media switch) in devices.xml

Figure 5 illustrates an example of a XML mode description. The multi-pipe mode on the Powerwall will be identified further on by an unique identifier string "id". After that, the parameter element of the mode indicates that a customizable parameter is required from the client. In this case, the location of the console where the user wants to connect the control terminal is necessary. Depending on the user role, the client implementation either uses a default value for the actual console location or asks the user to choose from a list of possible locations during a mode switch request. For the following mode description, the string "console" is substituted with the user value. The XML description is now followed by two main sections: one section with a set of actions for the activation of the mode (constructor), another section with a set of actions for the proper deactivation (destructor). Each action line represents a device command, for example the videomatrix (Line 5 and 6) to connect the video output signal of the Onyx to the input ports of the soft edge blending box. The sync attribute of the action element is used to control the multi-threaded execution of the device actions. Some of the actions are not critical and can be run in parallel to speed up the total mode switch time. Other operations require some other actions to be completed and the execution of the sync command waits until all previous actions have been performed.

```
1  <mode id="pwall_multipipe_mono">
2    <parameter id="console"/>
3    <activate>
4      <action device="pwall" cmd="power" parameters="stdby" sync="true"/>
5      <action device="videomatrix" cmd="connect" parameters="onyx3000.pipe0.channel1 pwal
6      <action device="videomatrix" cmd="connect" parameters="onyx3000.pipe1.channel1 pwal
7      <action device="pwall.edgeblending" cmd="channel" parameters="edgeblended" sync="fa
8      <action device="videomatrix" cmd="connect" parameters="onyx3000.pipe0.channel0 $con
9      <action device="keyboardmatrix" cmd="connect" parameters="onyx3000.keyboard1 $conso
10     <action device="serialmatrix" cmd="connect" parameters="onyx3000.ttyd2 $console.ser
11     <action device="serialmatrix" cmd="connect" parameters="onyx3000.ttyd3 $console.ser
12     <action device="onyx3000" cmd="Xserver" parameters="multipipe_mono" sync="true"/>
13     <action device="pwall" cmd="power" parameters="on" sync="true"/>
14   </activate>
15   <deactivate>
16     <action device="pwall" cmd="power" parameters="stdby" sync="true"/>
17     <action device="videomatrix" cmd="disconnect" parameters="onyx3000.pipe0.channel1"
18     <action device="videomatrix" cmd="disconnect" parameters="onyx3000.pipe1.channel1"
19     <action device="videomatrix" cmd="disconnect" parameters="onyx3000.pipe0.channel0"
20     <action device="keyboardmatrix" cmd="disconnect" parameters="onyx3000.keyboard1" sy
21     <action device="serialmatrix" cmd="disconnect" parameters="onyx3000.ttyd2" sync="fa
22     <action device="serialmatrix" cmd="disconnect" parameters="onyx3000.ttyd3" sync="fa
23     <action device="pwall.edgeblending" cmd="channel" parameters="passthru" sync="false
24   </deactivate>
25 </mode>
```

Fig. 5. Example of a system mode in modes.xml

5 Sample Installation

Figure 6 illustrates a screenshot of a working draft for a sample client IPT installation with a three channel Powerwall. The main interaction paradigm of this client GUI is drag-and-drop. The application icons on the left can be dragged onto the visual representation of the Powerwall in the client's center area. If all needed resources are available, the application mode will be switched and a corresponding application image appears on the Powerwall. Otherwise the user gets information about the reason for the failure. This information is tailored to the current user role (i.e. knowledge and authorization level). Remote parts of the IPT installation are located in the right column. In this case, there are additional CAD workplaces in a nearby office where designers and stylists are able to use free graphic pipe resources of the Onyx to connect their CAD terminal to. In the lower area, single devices can be controlled using a set of controls. The availability of controls also depends on the current user role. If for example a user has no permission to change the settings of a device, the according control will not be visible for him.

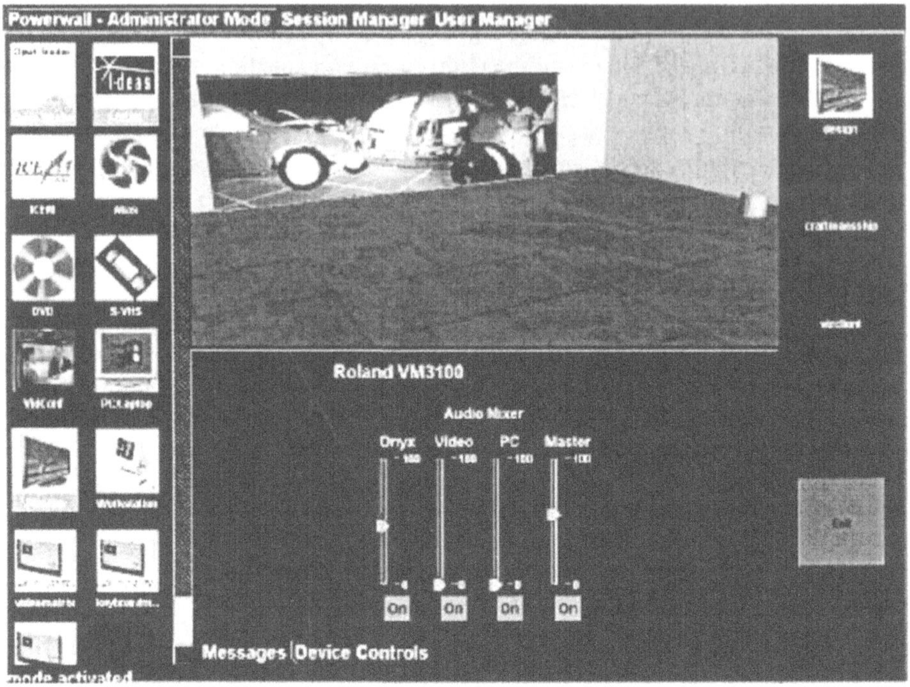

Fig. 6. Sample client GUI

A first commercial version of the software will be available in spring 2001. Future work can include dedicated functionality to support the daily work tasks of center operators. Examples are connectivity features of the center software to a calendar tool or an accounting system to keep track of the actual center usage times. There are some interesting Java Specification Requests (JSR 059) [5] proposed for the upcoming Java Releases. API extensions like XML Parsing (005), Preferences API (010), Logging API (047) and Network Launching API (056) are very interesting for the standardization of the RCMS software implementation. Some of the APIs can replace our own implementation (like logging) or external software modules (like Xerces-J [6] for XML parsing), others can extend the functionality (like the Java Network Launching Protocol).

6 Conclusion

In this paper we described a new kind of control software for IPT installations. It is in particular useful for distributed installations and enables engineers to focus on their work with the applications and tools rather than on the configuration and resource sharing of the hardware installation. The design of the software reflects the lessons we have learned while installing and operating Reality Centers for our customers. We are sure that this software approach is a step towards more user friendly and hence productive industrial IPT installations.

Acknowledgements

We'd like to thank all our partners and colleagues at SGI, especially the RCMS development team, for their enthusiasm and effort bringing the software to life. Finally, many thanks to all the reviewers for their valuable input.

References

1. DaimlerChrysler Virtual Reality Center (VRC).
   http://www.daimlerchrysler.com/index_e.htm?/specials/virtual/virtual5_e.htm
2. SGI Reality Center™ Advanced Visualization Facilities.
   http://www.sgi.com/realitycenter
3. Crestron Remote Control Systems.
   http://www.crestron.com
4. Sun Java Technology.
   http://www.javasoft.com
5. Java Specification Request (JSR).
   http://java.sun.com/aboutJava/communityprocess/jsr
6. Apache XML project.
   http://xml.apache.org

Novel Shutter Glass Control for Simultaneous Projection and Picture Acquisition

Andreas M. Kunz Christian P. Spagno

Swiss Federal Institute of Technology Zurich
Center of Product Development
kunz@imes.mavt.ethz.ch

Abstract. Virtual reality offers completely new possibilities for collaborative work over distributed environments. To enable collaborative work, it is necessary that both, virtual objects as well as the other users, can be seen simultaneously in real-time. A novel technique is necessary to overcome the contradiction of darkness and light for image projection and video acquisition, respectively. A stroboscopic light and a camera system are added to the existing VR-system and a few modification are made to existing shutter glasses. In such a solution, the method of projection in the VR-system remains unmodified. This paper describes how to resolve this contradiction with the constraint to make as few changes as possible to existing VR-systems. Furthermore the timing of the different devices is discussed.

1 Introduction

More and more VR installations are set up worldwide [1], [2]. Most of these installations are stand-alone, where the user is shown synthetic, computer-generated objects. Although present computing tools support information exchange and simple communication fairly well, collaboration on complex issues - be it models of functions, form or behavior - is not well supported. Current VR systems use projectors to display full-color, computer-generated stereoscopic images on the walls of a cube. Software synchronizes all the devices and calculates the correct perspective for each wall. In the CAVE [5]; [6] all perspectives are calculated from the user's point of view. Offset images are calculated for each eye to create the stereoscopic effect. The user can only experience this stereoscopic effect by wearing active stereo glasses, which alternately block the left and right eye.
Stand-alone installations lack the functionality for collaborative work among networked users and are thus not well suited for distributed teamwork. Most systems today do not allow interactions between multiple users and an object under design. In virtual meetings, humans are represented inadequately and disembodied through text, voice, or two-dimensional video projections. By integrating human representations in computer modeling environments, many of today's simulation techniques can be improved and new ones invented. Furthermore, the projects that use picture acquisition for rendering and gesture recognition not only face the problem of creating an effective team-working environment, but usually do not make use of a network [7];

[8]; [9]. In order to enable collaborative work in a distributed environment, a picture acquisition of the person must work together with the projection of both, the virtual objects and the other users, all in real-time [3], [4].
A new project called „blue-c" [10] proposes to build a system that achieves the following two major goals. The first goal is to enable a number of participants to interact in a virtual meeting and a collaborative setting, where the representation of people and objects is as complete as possible, in other words all objects and persons are fully rendered in three-dimensions with real-time movement and speech. The second goal is to provide an interaction between all the users and the simulated artifacts, be they models of function, form, behavior or their combination. The advantage of such simulations is the improvement of telepresence in conference meetings and the creation of immersive, virtual multi-user environments.
The key problem with simultaneous projection and picture acquisition is the illumination of the scene. On the one hand, to achieve a high quality image acquisition, a well-lighted scene is necessary. On the other hand, the projection system requires dark surroundings for a bright and sharp picture.
In order to overcome these conflicting lighting requirements, a new approach is used in the „blue-c"-project. The basic idea is to illuminate the „blue-c" actively with a stroboscopic light source during video image acquisition. The stroboscope is synchronized with the cameras, the projectors and the shutter glasses, that are needed to generate stereoscopic views in such VR Caves.

2 Contributions

In order to simultaneously provide a good projection and a good image acquisition, two different illumination phases are necessary. In a dark phase the spectator can watch the projection and in a light phase the camera can acquire the person's texture.
Our approach uses a flash to illuminate the person in order to get the texture. During the flash, the spectators eyes are covered by a new, third phase of the shutter glasses, where the glasses become opaque. If the phase sequence is done fast enough, human perception fails to follow the oscillation from light to dark.
Thus, the basic idea of the presented concept is to make as few changes as possible to an existing technical setup. The projection system is the most critical part in a VR setup and so it should not be modified to accommodate the video acquisition. Furthermore, stereoscopic viewing should still be possible and not be affected by the stroboscopic illumination. These constraints lead to a solution shown in Figure 1.
The original two states of the shutter glasses are thus supplemented by a third state, which darkens both the left and the right lenses simultaneously. This dark phase is used to shield the user's eye from the stroboscopic illumination. Each of the original states, one for the left and the other for the right eye, is shortened in order to create a third state. If this third state is kept very short, it will not be detected by the spectator's eye. However, regardless of how short the new state is, the overall picture will appear slightly darker because of the decreased light integration (exposure) time for the left and the right eye. Consequently, the dark phase is made to be as short as possible. The actual value for the dark phase is constrained by the following aspects:

- the minimum required time (to grab a video frame) for a picture (dictated by the shutter speed)
- the maximum switching frequency of the shutter glasses
- the minimum time of the flash (including the afterglow time)
- the maximum rise time of the flash
- the latency time of the additional electronical circuitry

These constraints were verified by the preliminary, basic measurements.

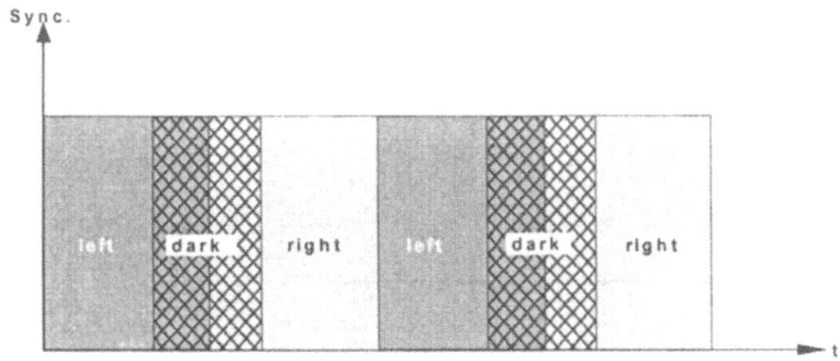

Figure 1 Time multiplexing diagram

3 Basic measurements

The shutter glasses and their triggering via the infrared link is the only part of the whole VR-system that has to be changed. Therefore, the following basic measurements have been made to verify that the requirements, listed in the above, can be fulfilled by the shutter glasses and the active illumination.

Shutter glasses (LCD): First of all, the time behavior of the glasses must be examined in order to get the maximum usable frequency and the shortest switching time from transparency to opacity. The measurement gave the following results:

- the LCD-shutters are fast enough to work on the required frequencies up to 60 Hz
- increasing the driving voltage has no effect on the opacity of the glasses
- it is possible to shorten the transparency phase of the glasses

Shutter glasses (electronic): In a next step the driving signals for the glasses itself have to be analyzed.

Figure 2 shows the two channels for the left and the right lens. The decoding and signal-processing unit within the shutter glasses generates a bipolar signal that is used to operate the LCD shutters. This bipolar signal is used to charge and discharge the LCD shutters since they behave like a capacitor. This implies that only the absolute value of the signal is used to darken the LCD shutters.

In order to use the already existing circuitry within the glasses that decodes the emitter's infrared signals, an additional electronic circuit was added to delay the rising edge for the left eye impulse and to start the falling edge of the right eye impulse earlier. This modification of the pulse widths causes an overlap and thus creates the third, dark phase.

Active illumination: Next, a suitable stroboscopic illumination was chosen and it's performance was measured. To provide such a high flash frequency only semiconductors or gas-filled light bulbs can be used. In the test setup a stroboscope and an array of white light emitting diodes (LEDs) were used. This illumination is bright enough to overpower the normal projection making changes to the projection system unnecessary.

The tests gave the following results:

- the stroboscope has sufficient light intensity.
- the pulse-width of the scope-flash is very small.
- active illumination using a stroboscopic light is very noisy.
- white light emitting diodes have lower intensity and need a wider pulse-width of the flash.

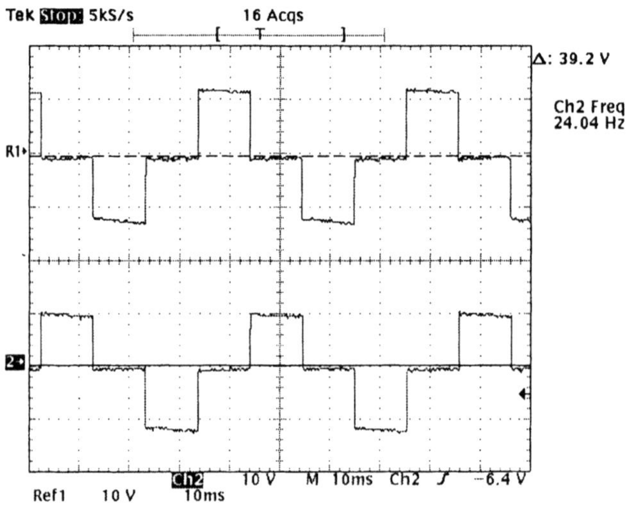

Figure 2 Driving signal for the glasses

4 Generating the third phase

For human perception, it is important that the new dark phase is symmetrical to the original phases for the left and the right eye. This must be taken into account when placing a third state into the operational cycle of the shutter glasses. In order to retain the system's symmetry, the third phase is placed during the transition from the original dark phase of the left eye to the dark phase of the right eye. Figure 3 shows the timing diagram of the prolonged signal for both glasses, compared to the original signal. In the chosen example, the picture refresh frequency is $f_w = 60$ Hz. Therefore, each eye will see 60 pictures per second and the dark phases for the left and the right eye can be calculated as:

$$T_D = T_L = 1/(2 * f_w) = 8{,}33 \text{ ms}$$

T_D = period of the dark phase

T_L = period of the light phase

In order to keep the symmetry, the frequency f_3 of the third phase must be either an integral multiple or an integral factor of fw. The following options are available for the period length T_3 of the dark phase:

$f_3 = 2*n*f_w$; $0 \leq T_3 \leq 1/(2*n*f_w)$; $1n = 1, 2, 3,...$ (case 1)

In case 1, the dark phase can be placed anywhere without distortion of the symmetry, since the third phase takes an equal amount of time from the right and the left eye.

$f_3 = f_w$; $0 \leq T_3 \leq 1/f_w$ (case 2)

In order to use the same amount of time from the left and the right eye in case 2, the dark phase must be placed symmetrically during the transition from the left to the right eye.

$f_3 = f_w/n$; $0 \leq T_3 \leq 1/f_w$; $n = 2, 3,...$ (case 3)

In case 3, the dark phase must be placed symmetrically during the change from the left to the right eye, as well.

Especialy case 3 was further examined. A higher frequency f3 did not give better results than case 2, because the person will still see the lower screen refresh frequency.

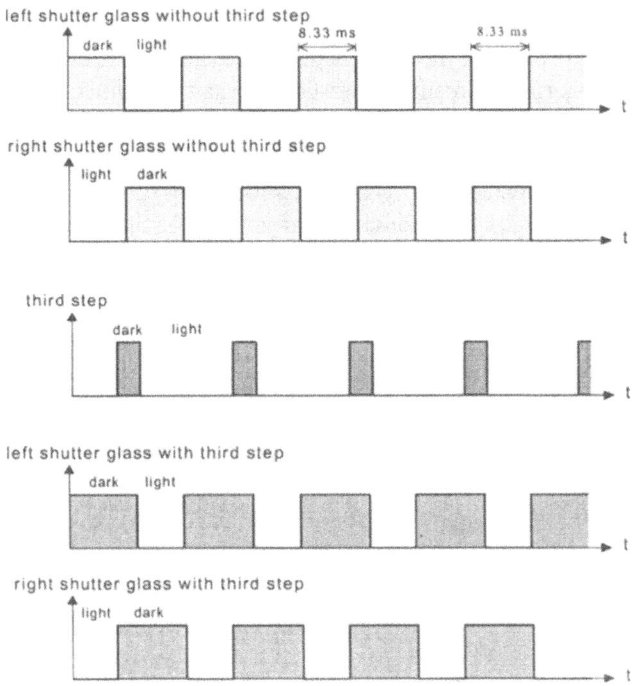

Figure 3 Signal diagrams for the shutter glasses

5 Modifications on the existing system

First experiments have been done with the CrystalEyes shutter glasses. This shutter glasses work with two LCDs. The additional circuit for the third phase is integrated between the original circuit of the shutter glasses and the two LCDs. Figure 4 shows the block diagram for this additional circuit.

The original bipolar signal coming from the shutter glasses is given to a rectifier stage since only unipolar signals will be processed. In the following, pulse-duration stage the rectified pulses are modified. The counter stage controls the number of pulses to be prolonged. This number can be chosen from one prolonged pulse within every period to one prolonged pulse only every 15th period. The third phase signal is combined with the original signals for the left and the right lens to generate the new signal for the glasses. Finally the signal passes to a flip-flop stage, which generates the bipolar signal.

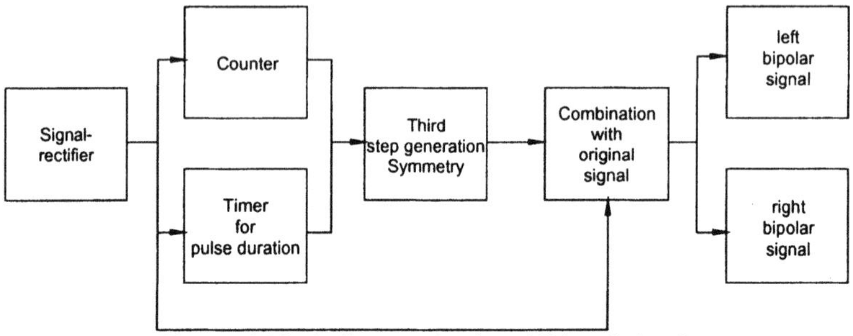

Figure 4 Block diagram for the additional circuit

Figure 5 shows the signal rectifier, the counter and the timer. Sig 1 is the signal coming in from the shutter glasses. The counter and the timer define when and how often the third phase is generated. The duration and the timing of the third state (the dark phase of the shutter glasses) are generated within this stage. The signal, sig 3, coming out of this stage corresponds to only a half of the third phase and will be completed in the following stage.

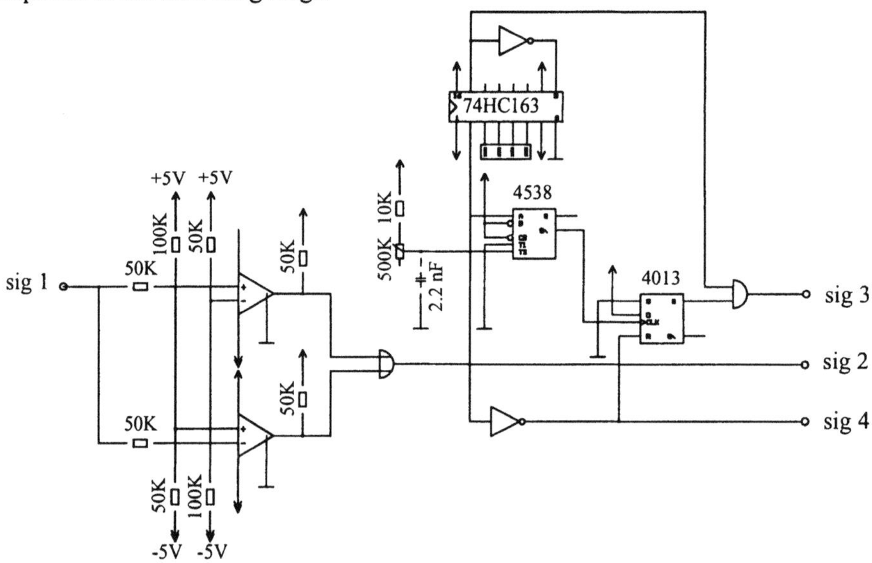

Figure 5 Signal rectifier, counter and timer

In the next stage, the symmetry of the third phase is generated. In Figure 6, signal sig 3 is coming in from the previous stage and sig 5 corresponds to the third phase.

To create the required symmetry, a capacitor is charged and discharged with a constant DC current. The input (sig 3) is at 0 V when charging the capacitor and at + 5 V when discharging the capacitor. The positive input of the first op-amp is regulated to 2.5 V. The capacitor is charged and discharged over the resistor that is connected to signal sig 3. A diode is connected in parallel to the capacitor to ensure that the op-amp does not saturate. In the last stage, the third phase signal sig 5 is combined with the original signals for the left and the right LCDs as shown in Figure 6 The new signals are then amplified. The alternation between positive and negative voltage prevents the LCDs from showing a memory effect. The LCDs for the left eye is connected to the signals sig 6 and sig 7 while the one for the right eye is connected to sig 8 and sig 9.

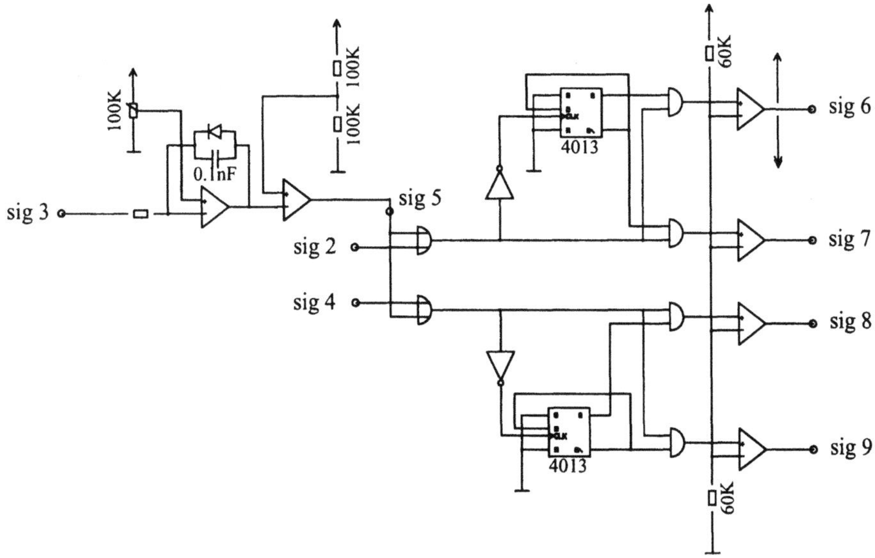

Figure 6 Symmetry generator of third phase and r output signal

6 Test setup

In order to verify the functionality the system, its components were assembled and integrated into a test setup as shown in Figure 7.

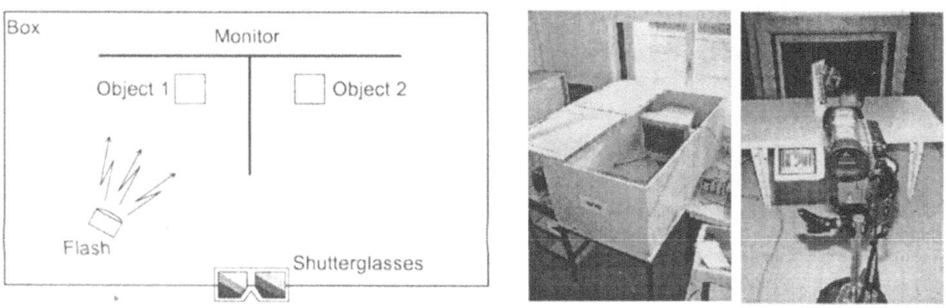

Figure 7 Test setup

The test setup is a chamber, which can be completely darkened. Inside the chamber, there is a monitor to provide a stereoscopic projection, combined with a standard infrared transmitter. The stereoscopic image can be viewed from outside through the modified shutter glasses, which are triggered via the infrared emitter. The chamber can be illuminated by stroboscopic light to illuminate the objects found inside. These objects can be acquired via a camera, which is installed in the chamber.

7 Experimental results

The chamber was used to test the feasibility of the whole system. The following points were of main interest:

- the subjective impression to the user
- the interference between the video image an the flash
- the need to synchronize the flash with the picture acquisition

In order to demonstrate the effectiveness of the modifications, the illumination of the object was viewed with and without a third phase. Figure 8 shows the difference between these two results.

Both images have been taken through the shutter glasses. In the left image, the shutter glasses were not modified, while in the right image the third phase was added. The illumination was the same for both images, i.e. the left object was illuminated with a flash while the right was illuminated with diffuse light.

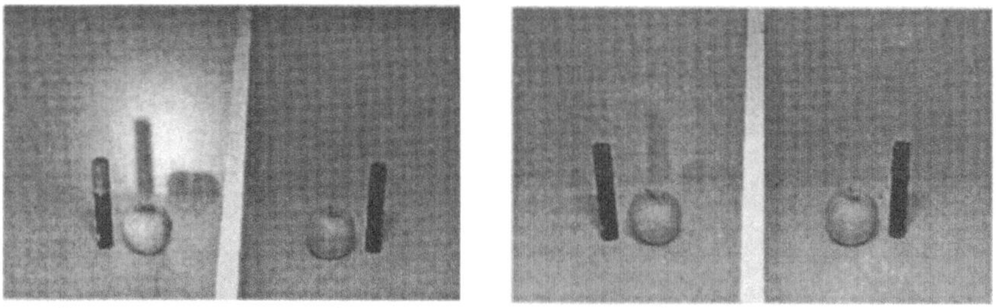

Figure 8 Illumination viewed without (left) and with the third phase (right)

Figure 8 shows that the flash illumination fades out almost completely. Tests with lower intensity flashes brought even better results in fading out the illumination. In both cases, the video image is bright enough to acquire good texture of the object.

Several tests were made in order to find out if the camera needs to be synchronized. A CCD-camera was installed within the test-setup of Figure 7. The camera was able to take video pictures every 1/50 s and was not synchronized with the stroboscopic flash, running at 48 Hz. Figure 9 shows typical results of such video acquisition.

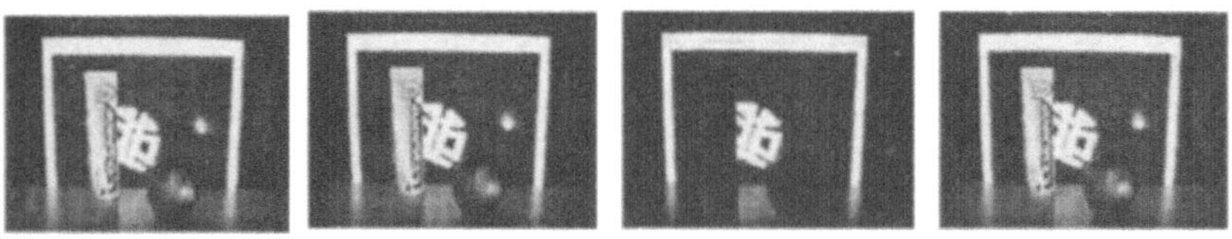

Figure 9 Typical video acquisition sequence with a CCD-camera and a stroboscopic flash

It can be seen from Figure 9 that there is one picture frame with poor illumination. This frame repeats after 0.5 s.

Figure 10 Typical video acquisition sequence with a CCD-camera and a LED flash

Using a LED's instead of the flash gives much better results. It can be seen from Figure 10, that the illumination differs. However, there is no picture frame without illumination.

The period of the flash is slightly longer than the period of picture acquisition. Assuming the flash illumination is a dirac impulse, there will be frames without illumination. The width of the stroboscopic flash is very similar to such a dirac impulse, while the LED illumination is not. This causes that every 25th picture appears dark when the stroboscopic flash is used. In order to avoid interference between the flash frequency and the picture frequency of the camera, the camera must be synchronized with the flash frequency.

This initial test set-up proved that the stroboscopic light could be used together with the video acquisition system. Furthermore, it has been shown that the third phase of the shutter glasses shields the user's eyes sufficiently from exposure to active scene illumination.

8 Conclusions

The basic measurements and the first test results from the setup proved that it is possible to integrate active illumination into a stereoscopic viewing system and perform texture acquisition of objects and people inside the system. A third phase (dark phase for both eyes) within the shutter glass protects the user's eyes from this additional illumination. The timing frequency of this third phase can be chosen to be fast enough so that the human eye cannot resolve it.

The new technology is compatible with existing VR-systems and incurs low additional costs from the modified shutter glasses.

This basic technology will allow the development of new applications of virtual reality within a collaborative framework.

9 Future work

In addition to the small test chamber, the system needs to be tested within a full-size test setup. This will give the user a better impression of a modified VR-system.

The tests have shown that the stroboscopic illumination is needed at every display cycle. Therefore the counter in the electronic circuit is no longer necessary.

Further work will also be focused on the stroboscopic illumination. The stroboscope used in the initial set-up was very noisy; a semiconductor flash could be used instead. This semiconductor flash can be made from a number of LED's placed all over the projection room. This will create sufficiently diffuse light, as required.

In addition we will work on an illumination with infrared light, that can be used in parallel to the projection and the active illumination. The infrared light together with specialized cameras will allow an easy silhouette extraction of the person inside the system.

10 Acknowledgements

The research work is funded by the ETH research contract 0-23803-00. We would like to thank all members of the project team.

11 References

1. C. Cruz-Neira, D.J. Sandin, and T.A. DeFanti, „Surround-screen projection-based virtual reality: The design and implementation of the cave." *Proceedings of SIGGRAPH 93*, pages 135-142, August 1993.

2. E: Lantz. „The future of virtual reality: head mounted displays versus spatially immersive displays (panel)." *In Proceedings of SIGGRAPH 96, Computer Graphics Proceedings*, pages 485-486, Aug. 1996.

3. V.D. Lehner and T.A. DeFanti. „Distributed virtual reality: supporting remote collaboration in vehicle design." *Computer Graphics & Applications, 17(2)*: 13-17, 1997.

4. R. Raskar, G. Welch, M. Cutts, A. Lake; L. Stesin, and H. Fuchs. „The office of the future: A unified approach to image-based modeling and spatially immersive displays." *Proceedings of SIGGRAPH 98*, pages 179-188, July 1998.

5. C. Cruz-Neira, D. J. Sandin, T. A. DeFanti, R. V. Kenyon, and J. C. Hart. „The cave: Audio visual experience automatic virtual environment." *Communications of the ACM, 35(6)*: 65–72, June 1992.

6. T. Disz, M. Papka, M. Pellegrino, and R. Stevens. „Sharing visualization experiences among remote virtual environments." *In Proceedings of the International Workshop on High Performance Computing for Computer Graphics and Visualization*, July 1995

7. J. W. Davis and A. F. Bobick. „Sideshow: A silhouette-based interactive dualscreen environment." *Technical Report 457*, MIT Media Lab, 1998.

8. H. Fuchs, G. Bishop, K. Arthur, L. McMillan, R. Bajcsy, S. Lee, H. Farid, and T. Kanade. „Virtual space teleconferencing using a sea of cameras." *Technical Report TR94-033*, The University of North Carolina at Chapel Hill, Department of Computer Science, 1994.

9. T. Kanade, P. J. Narayanan, and P. W. Rander. „Virtualized reality: Concepts and early results." *In Proceedings of the IEEE Workshop on the Representation of Visual Scenes*, June 1995.

10. W. Elspass, L. VanGool, M. H. Gross, A. Kunz, M. Meier, G. Schmitt, O. Staadt, P. Stucki „The BlueCave"; *ETHZ-internal research proposal*; Swiss Federal Institute of Technology (ETH) Zurich, Switzerland and University of Zurich, Switzerland

11. A. Kunz, C. Spagno „Modified Shutter Glasses for Projection and Picture Acquisition in Virtual Environments.", extended abstract to appear in IEEE VR 2001

Round Table: A Physical Interface for Virtual Camera Deployment in Electronic Arenas

Michael Hoch

ZKM | Institute for Visual Media,
Karlsruhe, Germany

mpunkt@zkm.de

Kai-Mikael Jää-Aro, John Bowers

Royal Institute of Technology (KTH),
Stockholm, Sweden

[kai,bowers]@nada.kth.se

Abstract.
In this paper, we describe a physical input device for the control of virtual cameras. The so called *RoundTable* has a round projection area where physical icons are used to stipulate the position of virtual cameras. With this scenario we propose a hybrid mixed reality environment for use by production personnel for real-time camera control during a live-broadcast. We present first results of using the RoundTable to support the managing of events in electronic arenas and compare them with traditional interfaces for camera control. We also comment on findings from a scenario in the field of sound mixing and sound composition.

1 Introduction

A number of applications of Virtual Reality (VR) technology exist where multiple cameras are deployed and switched between to take in the virtual environment (VE) from a number of viewpoints. Notably in so-called 'inhabited television' (iTV) applications, where a multi-user VE provides some of the input to a broadcast program [2, 7], virtual cameras may need to be deployed and selected in real-time in a manner similar to the direction of TV. This work takes as its starting point the argument that *finding the action* is one of the core problems in producing events in large-scale participatory settings, especially live events. When many participants are involved and the action can become distributed and is not necessarily governed by a strongly constraining script, it is easy for events of interest to be missed. Accordingly, effort has been devoted to develop a tool which might enable production personnel to gain an overview of the action in an electronic arena and, through this, to support the deployment of resources such as virtual cameras and virtual microphones to pick up happenings of interest. In this paper we describe an approach using a round table as a physical input device to support event management in such electronic arenas via a notion of activity oriented virtual camera deployment and control. That is, it is the activity of participants in an electronic arena which serves as a resource to guide the deployment, direction and control of the views which are made available for broadcast or other forms of dissemination.

It has been an important emphasis of this work that technical systems be proposed and developed which are capable of real-time operation in settings which have a considerable degree of unpredictability. The application is able to receive and visualize a real-time stream of position, orientation and activity data from an electronic arena. An application, for example, which would require time consuming activity at the interface selecting from hard to access menus or with physical interfaces which could not be used dexterously would be unlikely to be acceptable.

This paper, describes our initial development work of a novel *physical interface* (embedded within a *room-sized environment*) for the control of virtual cameras in applications in electronic arenas. Several usability issues have prompted this proposed solution, including the following.

1. Interaction using conventional desktop input devices such as mice, joysticks and keyboards is often too slow when time-critical selections are required (to move icons or make selections with a mouse requires the user to first grasp the mouse, then make a controlled movement on screen to the target, engage with the target, and then execute the appropriate function).
2. Image direction in the settings of interest to us is a cooperative activity, where multiple users (directors, camera operators and other production members) need to sustain awareness of each other's gestures around shared artifacts— such forms of mutual awareness being very commonly documented as an essential feature of co-operative work in time-critical settings (see, e.g., [9]).
3. Real-world space needs to be recognized and reserved for participants to bring freely whatever real-world documents and other artifacts they wish allowing interaction with these to be interleaved with technically-mediated interaction. These phenomena tend to speak against fully immersive solutions.

2 Mixed Reality / Shared Environments

Several approaches to integrate physical and virtual space in a shared environment have been proposed, for example, DigitalDesk [13], Bricks [6] and phicons [8]. Based on these foundations some applications have been shown to successfully integrate physical interaction handlers and virtual environments or tasks, as in the System BUILD-IT [10], where engineers are supported in designing assembly lines and building plants, or in URP [12] where a physical interface is used for urban planning, or the concept of 'Embodied User Interfaces' [5] where the user physically manipulates a computational device.

In the table environment BUILD-IT described in [10] a menu area is proposed for object selection that, thereafter, can be placed on the virtual floor plan by moving the interaction handler. This approach uses the physical object as a general interaction device. The physical objects that are used in [12] for the urban planning example are mostly used in a less generic but more specific way which lowers the chances of errors due to user input, e.g. a building phicon would less likely be used as something else than a generic brick object. Another approach is reported in [11] where physical objects, the so called 'mediaBlocks', are used as digital containers that allow for physical manipulation outside of the original interaction area.

The input devices proposed in this chapter extend these approaches in a number of ways. First, we introduce a context sensitive functionality to the physical objects a user interacts with. That is, the exact significance of an action on a physical object can change in relation to the context in which the action is performed. This enables us to support several different kinds of user action without proliferating the number of phicons which need to be used and identified. Second, we propose a setup that combines physical interaction with abstract visualization in an application that is not concerned with the off-line design of an environment, but real-time intervention in an electronic arena. This combination of physical interface with abstract visualization and real-time consequences of interaction gives our work uniqueness within exploration of physical interfaces. Finally, we emphasize the overall working ecology in which the physical interface we have prototyped is designed to fit. We imagine a room-sized cooperative environment where physical interfaces might enhance and add to traditional interfaces and work activity. This concern for realistic cooperative working environments is rarely emphasized in the design-led demonstrations of physical interfaces and tangible bits which are commonly reported.

3 Round Table with Interaction Blocks

A round table with a projection screen in the middle is used to display a map of the electronic arena (see Figure 1a). The image on the table-screen is rear-projected— that is, projected from underneath the table using a projector and a mirror. The projection screen is approximately 80cm across with a table height of approximately 95cm.

Physical objects are placed upon the table-top projection screen to deploy cameras (figure 1b), select cameras for transmission (TX in broadcasting terminology), enable zooming of the display and the other operations we shall shortly describe. On a second projection screen next to the table (to the rear of Figure 1a), a 3D rendered scene can be displayed from the perspective of the deployed camera. Alternatively, the camera view, as well as the TX view, can be shown on additional monitors in a room-sized environment.

A pole mounted on the table holds a real camera with infrared light. It is used for tracking blocks that can be placed on the table screen (see Figure 1). These can signify the position of virtual cameras by means of positioning the interaction blocks on a representation of the virtual scene. For robust segmentation of the blocks on the projection table, we use retroreflective color attached to each block (made available by 3M, Neuss, Germany) and an infrared filter on the camera to eliminate visible light. In Figure 1c, a visualization of participant activity is shown with participants depicted as shaded triangles together with the, larger triangular, camera phicon and a small circular *probe* phicon, that are used to make selections in the display (indicated by darker, red highlighting).

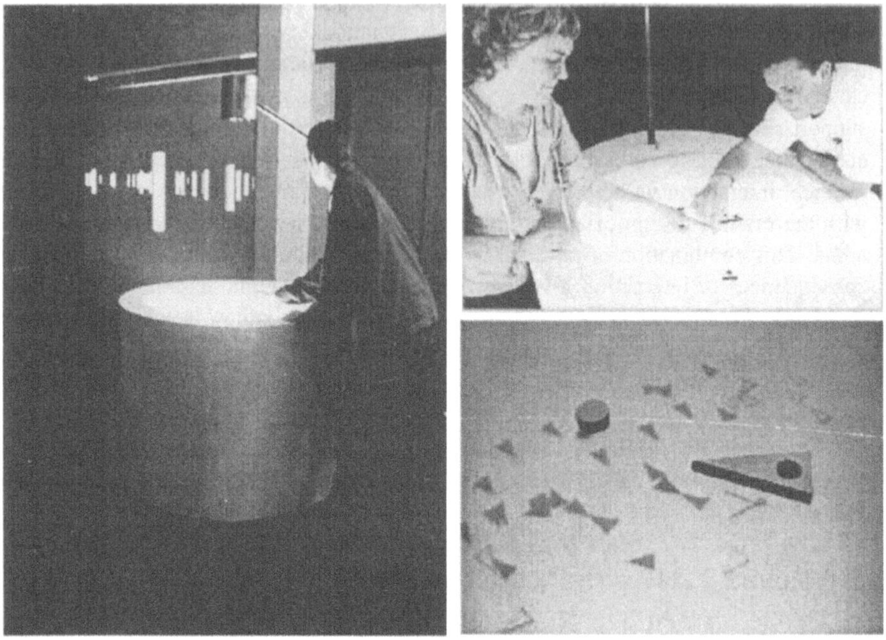

a) b), c)

Figure 1: a) Table with rear projection, b) deploying cameras on table surface, c) Top view of table with floor plan, abstract visualiz ation of avatars and interaction blocks

In the following we will describe two different application scenarios where the Round-Table has been applied to. We also evaluated a traditional interface approach using mouse and/or keyboard.

4 Application Scenario1: Camera Deployment

We have developed a prototype implementation of the principles we have described above, called SVEA (Sonification and Visualization for Electronic Arenas). SVEA implements the Spatial Model described in [1], it computes and displays awareness maps, and the support for simple mouse-based interaction. We place isosceles triangle shaped markers representing the participants of the electronic arena on a 2D projection of space with the color of these markers displaying a measure of the activity they show. Areas of high activity will thus be conspicuous as large, brightly-colored areas.

Once a new camera phicon is detected on the RoundTable, a virtual camera is assigned to the location indicated and pointing in the direction suggested. The view onto the electronic arena from this virtual camera can be selected for transmission (TX) by placing a small round *camera selector* phicon into the non-reflective hole in the middle of the triangle. Using the camera selector phicon is proposed as an intuitive and simple way for selecting cameras. The *probe* phicon is used to select a group of avatars in the projected visualization. Rather than attempt— using phicons— to replicate the mouse gesture of clicking and dragging used to select groups in the screen-based application, we decided to exploit and extend the awareness model underlying the visualization to enable context-sensitive selections to be made [4], i.e. exactly which avatars it selects, how many and in which configuration, is dependent upon the avatars' orientations and proximity with respect to the probe. We describe this use of the probe phicon as being 'context-sensitive' because exactly which avatars it selects, how many and in which configuration, is dependent upon the avatars' orientations and proximity with respect to the probe. Finally, the *zoom* phicon allows one to zoom into the visualization in a similar context-sensitive fashion. The group of avatars is determined corresponding to those which an object placed in the electronic arena at the location corresponding to the zoom phicon would be aware of. The display is rescaled so that it shows this group plus an area around them.

In the desktop version of SVEA, algorithmic camera deployment is actioned by dragging the mouse over the display to select a set of markers (i.e. participants). As soon as the mouse is released a camera is deployed to the algorithmically computed optimal location for that group according to whichever algorithm is set as a preference. In this, algorithmically enhanced way, camera deployment can be efficiently actioned by a single interface gesture. Also in in the desktop version of SVEA, the 2D display can be magnified up to 16 times by selection of a menu option to zoom in on a selected group of interest with the center of that group being the center of the zoom. Zooming rescales the relative separation of markers in screen distances but not the size of the triangles themselves. Zooming, therefore, can clarify the relative positions of participants that are so close to each other as to appear overlapping when in a 'wide angle' view.

In the RoundTable production environment, we have had to make important design decisions over issues to do with the relationship between inserting a new camera phicon into the vision system's field of view and the 'lifecycle' of a corresponding virtual camera. Does deploying a phicon create a new camera at the designated location? Or does it merely re-deploy an available camera? Are there as many camera phicons as virtual cameras (and no more)? Or can virtual cameras be created without upper limit? Does the removal of a camera phicon cause the corresponding virtual camera to pass out of existence? Or does it cause the virtual camera to return to some default behavior? Ultimately, we feel that such questions have to be answered with respect to particular applications.

Our prototype, then, arbitrarily restricts the number of cameras to a user-preferred limit but does so without prejudice to alternative possibilities. Within this set of cameras, the default behavior is an autonomous one. That is, if a camera is not deployed through activity at the round table, it maintains behavior which is entirely algorithmically determined. This default behavior is to rove the space, following the gradient of increasing awareness, while avoiding other cameras. The introduction of a camera phicon will 'claim' the first available camera. Which camera is 'first' is determined in numerical order— thus retaining a sense of 'Camera 1', 'Camera 2' and so forth which could be explicitly referred to by users to individuate cameras. The assignment will pass over already assigned cameras. Amongst other desirable features, this method has the consequence that cameras already selected for TX will not be suddenly and mistakenly cut to another location.

Our introduction of a phicon controlled zooming functionality has some important consequences. After zooming, the projection of the virtual space will be transformed such that the position of a camera phicon may no longer correspond to the virtual camera previously associated with it. There are a number of design options here. Zooming could (i) forcibly deassign virtual cameras from phicons or (ii) the phicon and the associated camera become disjoint in their spatial location on the table or (iii) virtual cameras 'snap' to the new relative locations occupied by their phicons. In discussion with users, each of these options have been revealed as having benefits and drawbacks as general solutions, so again ultimately the choice should be made on application-specific grounds.

5 Application Scenario2: Interactive Compositional Machines

For this application we ported one piece of the CD-ROM "Small Fish" that has been created by Kiyoshi Furukawa, Masaki Fujihata and Wolfgang Münch at the ZKM in Karlsruhe to the RoundTable. Small Fish allows the user to manipulate a predefined set of musical algorithms, that stipulate what kind of relationships between visual graphics and musical time exist and how the player is able to influence the sounds via the screen. As a CD-ROM, Small Fish uses a traditional interface with mouse. For porting the application to the RoundTable we modified the mouse interface to actually get driven by the table output. We allowed three phicons, which did not get differentiated in shape, to stipulate the position of three different graphical objects. Hence, allowing three users to simultaneously interact with the system (see Figure 2a).

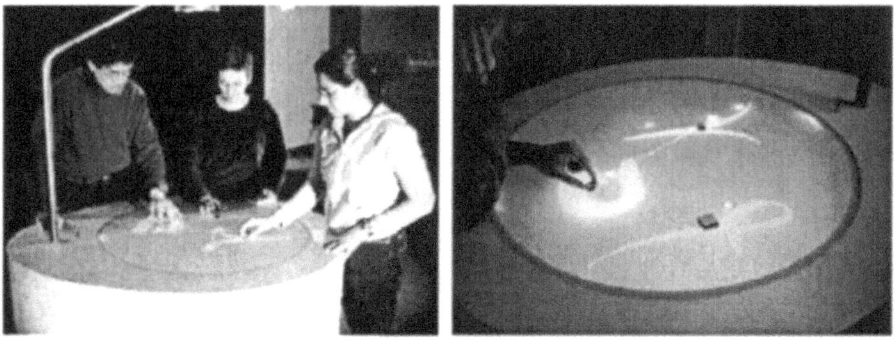

a) b)

Figure 2: RoundTable with Sound Mixing Application "Small Fish", a) three users interacting simultaneously, b) detail view of the graphical objects

By modifying the position of the phicons on the table surface, the graphical objects position gets stipulated (see figure 2b). Music is generated by producing a Midi stream of notes that gets influenced by the position of smaller circular objects that stick to the larger graphical objects (see small blue points in figure 2b). By moving the larger objects, the user can "catch" or remove the small objects from other objects. Another two small circular objects are special, they move around autonomously, touching the smaller objects in a predefined order. Whenever they touch a small (blue) objects, a Midi note is produced. Tone and the note itself is stipulated by the y-position of the "collision" (i.e. from lower left top upper right in figure 2b). Hence, notes and speed can be stipulated by the user by modifying the position of the objects in y-direction and spatially arranging the objects on the 2D display surface.

Our first results of evaluating the Small Fish Interactive Compositional Machine by showing this application to some 'players' were really positively. All users liked the tangible interface to the application. We noted that users did interact in an immediate and intuitive way. The interface allowed a single user to most easily change the position of the graphical objects at different spatial locations on the table. There is no more a point and click operation needed, no positioning of one interface handler to different graphical objects, but more a direct manipulation of graphical objects with the aid of the physical objects on the table surface. Even when more than three people where present, we noted that interaction did switch between users, i.e. showing collaborative behavior. Also users reported it being "fun" to interact with other users simultaneously.

6 Discussion and Results

The applications described in this paper have been trialed upon the RoundTable as well as in more conventional desktop variants. Using the RoundTable indicates how mixed reality technologies (here mixing the manipulation of physical objects with projected computer generated displays) can be deployed in support of production activities in an electronic arena. Our work has been marked by a focused concern to reflect upon its nature and evaluate its advantages and problems throughout design. Where possible we have put our technologies before both members of the public and media professionals. We believe that our emphasis on combining physical interfaces and virtual displays within a shared environment designed to support cooperative work is novel, and that physical interfaces for virtual camera control in electronic arenas is a unique application area.

Currently, we have built a functional prototype for deploying virtual cameras that shows the applicability of our approach. We introduced a novel context-sensitive use of physical objects and presented novel selection and zoom operations using this technique. We have presented the RoundTable to a number of persons independent of the development group so as to evaluate it as a means for presenting production support tools. Users of the RoundTable have included a number of media professionals as well as students and visitors to our lab. Most importantly, several production personnel who were practically involved in the inhabited TV events have been presented with the table and the concepts it embodies. These evaluation sessions have been informal and discussive, rather than based around controlled experimentation. This is appropriate given the kind of technology it is and the prototype standing of the applications we have developed for it.

The main advantages with using the RoundTable that have repeatedly come to light are twofold:

1) Giving both a position and an orientation using a physical block is noticeably faster than using a mouse, since mouse-based positioning requires one operation for indicating the position and a second for indicating the direction – this latter requires dragging and thus takes longer time than just placing an item. (The mouse operations can be combined into one physical movement, so that the position at mouse-down is taken to be the origin of the camera and the position at mouse-up to indicate the end of a direction vector. However, it is very hard to do this with the same speed and precision as with a phicon.)
2) Several people can stand around the table and easily do adjustments or new placements of cameras, thus supporting mutual awareness among the production personnel as they engage with a shared artifact. Conventional screen-based, desktop solutions are more cumbersome in this regard.

Problems we encountered concern the way users touch the objects, i.e. when users grasp objects from above they often partly (or fully) occlude the objects from the camera. This can make the tracking erroneous. However, once the user gets instructed how to handle the objects we do not encounter this as a major problem. Indeed, we have noticed users spontaneously discover that covering an interaction object is a gesture that can be creatively used (e.g. to simulate the momentary removal of an object). Again, if such occlusion problems become excessive, it is possible to consider siting the camera beneath the table. However, this solution can lead to misunderstandings if users think that triangular phicons always represent the presence of a camera in the electronic arena. For our method of camera allocation, this would be an inappropriate 'user-model'. Rather, the camera phicons should be regarded as *tools with which to deploy virtual cameras*, not representations of those cameras themselves. It is clear, though, that this is a less natural model than expecting a one to one correspondence between virtual camera and camera phicon.

It is important to observe that similar issues arise for most attempts to physically interface to the virtual and are not specific to our application or our particular design decisions. Only in the extreme case of a completely strict coupling between physical activity and consequences in the virtual world *(and vice versa*) would it be possible to think that a physical object could non-problematically represent a virtual one. As soon as the coupling is relaxed the relationship between the physical and the virtual has to be *achieved in users' practical understandings* rather than technically mandated (see [3]). In a sense, this argument presents a limit case on the use of tangible mixed reality interfaces. When using simple 'inert' physical objects like blocks, many simple user-interface operations will cause problems with the significance of the physical objects. Rescaling and scrolling a display will make the objects disjoint from anything they are to represent.

In the case of a production tool intended to be shared by personnel, with individuals possibly attending to different parts of the display at the same, there may be good arguments for disallowing operations such as zooming and scrolling. Changing the viewpoint in the display places fairly strict restrictions on the type of collaboration between production personnel as any zoom or scroll would potentially move an individual's work area out of sight. We conclude therefore that our concept of 'context sensitive zooming' supported by a phicon, while of some novelty (we know of no other work which has such an elegant, single phicon solution to such a fundamental interaction issue in tangible interfaces), is probably not of great practical utility in our target domain (production work for electronic arenas). In our domain, on the occasions when zooming etc are required, conventional desktop solutions seem more appropriate.

One of the directors of the inhabited TV events envisaged problems in using a device like the RoundTable because it suggested to her that she would have to disengage with inspecting view monitors (both of TX and sources) in order to use it. To be sure, in conventional TV practice, a director will be continually attending to her sources and to TX with, if she is also doing vision mixing, fingers poised on pre-programmed buttons to bring about transitions between sources. SVEA on the RoundTable is a very different setting from this. In our current design, the selection of a camera requires the placing of a small peg into a camera phicon. This is not a faster gesture than pressing a button ones finger is already poised over.

A technology like ours could still be used by non-directors. Indeed, typically in a large-scale distributed live real-world event, a director will be assisted by several assistants who submix or pre-select views for her. A RoundTable production suite could well have a specific role in browsing and homing in on action in electronic setting analogous to that one. Selecting a camera with the peg would not necessarily select TX but would sub-edit a shot for directorial consideration.

7 Conclusion

Our initial motivation for the physical interaction solution that the RoundTable embodies was based on the claim (often articulated in the literature) that interaction with phicons is commonly faster than with conventional desktop widgets. This claim is critically interrogated since we were able to compare RoundTable with conventional workstation implementations of essentially the same applications. Some operations are noticeably quicker, but others seem slowed. This again enables us to know the limitations of the RoundTable as a solution. Our overall view is that a tangible physical interface (like the RoundTable) enables some interaction capabilities while inhibiting others. And the converse is true for conventional desktop interfaces. The RoundTable enables some kinds of gestures to be made much more swiftly than others (e.g. the simultaneous specification of an orientation and a position). Other gestures may be slowed (e.g. those which require an object to be visually searched for on the table before an action, like selection with a peg, can be initiated). The RoundTable permits multiple viewers to experience its information visualization more readily than a screen on a personal workstation. This facilitates certain patterns of collaboration and inter-working between personnel.

Commands can be actioned from the keyboard, by mouse-gesture, by menu selection and so forth. On the RoundTable, we have tried to avoid simulating or reproducing such widgets, preferring a consistent physical interaction approach throughout. Accordingly, we have a limited number of blocks with basic functionality. This works well. Our attempts to go beyond this and trying to support classic operations such as zooming and scrolling have introduced tensions and inconsistencies in our design approach and given users difficulties in finding the appropriate 'model' for understanding what's going on. In short, the RoundTable is an elegant interface for applications that need a small repertoire of commands to be supported.

Our overall appraisal of the RoundTable, then, is nuanced. In contrast to much of the HCI literature at the time of writing, we do not think that physical-tangible interaction methods offer categorical advantages over conventional desktop-workstation-based solutions. At least, not so in all contexts. Our experience has enabled us to articulate the boundary conditions on the applicability of such interaction techniques. We conclude that gestural interaction in relation to an interaction surface is an idiomatic way for supporting participants' engagement within an electronic arena.

8 REFERENCES

1. Benford S, Fahlén L (1993), *Awareness, Focus and Aura, a spatial model of interaction in virtual space*, Proceedings of HCI International '93, Orlando, August 1993.
2. Benford S, Greenhalgh C, Brown C, Walker G, Regan T, Morphett J, Wyver J and Rea P (1998), *Experiments in inhabited TV*, Proceedings of CHI'98, pp 289–290.
3. Bowers J, Pycock J, O'Brien J (1996), *Talk and Embodiment in Collaborative Virtual Environments*, Proceedings of CHI'96, pp 58-65.
4. Bowers J, Hellström S-O and Jää-Aro K-M (1999), *Issues in management of Inhabited TV broadcasts*, eRENA Deliverable 4.3. 1999.
5. Fishkin K, Moran T, Harrison B (1998), *Embodied User Interfaces: Towards Invisible User Interfaces*, Proc. EHCI'98 Conference on Engineering for Human-Computer Interaction, Crete Greece, 1998
6. Fitzmaurice G, Ishii H, Buxton W (1995), *Bricks: Laying the Foundations for Graspable User Interfaces*, ACM Proceedings CHI'95, Denver, Colorado, 1995.
7. Greenhalgh C, Benford S, Tylor I, Bowers J et. al. (1999), *Creating a Live Broadcast from a Virtual Environment*, SIGGRAPH '99, Conference Proceedings, Los Angeles, 1999.
8. Ishii H, Ullmer B (1997), *Tangible Bits: Towards Seamless Interfaces between People, Bits and Atoms*, ACM Proceedings of CHI'97, pp. 234-241.
9. Martin D, Bowers J, Wastell D. (1997), The interactional affordances of technology: an ethnography of human-computer interaction in an ambulance control centre. Proceedings of HCI'97.
10. Rauterberg M, Bichsel M, Fjeld M et. al. (1998), *BUILD-IT: A Planning Tool for Construction and Design*, Video Proc. + Summary CHI'98.
11. Ullmer B, Ishii H. Glas D (1998), *mediaBlocks: Physical Containers, Transport, and Controls for Online Media, Proc. SIGGRAPH'98, ACM 1998.*
12. Underkoffler J, Ishii H (1999), *Urp: A Luminous-Tangible Workbench for Urban Planning and Design*, Proc. CHI'99.
13. Wellner P (1993), *Interacting with Paper on the* DigitalDesk, CACM, Vol. 36, No. 7, July 1993, pp 87-96.

Color Plates

Grosjean and Coquillart (pp. 1–12)

Fig. 1. The C^3 on the Responsive Workbench

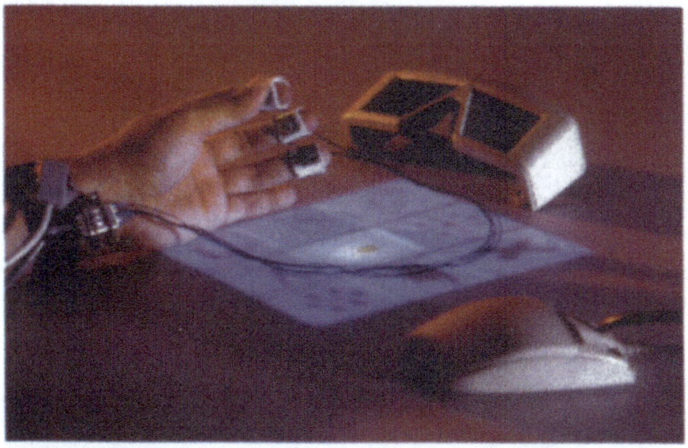

Fig. 3. The tracked buttons

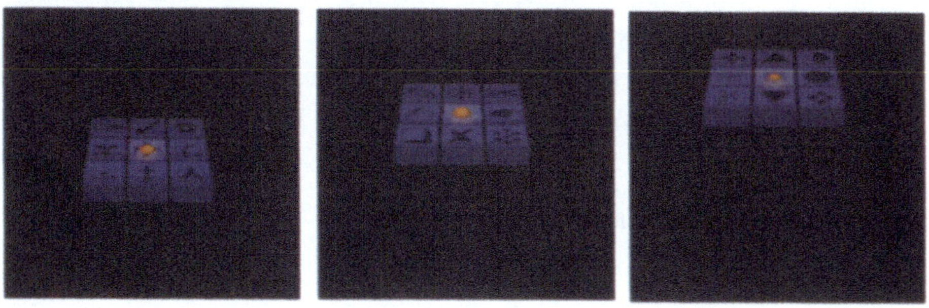

Fig. 5. The C^3 appearance when the user pinches and stands still, moves his hand down, or up

Koutek and Post (pp. 61–70)

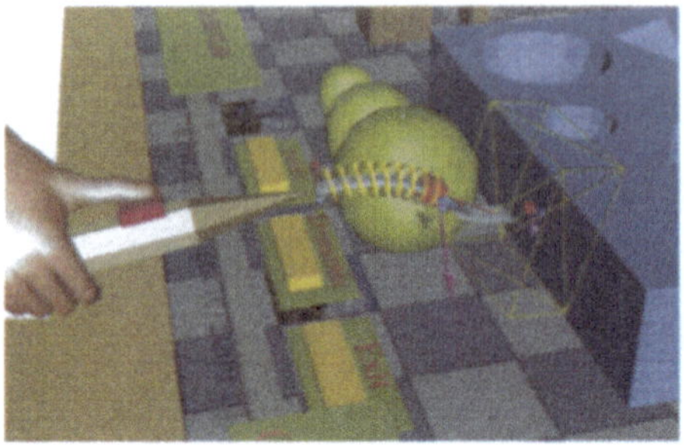

Fig. 14. Torsion resistant spring-fork

Fig. 15. Spring-fork in torsion

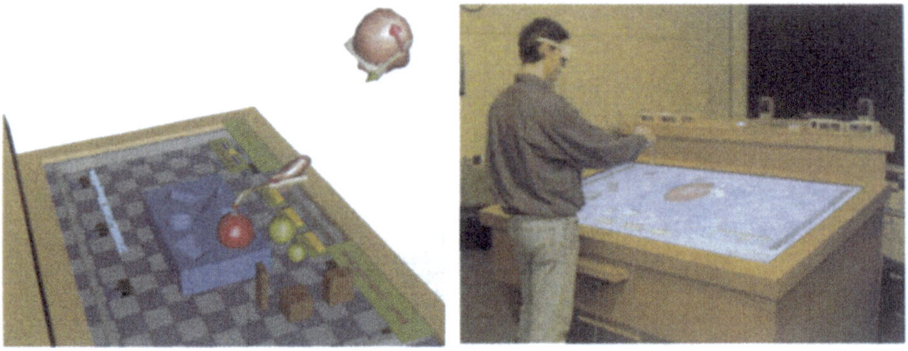

Fig. 16. RWB-overview: the spring-fork manipulation with objects in the mini-world left; left: RWB simulator; right: real RWB application

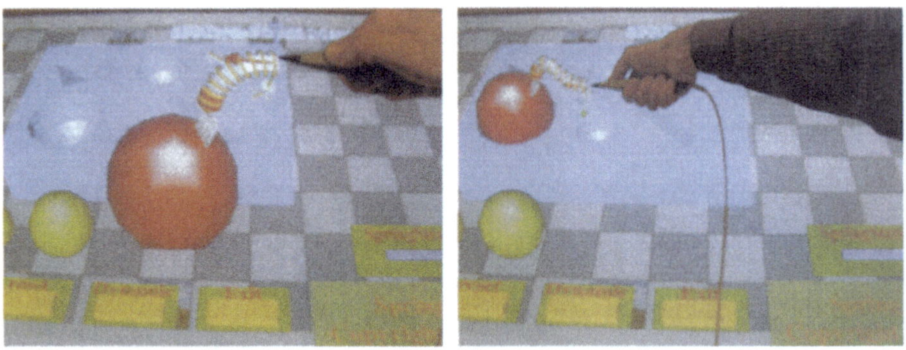

Fig. 17. RWB-detail: the spring-fork manipulation

El-Sana (pp. 175–184)

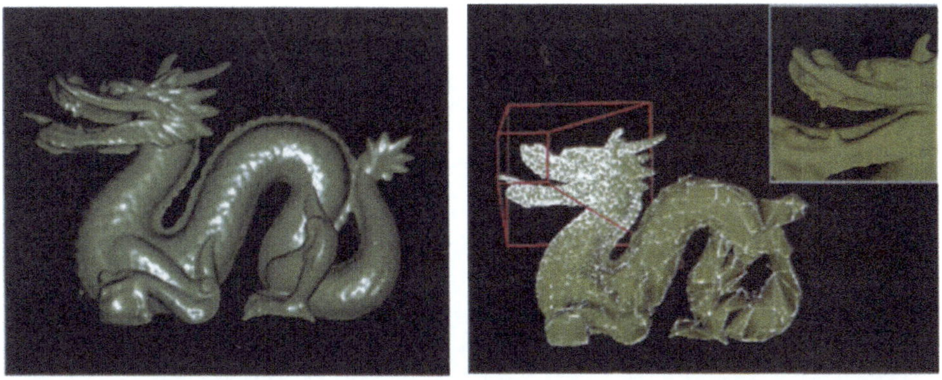

a Original model: 300K triangles **b** Selected view: 76K triangles

Fig. 4. View-dependent rendering of a Dragon model

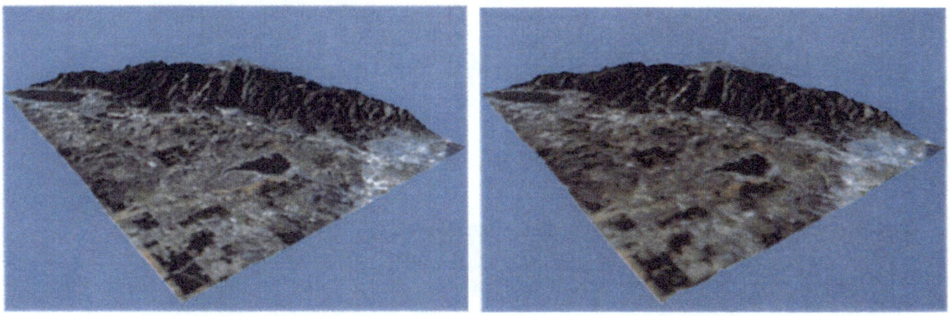

a Original mesh: 522K triangles **b** Low resolution: 32K triangles

Fig. 5. Uniform low resolution of a terrain model

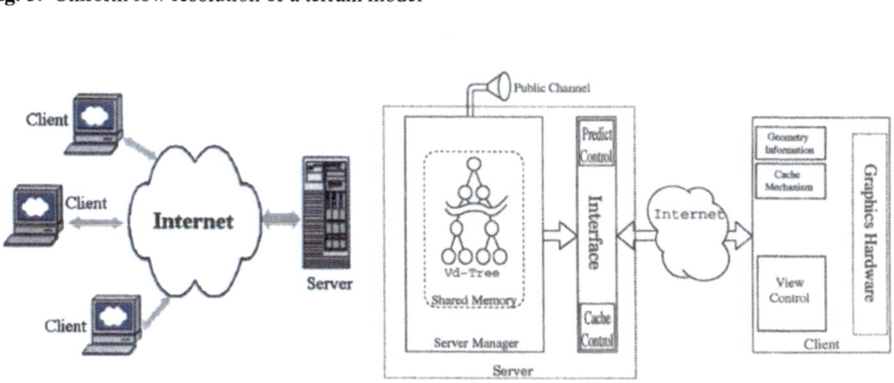

a Client-Server network **b** Client-Server view-dependent rendering

Fig. 1. System Configuration (a larger version of Fig. 1)

Schulze-Döbold et al. (pp. 187–198)

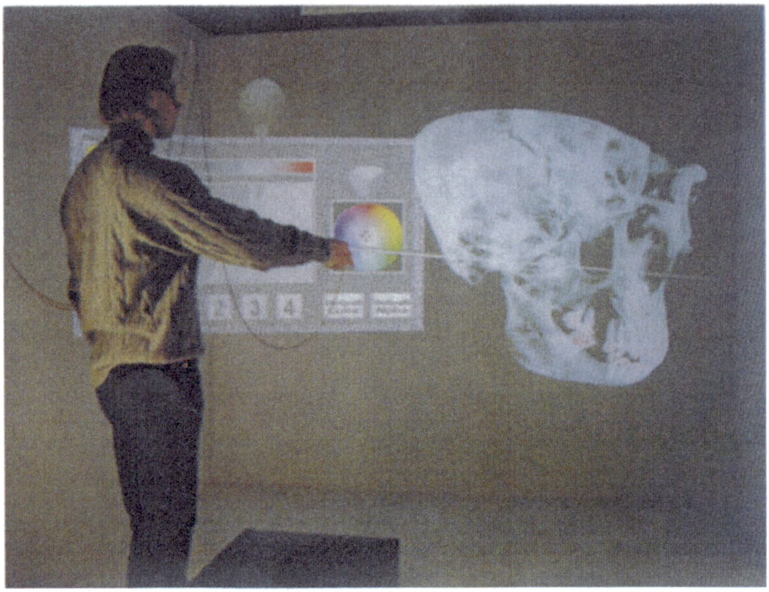

Plate A. Scenario 1: Visible human skull

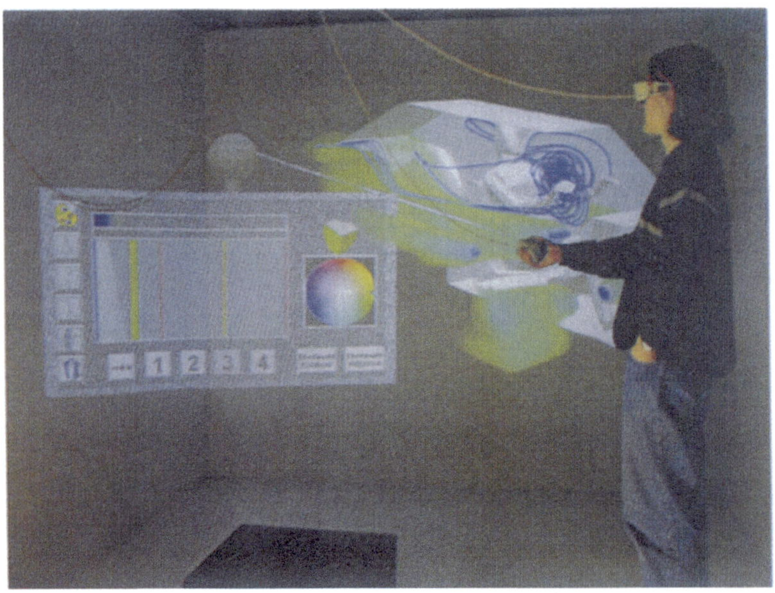

Plate B. Scenario 2: Air conditioning simulation

Majamder and Welch (pp. 209–217)

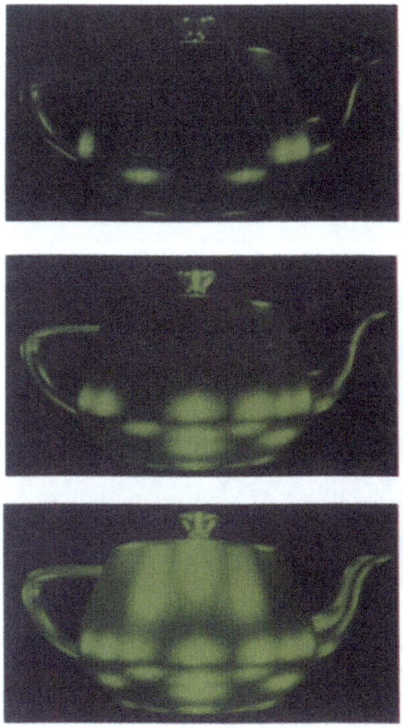

Highly Specular Scene: Top – One projector projecting the effects of 7 highly specular lights. Middle – Addition of one more projector projecting 7 different specular light sources. Bottom – A third projector projecting 6 more light sources

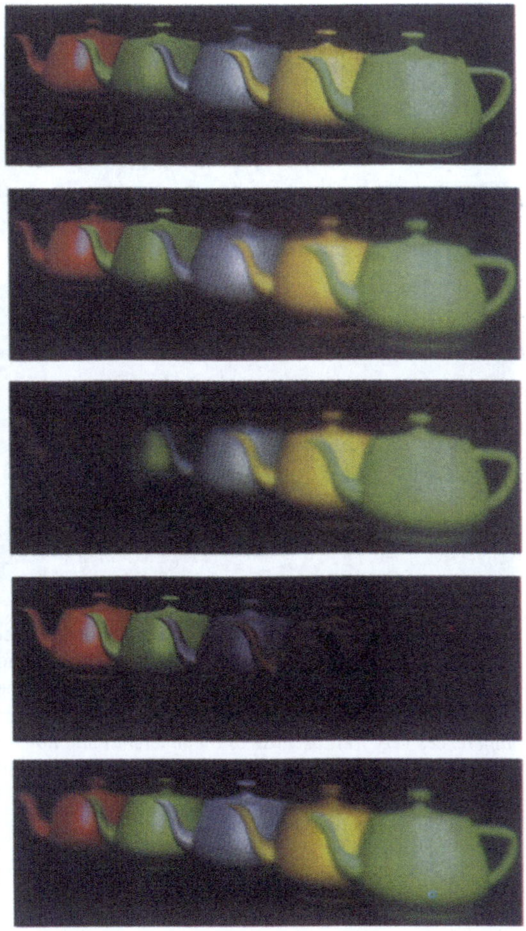

a Two superimposed projectors. Both are in focus. **b** One of the projectors is defocussed. The green teapot at the back is in focus. **c** This is the contribution of the defocussed projectors in **b**. **d** This is the contribution of the focussed projectors in **b**. **e** The silver teapot in the middle is in focus now

a b c d e

Top row. The circular inset is projected from one projector and the rest from another. Left: Both the projectors are in focus. Right: One of the projectors is defocussed. C
Bottom row. Left: A high dynamic range scene (1000:1) being projected by one projector. Right: The same scene being projected by a CGO display made up of three projectors. (*The pictures do not show the differences very well because of the inherent limitations of the involved devices like the camera and the printer. These should have similar color range and resolution to reproduce the result.*)

SpringerEurographics

David Ebert,
Jean M. Favre,
Ronald Peikert (eds.)

Data Visualization 2001

Proceedings of the Joint Eurographics - IEEE TCVG Symposium on Visualization in Ascona, Switzerland, May 28-30, 2001

2001. XI, 364 pages. 212 partly coloured figures.
Softcover DM 129,80, öS 913,–
(recommended retail price)
ISBN 3-211-83674-8
Eurographics

This book contains 33 papers presented at the Third Joint Visualization Symposium of the Eurographics Association and the Technical Committee on Visualization and Graphics of the IEEE Computer Society.

The main topics treated are:
- visualization of geoscience data
- multi-resolution and adaptive techniques
- unstructured data, multi-scale and visibility
- flow visualization
- biomedical applications
- information visualization
- object representation
- volume rendering
- information visualization applications
- automotive applications

SpringerWienNewYork

A-1201 Wien, Sachsenplatz 4–6, P.O. Box 89, Fax +43.1.330 24 26, e-mail: books@springer.at, Internet: **www.springer.at**
D-69126 Heidelberg, Haberstraße 7, Fax +49.6221.345-229, e-mail: orders@springer.de
USA, Secaucus, NJ 07096-2485, P.O. Box 2485, Fax +1.201.348-4505, e-mail: orders@springer-ny.com
Eastern Book Service, Japan, Tokyo 113, 3–13, Hongo 3-chome, Bunkyo-ku, Fax +81.3.38 18 08 64, e-mail: orders@svt-ebs.co.jp

Springer-Verlag and the Environment

WE AT SPRINGER-VERLAG FIRMLY BELIEVE THAT AN international science publisher has a special obligation to the environment, and our corporate policies consistently reflect this conviction.

WE ALSO EXPECT OUR BUSINESS PARTNERS – PRINTERS, paper mills, packaging manufacturers, etc. – to commit themselves to using environmentally friendly materials and production processes.

THE PAPER IN THIS BOOK IS MADE FROM NO-CHLORINE pulp and is acid free, in conformance with international standards for paper permanency.

GPSR Compliance

The European Union's (EU) General Product Safety Regulation (GPSR) is a set of rules that requires consumer products to be safe and our obligations to ensure this.

If you have any concerns about our products, you can contact us on ProductSafety@springernature.com

In case Publisher is established outside the EU, the EU authorized representative is:

Springer Nature Customer Service Center GmbH
Europaplatz 3
69115 Heidelberg, Germany

Batch number: 10584556

Printed by Printforce, the Netherlands